Language Learning and Deafness

THE CAMBRIDGE APPLIED LINGUISTICS SERIES
Series editors: Michael H. Long and Jack C. Richards

This new series presents the findings of recent work in applied linguistics which are of direct relevance to language teaching and learning and of particular interest to applied linguists, researchers, language teachers, and teacher trainers.

In this series:

Interactive Approaches to Second Language Reading *edited by Patricia Carrell, Joanne Devine, and David Eskey*

Second Language Classrooms – research on teaching and learning *by Craig Chaudron*

Language Learning and Deafness *edited by Michael Strong*

The Learner-Centred Curriculum *by David Nunan*

Language Learning and Deafness

Michael Strong

Center on Deafness
University of California, San Francisco

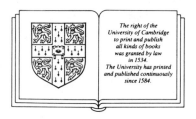

The right of the
University of Cambridge
to print and publish
all kinds of books
was granted by law
in 1534.
The University has printed
and published continuously
since 1584.

Cambridge University Press
Cambridge
New York   New Rochelle
Melbourne   Sydney

Published by the Press Syndicate of the University of Cambridge
The Pitt Building, Trumpington Street, Cambridge CB2 1RP
32 East 57th Street, New York, NY 10022, USA
10 Stamford Road, Oakleigh, Melbourne 3166, Australia

First published 1988

Printed in the United States of America

Cover design by Thomas Wharton

Library of Congress Cataloging-in-Publication Data
Language learning and deafness.
(Cambridge applied linguistics series)
Bibliography: p.
Includes index.
1. Deaf – United States – Means of communication.
2. Children, Deaf – United States – Language.   3. Deaf –
Education – United States – English language.   I. Strong,
Michael, 1945– .   II. Series.
HV2471.L35   1987   371.91'2   87–2974

British Library Cataloguing in Publication Data
Language learning and deafness. – (Cambridge
applied linguistics series).
1. Hearing impaired – Language
I. Strong, Michael, *1945–*
401'.9   HV2437

ISBN 0 521 34046 2 hardcover
ISBN 0 521 33579 5 paperback

Contents

Contributors

John A. Albertini, National Technical Institute for the Deaf, Rochester
Institute of Technology
Thomas Allen, The Gallaudet Research Institute, Center for Assessment
and Demographic Studies
Gerald P. Berent, National Technical Institute for the Deaf, Rochester
Institute of Technology
Joseph H. Bochner, National Technical Institute for the Deaf, Rochester
Institute of Technology
Carol J. Erting, Gallaudet University
Martha Gonter Gaustad, Department of Special Education, Bowling
Green State University
James Paul Gee, Applied Psycholinguistics Program, Boston University
Wendy Goodhart, Pennsylvania School for the Deaf
Diane Lillo-Martin, University of Connecticut, Department of
Linguistics
Mimi WheiPing Lou, Department of Psychiatry, Center on Deafness,
University of California, San Francisco
Steven Fritsch Rudser, Department of Psychiatry, Center on Deafness,
University of California, San Francisco
Arthur Schildroth, The Gallaudet Research Institute, Center for Assess-
ment and Demographic Studies
Hilde Schlesinger, Department of Psychiatry, Center on Deafness, Uni-
versity of California, San Francisco
Michael Strong, Department of Psychiatry, Center on Deafness, Univer-
versity of California, San Francisco
James Woodward, The Gallaudet Research Institute, Center for Assess-
ment and Demographic Studies

Series editors' preface

We are proud to include *Language Learning and Deafness*, edited by Michael Strong, in the Cambridge Applied Linguistics series. This series provides a forum for the best new work in applied linguistics by those in the field who are able to relate theory, research, and practice.

Strong has assembled a coherent collection of original research reports and position papers written especially for this volume by some of today's leading scholars in language and deafness. Researchers and practitioners will find up-to-date, accessible information on current problems and progress in language education for the hearing-impaired. The research presented herein links studies of language learning by the deaf and the insights these give into language learning in general.

In the introductions to individual chapters, Strong highlights issues of mutual concern to teachers and researchers involved with education in first or second languages, whether oral or manual. In so doing, he cuts across the traditional boundaries separating language acquisition in deaf and hearing populations.

We hope that in identifying areas of mutual concern this book will stimulate further cooperation and exchange of ideas among language professionals involved in the education of hearing, hearing-impaired, and other special needs populations.

Michael H. Long
Jack C. Richards
University of Hawaii at Manoa

Preface

There is good reason why a book on deafness should be included in a series devoted primarily to second languages in applied linguistics. The fact is that the prelingually deaf and speakers of other languages share many of the same problems in learning English; insights from work with either deaf or hearing populations, therefore, are often of interest to applied linguists working with the other group.

About 10% of the deaf population in the United States has at least one deaf parent (Rawlings and Jensema, 1977), and in a large majority of these families American Sign Language (ASL) is used in the home and is the children's first language. For this group English is learned either as a second language at school, just as it is for hearing speakers of other languages, or sometimes as another first language from bilingual parents.

About one third of all deaf children in the United States are enrolled in residential schools (see *American Annals of the Deaf*, 1985, p. 132). This figure includes most of the children of deaf parents and many other deaf children. In this environment, where Deaf culture predominates, ASL is usually the medium of social communication among peers.[1] Thus, the children of hearing parents not already fluent in that language learn it quickly as they are socialized into the deaf community. ASL then becomes their primary language, and English is reserved for academic purposes and for conversing with hearing teachers. In this way, the group for whom English is a second language expands to include many children whose parents do not use ASL at home.

The remaining deaf children who are educated in special programs in regular schools or who are mainstreamed learn English as their primary language. However, most, if not all, of these children have difficulty achieving native-like fluency in English, a fact reflected in the oft-quoted

---

1 Throughout this book, "deaf" (with a lowercase "d") is used to refer to the physical condition of hearing loss, whereas "Deaf" (with an uppercase "D") is used to refer to special collectivities and attitudes arising out of interaction among people with hearing losses. This distinction was first made by Woodward (1972) and has become standard in much of the literature on sociocultural aspects of deafness.

statistic that the average deaf student leaves high school with the ability to read at the fourth or fifth grade level (Trybus and Karchmer, 1977). Many deaf individuals, therefore, require remedial English in the same way that speakers of other languages require ESL instruction. Indeed, deaf learners make many of the same kinds of errors observed among hearing speakers of other languages (Quigley and Paul, 1984). Thus, even this third group, for whom ASL does not play a significant role, can be likened to ESL learners. A book on language learning and the Deaf, then, is indeed appropriately included in a series devoted primarily to second language issues.

Although the field of language learning and deafness is still relatively in its infancy, the last 15 years have seen a sharp increase in the attention scholars from a variety of disciplines have paid to the issues connected with deafness. Linguists are studying the grammar of ASL and are attempting to describe and categorize the varieties of sign language that are used by both deaf and hearing people when they communicate with one another. Neuropsychologists are studying the effects of deafness on the human brain. Educators are interested in the degree to which hearing-impaired children might be taught in classes with hearing children, and how their needs compare with those of children with other kinds of handicap. Physicians are experimenting with cochlear implants, which reverse some of the effects of hearing loss, and psychologists are considering, among other things, the ramifications of this procedure for the mental health of the recipients.

Of particular relevance to applied linguists are the ways in which language acquisition among deaf people compares with that among hearing people, and how the learning of English among the deaf relates to the acquisition of English by speakers of other languages. This book focuses on theoretical issues and research that form this bridge between the disciplines of deafness and applied linguistics. It will be of interest to anyone wishing to understand the complex issues involved in language learning among deaf children and adults, particularly to those who will be working with the deaf as teachers, interpreters, educational administrators, clinicians, or researchers. It will also provide an introduction to issues of language and deafness for other students of applied linguistics, and several chapters present familiar concepts (such as nativization and interlanguage) from a different perspective. The book is aimed at graduate-level readers, and the chapters are about evenly divided between those that summarize existing research, express theoretical positions, or define critical problems and those that report on new, original research. American Sign Language receives somewhat more attention than other kinds of communication, partly as a reflection of the interests of the editor and partly because ASL is increasingly at the center of educational, social, and linguistic polemics concerning deaf people in the United States and elsewhere.

Michael Strong

References

Quigley, S., and P. Paul. (1984). *Language and Deafness*. San Diego, Calif.: College Hill Press.

Rawlings, B., and C. Jensema. (1977). Two studies of the families of hearing impaired children. Gallaudet College, Office of Demographic Studies, ser. R, no. 5. Washington, D.C.

Trybus, R., and M. Karchmer. (1977). School achievement scores of hearing impaired children: National data on achievement status and growth patterns. *American Annals of the Deaf Directory of Programs and Services*, *122*, 62–69.

Woodward, J. (1972). Implications for sociolinguistic research among the deaf. *Sign Language Studies 1*, 1–7.

SECTION I:
THEORETICAL ISSUES

1 Language varieties in the deaf population and their acquisition by children and adults

Joseph H. Bochner *and* John A. Albertini

Editor's introduction

In this chapter, Bochner and Albertini take on the ambitious task of reviewing the central issues in the acquisition of language by deaf individuals in North America. They adopt a self-described "sociolinguistic" perspective by viewing language acquisition by the deaf as occurring under conditions of restricted intake that result in learning patterns resembling those of pidgin and creole speakers.

In order to explore this analogy in depth, the authors first provide an overview of research on the "products" or linguistic output of deaf learners, including written and spoken English, manual English, Pidgin Sign English (PSE), and American Sign Language (ASL). They then consider various aspects of the acquisition process, particularly those related to the interplay between the organism and the environment, the relationship between communication channel and the mind, and the influence of age on intake.

Apart from the thoroughness with which Bochner and Albertini treat their topic, what makes this chapter an important contribution to applied linguistics is their insights on the relationship between language acquisition among the Deaf and among other speech communities and the implications they draw from the linguistic evidence for the education of deaf children. The importance of primary language acquisition (whether ASL or signed or spoken English) and of the quality of language input/intake for educational advancement is lent an added urgency by the evidence and arguments put forward by these authors.

Language acquisition research with deaf persons over the past 20 years may be characterized as a search for an appropriate metaphor. Some in the United States view instruction in English as remediation to ameliorate the effects of a pathological condition. Others see it as providing students from a subculture access to the academic and employment mainstream. For many adult deaf students, it is sometimes viewed as instruction in a second language, despite the fact that English is their first language.

In this chapter, a sociolinguistic metaphor is suggested: The acquisition of spoken and signed languages most often occurs under conditions of restricted intake, and deaf learners of English, American Sign Language (ASL), or other varieties of signing behave in much the same way as speakers of pidgins and creoles.

The practice of applying sociological terms such as *culture* and *ethnic group* to deaf people is hardly new. At a conference on the social aspects of deafness at Gallaudet College in 1982, Joshua Fishman praised the borrowing of concepts and hypotheses from the social sciences to describe the socialization of the deaf child. At the same time, he warned that metaphors, while usually enlightening, are also somewhat misleading. However instructive, metaphors have their limitations. Mindful of Fishman's warning and cognizant of the limitations of our chosen metaphor, we apply the constructs of pidginization and creolization to the process of language acquisition in deaf individuals much as they have been used recently to describe acquisition by a variety of hearing populations (Andersen, 1983b).

Any overview of language learning in the deaf population must take into account at least three languages or varieties (English, American Sign Language, and Pidgin Sign English), two sensory modalities (audition and vision), and three types of signals (speech, sign, and print). Our task is twofold: first, to conceptualize the range and diversity of language varieties used by deaf children and adults (the products); and, second, to explain how and why these varieties might be acquired (the process). For both parts of the task, the constructs derived from the field of sociolinguistics appear to be useful tools. First, great diversity in language use and form is the rule in communities where pidgins and creoles have evolved. Second, researchers in child language and second language learning have repeatedly noted parallels to the processes of pidginization and creolization.

In this chapter, we have kept discussion of the diverse products of acquisition to a minimum. We focus mainly on the process of acquisition. The interaction between the organism and the environment, the relationship between the communication channel and the mind, and issues related to age, intake, and attainment are discussed in some depth. This discussion holds implications for the instruction of deaf students and for future research. Some of these implications are discussed in the concluding section of the chapter, where it is suggested that acquisition research with deaf students, rather than being tangential, has much to offer mainstream research in language acquisition.

The products of acquisition

We begin with a brief description of the language varieties used by members of the deaf population. These include various manifestations of English (e.g., spoken and written) and of manual languages (e.g., Pidgin Sign English and American Sign Language).

English

READING

Reading achievement tests standardized on normally-hearing students are routinely considered indirect estimates of the English skills of hearing-impaired individuals since English language proficiency is a necessary prerequisite for reading comprehension. The results of numerous studies have consistently demonstrated that the reading comprehension skills of hearing-impaired students are considerably lower than those of normally-hearing children of comparable age, with about half of the population of deaf 18-year-olds reading at or below a fourth grade level and only about 10% reading above the eighth grade level (Conrad, 1977; DiFrancesca, 1972; Gallaudet Research Institute, 1985; Trybus and Karchmer, 1977). On the average, the reading achievement of hearing-impaired students tends to increase at a rate of less than 0.3 grade equivalents per year (Trybus and Karchmer, 1977).

Although proficiency in the English language is necessary for reading comprehension, it is not sufficient since comprehension may vary as a function of extralinguistic factors, such as the reader's familiarity with the subject matter of the text. Consistent with reports from adult second language acquisition, English language proficiency and reading comprehension have been found to correlate at approximately .70 in deaf young adults (Albertini et al., 1986; Bochner, Meath-Lang, and Lichtenstein, personal communication); these results indicate that reading comprehension and English proficiency are distinct but related skills. Similarly, other research indicates that deaf students do not possess English language abilities comparable to those of younger normally-hearing children with equivalent reading achievement (Moores, 1970).

WRITING

The writing of deaf individuals has been compared to that of normally-hearing controls in numerous studies, which have consistently revealed differences in performance indicative of deaf subjects' English language deficiencies. Sentences written by deaf children and adolescents tend to be shorter (i.e., contain fewer words) than those written by normally-hearing controls of the same age and contain fewer conjoined and subordinate clauses (Heider and Heider, 1940; Myklebust, 1964). Deaf individuals also tend to reiterate words and phrases within a discourse (Heider and Heider, 1940; Myklebust, 1964; Simmons, 1962) and use more articles and nouns and fewer adverbs and conjunctions than normally-hearing children matched for age (Myklebust, 1964; Simmons, 1962). With increasing age, however, the length of their sentences and compositions tends to increase, as does the diversity of their word usage (Stuckless and Marks, 1966).

Grammatical errors frequently appear in the writing of deaf children and youth, their number decreasing slightly as age increases (Stuckless and Marks, 1966). Among the most common errors that these individuals make is the recurrent use of patterns that do not correspond with the inflectional morphology (e.g., in verb tense and agreement), the misuse of function words (e.g., articles and prepositions), and various other errors (e.g., incorrect subcategorizations, inappropriate use of coordinating and subordinating conjunctions, and/or anomalies in constituent structure). (See Greenberg and Withers, 1965, for numerous examples of the types of grammatical errors appearing in the writing of deaf individuals.) Some of these errors are related to the fact that, traditionally, deaf children have been taught written language sentence by sentence and not in discourse form (Kretschmer and Kretschmer, 1978; Wilbur, 1977).

GRAMMAR

In the past two decades, a number of studies have examined the status of various syntactic structures in the English of deaf children, adolescents, and young adults, focusing attention on the nature of errors in comprehension, production, and acquisition. The results of such studies help to characterize the linguistic competence of hearing-impaired individuals. In addition, they provide a foundation for the study of acquisition by demonstrating the degree to which various constructions have been acquired and by yielding descriptive information about aspects of the structure and processing of language.

The results of numerous studies involving a diverse array of sentence structures, subjects, and experimental procedures have shown that function words and morphology pose considerable difficulty for hearing-impaired children and adults. These components of grammar, which are readily acquired by normally-hearing children as well as by adult second language learners, constitute major obstacles to the successful acquisition of English and attainment of proficiency in the hearing-impaired population. Articles, prepositions, conjunctions, pronouns, verbal auxiliaries, and inflectional and derivational suffixes are among the most persistent and pervasive sources of error observed in their spoken and written English and on experimental tasks (Bochner, 1982; Quigley and Paul, 1984). The difficulty hearing-impaired individuals experience with function words and morphology can be seen in the way they process and acquire a variety of English syntactic structures; this difficulty persists in the adult population despite years of formal instruction. In simple, active, declarative sentences, errors in function words and morphology indicate faulty choice or interpretation of grammatical markers. In multiple-clause, interrogative, and passive sentences, however, the errors often seem to involve anomalous structural configurations or overgeneralized processing strategies (Albertini and Samar, 1983; Bochner, 1978, 1982).

The problems deaf individuals encounter with passive, interrogative, and relative clause sentences, for example, are clearly associated with difficulties pertaining to the use of verbal auxiliaries, participles, prepositions, and relative pronouns. Passive sentences frequently are interpreted as active and produced with errors in the auxiliary *be,* the preposition *by,* and/or the passive participle *-en* (Power and Quigley, 1973; Tervoort, 1970). The insertion of *do* and inversion of subject and auxiliary tend to be major sources of difficulty with interrogatives (Quigley, Wilbur, and Montanelli, 1974). With regard to relative and other subordinate clause constructions, the function words that characterize them are frequently used inappropriately, and subordinate clauses tend to be treated as or confused with coordinate constructions (Bochner, 1978, 1982). These examples illustrate how errors in function words and morphology are manifested in various constructions, but they do not indicate the cause of these errors.

Constructions that include strings deviating from the canonical subject-verb-object (agent-action-patient or noun-verb-noun) word order are especially difficult for hearing-impaired individuals to comprehend and produce correctly and reliably. This difficulty is evident in various types of embedded and subordinate clause environments, especially in those containing discontinuous constituents where a subject noun phrase does not immediately precede the verb with which it is associated (Albertini and Forman, 1985; Berent, 1983; Bochner, 1978, 1982; Quigley and Paul, 1984). Similarly, this difficulty is manifested in simple sentences containing alterations in underlying SVO word order, specifically in the interpretation of passive and production of interrogative sentences, as noted earlier. One explanation for this behavior may be a preference for arranging English phrases and clauses in a linear-sequential manner, and this preference may in turn stem from tendencies toward parataxis and the simple concatenation of elements without specifying hierarchical relationships among them (Bochner, 1978, 1982; also see Bickerton, 1981 and Givón, 1979). Again, it is noted in passing that traditional instructional practices may have unintentionally limited hearing-impaired students' exposure to complex sentences (Kretschmer and Kretschmer, 1978).

SPOKEN LANGUAGE

The oral language of hearing-impaired individuals has been compared to that of normally-hearing controls in various studies. Results of these studies indicate that hearing-impaired children tend to utter fewer words and shorter sentences and commit more errors than controls of the same age or younger (Brannon, 1966, 1968; Brannon and Murray, 1966; Elliott, Hirsh, and Simmons, 1967; Simmons, 1962). The fact that their spoken utterances tend to consist primarily of nouns and verbs, suggests that function words are used sparingly (Brannon, 1966, 1968; Elliott et al., 1967; Goda, 1964); in addition, their spoken utterances appear to contain fewer total words per sentence than their written counterparts (Goda, 1959). In general, the performance of deaf children on oral language production and comprehension tasks tends to improve rather slowly as a function of age (Pressnell, 1973).

ENGLISH-BASED (AUXILIARY) MANUAL SYSTEMS

Prior to 1960, little descriptive or comparative work was done on the educational use of manual communication owing to the predominance of oral methods of instruction (Moores, 1978). Since then, however, interest in the use of signing and fingerspelling in educational settings and discussion of it in the literature have increased dramatically. Today, any discussion of modes of English used in educational settings must include English-based systems of manual communication, specifically fingerspelling (Visible English, as used in the Rochester Method), and the auxiliary sign systems known as Seeing Essential English (SEE 1), Signing Exact English (SEE 2), and the Gallaudet Preschool Signed English System (see Caccamise, Brewer, and Meath-Lang, 1983). Another major system, which deserves mention but lies outside the scope of the present overview, is the Paget-Gorman Systematic Sign (PGSS) developed and used in Great Britain (Paget and Gorman, 1971; Wilbur, 1979). These forms of manual communication are treated here as auxiliary languages in the sense that they are contrived (artificial) codes purposely invented to serve specific communicative and educational functions (see McQuown, 1950; Sapir, 1931).

Since several comprehensive descriptions of these systems are available in the literature (see, for example, Caccamise and Newell, 1984; Wilbur, 1979), the discussion here is limited to common goals and characteristics of the auxiliary systems and to the psycholinguistic and pedagogical issues surrounding their use. All of these systems were invented to provide students and teachers with visible, manual equivalents of English words and affixes (Caccamise and Newell, 1984). The most literal representation of English in these systems is provided by fingerspelling, which, in the context of the Rochester Method, is seen as an adjunct to oral educational procedures (Scouten, 1963, 1967).

Inventors of the auxiliary sign systems have generally justified their choice of signs by appealing to spoken and written English. Decisions in each system are based on the pronunciation and meaning of the

English word as well as its spelling (Caccamise and Newell, 1984). For example, inventors of SEE 2 adhere to a "two-of-three rule" that states that if two of three parameters (spelling, pronunciation, and meaning) are the same for a pair of English words, then the same sign will be used to represent those words. Thus, the same sign is used in SEE 2 for *right* (meaning *correct*) and *right* (meaning *privilege*) but not for *write*. What such a rule does is create sign homonyms, and although it is expedient for the inventors of a system, it seems unwarranted and unnecessary. It is unwarranted because homonyms may, in fact, make comprehension more difficult and unnecessary since there may already be attested separate forms (as there are for *correct* and *privilege* in ASL).

The primary issue regarding the use of fingerspelling or an auxiliary sign system is, of course, whether or not its use promotes the learning of English. Given that speech, when processed by audition and/or lip-reading, is usually an insufficient source of input and that deaf children rely to a great extent on the visual processing of information, one must scrutinize not only the integrity of each system's representation of English, but also the degree of synchrony between speech and manual representations (since many educational programs use speech simultaneously with signs and/or fingerspelling) and the manner in which parents, teachers, and others employ the system as a source of linguistic input in language acquisition.

Few proponents of auxiliary manual systems claim that such systems are "complete" representations of English. Some (e.g., Hsu, 1978, 1979) come perilously close, however. Hsu states that fingerspelling encodes the same information as "vocal articulation" (1979, p. 30). Since fingerspelling is a representation of orthography, the assumption that it is equivalent to speech and somehow encodes more information than print is unwarranted. However, it must be noted that as an educational methodology, the Rochester Method employs fingerspelling as an adjunct to speech, making it an oral multisensory approach (Scouten, 1963, 1967).

With regard to synchrony, Bellugi and Fischer (1972) found that nearly twice as many words as signs were used by their subjects to relate spoken and signed versions of the same story. This would suggest that a one-to-one, word-to-sign representation would require extremely rapid signing, a reduction in the rate of speech, or both, to maintain synchrony. Bellugi and Fischer also found that the rate of transmission of propositions ("underlying elementary sentences") in American Sign Language and spoken English were not appreciably different. Thus, it is conceivable that the more an auxiliary system borrows from the lexicon (and grammar) of ASL, the more synchrony could be achieved. However, achieving synchrony in this way might lessen the integrity of the system's representation of English. With the introduction of grammatical devices from ASL into manual representations of English, we leave the realm of in-

vented systems and enter that of pidginized varieties, specifically Pidgin
Sign English (PSE), the discussion of which is reserved for a later section
of this chapter.

Studies in the literature have compared oral and manual production
of English by parents (e.g., Crandall, 1978) and by teachers (e.g., Marmor and Petitto, 1979). These studies concluded that function words
(e.g., articles and prepositions) and inflections (e.g., past tenses) were
often omitted in the manual production of the normally-hearing adults
observed. Crandall further concluded that the accuracy of a child's sign
production correlated highly with that of the mother. In support of
Marmor and Petitto's findings, Geers, Moog, and Schick (1984) observed
considerable variability in the manner and degree to which teachers used
manually coded English. In their study of 327 profoundly deaf children
(5 to 9 years of age) from oral-aural and total communication programs
across the United States, they assessed the effect of communication mode
(and age) on signed and spoken production of selected English language
structures. They examined elicited and imitated production of 16 target
structures and found that the overall signed and spoken production of
the total communication children did not differ significantly from spoken
productions of the oral-aural children. The quality and/or consistency
of signing is generally recognized as an important educational variable
in these debates, but the quality and/or consistency of oral modeling is
equally important and needs to be recognized as such since language
acquisition depends more on the integrity or quality of verbal intake
than on its modality. Also, the amount of training necessary to produce
skilled talkers, fingerspellers, and signers, and the effect of age on acquisition of these skills need to be considered (see, for example, Caccamise, Garretson, and Bellugi, 1981).

In summary, research reports on the ability of children and adults to
process English through fingerspelling or auxiliary sign systems (Wilbur,
1979; Caccamise, 1978; Caccamise et al., 1983;) indicate that English
can be received effectively when speech is used with signing and/or
fingerspelling. However, when speech is not used, it is not entirely clear
how much grammatical information is processed by the student (and
under what conditions).

Pidgin Sign English and American Sign Language

VARIETIES

In 1969, Rainer, Altschuler, and Kallman estimated that approximately
75% of deaf adults used American Sign Language. More recent estimates, however, indicate that the actual proportion of ASL users may
be considerably lower. With hearing persons (primarily educators) who

do not know ASL, deaf individuals tend to use a variety sometimes called Pidgin Sign English (Woodward, 1973; Woodward and Markowicz, 1980; cf. "Ameslish" in Bragg, 1973). Deaf adults vary greatly with respect to the amount of English vocabulary and structure used in their signing. Not surprisingly, deaf users of ASL have been viewed as a minority language community that has come into close and prolonged contact with the linguistically and socially dominant group of English speakers. Woodward and Markowicz (1980) have described the relationship between ASL and English as one of "diglossia with bilingualism," with ASL used in informal interchanges involving family and friends and English in more formal contexts such as educational settings. Although sometimes regarded as inferior to English by its users, ASL is nevertheless a badge of in-group solidarity. It has changed rapidly over the years, especially in the area of vocabulary, and exhibits a great deal of interuser variation. As Fischer (1978) points out, these characteristics could well describe the sociolinguistic situation in a creole community. Fischer, like Woodward (1978), regards ASL as the "basilect" (cf., "Ameslan" in Fant, 1972) on a linguistic (postcreole) continuum that ranges from varieties bearing little resemblance to English to varieties very close to standard English, the "acrolect." Included at the acrolect end of the continuum are what Fant calls "Siglish," Visible English, and the auxiliary sign systems. On such a continuum, PSE constitutes a large middle range, the "mesolect."

In this chapter, a sharper distinction has been drawn between ASL and PSE on the one hand and the auxiliary manual systems on the other. We argue that, although they share the same modality, Visible English and the auxiliary sign systems should be differentiated from varieties of PSE and ASL on socio- and psycholinguistic grounds that set auxiliary languages apart from natural languages.

Circumstances surrounding the use of the auxiliary manual systems in some ways resemble those of oral pidgins. Most of the world's pidgins originated in seaports and marketplaces where they served mercantile purposes among individuals having limited, transitory contact; the auxiliary manual systems were created for use in educational settings to serve instructional purposes among teachers and students. These systems, like pidgins, are typically limited to an instrumental function as opposed to older, more developed languages that serve expressive and integrative functions as well within a cultural context (Smith, 1972; see also Lyons, 1977). In one crucial respect, however, auxiliary manual systems differ from pidgins: They were created systematically by educators and are perpetuated by educational intervention. In contrast, pidgins are inherently unstable varieties that are created by their users and tend either to develop into creoles or to disappear after a few generations.

A second point is that striking parallels have been noted between learner-languages and pidgins/creoles and, what is more important, in the processes underlying their development (e.g., Andersen, 1983a; Cokely and Gawlik, 1980; Ferguson, 1971). In these cases, the learner participates directly in the creation of the language system. Modifications in auxiliary manual systems brought on by children learning them are not incorporated into the systems and passed on to subsequent generations of learners by educators. In other words, natural psycholinguistic processes that operate during language acquisition and change (Slobin, 1973, 1977) are prevented from affecting auxiliary systems of manual communication. This is because these systems are not natural languages per se, but are contrived (artificial) representations of spoken English. The learner's participation in the acquisition process is therefore an important factor serving to differentiate PSE and ASL from auxiliary manual systems.

PIDGIN SIGN ENGLISH

In some respects, the language varieties referred to as PSE (Woodward and Markowicz, 1980) seem to fit the traditional definition of a pidgin language (DeCamp, 1971). Sociologically, they serve the instrumental communicative function in contact situations involving members of a minority group. Linguistically, they share structural features with oral pidgins, and such features have been considered simplifications and reductions of English structure. There are, however, differences between these sign varieties and the typical oral pidgin.

Whinnom (1971) provides a framework for considering the differences as well as similarities between PSE and spoken pidgins. To describe pidgins and the process of pidginization itself, Whinnom compares the contact of language communities, and their intermingling, with the interbreeding of different species; in this biological analogy, he calls pidginization "tertiary hybridization" (1971, p. 5). In biology, "primary hybridization" refers to the breaking up of a species into races; applied to language, it refers to dialectal fragmentation. "Secondary hybridization," or the interbreeding of distinct species (1971, p. 92), is what is commonly meant by the unqualified term *hybridization*. This results from language-switching situations, where one language may be superimposed over another, as in the case of *cocoliche* in Argentina. In *cocoliche*, Italian immigrants imported Spanish lexical items into an Italian morpho-syntactical system without interfering with the native (Italian) phonological system. The formula of this mixture – the vocabulary of one language and the grammar of another – has been used, as Whinnom points out, as a simplistic description of pidgins. True pidgins, he argues, are more complex and should be understood as cases of tertiary hybridization. In other words, a third term (a language or set of languages) is required in the formula for a true pidgin: A pidgin arises from a situation involving at least three source languages, one superstrate language and two or more substrate languages (1971, p. 106). In Hong Kong, for example, Chinese Pidgin, an English-based language, was used among domestic servants, taxicab drivers, and shopkeepers who shared no common Chinese dialect. As Whinnom suggests, a geographical designation, such as *China Coast Pidgin English,* might be more descriptive of this variety.

It is difficult to draw a clear parallel between the sociolinguistic situations that have spawned oral pidgins and the situation surrounding PSE as described by Woodward and Markowicz (1980). Whinnom maintains that a (synchronic) stability of grammatical features exists across users of a true pidgin. Woodward and Markowicz, however, draw a sharp distinction between hearing and deaf signers of PSE and seem to assume linguistic stability within the population of deaf PSE signers only, a distinction similar to that assumed by Bickerton (1981) in his analysis of Hawaiian Pidgin English.

Woodward and Markowicz do not clearly indicate what the third term (the third source language) in this language environment might be. Unless we consider home-signing and regional varieties as divergent substrate sign systems, we have here at best a bilingual and not a multilingual situation. Another difference is that contact with ASL in many cases may not even exist. In Whinnom's definition, distance from an existing norm, in this case ASL, is crucial. However, he allows (albeit in a footnote, no. 16) that pidginization could occur within groups as well (perhaps for reasons of subgroup identification as Woodward and Markowicz suggest). We must therefore ask to which groups of signers the distance criterion applies. It may be that young deaf adults who have had limited access to or who are "distanced from" oral English and have not had childhood contact with other signers would form one such subgroup. The members of this subgroup (forming at a college or on the job, say) could develop a variety that in Hymes's words was simplified in outer form, reduced in inner form, restricted in role, and separated from the norm by exclusion and disassociation (1971, p. 67), a variety that was relatively stable within the subgroup only.

Considering the great variety in signing among deaf adults, it is probably an overgeneralization to say that "almost all deaf persons in the U.S. and most of Canada use ASL" (Quigley and Paul, 1984, p. 7). It may yet be an oversimplification to state that almost all use two stable varieties, ASL and PSE. A more accurate statement may be that, "distanced from" the norms of ASL and English, a pidgin may be developing in North American schools and workplaces among users of mutually unintelligible sign systems. Indeed, Whinnom is careful to distinguish between pidginization and a pidgin. What Woodward and Markowicz describe may be features of a "pre-pidgin continuum" (Hymes, 1971) rather than an established pidgin. We are witnessing perhaps the process of pidginization. Objective and detailed descriptions of the structure and function of signing being used in these situations would clarify the picture (see Chapter 5).

AMERICAN SIGN LANGUAGE

A number of detailed descriptions of the structure of ASL are available in the literature (see Klima and Bellugi, 1979, and Wilbur, 1979, for comprehensive treatments of structural similarities between ASL and spoken languages at sublexical, morphological, syntactic, and discourse levels). Also, descriptions of the acquisition, processing, and social functions of ASL are available (see, for example, Lane and Grosjean, 1980). Such studies are based on the production and judgments of native users of the language; that is, deaf signers who are children of deaf parents. The syntactic, lexical, and sublexical (phonological and morphological) levels of ASL have been studied, and striking parallels between it and spoken creoles have been noted.

The history of ASL is difficult to reconstruct. Yet, observations of a modern situation (on Providence Island in the Caribbean) that parallels the language situation in the United States before 1816, knowledge of French Sign Language (FSL), and glottochronological estimates of divergence between related languages (ASL and FSL) have led Woodward (1978) to suggest that initial creolization of ASL occurred in the early 1800s. For Woodward, its structural characteristics, current status, and use warrant calling modern ASL a creole. According to Fischer (1978), the sociolinguistic environment of most deaf children explains why ASL continues to be a creole. Since children use language for other than merely instrumental functions and since many hearing parents and educators use a variety like PSE, deaf children tend to "recreolize" or expand pidginized sign input into ASL each generation.

More recently, sign language researchers have included other sign languages in this comparison. Deuchar (1983) treats ASL, British Sign Language (BSL), and FSL as "newly emerging creoles" and suggests that, although some constraints may be modality-specific, others operate on spoken and signed creoles independently of modality (her term is "medium"). Edwards and Ladd (1983) examine the parallels between the structure of BSL and West Indian Creole, both minority languages used in Britain, and suggest changes in the education of deaf children on the basis of experience with West Indian Creole–speaking children. In this chapter we take into account Bickerton's claim that creoles tend to have certain types of grammatical rules (1981, p. 50) and preliminary data in these and other studies indicating that ASL shares some of these rules, and proceed on the assumption that ASL is a creole, and, more important, that it is acquired through a process analogous to creolization.

Before considering the character of acquisition with deaf learners, we propose a model describing the interaction between the learner and the linguistic environment and the channels providing access to that environment.

The process of acquisition

The organism and the environment: the ecology of acquisition

Language acquisition may be viewed in a biological context as a dynamic interaction between the organism and the environment. In this view, the process and product of acquisition are influenced by states inherent in the learner and the environment, and by diachronic changes in these states. During maturation, for example, the developing child undergoes a series of ontological changes that affect, most notably, the plasticity of the central nervous system. The time of these maturational effects constitutes the critical period for primary language acquisition. In order to acquire language, however, the learner must also have access to a suitable linguistic environment and be able to process signals and to associate percepts with meaning through the construction of abstract mental categories.

AN ECOLOGICAL MODEL

The ecological model sketched here is rooted in the belief that the organism and the environment interact in ways that make them inseparable (see Eibl-Eibesfeldt, 1970; Liberman, 1980; Piaget, 1971). The model takes into account the role of the verbal environment in language acquisition (Andersen, 1983a; Broen, 1972; Bruner, 1981; Krashen, 1980; Lewis and Rosenblum, 1977; Snow and Ferguson, 1977), but places heavier emphasis on the learner's contribution to the acquisition process (Bickerton, 1981, 1984; Chomsky, 1965, 1975; Cromer, 1981; Karmiloff-Smith, 1979a, 1981; Krashen, 1982; Lenneberg, 1967; Shatz, 1981, 1982; Slobin, 1977, 1983). The model purports to describe the primary variables affecting acquisition and offers an initial characterization of the relationships among them (see Gleitman and Wanner, 1982; Maratsos, 1983; Waterson and Snow, 1978), in order to provide a highly general and integrated account of the acquisition process and to explain the causes of linguistic variation across a wide range of diverse learner populations (see Andersen, 1983b).

The interaction between the organism and the environment is regulated by both physiological and cognitive mechanisms, as depicted in Figure 1. The sensory-perceptual and motor mechanisms constitute phys-

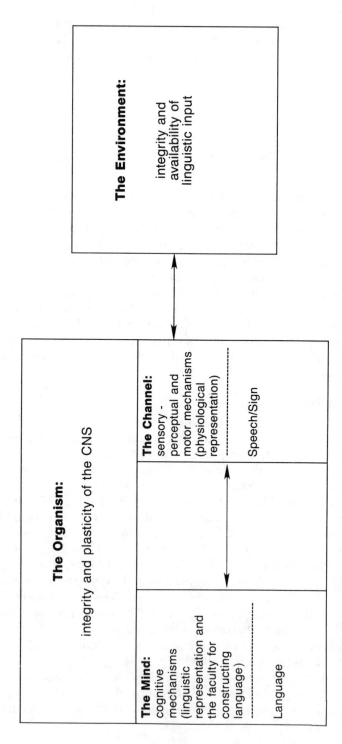

Figure 1. Relationships among variables affecting language processing and acquisition

iological levels of representation intrinsic to auditory and visual processing (reception) and to neuromuscular activity (expression). Some components of the physiological mechanisms may be considered innately predisposed toward the reception and expression of linguistic signals and thus may be said to guide the organism in its interaction with the environment and prepare it to respond in specific ways. In contrast, cognitive mechanisms function at the mental level of representation. The mental level is considered to be more general than the physiological level, and hence is not necessarily specifically or exclusively adapted to the acquisition of language. Both physiological and cognitive mechanisms operate in conjunction with environmental stimulation to shape the child's responses during a critical period. In this scheme, sensory-perceptual and motor mechanisms govern the acquisition of speech/sign, whereas cognitive mechanisms govern the acquisition of language.

It has been proposed that innate auditory structures guide the development of specific perceptual and motor functions in the acquisition of speech. The existence of such structures, referred to as auditory templates, has been hypothesized by Marler (1975, 1977a, b) on the basis of observations of vocal learning in birds and its similarity to vocal learning in humans. Citing categorical perception and cerebral lateralization as factors that distinguish the auditory processing of speech from other (nonspeech) acoustic signals, Marler hypothesizes that humans are predisposed to respond to vocalizations characteristic of their species during a critical period. The developing perceptual and motor skills are therefore shaped by the interaction between the organism and its environment, with auditory feedback contributing to the development of motor control (see Fourcin, 1978; Fry, 1975). The development of speech motor control is also thought to be facilitated by endogenous mechanisms of motor behavior that may be referred to as articulatory templates. These templates are conceived as preparing and enabling the organism to respond to auditory stimulation and/or initiate speech events (Fentress, 1983; Kent, 1981; Studdert-Kennedy, 1983a; Summerfield, 1980).

Auditory and articulatory templates are thought to influence the way children segment utterances and develop phonetic categories. The effects of such mechanisms may help explain the ability of human neonates and infants to process speech prosody (Crystal, 1973) and the segmentation and categorization of utterances into primal units of phonetic analysis, specifically breath groups, syllables, and/or phones (Liberman and Pisoni, 1977; Lieberman, 1967; Studdert-Kennedy, 1976, 1977). The auditory and articulatory templates are modified in the course of vocal learning and give rise to a linguistic (phonetic) level of representation (see Fourcin, 1978). Data pertaining to the acquisition of native-like pronunciation in second language learners is consistent with this view of vocal learning since pronunciation, more than any other linguistic skill, is known to be directly associated with maturation (Scovel, 1981; Seliger, 1981).

Cognitive mechanisms, on the other hand, are related to the general character of the organism's mental capabilities (Piaget, 1971), and language acquisition is thus considered largely a form of problem-solving activity (Cromer, 1981; Karmiloff-Smith, 1979a; also see Anderson, 1983). Contrary to the view that humans possess one innate cognitive mechanism devoted solely to the processing and acquisition of language (Chomsky, 1966, 1972, 1975; Wexler and Culicover, 1980), we hypothesize that hierarchically organized systems of enormous complexity, among them natural languages, are derived from general cognitive principles. These principles may be characterized as universal problem-solving heuristics (Simon, 1981). Citing examples ranging from the structure and development of atoms, molecules, and cells to the structure and development of social organizations, cognitive processes, and machines, Nobel laureate Herbert A. Simon espouses two theses pertinent to this discussion: (1) that "a large proportion of the complex systems we observe in nature exhibit hierarchic structure" and "evolve from simplicity" (1981, p. 229); and (2) that "man, viewed as a behaving system, is quite simple," with the apparent complexity of his behavior over the time being "largely a reflection of the complexity of the environment in which he finds himself" (1981, p. 65). Simon's ideas are in general compatible with those expressed in this chapter pertaining to the contributions of the organism and the environment to the acquisition process (1981, pp. 89–95).

The model outlined in this chapter represents an initial attempt to formulate a general unified account of the language acquisition process, one that can explain development under a variety of circumstances and in a variety of populations. Such a model is needed to characterize acquisition in the hearing-impaired population, where there is considerable linguistic diversity. The two most important factors to account for in any theory of language acquisition are (1) the effects of age, and (2) the relative contributions of the organism and the verbal environment to acquisition.

THE EFFECTS OF AGE

The effects of age have been explained in terms of a critical period for primary language acquisition extending approximately from 2 to nearly 15 years of age (Curtiss, 1977; Lenneberg, 1967). However, the critical period does not appear to be strongly associated with cerebral lateralization, as Lenneberg originally hypothesized, since more recent studies suggest that lateralization may be firmly established by about 5 years of age (Krashen, 1982). As a result of these findings, the critical period has instead been related to variation in neuronal plasticity as a function of age. Plasticity refers to the specialization for and localization of specific neurological functions in the central nervous system (CNS). The functions of certain neurons, specifically the variety classified as Golgi Type II, can be modified by nervous activity resulting from environmental stimulation. The functional capability of such neurons is greatest in the early phases of maturation but diminishes progressively during later states of ontogeny (Jacobson, 1975).

The effects of maturation on neuronal plasticity have been well documented and strongly suggest that during the critical period the neurons subserving linguistic functions undergo a progressive loss of plasticity, at least through adolescence (Milner, 1976; Seliger, 1978). This might explain observations of effects of age on acquisition in various populations, including the deaf (Bochner, 1982), second language learners (Patkowski, 1980; Scovel, 1981; Seliger, 1981), pidgin and creole users (Bickerton, 1981; Andersen, 1983b; Slobin, 1977), and individuals with brain damage as a result of mental retardation and aphasia (Lenneberg, 1967). The critical-period hypothesis, therefore, offers a coherent, integrated account of a wide array of data that could not readily be explained by other constructs (e.g., the construct of an affective filtering mechanism designed to govern the processing and intake of linguistic information in second language learners [Krashen, 1980, 1982]).

INPUT AND INTAKE

Languages cannot be learned in the absence of linguistic input. The appropriateness of the input, however, varies in relation to the processing capabilities of the learner, and these capabilities, in turn, vary as functions of development and maturation, generally increasing with age from childhood to adulthood. Research results indicate that utterances addressed to child and adult language learners typically are modified in ways that seem to facilitate their processing (Hatch, 1983; Larsen-Freeman, 1983; Snow and Ferguson, 1977; see also Gass and Madden, 1985). The modifications or linguistic adjustments involved in the use of special simplified registers, such as baby and foreigner talk, have led researchers to distinguish between input and intake. Input may be characterized as representing the verbal environment, whereas intake may be construed as the learner's selective processing of input. A variety of factors, both internal and external to the learner, affect the processing of linguistic input and, as a result, affect language acquisition. Among the internal factors are cognitive and affective variables, sensory capabilities, and, at least in the deaf population, limitations on verbal memory that affect the processing of printed English through reading (Conrad, 1979; Hanson, 1982; Lichtenstein, 1984). Some of the external factors include the linguistic structure of the input, the integrity and channel of the signal, and pragmatic variables such as situational context and the availability of message feedback. Another external factor that affects language acquisition is the quantity of input.

Internal and external influences interact in complex ways. Not only do factors internal to the learner influence intake, they also appear, to a certain degree, to shape the character of the verbal environment since the learner may selectively elicit input (e.g., Hatch, 1983). The constructs of input and intake are strongly associated with sociolinguistic variables pertaining to patterns of communicative interaction, language contact, and variation. Language acquisition therefore occurs within a social milieu in which the learner is an active participant, eliciting and selectively processing input in the course of communicative interactions and constructing language with the assistance of physiological and cognitive mechanisms.

When learners cannot gain exposure to appropriate input, they sometimes are able to create novel linguistic structures, as occurs in creolization (Andersen, 1983a; Bickerton, 1981). Creolization occurs only with children acquiring their primary language under conditions of restricted input, and differs from pidginization mainly in that children appear to be more creative in language learning than adults. The creativity exhibited by children may be attributed to their having a greater creative capacity and/or a greater need to expand and elaborate upon their input than adults. Whatever the case, creolization, conceived as "first language learning with restricted input," is typically differentiated from pidginization, conceived as "second language learning with restricted input" (Bickerton, 1977, p. 49). Bickerton's definitions are generally compatible with those employed in this chapter, as is his view that "the difference between arriving at a pidgin and arriving at a reasonably accurate version of a standard language lies mainly in the availability of target models and the amount of interaction with speakers of the target language" (1977, p. 55).

The channel and the mind: speech/sign and language

The various levels of linguistic analysis, from phonology to syntax and semantics, exist entirely in the form of abstract mental constructs, and as such must be distinguished from the concrete, physical signals that embody them. Cognitive mechanisms are said to regulate the acquisition of linguistic constructs, and sensory-perceptual and motor mechanisms are said to regulate the acquisition of the skills needed to transmit and receive linguistic signals at the physiological level. The distinction between abstract levels of linguistic structure and concrete physical signals, the distinction between language and speech/sign, is important for two reasons.

First, the sensory-perceptual and motor capabilities of the organism are provided a basis for language acquisition. Language could not have evolved in the human species without its capacity for transmitting and receiving signals, nor can it develop in individuals unless they have the capacity at least to receive these signals. The human organism is biologically prepared for auditory-vocal communication, as indicated by the structure of its vocal tract, which has been shaped through the course of evolution to facilitate speech production, as well as by the special status afforded speech perception and production in the brain and by the role of audition in vocal learning (Lieberman, 1984). Although predisposed toward auditory-vocal communication, the human organism also possesses the capabilities for visual-gestural communication. The fact that the organism can acquire language in a domain of perceptual and motor experience for which it is not genetically prepared attests to the striking plasticity of the central nervous system.

Second, differences between speech and sign appear to stem primarily from differences between the auditory-vocal and visual-gestural modalities (Studdert-Kennedy and Lane, 1980; see also Jakobson, 1967). Owing to the character of the auditory-vocal modality, speech consists of a serial ordering of linguistic units that are encoded in continuous intervals of sound and, as a result, are arranged in a temporal sequence. In contrast, the units of sign are produced in a more parallel and simultaneous arrangement (Bellugi and Fischer, 1972; Stokoe, 1960). These differences are relative rather than absolute, since speech is not entirely serial and continuous, nor is sign entirely parallel and discrete (Studdert-Kennedy and Lane, 1980). The greatest contrasts, we believe, occur at the level of the signal.

According to Liddell (1984), however, the view that signs are parallel arrangements of units may have given rise to inadequate representations of obligatory features. He offers the example of the ASL sign for *know,* which is normally described as a "B handshape which makes contact with the forehead, palm towards the forehead." The feature "contact with the forehead," he points out, is often deleted in noncitation forms, but what always remains and seems an essential underlying feature is "movement towards the forehead." Although previous research has noted the salience of movement in particular cases (e.g., see Stokoe's treatment of *Chicago,* 1960; and Supalla and Newport's distinction between certain noun-verb pairs, 1978), Liddell postulates that movement is a regular feature of signs (just as "obstruction" is considered a regular feature of consonants) and presents a case for treating signs as sequences of movement (M) and hold (H) segments. For him, these segments are analogous to the syllable-forming segments of spoken language, vowels and consonants, and each is thought of as a set or bundle of features (handshape, orientation, location, and contact). The arrangement of sign segments, however, appears to conform to "fairly rigid morpheme structure constraints" (1984, p. 395). Specifically, Liddell reports that his sampling of ASL citation forms revealed three basic patterns: for signs consisting of one M and one H, the predominant pattern was M + H; for those consisting of three segments, the order was H + M + H; and for four-segment signs, the pattern was M + H + M + H (p. 396).

The phonetic segments of spoken language are linguistic elements encoded in continuous intervals of sound; however, their boundaries are neither acoustically, auditorily, nor articulatorily salient. Children learning spoken languages, therefore, must rely heavily on meaning to discover the boundaries of sound segments, as well as the boundaries of morphemes and words in continuous speech (Bowerman, 1982; Kent, 1981; Menyuk and Menn, 1979). In general, it appears that meaningful elements are easier for learners to segment, discover and/or create than those having no meaning (see Kent, 1981; Menyuk and Menn, 1979; Slobin, 1977, and 1983). The accessibility of units at various levels of linguistic structure then must be related to the manner in which they affect meaning, and units that possess meaning must be more accessible to learners than those that do not (Slobin, 1977). Thus, manual signs and spoken words should be more accessible to learners than the intrinsically meaningless elements that comprise them. Consequently, it should be easier for learners to represent signs and spoken words as holistic units than as sets of phonemelike and/or morphemelike elements (Kent, 1981; Menyuk and Menn, 1979). Likewise, learners sometimes represent phrases as unanalyzed chunks, and only later do they segment them into lexical and morphological components (Bowerman, 1982; Clark, 1977; Peters, 1983).

The level of proficiency attained by learners of sign seems to be related to the manner in which they represent sublexical structure. It appears that less skilled signers tend to treat signs as unanalyzed holistic units, whereas more skilled signers tend to create or discover sublexical elements of structure. As a result, the greatest differences between speech and sign seem to occur when advanced stages in the acquisition of speech are compared to early stages in the acquisition of sign.

Since the phonemes of speech are abstract units of linguistic structure having no intrinsic meaning and a highly variable acoustic identity, they presumably would be exceedingly difficult to process and learn without endogenous auditory and articulatory mechanisms. These mechanisms are thought to serve as an interface between generalized auditory-articulatory processing and speech perception and production, between primitive levels of sensation, perception, and motor behavior and the more abstract mental levels of linguistic representation. Specifically, it is hypothesized that innate auditory and articulatory mechanisms facil-

itate the transition from perceptual-motor to phonetic levels of representation in vocal learning (Fourcin, 1978; Marler, 1975, 1977a, b).
The phonetic level is purely linguistic and must be distinguished from
the more primitive perceptual-motor (physiological) level of representation, much as a mynah bird's imitations of human speech cannot be
assumed to be based on any phonetic (linguistic) knowledge of or mental
capability for language, although the bird surely possesses the requisite
perceptual-motor apparatus for imitating sounds (Studdert-Kennedy,
1983a).

While innate auditory-articulatory templates have been hypothesized
to facilitate the processing of speech and acquisition of phonetic representations, regulatory mechanisms of comparable specificity have not
been posited for sign. It is felt that such mechanisms are not necessary
for sign because the articulation of phonetic segments in the visual-
gestural modality is manifested in the signal itself and is apparent to the
learner. In contrast, vocal articulation is not manifested in the speech
signal, with the result that speech is received as an acoustic event, not
an articulatory one. In other words, manual signals comprise articulatory
gestures that are directly observable to the learner. Speech, on the other
hand, comprises acoustic signals, and as such, its articulation is not
directly observable to the learner. Speech and sign, therefore, are both
products of neuromuscular activity that are processed by the senses.
However, they differ from one another in that the articulatory gestures
of speech are not manifested in the signal whereas those of sign are.

Although auditory and articulatory mechanisms are thought to facilitate the acquisition of speech and, to a limited extent, the linguistic
(phonetic) representation of sound, they are not employed directly in
the acquisition and processing of morphological, syntactic, and semantic
levels of representation. However, auditory and articulatory mechanisms
may indirectly facilitate the acquisition of syntactic structure because of
the correlation between phonetic and syntactic boundaries. Major syntactic boundaries (i.e., clause and subject-predicate boundaries) tend to
be marked by distinctive prosodic characteristics in the speech signal
(Nooteboom, Brokx, and de Rooij, 1978) and these acoustic properties
of speech affect sentence processing in children (Bochner, in press; Read
and Schreiber, 1982).

The processing and acquisition of speech and language involve the
complementary operations of segmentation (analysis) and combination
(synthesis) (see Newport, 1982; Slobin, 1977). That is, linguistic systems
comprise identifiable units at various levels of structure (e.g., phonemes,
syllables, words, phrases, and clauses). These units must be assembled
in production, disassembled in comprehension, and discovered or created
in acquisition. The operations of segmentation and combination implicit
in the hierarchical structuring of speech, therefore, may serve as pre-

cursors or correlates of syntax (Cooper and Paccia-Cooper, 1980; Jones, 1976; Lashley, 1951; Lenneberg, 1967; Liberman, 1970; Martin, 1972; Studdert-Kennedy, 1983b). However, hierarchical structuring is a characteristic of complex systems in general, and hence is not unique to speech and language (Simon, 1981).

The physical correlates of hierarchical structure in spoken languages are manifested primarily in time and embodied in the abstract construct of rhythm (Lashley, 1951; Lenneberg, 1967; Martin, 1972), whereas those of manual languages are manifested in both time and space and do not appear to be related to any nonlinguistic construct (Studdert-Kennedy and Lane, 1980), except perhaps to an abstract rhythmically based motor program for the execution of manual gestures over time. It is therefore possible that subtle differences in structure between speech and sign might be correlated with differences between auditory and visual processing (see Bellugi, 1983; Newport, 1982). Such potential differences would presumably be minor since research results indicate great similarity in structure between spoken and signed languages and since hierarchical organization is an inherent property of natural languages and other complex systems, a property not constrained by the character of the physical signal or sensory channel. Therefore the structure and acquisition of language are primarily associated with properties of the human mind, with general properties of the perceptual and motor systems having less of an influence, but still serving an essential role in the ontogenesis and evolution of language. The study of language can help reveal these properties and the manner in which they constrain linguistic form.

Age, intake, and attainment

A number of physiological, social, cognitive, affective, situational, communicative, and linguistic variables influence the language acquisition process and hence can affect the level of language proficiency attained by learners. However, some of these variables clearly influence acquisition more than others. Of all the variables thought to affect the language acquisition process, two seem primary: age and intake. As noted earlier, age relates to both the physiological maturation of the central nervous system and cognitive development; that is, neuronal plasticity decreases as cognitive abilities develop. Intake refers to both the integrity of input from the verbal environment and the learner's differential sensitivity to and selective processing of aspects of input signals. Defined in this way, the variables of age and intake encompass physiological, cognitive, environmental, and linguistic domains.

AGE AND INTAKE

The effects of age and intake may be observed in primary language acquisition in a diverse and unrelated array of special learner populations, specifically, in pidgin and creole communities, in mentally retarded and aphasic individuals, and in the deaf population. The acquisition of pidgins and creoles differs from that of more established languages in that they are constructed from incomplete input, pidgins being acquired by adult learners and creoles by children in a restricted verbal environment (Andersen, 1983a; Hymes, 1971). Language development in the mentally retarded population and in individuals recovering from aphasia is associated with age such that primary language learning in children with these disabilities proceeds in a much more efficient and effective manner than in adults, and the acquisition process in adult members of these populations is seemingly suppressed short of nativelike proficiency (Lenneberg, 1967; Rosenberg, 1982). Since mental retardation and many types of aphasia affect the ability to process linguistic input, they cause the intake of linguistic information to decrease and the mental faculty for constructing language to become inhibited. In the deaf population, the availability of language input via the auditory-vocal channel is reduced. Primary language acquisition in many hearing-impaired individuals generally appears to be suppressed to the point where nativelike proficiency in English, if not achieved in childhood, is rarely obtained in adulthood (Bochner, 1982; Lenneberg, 1967).

The hypothesized effects of age and intake on language development are illustrated in Figure 2. In this illustration, the parameter of language attainment is conceived as an acquisition continuum representing a hierarchy of proficiency levels. Unlike the sociolinguistic continua used to describe variation in communities where contact has spawned linguistic hybrids (i.e., pidgins and creoles), the continuum employed in Figure 2 is intended to characterize variation in the level of language proficiency attained by individuals learning one specific language independent of any others (see Schumann and Stauble, 1983). As such, this continuum may be used to characterize individual attainment in the primary or nonprimary acquisition of English, ASL, or any other language. This continuum of acquisition, then, does not necessarily imply language contact. Deaf individuals who in adulthood have acquired a meso level/ variety of English may also have independently acquired a meso level/ variety of ASL. A substantial portion of the deaf population probably falls into this category, attaining native proficiency in neither English nor ASL.

Many deaf adults are viewed as having acquired a variegated primary language, one of a series of pidginized/creolized varieties of English. The term PSE, as described by Woodward and Markowicz (1980), denotes a range of such linguistic hybrids stemming from the mixture of English and ASL. However, the view that PSE is a contact vernacular arising from a mixture of English and ASL, while a useful heuristic having some sociolinguistic validity, does not appear to be completely accurate, since

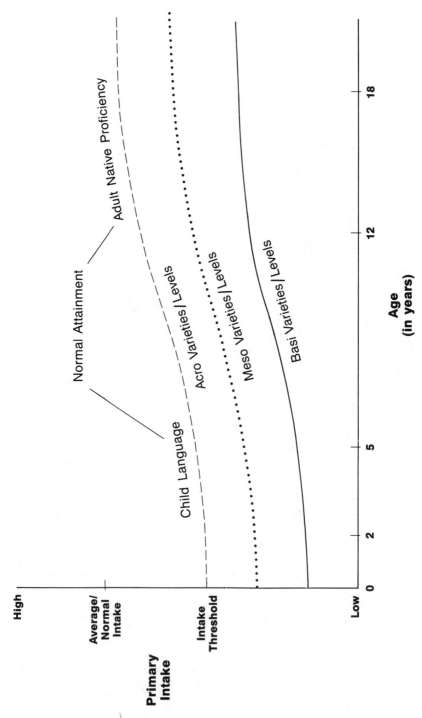

Figure 2. *Hypothesized effect of variation in age and intake on attainment in primary language acquisition*

PSE regularly arises independently of direct contact with ASL, and, as a result, does not satisfy the sociolinguistic conditions for the development of a pidgin. Rather than being a pidgin per se, PSE is more precisely a language developed from the pidginization/creolization process. Therefore, we do not view it as a contact vernacular directly influenced by the structure of ASL, but as the outcome of an acquisition process based on restricted linguistic intake, yet strongly influenced by the norms of standard English.

PSE and ASL exhibit structural characteristics similar to one another and to traditional pidgins and creoles, as described in the next section. However, PSE differs from ASL in that it has, to a far greater degree, been influenced by the norms of an external target language (English). Consequently, PSE may be viewed as a range of partly acquired varieties of standard English, similar to the varieties of spoken and written English acquired by deaf individuals. All of these varieties may be represented as levels of attainment on the acquisition continuum for English. The pidginization/creolization process can help to account for variation in levels of English and/or ASL proficiency. This process can also account for the remarkable similarities observed within and between spoken, written, and signed varieties of English despite wide variation in the ability of individuals to process speech and utilize manual communication.

In contrast, ASL, since it has not developed toward the norms of an external target language, may be considered a language created by its users, as in pidginization and creolization. It is a language with a wide array of varieties that must be represented on an acquisition continuum separate and distinct from that of English. The premise underlying Figure 2 and the ensuing discussion of age, intake, and attainment is that language acquisition in the deaf population, and in fact any population, can be explained parsimoniously by general principles characteristic of the processes of pidginization and creolization and the related constructs of depidginization and decreolization (see Andersen, 1983a). The acquisition continuum incorporated into this diagram extends from the initial stages of language development through more advanced stages, from pidginization and the beginnings of creolization and first language acquisition at basi (basal) levels through depidginization/decreolization at meso and acro levels. This continuum, therefore, accounts for child and adult acquisition under a variety of diverse circumstances ranging from first and second language acquisition to creolization, and, of course, to language development in the deaf population.

The two most prominent developmental milestones are highlighted in Figure 2. The interval from birth to about 5 years of age marks a period of exceptionally rapid language development in which a large portion of primary acquisition occurs, especially between the ages of 2 and 5

(Brown, 1973; Dale, 1976; Gleitman and Wanner, 1982; Maratsos, 1983). The fifth year is commonly considered a natural dividing line between initial/intermediate phases of acquisition and more advanced phases. Prior to age 5, the child's mastery of many linguistic constructs is incomplete, whereas after age 5, his/her internal representation of language structures and functions is refined, integrated, and reorganized to conform more closely to adult norms (Karmiloff-Smith, 1979b). The fifth year also marks the point at which cerebral lateralization is thought to become firmly established (e.g., Krashen, 1982) and has sometimes been considered an upper boundary for distinguishing pre- from post-lingual onset of deafness (e.g., Thompson, 1936).

The interval from the fifth to the twelfth years defines a period in which development and maturation near completion. Between the ages of 5 and 8, children bring their internal representation of the language closer to adult norms, and at about 8 years of age begin to acquire the ability to conceptualize and consciously reflect upon linguistic constructs as the objects of their own thought (Hakes, 1980; Karmiloff-Smith, 1979b). The child's emerging metalinguistic awareness may reach adult levels by 12 years of age and coincides with the onset of the stage of cognitive development known as formal operations (Hakes, 1980; Krashen, 1982). The age of 12 has been proposed as the boundary between child and adult language learning on the basis of reports that the initial stages of second language acquisition in learners over twelve generally progresses at faster rates than in younger learners (Krashen, Long, and Scarcella, 1982; Krashen, 1982). The age of 12 also marks the beginning of adolescence and the end of the critical period for primary language acquisition (Lenneberg, 1967).

The term *intake threshold* (see Figure 2) refers to a hypothetical measure of intake quantity and quality (i.e., a measure of intake integrity) and is intended to denote the minimum intake the learner needs to achieve mastery of the target language. The average of normal level of learner intake is hypothesized to be somewhat greater than the threshold level in order to allow for the possibility of individual differences among learners within the normal ranges of intake and attainment. The intake threshold varies as a function of age and gradually increases to reflect the organism's progressive loss of neuronal plasticity during maturation. The slope of this hypothetical function changes at about 5 and again at about 12 years to account for changes in the acquisition process associated with development. It is steepest in the interval between 5 and 12 years of age and approaches asymptote in the years following adolescence.

The mastery of a first language in childhood, it would seem, establishes the neurological basis for language learning in adulthood. When mastery of a first language has not been attained by the onset of adolescence, as typically occurs in the deaf population, progress in acquisition is inhibited or suppressed because the neurological foundations for language processing have not been sufficiently developed to support the intake of linguistic information. To the degree that the learner has not mastered a first language by the onset of adolescence, the neurological and cognitive substrates of language processing will fail to develop (see Curtiss, 1977). Those neurological and cognitive functions associated with primary acquisition are referred to here as the faculty for constructing language, or simply the language faculty (see Figure 1).

The language faculty filters the organism's input. However, since it is associated with primary language development and the progressive loss of neuronal plasticity, the language faculty is discernible only in situations where adequate mastery of a primary language has not been achieved by the onset of adolescence. Furthermore, the language faculty may become differentiated from other forms of symbolic activity, such as general problem-solving ability, in the course of acquisition.

A PIDGINIZATION/CREOLIZATION FRAMEWORK

The relationship between English and ASL is depicted in Figure 3 as the intersection of two acquisition continua. The premise underlying this diagram is that English and ASL spring from a common source, a primitive prototype that emerges in the initial state of pidginization and extends through much of the basi phase of acquisition. This earliest phase, which serves as a precursor of and basis for the development of syntactic structure (Givón, 1979, 1984), is characterized by a distinct lack of grammatical competence. The arrangement of constituents is dictated primarily by pragmatic discourse functions and characterized by strong tendencies toward parataxis (linear-sequential ordering) in lieu of syntactic devices, such as subordination and grammatical morphology (Givón, 1984; Schumann, 1982, 1987). At the basi level of acquisition, then, English and ASL are virtually indistinguishable.

Presyntactic development is a general phenomenon occurring in the earliest stages of both first and second language acquisition (e.g., in children's two-word utterances and at basi levels of adult second language proficiency), as well as in the development of pidgins and possibly even in the evolutionary origins of human language (Givón, 1979, 1984; Schumann, 1982). This phase of development is therefore universal and not unique to deafness. Differences in presyntactic development within and between groups of individuals are hypothesized to result from variation in the factors of age and intake, which appear to cause some learners to pass through the presyntactic phase more rapidly and completely than others. Vestiges of the presyntactic phase seem to persist in the English of a number of deaf adults and are especially evident in their incomplete acquisition of subordinate clause constructions and gram-

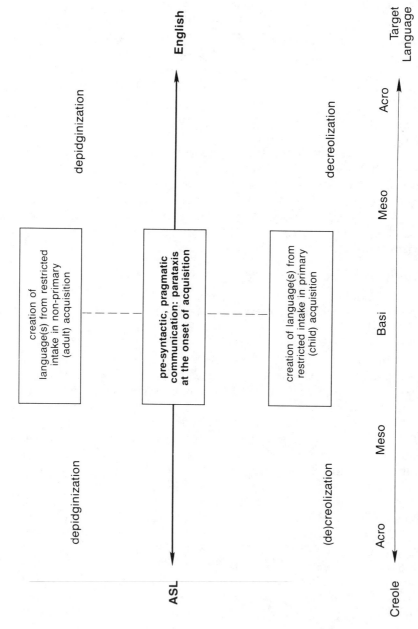

Figure 3. *Relationship among language varieties and acquisition continua in the deaf population*

matical morphemes, that is, in their tendency to concatenate constituents in linear-sequential order (Bochner, 1978, 1982). Similarly, in basi ASL, symbols tend to be juxtaposed in linear-sequential order, as in classical Chinese orthography. The juxtaposition of ideographic characters in classical Chinese writing represents a type of metaphorical expression that, like basi levels of ASL and English, does not involve conventional syntax (Fenollosa, 1962). Since the suspension of surface syntactic constraints characterizes metaphor, figurative usage in all human languages may be viewed as the vestiges of parataxis and pragmatic communication. Metaphorical language, while circumventing and defying the linguistic parameter of grammaticality, represents a primal level of symbolic functioning at the root of creative expression in the arts and sciences and in other epistemological systems (Cassirer, 1944; Langer, 1951; Turbayne, 1971). Thus, pre- or nonsyntactic representation may be associated with metaphor, and hence, considered a universal property of language and symbolic functioning common to deaf and normally-hearing individuals alike.

For hearing-impaired individuals, intake tends to be restricted by both internal and external sources (see Figure 1). First, hearing loss restricts the organism's ability to process speech input at the level of sensation, and despite the benefits of acoustic amplification, speech intake generally remains fragmentary and incomplete since hearing aids and lipreading cannot sufficiently compensate for most severe to profound hearing losses (Erber, 1983; Niemoeller, 1978; Perry and Silverman, 1978). Second, manual communication, when used in conjunction with speech, frequently does not complement or supplement acoustic input very well. This is because the simultaneous manual representations produced by normally-hearing individuals are often truncated versions of their spoken messages (Nienhuys, Cross, and Horsborough, 1984; Swisher, 1984). Such truncated input may not be adequate for normal language learning. Even when adequate and accurate manual depictions of spoken English are available, they may not be processed completely and reliably by some hearing-impaired learners because certain features (e.g., inflectional suffixes in SEE 1 and SEE 2 and portions of rapidly fingerspelled messages) may not always be perceptually salient or linguistically significant to them.

Finally, printed English can at best only complement or supplement its spoken counterpart as a source of linguistic input since it does not allow for fluid social interchanges as does speech, nor does orthography have an adequate analog to speech prosody. In addition, deaf individuals tend to have difficulty maintaining sequences of words in working memory while reading (Conrad, 1979; Hanson, 1982), and such limitations on memory capacity are associated with the tendency to exclude functors and grammatical morphemes from processing (Lichtenstein, 1984). Restrictions on the integrity of linguistic intake such as these, when coupled with the effects of age, are hypothesized to influence the level of proficiency attained by learners.

English

The most primitive level of basi English is characterized by a tendency to concatenate nominal elements and use verbs sparingly, and is evidenced in paratactic naming behavior in the writing of deaf children (Myklebust, 1964; Walter, 1955). This level of acquisition is comparable in many respects to children's early one- and two-word utterances and to primitive pidgins, and it parallels a stage of second language acquisition in which nouns outnumber verbs by a ratio of greater than two to one (Kelly, 1983; Schumann, 1982). Another form of parataxis characterized by a nearly one-to-one ratio of nouns to verbs seems to emerge in the spoken language of deaf children (Goda, 1964), as well as in early stages of normal first language acquisition and in the development of pidgins (Givón, 1979). Both types of parataxis appear to be widespread in language development, and not limited to any particular channel or modality of communication employed by members of the deaf population. In general, parataxis would appear to be more common in spontaneous face-to-face communication than in writing owing to the facilitating effects of an ongoing and shared communicative context (see Givón, 1979).

As development proceeds, the primitive features characteristic of the lowest end of the acquisition structures, with vestiges of the presyntatic phase persisting to various degrees as errors committed by learners at the meso level. The latter stages of basi English are characterized by the emergence of simple SVO clauses, coordinate structures, and the precursors of grammatical morphology, all of which are interrelated and correspond to features of pidgins and creoles and the early development of first and second languages (Bickerton, 1981, 1984; Givón, 1979, 1984; Schumann, 1982, 1987; see also Curtiss, 1977). Permissible deviations from the canonical SVO word order, such as passive and interrogative sentences, are rarely produced and exceedingly difficult for individuals at the basi level to comprehend correctly (Power and Quigley, 1973; Quigley et al., 1974; Tervoort, 1970). Syntactic passives and interrogatives are also rare in pidgins and creoles (Bickerton, 1981). In addition, phrases and clauses tend to be concatenated rather than hierarchically arranged, with subordinate clauses, grammatical morphology, and null anaphora being sources of considerable difficulty and the complementizer *to* frequently being omitted from infinitive constructions (Albertini and Forman, 1985; Bochner, 1978, 1982; Odom and Blanton, 1967; Wilbur, 1977). Grammars of pidgins and creoles are likewise characterized more by verb serialization and paratactic coordination than by subordination (Bickerton, 1981). Finally, errors in the formation of the English passive, interrogative, and complement constructions are in part reflections of the tenuous status of the category of verbal auxiliaries (Bochner, 1982; see also Ivimey and Lachterman, 1980). This category is typically absent from pidgins (Bickerton, 1981).

The meso and acro levels are distinguished from the basi level of attainment by the emergence of complex syntax. The transition from the basi to the meso level is marked by the transition from coordination to subordination, the development of grammatical morphology, and the emergence of a category of verbal auxiliaries (Bickerton, 1981; Givón, 1979; also see Schumann, 1987). The onset of the acro level, although difficult to locate and define precisely, represents a point where the major syntactic structures of the language have clearly emerged and lapses into parataxis are quite rare. Progression through the acro level then constitutes a process of increasing refinement and conformity toward the norms of the target language, especially with regard to the acquisition of marked forms.

AMERICAN SIGN LANGUAGE

Fischer (1978), Woodward (1978), and others have proposed sociolinguistic continua to explain the relationship among varieties of signing in North America. On these continua, the variety closest to English constitutes the acrolect and the one furthest from English the basilect ("pure" ASL). Turning now to the acquisition of ASL, *the process,* we proposed a wholly different sort of continuum in order to capture the various levels of proficiency evident among adult deaf signers (Figure 3). The acro level on this psycholinguistic continuum refers to varieties exhibiting the hallmarks of ASL grammar (e.g., a rich aspectual system and SVO word order); whereas the basi and meso levels are defined as systems exhibiting these characteristics to lesser degrees. As with English, the basi and meso levels are considered substandard varieties of ASL.

The acro level is typically used by deaf (and hearing) children of deaf parents. As discussed in "The Process of Acquisition," this variety exhibits striking structural parallels to spoken creoles. At the morphological level, one similarity is that the ASL verb is inflected for temporal aspect (e.g., punctual or durative) but seldom for tense (Bickerton, 1981); tense is indicated lexically by using such signs as WILL, PAST, and NOW (Newport and Meier, 1986). The canonical word order of ASL is subject-verb-object. Question word order is identical to that of statements in ASL, as is the case in spoken creoles; an interrogative morpheme is either pre- or postposed in ASL for wh-questions. According to Bickerton (1981), passive constructions are extremely rare in creoles, and this is the case in ASL; given any transitive verb, an N-V-N sequence will be interpreted as agent-action-patient, while an N-V sequence will be interpreted as patient-action (Fischer, 1978, refers to this latter construction in the ASL sentence, PICNIC POSTPONE BECAUSE RAIN, as a kind of "middle voice"). A notable departure from standard SVO word order occurs when constituents other than the subject NP are topicalized. As in Guyanese Creole and Hawaiian Creole English, ASL appears to have a discourse-motivated rule that moves topicalized constituents to sentence initial position.

There are lexical similarities as well. Content words sometimes assume unique and distinctive grammatical functions in creoles. The same lexical item (get/have), for example, is used for existentials and possessives in Hawaiian Creole English and ASL:

get wan wahini shi get wan data
"There is a woman who has a daughter." (Bickerton, 1981, p. 67)

HAVE SOMEONE HOME?
"Is there anyone home" (Fischer, 1978, p. 319)

Basi and meso varieties are used by children at early stages of acquisition and by adults who have not learned ASL at an early age. Without sufficient sign input at an early age, children tend to create idiosyncratic home-signs (Goldin-Meadow, 1979, 1982). Such children are thought to recreate or "recreolize" ASL in each generation (Fischer, 1978). Their attainment in ASL is determined, again, by amount, type, and age of first exposure to the language (see Figure 2).

The variables of age and attainment in PSE and ASL have been examined by Hatfield (1982). She used four tasks to assess fluency in ASL and manually coded English (MCE): a reaction time fluency test, self-rating scales, interviewer rating scales, and a language background questionnaire. MCE is defined as all forms of signing that approximate English structure, including Pidgin Sign English. Her subjects were 51 deaf and 10 hearing adults. The deaf students had a mean age of 20 years at the time of the study. Her results indicate a strong correlation between age of acquisition and attainment. Students who were exposed to ASL or MCE before the age of 12 years performed best in both, whereas those who learned ASL or MCE after the age of 12 performed poorly.

Over the last fifteen years, much attention has been focused on the acquisition of ASL (e.g., Fischer, 1973; Hoffmeister, 1982; and Newport and Meier, 1986; Prinz and Prinz, 1979; Schlesinger and Meadow, 1972; Wilbur, 1979). One is struck first by the similarities between the acquisition of ASL and spoken languages. Children learning ASL appear to pass through stages of sign babbling, single sign (or utterance) production, and holophrastic signing between the ages of 8 and 22 months. Errors in child sign are similar in kind to those made by children learning English, for example. There is morpheme reduction or deletion (Loew,

1984; Newport and Meier, 1986), overgeneralization of rules (Fischer, 1973; Hoffmeister, 1982), and avoidance of highly marked forms (hand-shapes) (Hoffmeister, 1982, McIntire, 1977).

Studies like those mentioned above indicate that deaf children appear to attend more to the formal properties of signs than to iconic associations even in a language where such associations are plentiful. A question often asked is what role, if any, the difference in modality plays in the acquisition of ASL. One apparent difference of interest in this chapter is the precocious appearance of the first intelligible signs as opposed to words. In one study (Bonvillian, Orlansky, and Novack, 1983), the early sign production of 10 hearing children of deaf parents and one deaf child of deaf parents was recorded. The mean age for producing the first intelligible sign was 8.5 months and, by 1 year of age, mean vocabulary size was 10.0 signs. As Newport and Meier point out, the earliest reports of 10 intelligible spoken words are around 15 months (e.g., Nelson, 1973). Hoffmeister (1982) cities one study that reported a subject's first sign at 7 months. Interestingly, subsequent milestones in the acquisition of ASL do not appear to be achieved earlier than those of the spoken language (English). One explanation offered for this early sign production is the earlier maturation of the gross motor or visual receptive systems; further, precocious signing may suggest that the age at onset of sign production in deaf *and* hearing children of deaf parents is earlier than previously supposed, given "... access to a modality which favors their earliest attempts" (Newport and Meier, 1986). As suggested earlier in this chapter, the nature of the signals themselves may influence the reception and onset of production. The appearance of intelligible signs may be due, in part, to a child having greater access to the segmentation of morphological units in the stream of signing as opposed to such units in the stream of speech.

Finally, there is one significant difference between the Deaf community and other language communities that complicates studies of acquisition and accounts for the varieties of ASL. Unlike most creole situations, where the parents almost invariably provide the primary language environment, there are two paths to the acquisition of ASL. The first is that of second- and third-generation Deaf children for whom ASL is a native language acquired in childhood; the second, more varied, path is followed by first-generation deaf children (children of hearing parents) whose contact with ASL may be very limited (Newport and Supalla, 1980). One wonders what happens when a first-generation signer attempts to communicate with second- or third-generation signers. Presumably, the native signer pidginizes or simplifies his/her variety. Although such contact occurs frequently, this hypothesized simplification of register (see Ferguson, 1971) has not been studied. It would seem a crucial area for establishing the nature of language change in ASL.

Here is a case where users of the acrolect constitute the minority, and as such must frequently adapt to the communication needs of the majority, who are users of basil and meso varieties. Such a situation might restrain structural change arising from second- and third-generation signers.

Educational implications and conclusions

As we explained in the preceding section of this chapter, the process of language acquisition is affected greatly by the interaction between age and intake. The effects of this interaction on the attainment of language proficiency provide the rationale for parents and teachers to consciously and systematically strive, from the moment hearing loss is diagnosed in a child, to create an appropriate language environment. A crucial step in creating such an environment is to make the speech signal more accessible by fitting the child with an appropriate hearing aid and fostering the use and development of lipreading. In addition to acoustic amplification, lipreading, and other features of oral education, some form of manual communication should be considered either a complement to or substitute for oral English. Where proficient models of ASL are available, parents should consider providing their child with early exposure to ASL in a bilingual environment.

In designing an appropriate language environment for a given hearing-impaired child, both the quality and quantity of language intake must be considered. Attention must be paid not only to the form of language input (e.g., to the syntactic structure of the input), but also to its meaning and function (Halliday, 1975). For example, although orthographic signals may be of sufficient quality to complement or supplement other forms of input, print neither readily serves social interactive functions nor permits the immediacy of interpersonal feedback that spontaneous face-to-face communication does. However, the written mode may be consciously adapted to accommodate more fluid interpersonal interchanges through informal, conversational written registers, for example, through dialogue journals (Albertini and Meath-Lang, 1986; Staton, Shuy, and Kreeft, 1982).

The virtue of auxiliary systems of manual communication is that they serve instrumental functions and provide accessible input. Limitations in their use, however, need to be recognized. As models of English, they require a high degree of proficiency if simultaneously spoken messages are to be adequately represented. Even when adequate models are available, many children will tend to digress from the established conventions of auxiliary systems in classroom communication. Such digressions raise the issue of whether strict adherence to the conventions of an auxiliary system facilitates or inhibits the attainment of English in deaf children. Should these digressions be prohibited because they are errors in standard English or should they be permitted because they are meaningful and creative usages? In order to answer this question, researchers and educators must recognize that creative excursions are a natural part of language acquisition and language change. Measures taken to prohibit such digressions and preserve the integrity of an auxiliary system, therefore, may have a detrimental effect on acquisition in some children. There is, of course, a need to maximize accuracy and synchrony with English, but this need must be balanced against the more basic need to foster meaningful, rewarding communication.

A diverse array of educational methods and approaches to communication is available, none of which would be appropriate to use with every hearing-impaired child. The question is not which method, approach, or philosophy is best suited to the general needs of a widely diverse population, but which best serves the actual needs of specific individuals in that population. This question presupposes that some hearing-impaired children will be best served by high-quality oral education and communication methods, whereas others will be best served by the Rochester Method, or by more general approaches falling under the auxiliary sign/total communication rubric. Still others may be served best by an ASL-English bilingual approach. The challenge educators face is to find valid and reliable ways of predicting how well individual students will perform under various educational alternatives and to inform them and their parents of available resources and reasonable expectations. A further, and perhaps more significant challenge is to ensure that educational and communicative practices are employed with high degrees of skill and understanding since these are areas in which practice is as important as theory and quality is more important than dogma.

Assuming that neuronal plasticity diminishes with increasing age and that mastery of a primary language serves as a basis for acquisition in adolescence and beyond, some researchers have hypothesized that the level of proficiency that may be attained by adults (i.e., learners over 15 years of age who have not yet mastered a primary language) is suppressed in an absolute sense to levels well below those considered indicative of native proficiency (Bochner, 1982). This hypothesis asserts only that the attainment of native proficiency is suppressed, and does not imply that adult learners falling into this category cannot improve their language proficiency, especially their skills in functional communication. Specifically, it is felt that adult learners can make tangible improvements in their primary language ability, but that attainment becomes suppressed as higher (acro) levels of proficiency are reached. The suppression hypothesis explicitly pertains to group tendencies and does not preclude the possibility of exceptions in the form of individuals who make great progress in acquiring their primary language in adulthood. The existence of such exceptional cases may be explained in part by individual differences in the loss of neuronal plasticity (see Seliger, 1981), the implication being that individuals may differ in the manner in which they are affected by the factor of age much as they differ in cognitive/learning style and motivation.

The level of proficiency attained in the primary language(s) has such a profound and lasting impact on an individual's development that its educational importance cannot be overemphasized. The effects of age indicate that the years prior to the close of the critical period, especially the preschool years, are vital to primary acquisition. The effects of intake indicate that its quality and quantity must be maximized in order to facilitate development and learning. The environment, the channel, and the mind each play a crucial role in the processing and acquisition of language and must be considered in the design of educational and communication programs for hearing-impaired children. In emphasizing the importance of age and intake, the constructs of pidginization and creolization enhance our understanding of the language acquisition process in ways that hold direct implications for the education of deaf people.

References

Albertini, J., J. Bochner, C. Cuneo, L. Hunt, R. Nielson, L. Seago, and N. Shannon. (1986). Development of a writing test for deaf college students. *Teaching English to Deaf and Second Language Students* 4 (2), 5–11.
Albertini, J. A., and J. Forman. (1985). The use of elicited imitation to assess competence in English as a second language. In S. Jones, M. DesBrisay, and T. Paribakht (Eds.), *Proceedings of the 5th Annual Language Testing Colloquium*. Ottawa: Carleton University.
Albertini, J., and B. Meath-Lang. (1986). An analysis of student-teacher exchanges in dialogue journal writing. *Journal of Curriculum Theorizing 7*, 1–14.
Albertini, J. A., and V. J. Samar. (1983). Early instruction of object complements to hearing-impaired college students. *Journal of Applied Psycholinguistics 4*, 345–357.
Anderson, J. R. (1983). *The Architecture of Cognition*. Cambridge, Mass.: Harvard University Press.
Andersen, R. W. (Ed.). (1983a). *Pidginization and Creolization as Language Acquisition*. Rowley, Mass.: Newbury House.
   (1983b). Introduction: a language acquisition interpretation of pidginization and creolization. In R. Andersen (Ed.), *Pidginization and Creolization as Language Acquisition*. Rowley, Mass.: Newbury House.
Bellugi, U. (1983). Language structure and language breakdown in American Sign Language. In M. Studdert-Kennedy (Ed.), *Psychobiology of Language*. Cambridge, Mass.: MIT Press.
Bellugi, U., and S. Fischer. (1972). A comparison of sign language and spoken language. *Cognition 1*, 173–200.

Berent, G. P. (1983). Control judgments of deaf adults and by second language learners. *Language Learning 33*, 37–53.

Bickerton, D. (1977). Pidginization and creolization: Language acquisition and language universals. In A. Valdman (Ed.), *Pidgin and Creole Linguistics*. Bloomington: Indiana University Press.

(1981). *Roots of Language*. Ann Arbor, Mich.: Karoma.

(1984). The language bioprogram hypothesis and second language acquisition. In W. E. Rutherford (Ed.), *Language Universals and Second Language Acquisition*. Amsterdam: John Benjamins.

Bochner, J. H. (1978). Error, anomaly, and variation in the English of deaf individuals. *Language and Speech 21*, 174–189.

(1982). English in the deaf population. In D. G. Simms, G. G. Walter, and R. L. Whitehead (Eds.), *Deafness and Communication: Assessment and Training*. Baltimore, Md.: Williams and Wilkins.

(In Press). Children's comprehension of time-altered sentences. *Language in Speech*.

Bonvillian, J., M. Orlansky, and L. Novack. (1983). Early sign language acquisition and its relation to cognitive and motor development. In J. Kyle and B. Woll (Eds.), *Language in Sign*. London: Croom Helm.

Bowerman, M. (1982). Reorganizational processes in lexical and syntactic development. In E. Wanner and L. R. Gleitman (Eds.), *Language Acquisition: The State of the Art*. Cambridge: Cambridge University Press.

Bragg, B. (1973). Ameslish—Our American heritage: A testimony. *American Annals of the Deaf 118*, 672–674.

Brannon, J. B. (1966). The speech production and spoken language of the deaf. *Language and Speech 9*, 127–136.

(1968). Linguistic word classes in the spoken language of normal, hard-of-hearing, and deaf children. *Journal of Speech and Hearing Research 11*, 279–287.

Brannon, J. B., and T. T. Murray. (1966). The spoken syntax of normal, hard-of-hearing, and deaf children. *Journal of Speech and Hearing Research 9*, 604–610.

Broen, P. (1972). *The Verbal Environment of the Language-Learning Child*. American Speech and Hearing Association Monographs no. 17. Washington, D.C.

Brown, R. (1973). *A First Language: The Early Stages*. Cambridge, Mass.: Harvard University Press.

Bruner, J. (1981). The pragmatics of acquisition. In W. Deutsch (Ed.), *The Child's Construction of Language*. London: Academic Press.

Caccamise, F. (1978). Sign language and simultaneous communication: Linguistic, psychological and instructional ramifications. *American Annals of the Deaf 123*, 797–902.

Caccamise, F., L. Brewer, and B. Meath-Lang. (1983). Selection of signs and sign languages for use in clinical and academic settings. *Audiology 8*, 31–44.

Caccamise, F., M. Garretson, and U. Bellugi. (Eds.). (1981). *Teaching American Sign Language as a Second/Foreign Language*. Silver Spring, Md.: National Association for the Deaf.

Caccamise, F., and W. Newell. (1984). A review of current terminology used in deaf education and signing. *Journal of the Academy of Rehabilitative Audiology, 17,* 106–129.

Cassirer, E. (1944). *An Essay on Man.* New Haven, Conn.: Yale University Press.

Chomsky, N. (1965). *Aspects of the Theory of Syntax.* Cambridge, Mass.: MIT Press.

(1966). *Cartesian Linguistics.* New York: Harper & Row.

(1972). *Language and Mind.* New York: Harcourt Brace Jovanovich.

(1975). *Reflections on Language.* New York: Pantheon.

Clark, R. (1977). What's the use of imitation? *Journal of Child Language 4,* 341–358.

Cokely, D., and R. Gawlik. (1980). Childrenese as pidgin. In W. Stokoe (Ed.), *Sign and Culture.* Silver Spring, Md.: Linstok Press.

Conrad, R. (1977). The reading ability of deaf school-leavers. *British Journal of Educational Psychology 47,* 138–148.

(1979). *The Deaf School Child.* London: Harper & Row.

Cooper, W. E., and J. Paccia-Cooper. (1980). *Syntax and Speech.* Cambridge, Mass.: Harvard University Press.

Crandall, K. (1978). Inflectional morphemes in the manual English of young hearing-impaired children and their mothers. *Journal of Speech and Hearing Research 21,* 372–386.

Cromer, R. F. (1981). Reconceptualizing language acquisition and cognitive development. In R. L. Schiefelbusch and D. D. Bricker (Eds.), *Early Language: Acquisition and Intervention.* Baltimore, Md.: University Park Press.

Crystal, D. (1973). Non-segmental phonology in language acquisition: a review of the issues. *Lingua 32,* 1–45.

Curtiss, S. (1977). *Genie: A Psycholinguistic Study of a Modern-Day "Wild Child."* New York: Academic Press.

Dale, P. S. (1976). *Language Development Structure and Function.* New York: Holt, Rinehart & Winston.

DeCamp, D. (1971). Introduction: The study of pidgin and creole languages. In D. Hymes (Ed.), *Pidginization and creolization of languages.* New York: Cambridge University Press.

Deuchar, M. (1983). *Negative incorporation in sign languages as creoles.* A paper presented at the Annual Meeting of the Linguistic Society of America, Minneapolis, Minnesota.

DiFrancesca, S. (1972). Academic Achievement Test Results of a National Testing Program for Hearing-Impaired Students: United States, Spring 1971. Washington, D.C.: Gallaudet College, Office of Demographic Studies.

Edwards, V., and P. Ladd. (1983). British Sign Language and West Indian Creole. In J. Kyle and B. Woll (Eds.), *Language in Sign.* London: Croom Helm.

Eibl-Eibesfeldt, I. (1970). *Ethology: The Biology of Behavior.* New York: Holt, Rinehart & Winston.

Elliott, L. L., I. J. Hirsh, and A. A. Simmons. (1967). Language of young hearing-impaired children. *Language and Speech 10,* 141–158.

Erber, N. P. (1983). Speech perception and speech development in hearing-impaired children. In I. Hochberg, H. Levitt, and M. J. Osberger (Eds.), *Speech of the Hearing Impaired.* Baltimore, Md.: University Park Press.

Fant, L. (1972). *Ameslan: An Introduction to American Sign Language (Teacher's Manual).* Silver Spring, Md.: National Association of the Deaf.

Fenollosa, E. (1962). The Chinese written character as a medium for poetry. In K. Shapiro (Ed.), *Prose Keys to Modern Poetry.* New York: Harper & Row.

Fentress, J. C. (1983). Hierarchical motor control. In M. Studdert-Kennedy (Ed.), *Psychobiology of Language.* Cambridge, Mass.: MIT Press.

Ferguson, C. (1971). Absence of copula and the notion of simplicity: A study of normal speech, baby talk, foreigner talk, and pidgins. In D. Hymes (Ed.), *Pidginization and Creolization of Languages.* New York: Cambridge University Press.

Fischer, S. (1973). Verb inflections on American Sign Language and their acquisition by the deaf child. A paper presented at the Annual Meeting of the Linguistic Society of America, San Diego.
    (1978). Sign languages and creoles. In P. Siple (Ed.), *Understanding Language through Sign Language Research.* New York: Academic Press.

Fishman, J. (1982). A critique of six papers on the socialization of the deaf child. In V. Christiansen and R. Meigegeier (Eds.), *Conference Highlights, National Research Conference on the Social Aspects of Deafness.* Washington, D.C.: Gallaudet College.

Fourcin, A. (1978). Acoustic patterns and speech acquisition. In N. Waterson and C. Snow (Eds.), *The Development of Communication.* Chichester, N.Y.: Wiley.

Fry, D. B. (1975). Phonological aspects of language acquisition in the hearing and the deaf. In E. H. Lenneberg and E. Lenneberg (Eds.), *Foundations of Language Development,* Vol 2. New York: Academic Press.

Gallaudet Research Institute (1985). *Gallaudet Research Institute Newsletter.* Washington, D.C.: Gallaudet College.

Gass, S., and C. Madden. (Eds.). (1985). *Input in Second-Language Acquisition.* Rowley, Mass.: Newbury House.

Geers, A., J. Moog, and B. Schick. (1984). Acquisition of spoken and signed English by profoundly deaf children. *Journal of Speech and Hearing Disorders 49,* 378–388.

Givón, T. (1979). *On Understanding Grammar.* New York: Academic Press.
    (1984). Universals of discourse structure and second language acquisition. In W. E. Rutherford (Ed.), *Language Universals and Second Language Acquisition.* Amsterdam: John Benjamins.

Gleitman, L. R., and E. Wanner. (1982). Language acquisition: the state of the art. In E. Wanner and L. R. Gleitman (Eds.), *Language Acquisition: The State of the Art.* New York: Cambridge University Press.

Goda, S. (1959). Language skills of profoundly deaf adolescent children. *Journal of Speech and Hearing Research 2,* 369–376.
    (1964). Spoken syntax of normal, deaf, and retarded adolescents. *Journal of Verbal Learning and Verbal Behavior 3,* 401–405.

Goldin-Meadow, S. (1979). Structure in a manual communication system developed without a conventional language model: language without a helping hand. In H. Whitaker and H. Whitaker (Eds.), *Studies in Neurolinguistics.* New York: Academic Press.
    (1982). The resilience of recursion: a study developed without a conventional

language model. In E. Wanner and L. R. Gleitman (Eds.), *Language Acquisition: The State of the Art.* Cambridge: Cambridge University Press.

Greenberg, B. L., and S. Withers. (1965). *Better English Usage: A Guide for the Deaf.* Indianapolis, Ind.: Bobbs-Merrill.

Hakes, D. (1980). *The Development of Meta-linguistic Abilities in Children.* New York: Springer-Verlag.

Halliday, M. A. K. (1975). Learning how to mean. In E. H. Lenneberg and E. Lenneberg (Eds.), *Foundations of Language Development.* New York: Academic Press.

Hanson, V. L. (1982). Short term recall by deaf signers of American Sign Language: Implications of encoding strategy for order recall. *Journal of Experimental Psychology: Learning, Memory and Cognition 8,* 572–583.

Hatch, E. (1983). Simplified input and second language acquisition. In R. W. Andersen (Ed.), *Pidginization and Creolization as Language Acquisition.* Rowley, Mass.: Newbury House.

Hatfield, N. (1982). An investigation of bilingualism in two signed languages: American Sign Language and manually coded English. Unpublished doctoral dissertation. Rochester, N.Y.: University of Rochester.

Heider, F., and G. Heider. (1940). A comparison of sentence structure of deaf and hearing children. *Psychological Monographs 52,* 42–103.

Hoffmeister, R. (1982). Acquisition of signed languages by deaf children. In H. Hoemann and R. Wilbur (Eds.), *Social Aspects of Deafness: Interpersonal Communication and Deaf People.* Washington, D.C.: Gallaudet College.

Hsu, C. (1978, 1979). Six years of observation of Visible English at Louisiana State School for the Deaf. *Teaching English to the Deaf 5,* 27–28; 6, 27–34.

Hymes, D. (1971). Introduction. In D. Hymes (Ed.), *Pidginization and Creolization of Languages.* New York: Cambridge University Press.

Ivimey, G. P., and D. H. Lachterman. (1980). The written language of young English deaf children. *Language and Speech 23,* 351–377.

Jacobson, M. (1975). Brain development in relation to language. In E. H. Lenneberg and E. Lenneberg (Eds.), *Foundations of Language Development,* Vol 1. New York: Academic Press.

Jakobson, R. (1967). About the relation between visual and auditory signs. In W. Wathen-Dunn (Ed.), *Models for the Perception of Speech and Visual Form.* Cambridge, Mass.: MIT Press.

Jones, M. R. (1976). Time, our lost dimension: toward a new theory of perception, attention, and memory. *Psychological Review 83,* 323–355.

Karmiloff-Smith, A. (1979a). *A Functional Approach to Child Language.* Cambridge: Cambridge University Press.

(1979b). Language development after five. In P. Fletcher and M. Garman (Eds.), *Language Acquisition.* Cambridge: Cambridge University Press.

(1981). The grammatical marking of thematic structure in the development of language production. In W. Deutsch (Ed.), *The Child's Construction of Language.* London: Academic Press.

Kelly, P. (1983). The question of uniformity in interlanguage development. In K. M. Bailey, M. H. Long, and S. Peck (Eds.), *Second Language Acquisition Studies.* Rowley, Mass.: Newbury House.

Kent, R. (1981). Sensorimotor aspects of speech development. In R. N. Aslin,

J. R. Alberts, and M. R. Petersen (Eds.), *The Development of Perception: Psychobiological Perspectives.* New York: Academic Press.

Klima, E., and U. Bellugi. (1979). *The Signs of Language.* Cambridge, Mass.: Harvard University Press.

Krashen, S., (1980). The input hypothesis. In J. Alatis (Ed.), *Current Issues in Bilingual Education.* Washington, D.C.: Georgetown University Press.

(1982). Accounting for child-adult differences in second language rate and attainment. In S. D. Krashen, R. C. Scarcella, and M. H. Long (Eds.), *Child-Adult Differences in Second Language Acquisition.* Rowley, Mass.: Newbury House.

Krashen, S., M. Long, and R. Scarcella. (1982). Age, rate, and eventual attainment in second language acquisition. In S. D. Krashen, R. C. Scarcella, and M. H. Long (Eds.), *Child-Adult Differences in Second Language Acquisition.* Rowley, Mass.: Newbury House.

Kretschmer, R., and L. Kretschmer. (1978). *Language Development and Intervention with the Hearing Impaired.* Baltimore, Md.: University Park Press.

Lane, H., and F. Grosjean. (1980). *Recent Perspectives on American Sign Language.* Hillsdale, N.J.: Lawrence Erlbaum.

Langer, S. (1951). *Philosophy in a New Key.* Cambridge, Mass.: Harvard University Press.

Larsen-Freeman, D. (1983). The importance of input in second language acquisition. In R. W. Andersen (Ed.), *Pidginization and Creolization as Language Acquisition.* Rowley, Mass.: Newbury House.

Lashley, K. (1951). The problem of serial order in behavior. In L. A. Jeffress (Ed.), *Cerebral Mechanisms in Behavior.* New York: Wiley.

Lenneberg, E. H. (1967). *Biological Foundations of Language.* New York: Wiley.

Lewis, M., and L. A. Rosenblum (Eds.) (1977). *Interaction, Conversation, and the Development of Language.* New York: Wiley-Interscience.

Liberman, A. M. (1970). The grammars of speech and language. *Cognitive Psychology 1,* 301–323.

(1980). An ethological approach to language through the study of speech perception. In M. von Cranach, K. Foppa, W. Lepenies, and D. Ploog (Eds.), *Human Ethology.* Cambridge: Cambridge University Press.

Liberman, A. M., and D. B. Pisoni. (1977). Evidence for a special speech-perceiving subsystem in the human. In T. H. Bullock (Ed.), *Recognition of Complex Acoustic Signals.* Berlin: Dahlem Konferenzen.

Lichtenstein, E. H. (1984). The relationship between reading processes and English skills of deaf college students. Working Paper. Rochester, N.Y.: National Technical Institute for the Deaf.

Liddell, S. (1984). THINK and BELIEVE: sequentiality in American Sign Language. *Language 60,* 372–399.

Lieberman, P. (1967). *Intonation, Perception, and Language.* Cambridge, Mass.: MIT Press.

(1984). *The Biology and Evolution of Language.* Cambridge, Mass.: Harvard University Press.

Loew, R. (1984). Roles and reference in American Sign Language: a developmental perspective. Unpublished doctoral dissertation. University of Minnesota.

Lyons, J. (1977). *Semantics.* Vol. 1. Cambridge: Cambridge University Press.

McIntire, M. (1977). The acquisition of American Sign Language configurations. *Sign Language Studies 16,* 247–266.

McQuown, N. A. (1950). A planned auxiliary language. *Language 26,* 175–185. Reprinted in D. Hymes (Ed.), *Language in Culture and Society,* New York: Harper and Row, 1964.

Maratsos, M. (1983). Some current issues in the study of the acquisition of grammar. In J. H. Flavell and E. M. Markman (Eds.), *Handbook of Child Psychology.* Vol. 3, New York: Wiley.

Marler, P. R. (1975). On the origin of speech from animal sounds. In J. F. Kavanagh and J. E. Cutting (Eds.), *The Role of Speech in Language.* Cambridge, Mass.: MIT Press.

  (1977a). Development and learning of recognition systems. In T. H. Bullock (Eds.), *Recognition of Complex Acoustic Signals.* Berlin: Dahlem Konferenzen.

  (1977b). Sensory templates, vocal perception, and development: a comparative view. In M. Lewis and L. A. Rosenblum (Eds.), *Interaction, Conversation, and the Development of Language.* New York: Wiley-Interscience.

Marmor, G., and L. Petitto. (1979). Simultaneous communication in the classroom: How well is English being represented? *Sign Language Studies 23,* 99–136.

Martin, J. G. (1972). Rhythmic (hierarchical) versus serial structure in speech and other behavior. *Psychological Review 79,* 487–509.

Menyuk, P., and L. Menn. (1979). Early strategies for the perception and production of words and sounds. In P. Fletcher and M. Garman (Eds.), *Language Acquisition.* Cambridge: Cambridge University.

Milner, B. (1976). CNS maturation and language acquisition. In H. Whitaker and H. A. Whitaker (Eds.), *Studies in Neurolinguistics.* Vol. 1. New York: Academic Press.

Moores, D. F. (1970). An investigation of the psycholinguistic functioning of deaf adolescents. *Exceptional Children 36,* 645–652.

  (1978). *Educating the Deaf: Psychology, Principles, and Practices.* Boston: Houghton Mifflin.

Myklebust, H. R. (1964). *The Psychology of Deafness.* New York: Grune & Stratton.

Nelson, K. (1973). Structure and strategy in learning to talk. Monographs of the Society for Research in Child Development, *38* (1–2, Serial no. 149).

Newport, E. L. (1982). Task specificity in language learning? Evidence from speech perception and American Sign Language. In E. Wanner and L. R. Gleitman (Eds.), *Language Acquisition: The State of the Art,* Cambridge: Cambridge University Press.

Newport, E., and R. Meier. (1986). Acquisition of American Sign Language. In D. Slobin (Ed.), *The Cross-linguistic Study of Language Acquisition,* Vol. 1. Hillsdale, N.J.: Lawrence Erlbaum.

Newport, E. L., and T. Supalla. (1980). Clues from the acquisition of signed and spoken language. In U. Bellugi and M. Studdert-Kennedy (Eds.), *Signed and Spoken Language: Biological Constraints on Linguistic Form.* Weinheim: Verlag Chemie.

Niemoeller, A. F. (1978). Hearing aids. In H. Davis and S. R. Silverman (Eds.), *Hearing and Deafness.* New York: Holt, Rinehart & Winston.

Nienhuys, T., T. Cross, and K. Horsborough. (1984). Child variables influencing material speech style: deaf and hearing children. *Journal of Communication Disorders 17,* 189–207.

Nooteboom, S. G., J. Brokx, and J. de Rooij. (1978). Contributions of prosody to speech perception. In W. J. M. Levelt and G. B. Flo·res D'Arcais (Eds.), *Studies in the Perception of Language.* New York: Wiley.

Odom, P. B., and R. L. Blanton. (1967). Phrase-learning in deaf and hearing subjects. *Journal of Speech and Hearing Research 10,* 600–605.

Paget, R., and P. Gorman. (1971). *An Introduction to the Paget-Gorman Sign System with Examples.* AEDE Publications Committee, c/o 13 Ashbury Drive, Tilehurst, Reading, Berkshire, England.

Patkowski (1980). The sensitive period for the acquisition of syntax in a second language. *Language Learning 30,* 449–472.

Perry, A. L., and S. R. Silverman. (1978). Speechreading. In I. H. Davis and S. R. Silverman (Eds.), *Hearing and Deafness.* New York: Holt, Rinehart & Winston.

Peters, A. (1983). *The Units of Language Acquisition.* New York: Cambridge University Press.

Piaget, J. (1971). *Biology and Knowledge.* Chicago: University of Chicago Press.

Power, D. J., and S. P. Quigley. (1973). Deaf children's acquisition of the passive voice. *Journal of Speech and Hearing Research 16,* 5–11.

Pressnell, L. M. (1973). Hearing-impaired children's comprehension and production of syntax in oral language. *Journal of Speech and Hearing Research 16,* 12–21.

Prinz, P., and E. Prinz. (1979). Simultaneous acquisition of ASL and spoken English. *Sign Language Studies 25,* 283–296.

Quigley, S., and P. Paul. (1984). *Language and Deafness.* San Diego, Calif.: College-Hill Press.

Quigley, S. P., R. B. Wilbur, and D. S. Montanelli. (1974). Question formation in the language of deaf students. *Journal of Speech and Hearing Research 17,* 699–713.

Rainer, J., K. Altschuler, and F. Kallman. (Eds.) (1969). *Family and Mental Health Problems in a Deaf Population.* Springfield, Ill.: Thomas.

Read, C., and P. Schreiber. (1982). Why short subjects are harder to find than long ones. In E. Wanner and L. R. Gleitman (Eds.), *Language Acquisition: The State of the Art.* Cambridge: Cambridge University Press.

Rosenberg, S. (1982). The language of the mentally retarded: development processes, and intervention. In S. Rosenberg (Ed.), *Handbook of Applied Psycholinguistics.* Hillsdale, N. J.: Laurence Erlbaum.

Sapir, E. (1931). The function of an international auxiliary language. *Psyche 11,* 4–15. Reprinted in D. G. Mandelbaum (Ed.), *Selected Writings of Edward Sapir in Language, Culture, and Personality.* Berkeley: University of California Press, 1949.

Schlesinger, H., and K. Meadow. (1972). *Sound and Sign: Childhood Deafness and Mental Health.* Berkeley: University of California Press.

Schumann, J. H. (1982). Simplification, transfer, and relexification as aspects of pidginization and early second language acquisition. *Language Learning 32,* 337–366.

(1987). The expression of temporality in basilang speech. *Studies in Second Language Acquisition 9,* 21–42.

Schumann, J. H., and A. M. Stauble. (1983). A discussion of second language acquisition and decreolization. In R. W. Anderson (Ed.), *Pidginization and Creolization as Language Acquisition.* Rowley, Mass.: Newbury House.

Scouten, E. (1963). The place of the Rochester Method in American education of the deaf. *Report of the Proceedings of the International Congress on Education of the Deaf,* pp. 429–433.

(1967). The Rochester method, an oral multisensory approach for instructing prelingually deaf children. *American Annals of the Deaf 112,* 50–55.

Scovel, T. (1981). The effects of neurological age on nonprimary language acquisition. In R. W. Anderson (Ed.), *New Dimensions in Second Language Acquisition Research.* Rowley, Mass.: Newbury House.

Seliger, H. W. (1978). Implications of a multiple critical periods hypothesis for second language learning. In W. Ritchie (Ed.), *Second Language Acquisition Research: Issues and Implications.* New York: Academic Press.

(1981). Exceptions to critical period predictions: a sinister plot. In R. W. Anderson (Ed.), *New Directions in Second Language Acquisition Research.* Rowley, Mass.: Newbury House.

Shatz, M. (1981). Learning the rules of the game: Four views of the relation between grammar acquisition and social interaction. In W. Deutsch (Ed.), *The Child's Construction of Language.* London: Academic Press.

(1982). On mechanisms of language acquisition: Can features of the communicative environment account for development? In E. Warner and L. R. Gleitman (Eds.), *Language Acquisition: The State of the Art.* Cambridge: Cambridge University Press.

Simmons, A. A. (1962). A comparison of the type-token ratio of spoken and written language of deaf children. *Volta Review, 64,* 417–421.

Simon, H. A. (1981). *The Sciences of the Artificial.* Cambridge, Mass.: MIT Press.

Slobin, D. (1973). Cognitive prerequisites for the development of grammar. In C. Ferguson and D. Slobin (Eds.), *Studies of Child Language Development.* New York: Holt, Rinehart & Winston.

(1977). Language change in childhood and in history. In J. MacNamara (Ed.), *Language Learning and Thought.* New York: Academic Press.

(1983). What the natives have in mind. In R. Andersen (Ed.), *Pidginization and Creolization as Language Acquisition.* Rowley, Mass.: Newbury House.

Smith, D. (1972). Language as social adaptation. *Language and Linguistics Working Papers, no. 4.* Washington, D.C.: Georgetown University Press, 61–77.

Snow, C. E., and C. A. Ferguson. (1977). *Talking to Children: Language Input and Acquisition.* Cambridge: Cambridge University Press.

Staton, J., R. Shuy, and J. Kreeft. (1982). *Analysis of Dialogue Journal Writing as a Communicative Event. Vols. 1 & 2.* Final Report to the National Institute of Education, NIE-G-80-0122. Washington, D.C.: Center for Applied Linguistics.

Stokoe, W. (1960). Sign language structure: an outline of the visual communication system of the American deaf. Studies in Linguistics, Occasional Papers, 8. Buffalo, N.Y.: University of Buffalo.

Stuckless, E. R., and C. H. Marks. (1966). *Assessment of the Written Language of Deaf Students*. University of Pittsburgh School of Education.
Studdert-Kennedy, M. (1976). Speech perception. In N. J. Lass (Ed.), *Contemporary Issues in Experimental Phonetics*. New York: Academic Press.
    (1977). Universals in phonetic structure and their role in linguistic communication. In T. H. Bullock (Ed.), *Recognition of Complex Acoustic Signals*. Berlin: Dahlem Konferenzen.
    (1983a). Perceptual processing links to the motor system. In M. Studdert-Kennedy (Ed.), *Psychobiology of Language*. Cambridge Mass.: MIT Press.
    (Ed.) (1983b). *Psychobiology of Language*. Cambridge Mass.: MIT Press.
Studdert-Kennedy, M., and H. Lane. (1980). Clues from the differences between signed and spoken language. In U. Bellugi and M. Studdert-Kennedy (Eds.), *Signed and Spoken Language: Biological Constraints on Linguistic Form*. Weinheim: Verlag Chemie.
Summerfield, A. Q. (Rapporteur). (1980). The structuring of language by the requirements of motor control and perception. In U. Bellugi and M. Studdert-Kennedy (Eds.), *Signed and Spoken Language: Biological Constraints on Linguistic Form*. Weinheim: Verlag Chemie.
Supalla, T., and E. Newport. (1978). How many seats in a chair? The derivation of nouns and verbs in American Sign Language. In P. Siple (Ed.), *Understanding Language through Sign Language Research*. New York: Academic Press.
Swisher, M. V. (1984). Signed input of hearing mothers to deaf children. *Language Learning 34*, 69–86.
Tervoort, B. (1970). The understanding of passive sentences by deaf children. In G. B. Flores D'Arcais and W. J. M. Levelt (Eds.), *Advances in Psycholinguistics*. New York: American Elsevier.
Thompson, W. H. (1936). An analysis of errors in written composition by deaf children. *American Annals of the Deaf 81*, 95–99.
Trybus, R., and M. Karchmer. (1977). School achievement scores of hearing-impaired children: national data on achievement status and growth patterns. *American Annals of the Deaf 122*, 62–69.
Turbayne, C. M. (1971). *The Myth of Metaphor*. Columbia: University of South Carolina Press.
Walter, J. (1955). A study of the written sentence construction of a group of profoundly deaf children. *American Annals of the Deaf 100*, 235–252.
Waterson, N., and C. Snow. (Eds.) (1978). *The Development of Communication*. Chichester, N.Y.: Wiley.
Wexler, K., and P. Culicover. (1980). *Formal Principles of Language Acquisition*. Cambridge, Mass.: MIT Press.
Whinnom, K. (1971). Linguistic hybridization and the "special case" of pidgins and creoles. In D. Hymes (Ed.), *Pidginization and Creolization of Languages*. New York: Cambridge University Press.
Wilbur, R. B. (1977). An explanation of deaf children's difficulty with certain syntactic structures of English. *Volta Review 79*, 85–92.
    (1979). *American Sign Language and Sign Systems*. Baltimore, Md.: University Park Press.

Woodward, J. (1973). Some characteristics of Pidgin Sign English. *Sign Language Studies 3*, 39–46.

(1978). Historical bases of American Sign Language. In P. Siple (Ed.), *Understanding Language through Sign Language Research*. New York: Academic Press.

Woodward, J., and H. Markowicz. (1980). Pidgin sign languages. In W. Stokoe (Ed.), *Sign and Culture*. Silver Spring, Md.: Linstok Press.

2 American Sign Language and the human biological capacity for language

James Paul Gee *and* Wendy Goodhart

Editor's introduction

In Chapter 2 Gee and Goodhart discuss the structure and acquisition of ASL in the light of the nativization/denativization hypothesis, arguing forcefully that the study of ASL improves our understanding of the innate aspects of human language, and, indeed, of the nativization hypothesis itself. They carefully explain, primarily through a morphological comparison, why ASL looks like a creole in some ways but not in others and how it can manifest itself in different forms. The authors then hypothesize that ASL derives from a locative/directional system, possibly determined by the visual perceptual data base from which the nativization process starts. They suggest that, confronted with Slobin's "four charges" to language (be clear, be humanly processible in ongoing time, be quick and easy, be expressive), users of the manual modality, employing cumbersome large muscles of the body, are forced to convey more information per unit of meaning and thus incline to a nonisolating morphology.

This argument is in line with studies that have shown that deaf children exposed to manual forms of English but not to ASL tend to innovate ASL-like forms, even with little or no input in that language. This movement toward ASL-like forms is explained by the innate linguistic biological capacity present in humans using the manual modality. In synthesizing ideas from the nativization hypothesis, pidgin and creole theorists, and Slobin's cognitive prerequisites of language, Gee and Goodhart have put forth an effectively reasoned explanation for the state of ASL and its varying manifestations among deaf subgroups.

Approaches to the human biological capacity for language

The central goal of linguistics is to characterize the human biological capacity for language. Some linguists have approached this task by studying native speakers' intuitions about grammaticality and by searching for properties of human languages that cannot reasonably be said to be learned. (Baker and McCarthy, 1981; Chomsky, 1965, 1976, 1981, 1986; Piattelli-Palmarini, 1980; Pinker, 1984). For example, all the data available to a child learning English would indicate that the following is a true generalization about the language: From any declarative sentence, one can form a content question by changing some noun phrase in the sentence into a question word and placing it at the front of the sentence (plus inverting the first auxiliary or adding a form of *do)*. However, this generalization is false (Ross, 1967). Although many pairs such as (1a,b) below follow the generalization, some pairs, such as (2a,b), break it:

1a. John knows that the man wants to marry <u>his sister</u>.
1b. Who does John know that the man wants to marry _____?
2a. John knows the man who wants to marry <u>his sister</u>.
2b. *Who does John know the man who wants to marry _____?

Adult speakers of English all know that (2b) is ungrammatical, but they could not have learned this from the data available to them as children. Children never utter sentences like (2b), and they are never explicitly told that such sentences are ungrammatical. Thus, linguists hypothesize that this knowledge is part of the innate human linguistic capacity for language. It is then up to the linguist to propose a constraint that will rule out such sentences, while allowing grammatical sentences like (1b). This constraint must be known to the child prior to language acquisition and, further, must be universal, since the human biological endowment is everywhere essentially the same.

This approach to the biological capacity for language allows the linguist to formulate hypotheses about language universals on the basis of the study of a single language. It has been supplemented by several other approaches, including the cross-linguistic comparison of diverse languages (Comrie, 1981; Foley and Van Valin, 1984) and the study of early child language, which in all cultures diverges significantly from adult language (Slobin, 1977, 1981, 1982, 1983; Wanner and Gleitman, 1982). In addition, creoles are a rich source for hypotheses about the basic design of human language. They represent cases in which children learn a native language on the basis of inadequate input, namely, pidgin (a simplified contact language used for restricted forms of communication, e.g., trade), rather than on the basis of input from their parents' native language(s). Historically, this process has been related to social upheaval, such as when Europeans separated slaves who spoke the same languages to avoid rebellion. That creoles are biologically interesting has been demonstrated by Dereck Bickerton (1981, 1982, 1984). Bickerton argues that children who acquire a creole on the basis of a newly developed pidgin are faced with input that is so highly variable and inconsistent as to be useless. In nineteenth-century Hawaii, as Bickerton points out, a large number of speakers of different languages were thrown together (to serve as a cheap labor force) with little access to native speakers of English. They quickly developed a pidgin to communicate among themselves and with their employers. Many children had to learn a native language based on this pidgin, for instance, if their parents didn't share a language. However, the pidgin was spoken differently by different speakers, each influenced by the phonology and syntax of their native language. Bickerton argues that the child, unable to draw consistent generalizations from the data, had to fall back on his or her innate language capacity (what Bickerton calls the "language bioprogram") for the construction of the emerging creole. Many have found Bickerton's views overstated, but few have denied that creoles across the world do bear remarkable resemblances to each other, despite the fact that they are based on pidgins of genetically and typologically diverse languages.

The nativization hypothesis

Recently, Roger Andersen (1983a,b; see also Meisel, 1983; Schumann, 1978a,b; Schumann and Stauble, 1983; Valdman, 1983) has proposed "the nativization hypothesis" to account for the *processes* involved in language acquisition, whatever the resultant forms (pidgins, early child language, creoles, standard languages, etc.). This hypothesis unifies the above approaches to the human biological capacity along with several others and is perfectly natural from a biological perspective (see Gould, 1977). It enables us to delineate two underlying processes in language acquisition, regardless of the conditions in which it occurs: *nativization* and *denativization*.

Nativization: When, for whatever reason, input is not accessible, the human being falls back on the biological capacity for language and constructs language according to the internal norms for language design specified by this capacity. The input may be inaccessible because of limited cognitive or processing capacities, limited social access to native speakers, or psychological resistance to learning. Nativization thus unites early child language (where the data are originally inaccessible owing to the limitations on the child's cognitive capacities), early second language acquisition (where the data are inaccessible because of processing limitations in the early stages, and, perhaps, because of psychological, social, or cultural factors at various later points), pidginization (which is just a form of second language acquisition with even worse access to the data owing to the lack of native speakers of the superstrate), and creolization (where the data may be inaccessible owing to the variability and inconsistency of the pidgin). To the extent that access to the data does not improve (for cognitive, psychological, or social reasons), then to that extent the final form is due to the continued work of the nativization process. Notice that no matter how good the data, they are never good enough to induce that (2b) above is ungrammatical; thus this knowledge must represent the nativization process.

Denativization: To the extent that data are accessible, human beings acquire language on the basis of those data. The learner changes his or her original nativized grammar to fit the norms of the external input and thus is said to denativize toward the norm represented by that external source. In the course of normal first language acquisition, children's access to the data gets better and better as their cognitive capacities grow, and in the normal case the data are rich and consistent. Thus, the child denativizes toward the norm of the external input and learns the target language. This is why early child language is more similar across languages than are the adult languages. However, in the case of a child trying to acquire a native language on the basis of an early and variable pidgin, although the child's cognitive capacities grow, the data are no good, and so access to usable data is still poor. Here, nativization continues, and denativization is limited to whatever generalizations the child can induce from the data. The situation in second language learning is similar (Klein, 1986). In some cases, as the learner's ability to process the language improves, the data get better and better, and denativization takes over. The learner acquires the target language. In other cases, the learner may be psychologically resistant to interacting with the second language culture or social restrictions may prevent the learner from doing so. Here, the learner gets fewer data (or resists the data), the denativization process is more limited, and nativization (construction of forms on the basis of the biological capacity) goes further, with the result that the learner's interlanguage fails to resemble the target language as much as it would otherwise (of course, in second language acquisition, the learner may transfer properties of the first language to the second; transfer represents learning based on an external norm, i.e., the first language).

The nativization hypothesis predicts commonalities among normal first language acquisition, pidginization, creolization, and early second language acquisition because they all involve a similar underlying process (see articles in Andersen, 1983b). Whatever the final outcome of language acquisition, it represents some balance of nativization and denativization processes, the balance being different in different cases (depending on the accessibility – in terms of amount, consistency, and quality – of the input).

The nativization–denativization framework raises the question of adult versus child language learning. Since the hypothesis posits commonalities between early second language learning and first language learning, it leads one to suppose that adults can still nativize (construct language on the basis of their internal specification for what a grammar must look like in the absence of external data). Some of the early generative linguists assumed that the child's language acquisition device (Chomsky, 1965) turns off some time around puberty. Thus they argued that adults can change language only in relatively superficial ways, whereas children alone can change language in significant ways, which often amount to a reorganization of the grammar (King, 1969). However, many linguists now believe that adults play a much less passive role in language learning and language change, so that students of second language acquisition are able to find substantive parallels between first and second language acquisition. The contribution of adults can be seen quite clearly in the fact that pidgin languages have existed for generations without being creolized – Tok Pisin being the best known example. This situation is quite different from the one Bickerton refers to. His cases involved children who had to acquire a native language on the basis of an early, undeveloped, quite simple and variable pidgin. Tok Pisin has existed for generations as a pidgin; it has only recently begun to be creolized owing to the growing urbanization that has forced people who are not members of a mutual language community into contact with each other (see Muhlhauser, 1980; Sankoff and Laberge, 1973). Such pidgins do not remain unchanged, nor do they change in only superficial ways. The difference between Tok Pisin and a first generation pidgin – for example, the first generation pidgin that existed in Hawaii and served as the basis of Hawaiian creole – is quite significant. Muhlhauser (1980) points out that pidgin expands in a number of ways under the influence of adults changing the language. Such pidgins eventually become what he calls "expanded pidgins" and constitute relatively complex languages. Thus, what contributions adults make to the acquisition process and what contributions children make becomes an open question. Muhlhauser notes that, although adults can add morphological complexity to language (expanded pidgins have a word formation component), only children add recursive morphology to a language (and thus only creoles show this trait). For instance, in Tok Pisin, pidgin speakers use a form of reduplication as an intensifier (*krugut*, "crooked"; *krukrugut*, "very crooked") and they use a morphological causative (*krugutim*, "to make crooked"), but only the newly emerging creole speakers (children) apply these morphological processes recursively and so produce forms like *krukrugutim*, "to make very crooked" (derived from *krugut* by first applying the reduplication process and then applying the causative process to the output of this).

The acquisition of ASL and nativization

We argue that the structure of ASL and the conditions under which it is acquired can be understood within the nativization–denativization framework. More important, we argue that the study of ASL and its acquisition can shed light on the human biological capacity for language and can deepen and extend the nativization hypothesis.

The nativization hypothesis suggests that the acquisition of ASL occurs as a continuum. In all cases, the quality of the input to deaf children is restricted in a way that resembles somewhat the creole situation. Deaf children of hearing parents (DCHP) may get next to no input, or they may face a wide variety of types of signing, of various degrees of fluency, depending upon the individuals to whom they are exposed and when. This signing may range from fluent ASL signed by deaf people, various types of L2 ASL (from unfluent to quite fluent), various constructed sign systems (e.g., SEE I, SEE II, LOVE, Signed English, etc.), Pidgin Sign English (in its various forms), and various types of signing that place ASL signs in English word order. Not only is this input quite varied, it is certainly not consistent – Signed English, oral English, and ASL are different systems with different rules (Wilbur, 1979), although they are often mixed in various ways (through pidgin ASL, code switching, mixed varieties, and simultaneous signing and speaking). The problem is further exacerbated by the fact that several of these signing systems share a large lexical stock but differ significantly in morphological, syntactic, and discourse rules (Klima and Bellugi, 1979; Wilbur, 1979). Of course, different children are exposed to different parts of this continuum and to different degrees. But surely a logician exposed to such data could never induce a consistent grammar any more than a child exposed to an early pidgin can. It is crucial to recognize that the situation to which the deaf child of deaf parents (DCDP) is exposed is not as different from that of the DCHP as has heretofore been claimed. The DCDP is exposed to all the same forms as the DCHP in the early preschool and school years. For those children whose parents sign ASL at home, this is un-doubtedly a rich source of data, although it is only one source available to the child. Remember too, that the vast majority of deaf parents of deaf children themselves had hearing parents. Thus, as children, they were exposed to the very problems we have just delineated for DCHP. (Although specially constructed manually coded English systems, such as SEE 1, SEE 2, LOVE, and Signed English, were only developed in the 1960s, a naturally evolved form of manual English, involving ASL signs produced in English order without inflections, as well as some form of Pidgin Sign English, have existed for some time; see Lane, 1984.) Thus, the nativization hypothesis leads us to believe that all deaf children are confronted with a variety of forms. In reality deaf children do not divide neatly into DCHP and DCDP; different children in each group have been exposed to different ranges of the possible continuum of input and to different degrees. There are, for instance, DCHP with a great deal of contact with deaf peers, including DCDP; on the other hand, there are DCDP whose parents do not sign or who sign poorly. In fact, nearly all serious empirical research in the area shows, as we should expect, a great deal of variation when we consider the whole gamut of deaf children and adults. The balance between nativization and denativization in the case of each child is different depending on just how variable and inconsistent the input is, but presumably always represents a fairly strong degree of nativization.

From the nativization perspective it follows also that there is in fact no privileged class of signers to study. In the case of DCDP, DCHP, and deaf adults learning to sign, the underlying process of nativization goes on. Since the input to some DCHP is liable to have been even more variable and inconsistent, we would expect their signing to show yet more clearly the effects of nativization, that is, the shape the biological endowment for language takes in the case of sign language.

Finally, the nativization hypothesis throws an interesting light on the nature of ASL as a language. All languages are variable and no child in any circumstance gets completely nonvariable input (in fact, children seem to need a linguistic system with variability that can be used for stylistic and social purposes; see Gee and Mounty, 1986). Some children in some circumstances (e.g., in the creole situation), however, receive input that is variable and inconsistent enough to trigger extensive and continuous nativization. ASL itself is a highly variable language, as we would expect of a language that is in contact with a national standard (English), that is spoken by a widely diffuse minority population, and that has next to no signers of even the third generation. Under these conditions, it may well be that ASL must stay close to the biological specification for basic language design in order to survive as a language. To the extent that denativization (movement away from the biological norm) can take place, we would expect ASL to denativize toward English as an external norm, since ASL exists in a culture that considers English a prestige norm (much the way that a creole in contact with its superstrate language decreolizes toward it as an outside norm). Of course, this can only happen to the extent that deaf people have access to English data (many of them have such access, at least through print). But it is important to recognize that ASL is becoming a prestige norm within many segments of the Deaf community. This means that signers with various sorts of signing, including signed English, will denativize toward ASL as an external norm, a norm for the Deaf community. Thus, there are two, sometimes conflicting, denativizing processes going on in the case of the acquisition and historical development of ASL. The denativization toward ASL as a community norm, however, supports the nativization process itself to the extent that ASL reflects a design close to the biological specification for language, as we have argued here and explain further in the next section (this situation may well be unique).

Nativization and the structure of ASL: a paradox

We claim then that ASL, owing to the conditions under which it is acquired, is deeply influenced by an extended degree of nativization. Indeed, a number of investigators have pointed out that ASL arises under situations similar to a creole and that a number of its linguistic features resemble those typically found in a creole (Deuchar, 1983; Feldman, Goldin-Meadow, and Gleitman, 1978; Fischer, 1974, 1978; Mayberry, Fischer, and Hatfield, 1983; Meier, 1984; Newport, 1981, 1982; Woodward, 1973). Bickerton lists many features that all "radical" creoles have in common (those based on early pidgins). Linguists are still unsure whether ASL has some of these features, or, at least, how they apply to ASL. Nonetheless, the amount of overlap between Bickerton's list and ASL grammar is impressive. In radical creoles, no distinction is made between tensed and infinitival clauses, and this is true of ASL. There are no subject–object asymmetries or pleonastic subjects, and transitive verbs with agent subjects may appear also as intransitives with Patient or Theme subjects in both radical creoles and ASL. Both have SVO word order as their favored neutral word order. Neither radical creoles nor ASL typically use prepositions to introduce oblique cases, but use serial verbs instead. Both radical creoles and ASL distinguish between specific and nonspecific NPs (cf. ASL's extensive system of indexing). In radical creoles verbal auxiliaries are preverbal free morphemes expressing tense, mode, and aspect, in that order. ASL has few free auxiliaries, but is growing a preverbal marker of completion (and eventually past tense) out of the sign meaning FINISH (Fischer and Gough, 1972; Mounty, 1984), a typical creole process. Neither has extraposition or true passives. Both can topicalize by movement to the front of the sentence, and may topicalize any phrase type, as well as the verb. Adjectives are a subclass of (stative) verbs in both radical creoles and ASL (note that adjectives in ASL take many of the same morphological markers as verbs). However, ASL has one salient property that no creole, radical or otherwise, has: a large amount of morphology, including inflectional morphology. Radical creoles do not have inflectional morphology, according to Bickerton. Klima and Bellugi (1979) list dozens of verbal and adjectival aspect markers, and other investigators have reported many additional markers. This is certainly a far richer system of aspect marking than any known creole. In addition, nearly every ASL linguist agrees that the language has a rich inflectional system for person and number for both subject and object (e.g., Padden, 1983; Supalla, 1982), a derivational process for deriving nouns from verbs (Supalla and Newport, 1978), morphological marking for topics, negatives, questions, and, perhaps, relative clauses and conditionals (Baker and Cokely, 1980), as well as a morphological means of incorporating a classifier (for some, a noun) into the verb (Gee and Kegl, 1982a,b; Supalla, 1982). As linguists study the language further, they consistently propose additional morphology.

Thus, we have a paradox. Nearly everyone agrees that ASL arises in situations much like those that give rise to creoles, and that it shares many substantive properties with creoles, including radical ones. But it differs from them in a crucial property. The resolution of this paradox may cast important light on the nativization hypothesis and the way we view the human biological capacity for language.

The morphological complexity of ASL

Let's take a simple case and see what issues arise in trying to account for the morphological complexity of ASL. For example, consider the sentence "John hit Mary" translated into ASL. The matter is not simple to start out with. First, there are a number of ways to sign this sentence. Second, ASL linguists do not agree on how to transcribe/represent any such sentence (Gee and Kegl, 1982a,b, 1983; Liddell, 1984; Newport, 1982; Newport and Supalla, 1980; Padden 1983; Supalla, 1978a,b, 1982). Third, many signers resist giving sentences out of context and prefer to sign examples only in a given discourse context.

Consider one way the sentence can be signed and one way it can be represented (we oversimplify a good bit here; the description follows Gee and Kegl, 1982a,b, 1983; Goodhart, 1984, but the basic point does not hinge on this). The signer can, using the right hand, sign (fingerspell) the name JOHN and then point to a location to the right of the center of the signing space, call it LOC_{10}. This pointing motion can be viewed as a verb meaning DIRECT-A POINT-TO. Thus, we get, in sequence, the signs JOHN, DIRECT-A POINT-TO, and LOC_{10}. LOC_{10} is, by this pointing motion, assigned to JOHN. If the signer later again points to LOC_{10} or forms a sign by moving from or to LOC_{10}, this is a way of referring to JOHN. Thus LOC_{10} functions like a pronoun for JOHN. The whole sequence can be represented as JOHN DIRECT-A POINT-TO LOC_{10} and has more or less the logical function of "JOHN = LOC_{10}." The signer can then, with the left hand, sign (fingerspell) MARY and point to a location to the left of the center of the signing space, call it LOC_{20}. This assigns LOC_{20} to MARY as a pronoun and can be rep-

resented as MARY DIRECT-A POINT-TO LOC_{20}. These identificational clauses need only be signed once per discourse. Thereafter, JOHN
and MARY can be referred to through the locations they have been
assigned (i.e., by using these as proforms for them). Next, the signer
places the index finger of the left hand in an upright position at location
20, the location assigned to MARY. This placing motion can be viewed
as a verb meaning BE-AT. The upright index finger is a classifier for
humans (and is used in many other signs). Thus, we have another clause:
HUMAN AT LOC_{20}. The classifier sign here, the upright index finger
of the left hand, stays in place now, while the signer moves the right
hand in the shape of a fist from LOC_{10}, the location assigned to JOHN,
to the surface of the upright index finger at LOC_{20} (i.e., it looks as
though the signer hits the upright index finger at LOC_{20} from LOC_{10}).
The fact that the movement starts at LOC_{10} indicates agreement with
JOHN and is equivalent to attaching a pronoun to the verb (he-hit);
and the fact that it terminates at LOC_{20}, the location assigned to MARY,
indicates agreement with MARY and is equivalent to attaching a pronoun for MARY to the verb (*hit-her*). The first shape of the moving
hand is a classifier for round solid objects (used for other sorts of round
solid objects in other signs). The movement of the hand is a verb meaning
to MOVE or GO and can be said to consist of the following parts: GO
FROM (LOC_{10}) and GO TO-ON (the classifier situated at LOC_{20}). Thus,
for "John hit Mary" we get

3a. JOHN DIRECT-A POINT-TO LOC_{10}
 b. MARY DIRECT-A POINT-TO LOC_{20}
 c. HUMAN BE AT LOC_{20} # LOC_{10}—GO FROM # GO TO-ON—LOC_{20}

(A ROUND SOLID OBJECT)

where GO FROM represents a movement away from a location (i.e.,
LOC_{10}) and GO TO a movement toward a location (i.e., LOC_{20}) and On
a placing on a location; and ROUND SOLID OBJECT represents a classifier
that is incorporated into the movement of the verb.

The "HUMAN AT LOC_{20}" part of (3c) functions phonologically as part
of the verb. It acts like an object clitic clitized to the main verb, and not
really much like a clause (the main verb then has a form something like):

"her(clitic) – he(subject agreement) – verb – him(object agreement)."

In spite of this fact, in other cases placing classifiers in a location clearly
functions like a clause.

 Many ASL linguists would not agree with the above representation.
hey would see (3a) as simply a noun with a morpheme attached to it

that functions, like a case marker, in setting up agreement. They would, of course, view (3b) the same way. They would see (3c) as one mono-morphemic form, HIT (a sign made by moving the first of one hand against an upright index finger of the other), together with agreement for subject and object (marked by the motion of the moving hand). They would represent the whole sentence as something like

4. JOHN$_{\text{index}-10}$ MARY$_{\text{index}-20}$ $_{\text{index}-10}$HIT$_{\text{index}20}$.

Thus, what one view sees as multiclausal – a mini-discourse – the other sees as a simple sentence. However, there is somewhat less disagreement than may first meet the eye. Most ASL linguists now agree that there are classifier morphemes, and locative verb stems, and motion verb stems, like those shown in (3). However, they disagree on how pervasive these are in the language as a whole. Many linguists believe that there are two separate lexical domains in ASL. First, there is a frozen lexicon, consisting of "single-morpheme signs well standardized among signers, typically listed in standard dictionaries of ASL, learned early by adults and children acquiring ASL, and borrowed for use in Signed English" (Newport, 1982). HIT would be an example of such a sign. Second, there is "another portion of the language which has been called 'mimetic.' ... These signs seem to reflect aspects of the real world in form: Hand-shapes often refer to shapes of objects, and movement of these hand-shapes through space in front of the signer is used to represent the motion of objects through real world space" (Newport, 1982). This "mimetic depiction" lexicon is composed of a set of morphemes that combine in a highly productive way to form an indefinitely large set of possible (morphologically complex) signs, although, as Newport shows, the vo-cabulary is in no true sense "mimetic." For example, such novel locative-motional meanings as VEHICLE-WANDER-UPWARD-ACROSS-HORIZONTAL-WIDE-STRAIGHT-SHAPE ("A car wanders uphill") can be signed with a combination of classifiers and locative and motional roots.

Most investigators would presumably agree that the frozen vocabulary is originally made up of the same morphemes as the mimetic depiction vocabulary, but that these morphemes have become frozen in these forms (much like *"con"* and *"ceive"* in *"conceive"*, which for all practical purposes is monomorphemic to an English speaker). There is, however, some linguistic evidence that even in the frozen vocabulary these mor-phemes still function as separate units. For instance, the form HUMAN AT LOC$_{20}$ in (3) (the upright index finger agreeing with MARY's lo-cation) functions as an object clitic. Consider the sentences below in-volving the verbs HIT and LIKE, both of which are considered part of the "frozen" lexicon (the data are from Kegl, 1985, although we do not follow fully her analysis):

5. John$_{10}$ Mary$_{20}$ $_{10}$HIT$_{20}$ "John hit Mary."
6. John$_{10}$ $_{10}$HIT   "John hit someone."
7. John$_{10}$ Mary$_{20}$ $_{10}$LIKE$_{20}$ "John likes Mary."
8. *John$_{10}$ $_{10}$LIKE   "John likes someone."

In (5), HIT agrees with JOHN and MARY. In (6) it agrees only with
JOHN, and the form means something like "John hit someone" (has an
interpretation in which the object slot is bound by an existential quan-
tifier, Ex JOHN HITx). But in the case of LIKE, where agreement with
the object is left off, we don't get a sentence meaning "John likes someone," but rather an ungrammatical sentence. The difference between
HIT and LIKE is that HIT has what we have called an object clitic,
whereas LIKE does not (agreement with the object is made by directing
the verb – a body-anchored verb – toward the location assigned to the
object, but no classifier is in the location of that object). Since both *hit*
and *like* are transitive, (6) is grammatical because the object clitic serves
as an object, but (8) is ungrammatical because there is no object either
by agreement, a clitic, or a full NP. This explanation only follows,
however, if we see HIT as multimorphemic, that is, if we see the upright
vertical finger not as a nonmorphemic part of HIT, but as a morpheme
(or set of morphemes) filling the role of an object clitic.

The fact is that ASL is probably in the process of freezing, so to speak.
That is, a transition may well be taking place from multiclausal mini-
discourses, made up of clauses with verbs having locative directional
meanings, to single sentences with phrases and a morphologically complex verb. The object clitic may be a good example of the whole process.
What was once a clause becomes a morpheme and eventually may become a nonmorphemic part of a monomorphemic sign (lexical).

Agreement in ASL

The agreement system of ASL is not typical of early creoles. Creoles
usually do not have any inflectional agreement for subject and object,
certainly not for the object. Thus, it is interesting to speculate how ASL
got this sort of agreement system. One common discourse pattern that
has given rise to subject agreement in many languages is "left dislocation" ("My father, *he* got mad" – Duranti and Ochs, 1979; Givón,
1976, 1979) Object agreement is rarer in the world's languages than
subject agreement, and probably has right dislocation as one of its possible sources ("I really let *him* have it my little brother"; Hyman, 1975).
ASL, as a very discourse-sensitive language, does use structures like these,
but this is probably not the source of subject and object agreement in
ASL. If it were, we would expect ASL to have gone through a stage in

which independent pronouns showed up (as in the examples above), eventually lost their phonetic form, and finally became inflections (e.g., "My father, *he* got mad" → My father, i-got mad"). No such stages have been observed for ASL, and, given that it has so little generational depth, it probably could not have undergone these stages so rapidly, and, in fact, could not continually reenact them (since it constantly renativizes). The source probably has a lot more to do with what we might call "locative agreement." ASL has a set of structures that are not at all common across the world's languages, that is, cases in which the verb agrees with a locative Source (beginning location) and Goal (final location). Padden (1983) shows that, in an ASL sentence that we might translate as "I walked from New York to New Jersey," the ASL verb will agree not with the agent *I* (as almost all other agreement languages would), but with the locative source *New York* and the locative goal *New Jersey* (i.e., the motion of the verb will move from the location assigned to *New York* to the location assigned to *New Jersey)*. In fact, ASL has pairs of verbs that differ as to whether they take this sort of locative agreement or whether they agree with subject and object. For example, GIVE must agree with subject and object, whereas the very similar sign CARRY-BY-HAND agrees with Source and Goal. Thus, in "I gave him the telephone number", ASL will have *I* agreeing with *him*, but in "I transferred by hand the telephone number from the table to him" it will have *I* agreeing with the initial and final locations of the telephone number, that is, *the table* and *him*. By and large, the mimetic depiction vocabulary also functions with locative agreement.

The above examples suggest how ASL may have developed its agreement system. A number of linguists (Anderson, 1972; Gruber, 1965; Jackendoff, 1978, 1983) have pointed out that humans tend to interpret "abstract" meanings spatially (e.g., we talk about time as if it were a form of space, "I'll see you *in* a minute", "I'll be there *at* 10"). We refer to this as "the locative hypothesis." To take an example that relates directly to our discussion of agreement in ASL, although *giving* need not involve actual physical transference through space, but only transference in the abstract realm of possession, humans still tend to think of giving and changing possession as a type of figurative movement in space. Thus, agreement in ASL may be always in a sense locative. It is just that in "John gave Mary a book," John and Mary are viewed as the beginning location (source) and the final location (Goal), but figuratively, that is, as locations in the realm of possession (possessors are then seen as places in this realm – many languages show evidence of this, for example, in saying things like "The book is at John" to mean John possesses the book, although he need not actually have it at his physical location). In "John transferred the book by hand to Mary," ASL agrees with the actual source and goal because the sentence is about actual movement in space. (For a fuller discussion, see Gee and Kegl, 1983.)

An example of nativization tactic in an adult DCHP

The nativization hypothesis suggests that it will be illuminating to look beyond DCDP for data. DCHP and even deaf adults who learn ASL later in life have less adequate input than many DCDP. Thus, they may show certain nativization tactics in a particularly clear fashion. For example, when a fluent signing deaf adult with hearing parents (a signer who has signed since he was an older child) was asked to sign the message "John gave Mary a book" (the message was set up as a scenario, the signer was not given the English sentence per se – data from Turley and Serber, 1984), the result was

$$\text{9. JOHN}_{10} \quad \text{MARY}_{20} \quad \overline{\text{BOOK}_{10}}^{\text{T}} \quad {}_{10}\text{GIVE}_{20}.$$

Looked at as in (9), this does not make much sense. This example is ungrammatical in ASL, both because three NPs are lined up before the verb and because of the agreement between BOOK and JOHN, with BOOK separated from JOHN by MARY. Looked at in the following way, the situation makes more sense:

10a. JOHN DIRECT-A POINT-TO LOC_{10}.
   b. MARY DIRECT-A POINT-TO LOC_{20}.
   c. $\overline{\phantom{\text{BOOK AT LOC}_{10}}}^{\text{T}}$.
      BOOK AT LOC_{10}
   d. LOC_{10} GIVE(A BOOK) LOC_{20}.

The signer signs two identificational clauses (for JOHN and MARY) and then places the sign for book on the location assigned to JOHN. BOOK AT LOC_{10} clearly means "JOHN has a book." This is not the standard form of this meaning in ASL (nor is it the only such form in the signing of this signer), but this sort of locative expression for possession shows up in many languages (e.g., Russian). The signer then signs "CLASSIFIER-FOR-BOOK-HANDLING GOES FROM LOC_{10} TO LOC_{20}" (i.e., GIVE(A BOOK)). The signer treats the whole thing as a mini-discourse, using devices that are identical to current ASL indexing procedures to express what seems to be a multiclausal expression.

A hypothesis about ASL based on the nativization hypothesis and the locative hypothesis

The following hypothesis then suggests itself: ASL historically and acquisitionally has its basis in a locative/directional system of literal locative meanings that are expressed in simple clauses and extended to abstract domains.

Much of this system is still readily apparent in the mimetic depiction vocabulary of ASL, although this may now be a specialized use of it. Both through time (historically) and throughout child language development this locative/directional and discourse-based system grammaticalizes (mini-discourses collapse into phrases and morphemes in single sentences) and formalizes; that is, meaning tends to lose its locative/directional moorings and to take on formal semantic values, as in the development of person agreement or the development of frozen lexical items. This process presumably takes place at different rates, and perhaps in somewhat different ways, in the different groups of deaf children, depending upon the interplay of input and the nativization process. But there is something special about the ASL case. All languages display some evidence for the locative hypothesis, as do hearing children acquiring language (because, as noted earlier, humans tend to think spatially). It appears that ASL is based on a locative/directional core in a much more direct way. The initial data available to the child may take on the locative/directional structuring it has in part because humans rely strongly on a system of perception. This input then determines to some extent how the nativization process works. We have argued that it gives rise to a good deal of morphological complexity. This may be determined by the visual perceptual data base from which the nativization process starts. But another factor may be partly or wholly responsible.

It is quite likely that the language capacity does not specify a single set of fixed options, but rather expresses itself in different ways given what material is available. For example, a language can display several types of morphological structure and can be classified according to which of these types are in preponderance. An *isolating* language has no morphology, and there is a one-to-one correspondence between words and morphemes. An *agglutinating* language may have several morphemes in a word but each morpheme is kept, in phonological shape and meaning, clearly separate from the others. Both of these systems have a one-to-one correspondence between sound and meaning. In a *fusional* language, however, there is often no clear-cut boundary between the morphemes in a word, and different semantic and grammatical categories are often fused together to give a single, unsegmental morph (e.g., in Russian, in the word *stolov*, "of tables," the form *-ov* is a single morph expressing both genitive case and plural number, as well as declension (Ia), and there is no way to segment it into one part that names one thing and another that names another; see Comrie, 1981). Some languages have not just fusional affixes, but allow a number of morphs to combine in a single word and blur the boundaries between these morphs by phonological rules. Thus, a one-to-one mapping between sound and meaning is obscured, more or less seriously, depending upon the amount of fusion. Of courses, languages are rarely if ever pure types, but rather show various degrees and mixtures of the three types of morphology. A lan-

64   *James Paul Gee and Wendy Goodhart*

guage like English is not very complex morphologically, although it is by no means a totally isolating language. It seems that both isolating and agglutinative forms are highly valued by the language capacity. Children learn either type rapidly and well (Ecmekci, 1979; Johnston and Slobin, 1979; Slobin, 1981, 1982). If a child is forced to innovate using the nativization process, which of these will turn up seems to depend upon what materials are available in the input. However, the fact that in pidgins each word tends to carry independent stress suggests that creole speakers will gravitate toward the isolating forms. But even in creoles one finds a limited amount of agglutinative morphology (see Valdman, 1983). We expect, on the other hand, that fusional morphology will not be highly valued and that children will not construct it on the basis of their nativizing strategies (although they will denativize toward it perfectly well as an external norm, if the input requires this and gives sufficient access).

The situation in ASL with respect to these morphological types is quite interesting. There is reason to believe that the manual modality may force nativization toward a synthetic (nonisolating) norm, despite the fact that creoles display an isolating norm. Slobin (1977; see also 1973, 1981, 1982) lists four "charges to language" that are based on human cognitive prerequisites for language: (1) be clear, (2) be humanly processible in ongoing time, (3) be quick and easy, (4) be expressive. It is not clear, however, that sign systems can meet these criteria in all the same ways oral ones can. Signs are made with the large muscles of the body, and thus take longer to deliver than speech. Therefore, if a sign system is to be both quick and expressive, it must convey more information per unit of meaning (word/sign) than an isolating language, for example (since the speaker of an isolating language can deliver several words in the time that an individual using the sign system delivers one sign). Indeed, Klima and Bellugi (1979) have found that ASL conveys the same amount of information per unit time as does English (a fairly isolating language). This immediately suggests that children learning a sign system will nativize toward nonisolating morphology (that is, toward a system with a fair degree of morphological complexity). They will want one form to carry several meanings. Thus, we would expect agglutinative morphology, this being the form of morphological complexity specified by the biological capacity. If this argument is correct, sign systems that serve as primary communicational systems should be morphologically complex (and thus not isolating), but will not have a fusional morphology. In fact, nearly all recent work on ASL grammar has described the language as being very complex morphologically (Bellman, Poizner, and Bellugi, 1983; Gee and Kegl, 1982a,b, 1983; Klima and Bellugi, 1979; Liddell, 1984; Newport, 1982; Padden 1983; Supalla, 1978a,b, 1982).

Two interesting issues arise here, however. First, is even agglutinative morphology fast enough to meet the needs of sign language? Fusional morphology is faster, because it allows a single morph to carry multiple meanings and relies on phonological rules to blend morphs together for ease of expression. If signing is sufficiently slow in comparison with speech, then perhaps the optimal solution specified by the language capacity (agglutinative morphology) is still not going to allow it to satisfy Slobin's requirements of language. In this case, the child is in something of a bind – the optimal solution will involve fusional morphology, a candidate that is not optimal (perhaps not even available) in terms of the internal norms set by the language capacity (however, this "bind" may be mitigated by the visual system's contribution to the acquisition of ASL). We do not know if this scenario is true, both because we do not know what counts as "sufficiently slow" and because linguists cannot agree on whether ASL is agglutinative or fusional – in fact, the question has not yet really been directly asked (the issue often comes down to how much sequentiality versus simultaneity there is in signing, but note that this is an issue of how much of each there is in surface structure, not in underlying forms, since surface structures are what children have to process).

A second issue arises in the contrast between manually coded English (in any form) and ASL (in any variety). Manually coded English is, like oral English, an "analytic" or fairly isolating language, without a complex morphology. In view of the considerations mentioned earlier, even if given as consistent input to a deaf child, it should not be entirely adequate as input (since it cannot meet Slobin's charges to language). Thus, we expect DCHP who have signed English input, even if it is rich and consistent, to modify that input toward complex morphology. This is indeed what we find. DCHP innovate forms that are more or less like those in ASL even without ASL input (see the next section and Goodhart 1984; Livingston, 1983; Strong, 1985; Suty and Friel-Patti, 1982). Incidentally, signing systems that involve signed English with simultaneous oral English should be worse yet, as the superimposition of oral English forces the signing to be even more isolating. Thus, we predict that DCHP, with either little input or with substantial signed English input, will innovate toward the sort of grammar that ASL has, and has for reasons that follow from the interaction of the cognitive prerequisites for language (Slobin's four charges to language) and the innate human linguistic capacity.

DCDP and DCHP: a comparison

We close this discussion of nativization in sign language by considering some data from deaf children. The nativization framework suggests that it is instructive to look at DCHP as well as DCDP. Both types of children nativize, and in fact they can be placed along a continuum that suggests something of the historical movement of ASL as a language, a movement that may be reenacted over and over under the influence of nativization processes and the shallow generational depth of sign language. The data below come from Goodhart (1984), and are discussed at greater length in Gee and Goodhart (1985). Pairs of DCHP and DCDP of various ages were asked to sign a Road Runner cartoon to each other. (DCDP to DCDP and DCHP to DCHP). In the scene we are concerned with here, the coyote (two-legged in the cartoon world) – with suction cups attached to its feet – is hanging upside down from a train tunnel made of white blocks. As the coyote hangs there, waiting for the Road Runner, one of the blocks slips out of the tunnel frame. The coyote is left with one foot and its suction cup dangling in midair, and the other foot attached to the tunnel. Of course, the other leg eventually comes undone too. The following informal representation illustrates how four children signed this message (the notes at the end of each example explain what the representation means):

11. DCPH (AGE 6;7)

    THEN THE BLOCK COME O-F-F OTHER ONE COME O-F-F

Notes: Nine "frozen" signs produced sequentially in neutral space. The signs are produced as gestalts and are typical English-based signs.

12. DCHP (AGE 5;8)

TUNNEL AT LOC$_4$	FLAT SURFACE AT LOC$_4$	Both legs in air	One leg drops then other leg drops	BY-LEGS GOES FROM LOC$_4$ TO LOC$_3$ (GROUND)

Notes: A sign for an arched shape tunnel is placed at Location "4," a plane at eye level, representing "above-ground level". Then, a classifier for "flat surface" is placed at Location 4. This classifier thus agrees in location with the tunnel. While perseverating this classifier at Location 4 (i.e., keeping it in place there), the child leans back and places his legs in the air. While continuing to perseverate the flat surface classifier, he then moves a classifier for "creature with legs," a V handshape with fingers oriented upward and touching the flat surface at Location 4, from Location 4 to Location 3, a plane at chest level representing the ground. This last part then means that it, the coyote, falls from the tunnel to the ground.

13. DCDP (AGE 7;9)

FLAT SURFACE AT LOC$_4$	BY LEGS (UP) ON LOC$_4$	LONG THIN OBJECT (UP) ON + FROM LOC$_4$

Notes: The child places a flat surface classifier at Location 4, a plane at eye level representing "above ground." While perseverating this flat surface classifier at Location 4, the child places a "creature with legs" classifier (a V-handshape) under and contacting the flat surface at Location 4. This means "it hangs upside down from a flat surface (= the tunnel)." Then, while continuing to perseverate the flat surface, the child drops the index finger (a classifier for long thin objects) of the V handshape (the finger goes *away from* being *on* the flat surface), indicating that the coyote is now hanging from the tunnel with one leg off and one on.

14. DCDP (AGE 8;10)

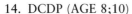

R + L FOREARM (UP) + INDEX/THUMB OPPOSED WARD LOC₄   R FALLS FROM LOC₄ TO LOC₃ (GROUND)

Notes: The child first orients both his left and right forearms, with index finger and thumb opposed on each hand, toward Location 4, a plane at eye level representing "above ground." The forearm represents a classifier for an "extended object." The index finger and thumb opposed represent a classifier for "square-ish object." Thus, each arm represents a leg with attached block. The child, while perseverating these classifiers at Location 4, then drops the right arm from Location 4 to Location 3, a plane at chest level representing ground level. See Figure 1 for a drawing of this example.

In (11–14) we see a continuum of forms, ranging from an English-based sign system in (11), which relies largely on input, to a very ASL form in (14), but one that is not predictable from what we have seen deaf children of deaf adults do with the same materials. The forms in (11–14) represent not only progressively deeper levels of morphological analysis of the component parts of signs and their possible meanings, but also a fulfillment of Slobin's charges to language. The forms in (11–14) become progressively more informative and at the same time progressively quicker and more efficient.

   We examine just one aspect of the continuous progression across (11–14). The sentence in (20), from a DCHP, contains nine frozen signs produced as gestalts and provides no evidence that the child sees the signs as having any parts. This child's sentence reflects the English-based sign input she has received from her hearing parents. We suggested earlier that given the speed of signing, such analytic systems as that displayed in (11) – even apart from their pidginlike properties – may not be fully adequate to meet Slobin's charges to languages. In any case, many deaf children of hearing parents go well beyond such forms.

   The sentence in (12), also from a DCHP, indeed goes well beyond

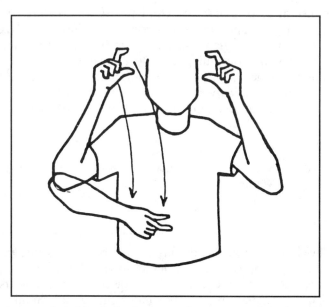

Figure 1.   Deaf child of deaf parents signing "While he (the coyote) hangs upside-down one foot (with block attached) slips and falls"

(11). It has all the structure of an ASL sentence, save for the fact that, in the middle of the sentence, the child uses his legs. Such a use of the legs is not characteristic of ASL, since the legs are not the normal articulators in the language. But note where the child has placed his legs, between FLAT SURFACE AT LOC_4 and the main verb (BY-LEGS GOES FROM LOC_4 TO LOC_3). This is just where such information would go in ASL. Further, he perseverates the FLAT SURFACE classifier through the whole use of the legs and the final verb complex. This is what characteristically marks a "phonological word" in ASL, marking everything from the FLAT SURFACE to the verb complex as one unitary phonological/morphological form. Thus, he has fully incorporated his use of legs into an ASL-like structure. From a purely informational point of view, he did not need to do this: Once the child used his legs to communicate that the coyote's legs come off one at a time in the cartoon, he communicated the message he intended to communicate, and he could have stopped there (we can infer that the coyote falls knowing that it is up in the air, as is communicated by what precedes the use of the legs in (12)). There is no informational reason to add the final verb. Thus, we can be reasonably confident that the child is operating with a linguistic system, despite having used his legs. Presumably he used his legs simply because he had not yet seen or innovated the full range of classifiers he needs.

The child who signed (13) is a DCDP. She signs the sentence in somewhat the same way an adult ASL signer might. But note that she has used grammatical material where the previous child used his legs, between FLAT SURFACE AT LOC₄ and the main verb. Where the previous child used his legs, the child in (13) places a BY-LEGS classifier on the bottom of a FLAT SURFACE, notating the coyote hanging upside down. Then, in the main verb, the child simply drops one finger of the BY-LEGS classifier to notate one leg falling. The previous child used his legs because he didn't yet see each of the fingers in the BY-LEGS classifier as separately standing for long thin objects (legs). That is, he had not yet analyzed the internal components of the classifier. The child in (13) is breaking down the forms into further meaningful parts, thereby gaining yet further classifier resources. As linguistic systems, however, what the child in (12) did and what the one in (13) did are very similar. Agreement, ordering, complex morphology, and a unitary higher-order phonological "word," marked by perseveration, are present in both cases.

The child in (14), also a DCDP, raises in an interesting way the whole question of innovation and input. He uses a form that we, at least, would not have predicted from the adult data we have seen. Instead of indicating the coyote's legs with one incorporated BY-LEGS classifier, this child uses two complex classifiers, and doubles both. Each raised forearm represents a leg of the coyote, while the thumb and index finger configuration on each hand specifies the size and shape of the blocks attached to each of the coyote's feet. These classifiers are oriented toward (WARD) the eye-level plane (notating ABOVE GROUND LEVEL). In the verb complex following, the child drops his right arm to indicate the coyote's leg is falling with a block attached to its foot. This child has used the morphological resources of the language in an innovative way to communicate yet more information than even the child in (13). Thus, in (12–14) both DCHP and DCDP fit into one continuum, operating with one system (ASL-like grammar), and both DCHP (12) and DCDP (14) innovate (nativize).

Conclusion

In our view, ASL is the product of extensive nativization, and that is why it looks a great deal like a creole. However, it has salient properties that are not like a creole (inflectional morphology and ASL's particular type of agreement system). These features, we have suggested, allow the system to meet Slobin's charges to language in the manual modality and perhaps are the unique contribution of visual perception. ASL is not a single form signed by some privileged group of speakers; rather, it is a continuum of forms within a system of a particular type, along which both DCHP and DCDP can be ranged, each balancing nativization and denativization in ways commensurate with their unique situations. All deaf children face a good deal of variability in input and produce a good deal of variability in their early output (Gee & Mounty, 1986; Goodhart, 1984). They ultimately converge on ASL-like forms and an ASL-like system because, we hypothesize, this system represents the expression of the human linguistic biological capacity in the manual modality. ASL has much to teach linguistic theorists, not only about parameters of the human linguistic capacity for language, but also about how locative/directional meanings form the basis for grammatical systems and their interpretation, and how discourse forms are progressively grammaticalized. If ASL, with its small generational depth, continually reenacts these processes, we may see here what we cannot see elsewhere.

Acknowledgments

We wish to thank Judy Mounty of Boston University, Judy Kegl of Northeastern University, and Michael Strong of the University of California at San Francisco for helpful comments at various stages of this work. Much of the theoretical approach to ASL grammar discussed here was originally worked out in collaboration with Judy Kegl. Although none of the above may agree with what we have made of their help, we appreciate it nonetheless.

References

Andersen, R. (1983a). A language acquisition interpretation of pidginization and creolization. In R. Andersen (Ed.), *Pidginization and Creolization as Language Acquisition.* Rowley, Mass.: Newbury House.
   (Ed.). (1983b). *Pidginization and Creolization as Language Acquisition.* Rowley, Mass.: Newbury House.
Anderson, J. M. (1972). *The Grammar of Case.* Cambridge: Cambridge University Press.
Baker, C., and D. Cokely. (1980). *American Sign Language: A Teacher's Resource Text on Grammar and Culture.* Silver Spring, Md.: T. J. Publishers.
Baker, C. L., and J. J. McCarthy. (1981). *The Logical Problem of Language Acquisition.* Cambridge, Mass.: MIT Press.
Bellman, K., H. Poizner, and U. Bellugi. (1983). Invariant characteristics of some American Sign Language morphological processes. In R. Hoffmeister and J. P. Gee (Eds.), Special Issue devoted to ASL, *Discourse Processes 6,* 199–223.
Bickerton, D. (1981). *Roots of Language.* Ann Arbor, Mich.: Karoma.
   (1982). Learning without experience the creole way. In L. K. Obler and L. Menn (Eds.), *Exceptional Language and Linguistics.* New York: Academic Press.
   (1984). The language bioprogram hypothesis. *The Behavioral and Brain Sciences 7,* 173–188.

Chomsky, N. (1965). *Aspects of a Theory of Syntax*. Cambridge, Mass.: MIT Press.
   (1976). *Reflections on Language*. New York: Pantheon.
   (1981). *Lectures on Government and Binding*. Dordrecht, Holland: Foris.
   (1986). *Knowledge of Language: Its Nature, Origin, and Use*. New York: Praeger.
Comrie, B. (1981). *Language Universals and Linguistic Typology*. Chicago: University of Chicago Press.
Deuchar, M. (1983). Negative incorporation in sign languages as creoles. A paper presented at the 1983 annual meeting of the Linguistics Society of America, December 28–30, Minneapolis, Minn.
Duranti, A., and E. Ochs. (1979). Left-dislocation in Italian conversation. In T. Givón (Ed.), *Syntax and Semantics 12: Discourse and Syntax*. New York: Academic Press.
Ecmekci, O. F. (1979). Acquisition of Turkish: A longitudinal study on the early language development of a Turkish child. Unpublished doctoral dissertation. Austin: University of Texas.
Feldman, H., S. Goldin-Meadow, and L. R. Gleitman. (1978). Beyond Herodotus: The creation of language by linguistically deprived deaf children. In A. Lock (Ed.), *Action, Symbol, and Gesture: The Emergence of Language*. New York: Academic Press.
Fischer, S. (1974). Sign language and linguistic universals. In C. Rohrer and N. Ruwet (Eds.), *Actes du colloque Franco-Allemand de grammaire transformationelle. Band II: Etudes de semantique et autres*. Tubingen: Max Niemeyer Verlag.
   (1978). Sign language and creoles. In P. Siple (Ed.), *Understanding Language through Sign Language Research*. New York: Academic Press.
Fischer, S. D., and B. Gough. (1972). Some unfinished thoughts on *FINISH*. Working Paper, Salk Institute for Biological Studies. San Diego, Calif.
Foley, W. A., and R. D. Van Valin, Jr. (1984). *Functional Syntax and Universal Grammar*. Cambridge: Cambridge University Press.
Gee, J. P., and J. A. Kegl. (1982a). Semantic perspicuity and the locative hypothesis. *Proceedings of the Eighth Annual Meeting of the Berkeley Linguistic Society*. Berkeley, Calif.
   (1982b). Semantic perspicuity and the locative hypothesis: Implications for acquisition. *Journal of Education 164*, 185–209.
   (1983). ASL structure: Towards the foundation of a theory of case. A paper presented to Special Session on Sign Language, Annual Boston University Conference on Language Development, October 1983.
Gee, J. P., and W. Goodhart. (1985). Nativization, linguistic theory, and deaf language acquisition. *Sign Language Studies 49*, 291–342.
Gee, J. P., and J. L. Mounty. (1986). Navitization, variability, and style shifting in the sign language development of deaf of hearing children. A paper presented at the Conference on Theoretical Issues in Sign Language Research, June, University of Rochester.
Givón, T. (1976). Topic, pronoun, and grammatical agreement. In C. Li (Ed.), *Subject and Topic*. New York: Academic Press.
   (1979). *On Understanding Grammar*. New York: Academic Press.
Goodhart, W. (1984). Morphological complexity, ASL, and the acquisition of

sign language in deaf children. Unpublished doctoral dissertation, Applied Psycholinguistics Program. Boston University.

Gould, S. J. (1977). *Ontogeny and Phylogeny.* Cambridge, Mass.: Harvard University Press.

Gruber, J. S. (1965). *Studies in Lexical Relations.* Amersterdam: North-Holland, 1976 (originally, doctoral dissertation, MIT, 1965).

Hyman, L. (1975). On the change from SOV to SVO: Evidence from Niger-Congo. In C. Li (Ed.), *Word Order and Word Order Change.* Austin: University of Texas Press.

Jackendoff, R. S. (1978). Grammar as evidence for conceptual structure. In M. Halle, J. Bresnan, and G. Miller (Eds.), *Linguistic Theory and Psychological Reality.* Cambridge, Mass.: MIT Press.

(1983). *Semantics and Cognition.* Cambridge, Mass.: MIT Press.

Johnston, J. R., and D. I. Slobin. (1979). The development of locative expressions in English, Serbo-Croatian, and Turkish. *Journal of Child Language 16,* 531–547.

Kegl, J. A. (1985). Locative relations in American Sign Language. Unpublished doctoral dissertation. Cambridge, Mass.: MIT.

King, R. D. (1969). *Historical Linguistics and Generative Grammar.* Englewood Cliffs, N.J.: Prentice-Hall.

Klima, E., and U. Bellugi. (1979). *The Signs of Language.* Cambridge, Mass.: Harvard University Press.

Klein, W. (1986). *Second Language Acquisition.* Cambridge: Cambridge University Press.

Lane, H. (1984). *When the Mind Hears: A History of the Deaf.* New York: Random House.

Liddell, S. K. (1984). THINK and BELIEVE: Sequentiality in American Sign Language. *Language 60,* 372–399.

Livingston, S. (1983). Levels of development in the language of deaf children. *Sign Language Studies,* 40, 193–286.

Mayberry, R., S. Fischer, and N. Hatfield. (1983). Sentence repetition in American Sign Language. In J. G. Kyle and B. Woll (Eds.), *Language in Sign: An International Perspective on Sign Language.* London: Croom Helm.

Meier, R. P. (1984). Sign as creole. *The Behavioral and Brain Sciences 7,* 201–202. (A reply to Bickerton, 1984.)

Meisel, J. M. (1983). Strategies of second language acquisition. More than one kind of language simplification. In R. Andersen (Ed.), *Pidginization and Creolization as Language Acquisition,* Rowley, Mass.: Newbury House.

Mounty, J. (1984). Nativization and grammaticalization in American Sign Language: An analysis of the 'FINISH' sign. Unpublished manuscript. Program in Applied Psycholinguistics, Boston University.

Muhlhauser, P. (1980). Structural expansion and the process of creolization. In A. Valdman and A. Highfield (Eds.), *Theoretical Orientations in Creole Studies.* New York: Academic Press.

Newport, E. L. (1981). Constraints on structure: Evidence from American Sign Language and language learning. In W. A. Collins (Ed.), *Aspects of the Development of Competence: Minnesota Symposia on Child Psychology.* Vol. 14. Hillsdale, N.J.: Erlbaum.

(1982). Task specificity in language learning? Evidence from speech perception and American Sign Language. In E. Wanner and L. R. Gleitman (Eds.), *Language Acquisition: The State of the Art.* Cambridge: Cambridge University Press.

Newport, E. L., and T. Supalla. (1980). The structuring of language: Clues from the acquisition of signed and spoken language. In U. Bellugi and M. Studdert-Kennedy (Eds.), *Signed and Spoken Language: Biological Constraints on Linguistic Form.* Dahlem Konferenzen. Weinheim/Deerfield Beach, Fla./Basil: Verlag Chemie.

Padden, C. (1983). Interaction of morphology and syntax in American Sign Language. Unpublished doctoral dissertation. University of California at San Diego.

Piattelli-Palmarini, M. (Ed.). (1980). *Language and Learning: The Debate between Jean Piaget and Noam Chomsky.* Cambridge, Mass.: Harvard University Press.

Pinker, S. (1984). *Language Learnability and Language Development.* Cambridge, Mass.: Harvard University Press.

Ross, J. R. (1967). Constraints on variables in syntax. Unpublished doctoral dissertation. Cambridge, Mass.: MIT.

Sankoff, G., and S. Laberge. (1973). On the acquisition by native speakers of a language. *Kivung 6* 32–47. (Reprinted in G. Sankoff. *The Social Life of Language.* Philadelphia: University of Pennsylvania Press, 1980.)

Schumann, J. H. (1978a). *The Pidginization Process: A Model for Second Language Acquisition.* Rowley, Mass.: Newbury House Press.

(1978b). The relationship of pidginization, creolization and decreolization to second language acquisition. *Language Learning 26,* 391–408.

Schumann, J. H., and A-M. Stauble. (1983). A discussion of second language acquisition and decreolization. In R. Andersen (Ed.), *Pidginization and Creolization as Language Acquisition.* Rowley, Mass.: Newbury House.

Slobin, D. I. (1973). Cognitive prerequisites for the development of grammar. In C. A. Ferguson and D. I. Slobin (Eds.), *Studies of Child Language Development.* New York: Holt, Rinehart and Winston.

(1977). Language change in childhood and in history. In J. Macnamara (Ed.), *Language Learning and Thought.* New York: Academic Press.

(1981). The origins of the grammatical encoding of events. In W. Deutsch (Ed.), *The Child's Construction of Language.* London: Academic Press.

(1982). Universal and particular in the acquisition of language. In E. Wanner and L. R. Gleitman, (Eds.), *Language Acquisition: The State of the Art.* Cambridge: Cambridge University Press.

(1983). What the natives have in mind. In R. Andersen (Ed.), *Pidginization and Creolization as Language Acquisition.* Rowley, Mass.: Newbury House.

Strong, M. (1985). The language of young deaf children: ASL and English. A paper presented at the Annual TESOL Convention, April 12, New York.

Supalla, T. (1978a). Morphology of verbs of motion and location in American Sign Language. In F. Caccamise and D. Hicks (Eds.), *National Symposium on Sign Language Research and Teaching.* Washington, D.C.: National Association of the Deaf.

(1978b). Morphophonology of hand classifiers in American Sign Language. Working Paper. University of California, San Diego.

(1982). Acquisition of morphology of American Sign Language verbs of motion and location. Unpublished doctoral dissertation. University of California at San Diego.

Supalla, T., and E. L. Newport. (1978). How many seats in a chair? The derivation of nouns and verbs in American Sign Language. In P. Siple (Ed.), *Understanding Language through Sign Language Research*. New York: Academic Press.

Suty, K., and S. Friel-Patti. (1982). Looking beyond Signed English to describe the language of two deaf children. *Sign Language Studies 35*, 153–166.

Turley, K., and L. Serber. (1984). Data on a deaf of hearing subject for Language Universals class. Boston University, Fall term, 1984–1985.

Valdman, A. (1983). Creolization and second language acquisition. In R. Andersen (Ed.), *Pidginization and Creolization as Language Acquisition*. Rowley, Mass.: Newbury House.

Wanner, E., and L. R. Gleitman. (Eds.). (1982). *Language Acquisition: The State of the Art*. Cambridge: Cambridge University Press.

Wilbur, R. B. (1979). *American Sign Language and Sign Systems*. Baltimore, Md.: University Park Press.

Woodward, J. C. (1973). Inter-rule implication in American Sign Language. *Sign Language Studies 3*, 47–56.

3 The history of language use in the education of the Deaf in the United States

Mimi WheiPing Lou

Editor's introduction

In Chapter 3 Lou takes a well-balanced look at language issues as they have influenced the education of deaf children over the past 170 years. In her review of the changes that have taken place in the educational use of language and mode, Lou details the struggles that persisted between advocates of oral and manual, English and ASL approaches, and that have finally come to a rather uneasy truce under the flag of Total Communication. Lou concludes, as do others in this volume, that no single method can fit all deaf children. In addition, Lou warns that Total Communication in name only is of little benefit to anyone, and that the real solution lies in a greater variety of alternatives provided by teachers who are capable of instruction in oral English skills, as well as, or alongside teachers with the ability to communicate in both signed English and ASL. This solution implies a greater use of deaf teachers, especially at the elementary level, an issue that is raised in Chapter 8. A true Total Communication program, Lou points out, should have the facilities for catering to the needs of individual students, including language and mode requirements together with audiological and speech therapy services. Such a program would be expensive and labor intensive and is simply not available under the current rubric of Total Communication. As a result, says Lou, the students suffer, and so does society.

This chapter provides a historical and contemporary context from which to view the work reported in this volume. An understanding of the history of the languages and language modes used in the education of deaf children allows us to examine more critically the research and current approaches in language instruction for deaf students.

The history of language use in deaf education in America has passed through almost exactly one and a half sweeps of the pendulum between American Sign Language (ASL) and manual approaches at one end of the arc and oral English at the other end. At first, during the early decades

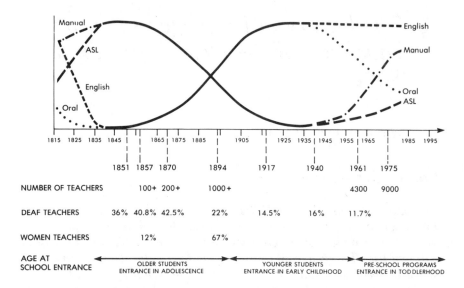

Figure 1. Graphic representation of ASL/English and manual/oral approaches in programs for the deaf, 1817–1980

of the nineteenth century, manual approaches and ASL were dominant. Then events moved steadily toward pure oral approaches and English, which became the standard language of instruction by the turn of the century. From the height of oralism in the first decades of the twentieth century, the pendulum swung slowly back in the other direction. At present the pendulum seems to have almost reached midpoint – both oral and manual systems are used, often in combination. Although the language of instruction is unquestionably English, the status of ASL is beginning to rise among Deaf and hearing communities (see Figure 1).

The period of manual approaches and American Sign Language: 1817 to 1860

A suitable starting point for this history is 1817 and the establishment of the first permanent American school for the Deaf in Hartford, Connecticut, by Thomas Hopkins Gallaudet (see Figure 2 for a time chart of major events discussed in this chapter). The school was the American School for the Deaf (originally named the Connecticut Asylum for the Education and Instruction of Deaf and Dumb Persons), and the first teacher there was Laurent Clerc, a deaf Frenchman. The mode of communication was manual, the language of instruction was a form of Signed

English (or an English-based revision of Signed French), and the language used outside the classroom was an early form of American Sign Language.

Thomas Gallaudet had gone to Europe in 1815 with the intention of studying both the oral methods developed by the Braidwood family in England, and the manual method used by L'Épée and Sicard at the National Institution for Deaf-Mutes in Paris. However, when the Braidwoods rejected Gallaudet's proposal that he try to learn their system in a few months, Gallaudet gave up his original plan to select the best from the two methods, and, instead, returned to America more than a year later, having trained only in the manual French method. He was accompanied by one of the best students of Sicard at the National Institution for Deaf-Mutes, Laurent Clerc, who was to teach at the new school for the Deaf that Gallaudet hoped to begin in New England.

Interestingly, the language initially used for instruction and taught at the first permanent school for the Deaf in the United States was Signed French, albeit in an anglicized form. This was the language taught at the National Institution for Deaf-Mutes in France and was based on signs taken from the natural sign language used by the Deaf community in Paris, although L'Épée had expanded it with methodical signs to capture aspects of French syntax, such as articles, gender, prepositions, and conjunctions. This artificial sign language enabled the Deaf to be "copyists" (as L'Épée described them) or to transliterate between signs and written French, but often without understanding.[1] Sicard, L'Épée's successor, tried to teach the meaning of the transliterated sentences by using the natural sign language of the Deaf community; however, the target language remained the Signed French developed by L'Épée. This was the language that Laurent Clerc learned as a student at the institution and that he, in turn, taught to another generation of French students and to Thomas Gallaudet. This language was modified somewhat before Clerc began teaching classes at the Connecticut Asylum; after Clerc learned English from Gallaudet, the two together "reformed certain signs which we thought would not well suit American customs and manners" (Lane, 1980, p. 125). It would appear, then, that the language of in-

---

1 The possibility of transliterating without understanding is made clear in this explanation from Lane: "In this system, which Epée called methodical signing, even the simplest sentence took on enormous complexity. One example: a line from Racine, 'To the smallest of the birds, He gives their crumbs,' required forty-eight signs from Epée's pupils. Gives alone required five signs: those for verb, present, third person, singular, and give. To the deaf pupil accustomed to expressing such an idea in five or six signs in a different order, the sentence in methodical signs lacked unity, was full of distractions, was far too long for a single unit of meaning, and in the end, was unintelligible. This did not prevent Epée's pupils from signing French sentences given a text and, conversely, from writing perfect French given a sentence in manual French; it just prevented them from understanding those sentences" (1984, p. 62).

MANUAL ORAL

1817	American School for the Deaf established in Hartford
1820's	Articulation instruction abandoned
1830's	ASL used: Methodical signs dropped
1844	Horace Mann report
1850	Convention of American Instructors of the Deaf holds first meeting
1850's	Some articulation instruction offered
1864	Gallaudet College (Columbia Institution) established
1867	First pure oral schools established: Lexington in New York, Clarke in Massachusetts
1868	Conference of Executives of American School for the Deaf organized
1869	First permanent day school established: Horace Mann in Boston
1870's	Arguments for "combined" method
1871	E. M. Gallaudet argues Sign Language used to excess
1872	Alexander G. Bell opens speech school for teachers of the Deaf in Boston
1874	Chicago Day Schools for the Deaf opened
1878	Rochester Method developed by Westervalt
1880	National Association of the Deaf organized
	International Congress on Education of the Deaf at Milan
1883	Bell "Memoir Upon the Formation of a Deaf Variety of the Human Race"
1890	A. G. Bell founds the American Association to Promote the Teaching of Speech to the Deaf (now the A. G. Bell Association)
1891	Gallaudet teacher training program established
1892	Clarke teacher training program opened

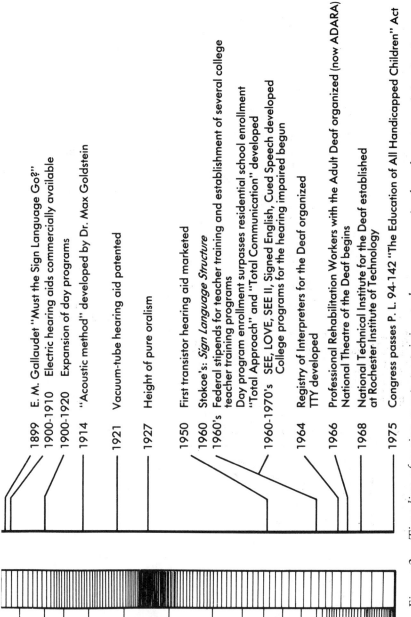

1899   E. M. Gallaudet "Must the Sign Language Go?"
1900-1910   Electric hearing aids commercially available
1900-1920   Expansion of day programs
1914   "Acoustic method" developed by Dr. Max Goldstein

1921   Vacuum-tube hearing aid patented

1927   Height of pure oralism

1950   First transistor hearing aid marketed
1960   Stokoe's: *Sign Language Structure*
1960's   Federal stipends for teacher training and establishment of several college
        teacher training programs
        Day program enrollment surpasses residential school enrollment
        "Total Approach" and "Total Communication" developed
1960-1970's   SEE, LOVE, SEE II, Signed English, Cued Speech developed
        College programs for the hearing impaired begun
1964   Registry of Interpreters for the Deaf organized
        TTY developed
1966   Professional Rehabilitation Workers with the Adult Deaf organized (now ADARA)
        National Theatre of the Deaf begins
1968   National Technical Institute for the Deaf established
        at Rochester Institute of Technology
1975   Congress passes P. L. 94-142 "The Education of All Handicapped Children" Act

Figure 2.   Time line of major events pertaining to language use in the education of the deaf

struction at the first permanent school for the deaf in America was a cross between Signed French and English.

Meanwhile, as in state residential schools today, the students used the different, more visually and manually based language of early ASL outside the classrooms. (See Woodward, 1978, for a discussion of the early development of ASL as a creolization of French Sign Language with indigenous sign languages in America.) Only two years after the establishment of the Asylum, Gallaudet suggested:

A successful teacher of the deaf and dumb should be thoroughly acquainted both with their own peculiar mode of expressing their ideas by signs and also with that of expressing the same ideas by those methodical signs which in their arrangement correspond to the structure of written language. For the natural language of this singular class of beings has its appropriate style and structure. They use it in their unrestrained communication with each other, [it is marked by] great abruptness, ellipses, and inversion of expression.... To take a familiar example ... "You must not eat that fruit, it will make you feel unwell." ... In [the deaf's] own language of signs, literally translated, it would be thus "Fruit that you eat, you unwell, you eat no." (Lane, 1980, p. 126)

It is most likely that Clerc also used (and helped to develop) this other "natural language" based only on signs when not teaching, since he himself had been a deaf student of a deaf teacher, Massieu, in a Deaf residential school community while growing up in Paris.

The first permanent school for the Deaf in the United States taught exclusively in the manual mode and offered no instruction whatsoever in articulation. This policy of excluding speech and speechreading was quite different from the current approach of Simultaneous and Total Communication. The second school established for the Deaf, in New York, had first tried to get a teacher trained in the Braidwood oral method, but when this turned out to be too costly it made do with only one articulation class in conjunction with an otherwise manual approach. This instruction proved to be unsuccessful, however, even when offered to "such of their pupils as retained a remnant of speech or of hearing" (quoted from Fay in Lane, 1980, p. 137), and so instruction in articulation was abandoned at the New York Institution in 1821.

With the complete abandonment of articulation instruction in the 1820s, American public schools for the Deaf moved more and more away from signed English and toward ASL as the language of instruction. Thus, by 1835 not only was the mode of communication at schools still completely manual, but the language used was ASL, not English. The methodical signs were dropped entirely and it was affirmed by the head of the American Asylum that "every teacher of the deaf must master ASL" (see Lane, 1980, p. 128). The same movement had occurred in France as well, for Bebian, who had studied under Sicard, argued that instructors should drop the elaborate system of methodical signs developed by L'Épée and use instead the natural sign language of the Deaf themselves (Lane, 1980). Thus, the period from 1835 to the 1860s was the only one in which ASL was the language of instruction for deaf children.

Characteristics of deaf education in that period other than the communication system are also relevant. One of these was the quality of the faculty. Between 1817 and the 1860s teachers in schools for the Deaf were typically male college graduates who learned to teach their deaf pupils through on-the-job training, with additional special instruction in Sign Language (Brill, 1974). The faculty at the American Asylum learned Sign Language from Laurent Clerc, and from their ranks came most of the principals and teachers of the other schools for the Deaf.

It was also during this early period that the proportion of deaf teachers was greatest: In 1851, 36% of the teachers were deaf themselves (Moores, 1978); in 1858, 40.8% (Gannon, 1981); in 1870, 42.5% (Moores, 1978). Thereafter the growing emphasis on speech and speech-reading instruction argued against the hiring of deaf teachers, with the result that their representation among faculty fell to 22% by 1895 and in the following years continued to decline.

The students were relatively mature during this period. The minimum age for admission to the American School's five-year program in 1817 was 14 years which dropped to 12 years sometime after that, and to 8 years in 1843. Nevertheless, the average age of the last 100 students entering the school in 1893 was still 10.8 years (Brill, 1974). Clearly, throughout this period the students were predominantly adolescents, not young children, and the willingness of parents to have their children taught manual English only or ASL may have been related to this factor.

Growing oralism: 1860 to 1900

The next period in the educational history of the Deaf is characterized by growing interest in and the ultimate domination of the oral methods, a trend that began in the 1850s. Horace Mann's glowing report of the success of oral methods after his visits to schools in Germany and the United Kingdom in 1844 probably marks the very beginning of the upsurge of oralist interests. Although no purely oral schools were established until 1867, the oralist stirrings were strong enough to prompt representatives from both the American Asylum and the New York Institution to hurry off separately to tour the European schools. They returned with impressions that differed greatly from Mann's, for they found that communication in these schools was accomplished primarily through Sign Language and that articulation was taught as an ancillary ability (Lane, 1980). They did recommend, nevertheless, that instruction in articulation be offered to those students with some residual hearing or speech. Thus, in the 1850s, some articulation instruction was attempted again in schools for the Deaf in America. In 1859, the American Asylum went so far as to hire the first speech teacher, but this foray into articulation training was short-lived. So little was accomplished that the speech teacher was fired in 1863 and the teaching of speech was, once again, completely dispensed with.

The failure to introduce components of oral instruction into the manual schools did not deter those who wanted to have oral schools only, and this to exclude manual communication completely. After some struggle, two such schools were established in 1867: the Lexington School in New York and the Clarke School in Massachusetts. At this point the oral-only schools did not view themselves as necessarily being in conflict or in competition with the manual schools. Gardner Hubbard, the man responsible for establishing the Clarke School, saw it as serving a different population from the American School – those who were hard-of-hearing and those who had lost their hearing at age 3 years or later: "This institution [Clarke] is especially adapted for the education of the semi-deaf and semi-mute pupils, but others may be admitted" (Hubbard, 1868, as quoted in Lane, 1980, p. 147).

During this period a growing number of advocates of sign language also began expressing increased concern over the lack of attention paid to oral training in the state schools for the Deaf. The foremost of these was Edward Miner Gallaudet, son of Thomas Hopkins Gallaudet and principal of Columbia Institution and the National Deaf Mute College (later renamed Gallaudet College). He led the principals of the manual schools to urge articulation and lipreading instruction as a complement to manual instruction, while reaffirming their preference for the manual method. E. M. Gaullaudet's great dedication to this approach led Donald Moores to claim: "If Thomas Hopkins Gallaudet is the father of education of the deaf in the United States, Edward Miner Gallaudet is the father of oral education" (1978, p. 59). In 1871 E. M. Gallaudet argued that sign language was used to excess (Moores, 1978), and he criticized the American School for doing too little to promote oral skills. E. M. Gallaudet consistently argued in favor of tailoring language teaching to the requirements and potential of the individual child, thus predating the thinking behind today's Total Communication revolution by over half a century. In his advocacy of a combination of methods for teaching deaf children, Gallaudet strongly encouraged speech and articulation training for those who could benefit by it, in addition to instruction by signed methods. The "combined method," as it was called, did not mean simultaneous use of oral and manual methods. This is an important distinction to note, for the combined method of the early 1900s did not imply the corruption of either signing or speech (or both), which occurs in simultaneous communication as practiced today (Marmor and Petitto, 1979).

The end of the 1860s saw not only the establishment of the first oral schools and the advocacy and beginning of permanent oral instruction in the previously manual-only residential schools, but also the founding of the first permanent day school in 1869. Horace Mann School opened in Boston that year as an oral-only day school, and since that time day schools (and later day classes, which began with the turn of the century) have been identified almost entirely with pure oral methods. This remained so until the late 1960s (Quigley and Paul, 1984).

The turning point in the language methods controversy occurred sometime in the 1880s, as the oral-only approach became the preferred and predominant method. A vigorous proponent of the method between 1870 and 1900 was Alexander Graham Bell, who not only taught Visible Speech, a method of articulation training developed by his father, but who also helped to organize oral instructors and the oral-only movement and wrote against isolating the deaf through intermarriage, culture, and residential schools. Bell was opposed to any use of sign language, feeling that it would hamper, if not prevent, the development of oral skills, as well as limit intellectual development, since he believed sign language to be ideographic and less abstract than spoken language (Lane, 1980).

The resolutions passed by the Second International Congress on Education of the Deaf in Milan in 1880 brought about the triumph of the oral-only methods:

1. The Congress, considering the incontestable superiority of speech over signing in restoring the deaf mute to society, and in giving him a more perfect knowledge of language, declares that the oral method ought to be preferred to that of signs for the education of the deaf and dumb. (Woodward, 1975, p. 8)
2. Considering that the simultaneous use of sign and speech has the disadvantage of injuring speech and lip-reading and precision of ideas, the Congress declares that the pure oral method ought to be preferred. (Lane, 1980, p. 155)

Although the Congress was, from the first, dominated by oralists, held in an oralist stronghold, and set up to showcase the best of oral education approaches (see Lane, 1980, for an eye-opening account of this and other "International" Congresses for the Deaf), its resolutions were taken to heart by educators of the Deaf, and soon after the Congress, all the countries of Europe adopted pure oral methods. Only five Americans attended the meeting, and all voted against the resolutions, but the Congress nevertheless had an overwhelming impact on educational methods in America too. Although America was the only country not to be completely swept by the oralist tide – sign language was not entirely rejected there as it was throughout Europe – the position of sign language in the education of deaf children in the United States was drastically weakened: "Almost without exception, American schools for the Deaf were officially oral from a relatively short time after the Conference until the last five years or so [from 1970 on]" (Woodward, 1975, p. 13).

The last half of the nineteenth century witnessed other significant developments that may have encouraged the movement toward oralism. For one thing, major changes occurred in the ranks of deaf educators through this period. The most significant change was the enormous increase in the number of teachers employed in the education of deaf children toward the end of the nineteenth century, from over 100 teachers in 1857 to well over 200 by 1870, to more than 1,000 by 1894. This enormous growth reflected the rapid establishment of many new schools for the Deaf and resulted in substantial changes in the character of the teachers. Whereas the faculty through the first half-century of deaf education from 1817 to 1860 had consisted predominantly of college-educated young men, the teachers that started in the next half-century were mainly more poorly educated women. There were only 3 women teachers of the Deaf in 1851 and 14 women teachers, or 12% of teachers of the Deaf, in 1857, but by 1894 the numbers of women in the field had increased almost fortyfold to 527 and constituted 67% of the profession.

This increase was due not only to the growing demand for teachers, but also to the Civil War and the loss of men, and to the substantial reduction in pay offered to those in the field. Thus, it would probably be accurate to assume that the quality of teaching deteriorated substantially in this period. The high failure rate for deaf students at this time, which, according to Gannon (1981), encouraged the shift to oral methods, might have been at least in part related to the poorer standards of teaching at the time.

The changing character of teachers in the field probably influenced the development of the teacher training program, which began to put more emphasis on speech and lipreading training. Not only was technical training in oral methods required of educated hearing persons intending to teach these skills to deaf children, but a limited program of such instruction could be offered to the more poorly educated women now swelling the ranks of educators for the Deaf. In previous years the well-rounded liberal arts education of the college graduates entering the teaching profession was relied on as the basis for teaching deaf children. Because the early teachers were few in number and were introduced to the profession gradually, they had the opportunity both to acquire on-the-job training in teaching their deaf pupils and to learn the sign language necessary for communicating with their students. The rapid influx of new teachers after the first half of the nineteenth century made it much more difficult for them to use sign language, even if they had wanted to.

Another development that was related to, and may have helped spur the swing to, oral instruction was the expansion of education downward to younger children. (Since public state schools were residential, they were unable to accept very young children; therefore, the trend toward earlier education began outside these programs.) The first educational program to admit young deaf children, down to age 4½ years, was established in 1852 by David Bartlett, a teacher with over 20 years' experience in residential schools. The program integrated deaf and hearing children, used all modes of communication, including sign and the manual alphabet, and followed a "natural" process of education. Such programs were rare and fairly short-lived, and for the most part, the young deaf children who did receive early instruction through the middle of the nineteenth century came from wealthier families who could engage private tutors. It is more than likely that most, if not all, such tutors use oral rather than manual methods since skilled signing teachers were unavailable and the families able to hire such tutors were usually hearing. In any case, it was Clarke, one of the original oral-only schools, that first extended the age of admission down to five years in 1867.

The younger starting age of deaf students, the establishment of day programs, and the "natural approach" are all factors that were linked with the growth of oralism during the last decades of the nineteenth century and the first decades of the twentieth century. The desire to begin instructing deaf children as early as possible certainly provided increased impetus for the establishment of day programs that would allow young children to continue living at home while attending school nearby. The first day programs were established in 1869, and they increased in number rapidly during the first two decades of the twentieth century with the rapid urbanization and suburbanization of the country (Moores, 1978). That day programs have consistently been identified with pure oral methods is not really surprising. Children attending day programs continue to live at home with their parents, over 90% of whom are hearing. Their nonclassroom time is not spent in a Deaf signing community of the sort that develops at a residential school. In fact, day programs do not offer the social opportunity required for such a community to develop.

It is also easy to see how the growing recognition of the importance of early education and of early parent–child communication led to an increased interest in "natural" approaches to language instruction: How could parents be expected to teach and their 4-, 5-, and 6-year-olds to learn grammar and analytical methods of English sentence construction? The push for early education, home teaching and communication, and "natural" approaches in language training would clearly favor oralism and English over manual communication and American Sign Language. The fact that only about 30% of deaf children have or had any deaf relatives (a proportion that has remained remarkably stable over the years, according to Moores, 1978) influenced this trend even further. Clearly, it is easier for hearing, English-speaking parents to try to communicate with their deaf children by speaking English and working on speech and lipreading skills than by using signs, and their children would seem the more "normal" and less handicapped if this proved successful.

The period of oral domination: 1900 to 1960

By the turn of the century, most of the day school and class programs and a number of private residential schools were using pure oral methods and were actively discouraging any manual communication; in addition, the public residential schools were in general committed to oral-only instruction, at least in the primary grades. The extent to which sign language was used in the state residential schools from this time on through the first half of this century is difficult to determine precisely. Some report that the use of sign language was permitted at the middle and upper grades in the majority of schools (see Garretson, 1976b), whereas others report the free use of sign language by all children and school personnel outside the classroom (Quigley and Paul, 1984); still others claim, on the basis of personal experience, that such schools banned signing in and out of the classroom (see Galloway, 1973). As Gannon (1981) explains, "[in 1892] the Pennsylvania School for the Deaf at Mount Airy abandoned the use of sign language for the pure oral method, . . . becoming the first large residential school to do so and setting a precedent which many other residential schools would follow" (p. 15). Although there was indeed a national trend against the use of any sign language, even at the state residential school level, the explanation for these apparent contradictions may be simply that the practice in individual schools varied and that some schools permitted continued use of some sign language. Woodward (personal communication) has noted that certain schools continued to have a significant percentage of deaf teachers on their faculties right through the first half of the twentieth century (e.g., Arkansas, with 40%–50% deaf faculty from 1900 to 1950; North Dakota, with 30%–55% deaf faculty from 1900 to 1950; and Kansas, with 30%–40% through the first half of the twentieth century).

E. M. Gallaudet, who had fought to include oral instruction in his combined approach, "felt constrained to defend the value of sign language in 1887 (E. Gallaudet, 1887) and clearly on the defensive, before the end of the century wrote an article entitled 'Must the Sign Language

Go?' (E. Gallaudet, 1899)" (Moores, 1978, p. 60). At the Fourth International Congress held in Paris in 1900, E. M. Gallaudet tried to have a resolution passed in support of a mixed or combined method of instruction and urged that the method be tailored to the aptitudes and needs of the individual student. At the same time that he favored oral instruction only for those who would benefit from it, he accepted and included in his motion the idea that initial instruction in schools should be oral for all (Lane, 1980).

The turn of the century witnessed the rapid expansion of both oral instruction and of English over ASL throughout the United States. In 1904, 18% of deaf pupils were instructed in programs that used purely oral methods; by 1917, this figure had reached 30% (Lane, 1980). These figures do not include the students enrolled in the state residential schools who were also taught by oral methods. From the small number of students enrolled in a handful of oral schools (Clarke, Lexington, Horace Mann, Mystic) in 1880 who were taught in English rather than in ASL, this figure rose to one-third of all deaf students in 1904, to two-thirds in 1917, to virtually all in 1978 (Lane, 1980).

These changes were matched by corresponding decreases in the percentage of deaf teachers on school faculties. By 1917 only 14.5% of teachers for the deaf were deaf themselves – a drop from the 22% in 1895 and from the 42.5% peak reported in 1870. The figure remained at about 16% between World Wars I and II and then declined again to 11.7% by 1961 (Moores, 1978). Throughout this period there were essentially no deaf teachers in any of the day schools or classes nor in any of the private schools. This decline in the numbers of deaf teachers is mainly attributable to the shift to oral instruction. The increased interest in articulation instruction and the optimism about the possibilities of speech and lipreading led to a demand for hearing teachers with specialized training in oral instruction. No longer was the model teacher a well-educated individual – either hearing or deaf – with sign language skills. Instead, special programs were developed to provide more poorly educated hearing women with the needed technical skills to teach articulation and lipreading. Gallaudet College was able to begin such a teacher training program for hearing students in 1891, and Clarke quickly followed by opening its previously internal oral teacher training program to would-be teachers for other schools in 1892.

At the same time that more hearing teachers were being hired because of the newfound hopes for oralism that surged toward the end of the nineteenth century, discrimination incited by the arguments of A. G. Bell, began to develop against deaf teachers. Bell believed that the Deaf could learn to speak, lipread, and integrate completely with the Hearing. Correspondingly, he opposed any segregation of deaf individuals or groups, whether self-selected or not. (Note that Bell was thus also opposed to oral-only deaf schools: He favored integration into the hearing schools over deaf-only schools of any form.) In order to combat the "formation of a deaf variety of the human race" (1883), Bell advocated several preventive measures, which included the suppression of Sign Language, the elimination of residential schools, the outlawing of deaf intermarriage, and the prohibition of deaf teachers. He opposed the establishment of a teacher-training program at Gallaudet, fearing that deaf students would be admitted to the program even though it was intended solely for hearing students. Thus, in addition to the de facto discrimination that resulted from the favored hiring of hearing speech and lipreading teachers, there was active discrimination against deaf teachers by oralists. By 1927, "probably the height of pure oralism in this country" (Gannon, 1981, p. 3), the situation was so bad for deaf teachers that Gallaudet College (the alma mater of most of them) openly discouraged deaf students from considering a teaching career.

Developments in amplification technology undoubtedly encouraged the enthusiasm and optimism for oral approaches at this time. Electric hearing aids became commercially available for the first time in the early 1900s, and the decade between 1902 and 1912 witnessed the production of several new carbon-type hearing aids (Berger, 1975). In 1914, Dr. Max Goldstein, founder of the Central Institute for the Deaf, developed the "acoustic method," which specifically trained those with residual hearing (Evans, 1982). These were the beginnings of the aural/oral approach in deaf education.

The oral method continued to dominate the education of the Deaf until the 1960s. Throughout these decades, pure oral instruction was preferred for all young deaf children, and many residential schools had at some period attempted to ban all use of sign language in or out of the classroom. When signing was used in the residential schools in classrooms, it was only in the upper grade levels, and then, most often with "oral failures."

Total communication approaches: 1960 to present

The status of ASL and manual approaches changed substantially in the 1960s. Many factors contributed to the change in attitude toward sign language. One was the publication of the first linguistic study of ASL, Stokoe's *Sign Language Structure: An Outline of the Visual Communication Systems of the American Deaf,* and the growing acceptance of ASL as a language. In addition, evidence was obtained showing that deaf children with deaf parents (who used ASL as a native language) achieve more academically than deaf children with hearing parents, and that early use of Sign Language did not, after all, retard speech development. Also, "the exposure of deaf people on television, a changing

national mood towards disabled Americans, and the increasing articu-
lateness and visibility of deaf leaders" (Gannon, 1981, p. 365) changed
American perceptions abut deaf persons. "[T]he increasing militancy of
deaf adults" helped, too (Moores 1978, p. 18). Some were also growing
dissatisfied with the failure of oral methods to help many profoundly
deaf children. Studies in the 1960s (Boatner, 1965; McClure, 1966;
Schein and Bushnaq, 1962; as reported in Evans, 1982, p. 10) provided
evidence of these failings: More than 30% percent of the deaf student
population was illiterate; 60% of deaf school-leavers achieved only at
the fifth grade level or below; and of the 5% who reached a tenth grade
achievement level or better, most were hard-of-hearing or adventitiously
deafened. In a wider context, it must be remembered, too, that the 1960s
was the period of the very active Civil Rights and minority power movements, a fact that no doubt influenced the developments in the Deaf
community as well.

Interestingly enough, although perhaps not surprisingly, religious
groups and clergy had already recognized the difficulty of communicating with the Deaf through oral-only methods. Thus, in the 1900s
clergy began learning sign language and religious groups began to go
on record as supporting the use of sign language. An interesting situation
developed at some schools, such as the New Jersey School, where teachers were required to use the oral method but clergy were permitted to
use sign language. By the 1940s an increasing number of seminaries were
offering sign language to those who would be working with the Deaf
community (Gannon, 1981). It appears that when communication was
a means to some other end – religious instruction in this instance, or
general education in the nineteenth century – then sign language was
accepted and used. When a particular communication system – that is,
English – was itself the goal of education, then manual approaches were
avoided, if not completely banned.

Another factor that might have made people more receptive to "new"
manual approaches during the 1960s could have been the increase in the
number of congenitally deaf students. Table 1 presents figures from various
sources for 1844–1973 and indicates the age of onset of hearing loss up
through the prelingual years. A comparison of the figures in Table 1 clearly
indicates an increase in the percentage of congenitally deaf in recent years. If
we include the figures of those reported as deafened in the first year or two
of life in the group of congenital deaf (very commonly, in the 1800s in particular, cases were not diagnosed until a child showed delays in expressive
language development, even when the hearing loss had occurred at birth),
then a very interesting pattern emerges. Calculated this way, the proportion
of those congenitally deaf rises to 64.5%–76% in 1856, and 63%–68% in
1880. The decrease in the proportion of congenital deafness through the
early decades of this century then appears to have occurred at the same time

90   *Mimi WheiPing Lou*

TABLE I. PERCENTAGE DISTRIBUTION OF DEAF ACCORDING TO AGE OF ONSET
UP THROUGH THREE YEARS

Age of onset	1844	1848	1856	1880	1910	1920	1970
Congenital	44	55	(50)	57.4	41.5	41.7	69
0–1 year	n.a.	n.a.	14.5	4.8	9	8.6	n.a.
1 year	n.a.	n.a.	11.3	6	13.1	12.3	n.a.
2 years	n.a.	n.a.	6.3	11.6	14.4	14.5	n.a.
3 years	n.a.	n.a.	n.a.	7.4	8.7	8.6	n.a.

Note: n.a. = not available. The figures for 1844 are reported by Weld in the Twenty-Eighth Report of the American Asylum at Hartford for the Education of the Deaf and Dumb (in Moores, 1978) from an examination of students at that school. The 1848 figures are based on students at that same school, reported by Turner ("Causes of Deafness," *American Annals of the Deaf,* 1848; in Moores, 1978). In 1856 Dudley Peet examined the causes of acquired deafness ("The Remote and Proximate Causes of Deafness," *American Annals of the Deaf,* 1856; in Moores, 1978), reporting the age of onset for 284 students in 13 schools for the deaf – 9 in Europe and 4 in the United States. If we calculate on the basis of the 1844 and 1848 reports that about 50% of the students were congenitally deaf, then we derive the percentages deafened at each of the first three years of life presented above. The next three sets of figures for 1880, 1910, and 1920 are reported by Best (1943) and taken from census reports. In some ways this is a broader population since it is not restricted to students at one particular school. At the same time, it is in other ways a bit narrower, being based on the population that experienced hearing impairment in only the first eight years of life. The 1970–1971 figures are taken from the Annual Survey of Hearing Impaired Children and Youth as reported by Ries (1973).

that pure oral approaches dominated. The recent increase in the proportion of congenital deafness occurs at a time when manual approaches are back in vogue.[2]

The first instructional use of sign language outside of the state resi-

2 What does not appear to be true is that there have been corresponding changes in the proportion of prelingually deaf across this past century. If hearing impairment in the first three years of life is taken to be prelingual, then the proportion of prelingually deaf among students enrolled in deaf programs in 1856 was about 82%, while the proportion of prelingually deaf among those with hearing impairment by 8 years of age was about 80% in 1880; 78% in 1910; and 77% in 1920. Although the contemporary period has seen an increase in the proportion of congenital deafness among the prevocationally deaf, it may be surprising that there has simultaneously been a significant decrease in the proportion of prelingually deaf. According to the National Census of the Deaf Population (Schein and Delk, 1974), the proportion of prelingually deaf among the prevocationally deaf population appears to be only about 50%. Even accepting a difference in figures because the Schein and Delk study was the only one not to be based on the more limited population of those enrolled in deaf educational programs, it seems safe to conclude that, contrary to the general belief, there does not appear to have been a substantial increase in the proportion of prelingually deaf in recent years – if anything, the opposite appears to be true.

dential schools occurred in the 1960s with high school students. In the early part of the decade, Dorothy Shifflet, a hearing mother of a deaf daughter and a public high school teacher, became disillusioned with the oral approach. She began using a multiple approach combining sign language and fingerspelling in addition to speech, speechreading, and auditory training for the deaf students in her school in Anaheim, California. She called this "the Total Approach" (Gannon, 1981). In 1968, in the same county in California, Roy Holcomb, a deaf educator and supervisor of an elementary school program for deaf children 3–12 years old, instituted the total approach for all the children in the program. He began publicizing this system, calling it "total communication" (Gannon, 1981). In 1968, Dr. David Denton, superintendent of the Maryland School for the Deaf, officially adopted the Total Communication philosophy for the school, including in that "the full spectrum of language modes, child-devised gesture, the language of signs, speech reading, fingerspelling, reading, and writing... [and] the development of residual hearing for the enhancement of speech and speech reading skills" (as quoted in Evans, 1982). In 1976 the Conference of Executives of American Schools for the Deaf officially defined Total Communication as "a philosophy incorporating the appropriate aural, manual, and oral modes of communication in order to ensure effective communication with and among hearing impaired persons" (Garretson, 1976a, p. 300).

Meanwhile, concurrent with the development of Total Communication, several systems of manually coded English were developed during the 1960s and 1970s to enhance the teaching of reading and writing to deaf children. In the early 1960s, David Anthony, a deaf teacher in Michigan, began working on a new sign system called Signing Essential English (Gannon, 1981). He borrowed signs that existed in ASL for English words, but he also created many new signs for English morphemes. Every English word was to be signed morphemically, so that a single word might require several separate signs (e.g., boy-ish-ly). His idea was to present manually the same information that was contained in written English, but without resorting to fingerspelling. Thus, many English homonyms share the same sign in SEE, even though their different meanings are conveyed by different signs in ASL. Anthony considered sound, spelling, and meaning in determining when different English words should be represented by the same sign. If different English words shared two of the three aspects, then they would be signed identically.

After beginning work on Signing Essential English, Anthony moved to a teaching position in Anaheim, California, where a group of other teachers and interpreters continued developing the system with him. The name of the system was changed to Seeing Essential English, downplaying the signing aspect so as to appeal more to hearing parents.

However, the group could not agree on how much should be retained from ASL and how much of the system should conform to English. Thus they broke up and two alternative signing systems were developed (Gannon, 1981). Dennis Wampler developed Linguistics of Visual English (LOVE) for use in preschool and kindergarten. The signs parallel speech rhythm and so are less close to ASL than those in Anthony's SEE system. LOVE is little used now (Quigley and Paul, 1984).

Gerilee Gustason, Donna Pfetzing, and Esther Zawolkow developed a system called Signing Exact English, or SEE II. This system differs from SEE I primarily in its treatment of compound and complex words. For example, SEE II borrows the ASL sign for butterfly where SEE I uses the two signs for butter and fly, even though this is conceptually misleading in terms of ASL. SEE II thus retains more of ASL than does SEE I. The developers of SEE II describe the system as consisting of 61% ASL signs, 18% modified ASL signs, and 21% newly invented signs.

Meanwhile, on the opposite coast, at Gallaudet College, Harry Bornstein along with Barbara Kannapell and Lillian Hamilton was developing yet another manually coded English system – Signed English. This system is a semantic representation of English covering the syntax and vocabulary commonly used with young deaf children, 1–6 years old. It is based on ASL with markers added to indicate the English inflectional system, and it remains the closest to ASL of the artificial sign systems just described.

Many have pointed out the similarity between the manually coded English systems and that developed by L'Epée two centuries ago when he added the methodical signs to the natural sign language in order to teach French. One important difference, however, is that the recent American systems are simultaneous systems in which English is meant to be spoken as it is signed. There is no indication that this was the case with Signed French. In fact, there are reports that until at least the 1900s it was considered quite rude by deaf people to sign and speak at the same time. Gannon (1981, p. 362) describes the signing of the late 1800s this way:

As sign language became outlawed in an increasing number of schools, there was a growing concern among deaf leaders that the beauty of the American Sign Language used by the masters of old would be lost. Those masters had a special delivery of their own, a poetic motion, a Victorian dignity, standing ramrod straight with their lips tightly shut as they graphically etched in the air spellbinding presentations of beauty. It was considered gross in those early days to mouth words; platform signers placed emphasis on signs. If fingerspelling could be avoided it was.

In the 1960s, the manual approach was even accepted in helping deaf children with speech reading and oral communication. Cued Speech, developed by Cornett (1967, 1969), is a manual representation of the phonetic elements of speech that are not readily visible for speechreading. It is meant to be used in conjunction with speechreading, and not as a linguistic system on its own.

There has also been renewed interest in the Rochester method, which was developed in 1878 by Westervalt and was also to offer manual-visual assistance to lipreading spoken English by the simultaneous fingerspelling of all spoken words. In 1953 the California School for the Deaf at Riverside adopted the method. New Mexico School for the Deaf was the first school to use the Rochester method in an early intervention program (Moores, 1978); and in the 1960s other schools began advocating this system as well (Brill, 1974).

Of these systems, SEE I and SEE II are most widely used today in the programs that ascribe to the Total Communication philosophy. Even more widely used, however, is a nonstandardized approach to the simultaneous communication of Signed English that has developed through the effort of teachers who later learned sign language and tried to use the two at the same time, in a "total" approach. This has meant that most deaf children in Total Communication programs are instructed in a form of English in which the spoken portion is distorted by simultaneous signing, which is incomplete and inconsistent at best. (See Kluwin, 1981; Marmor and Petitto, 1979; and Strong and Charlson, in press, for a discussion of the way teachers sign when using simultaneous communication; see Markowicz, 1974, for a discussion of the impossibility of communicating sentences in full simultaneous communication at the same speed as either oral English or ASL alone.)

Clearly, the attitude toward manual approaches in the education of deaf children has changed in the second half of the twentieth century. The decade between 1968 and 1978, in particular, saw the most rapid and consistent changeover of school programs to a Total Communication approach, with an average of 10 schools a year adopting it (Evans, 1982, reporting Garretson, 1976). By 1978 about 65% of all programs identified themselves as Total Communication, about 35% as pure oral programs, 0.5% as using the Rochester Method, and 0.2% as using Cued Speech (Jordan, Gustason, and Rosen, 1979, 1976).

In some ways these developments were enormous, as public day school programs were permitting and using manual communication for the first time. These programs had been strongholds of the pure oral approaches for almost a century. In the mid-1960s the enrollment in day programs surpassed that in the residential schools, and one may surmise that the difficulty of educating or, at least, coping with so many more hearing-impaired children may have had something to do with the addition of manual approaches in many of these programs by the end of the 1970s. The acceptance of simultaneous communication in the education of deaf children also had a significant impact on residential schools. Not only was signing in the classrooms permitted and even more, encouraged, but a freer, more open use of ASL, particularly outside of the classrooms, ensued.

In other ways the changes during the last two decades may appear larger than they actually were. There is no question that the pendulum has begun to swing back toward manual language and ASL, but it has not swung as far as many have feared and others have hoped. The language of instruction is still English. There are very few programs (for example, the experimental one referred to in Chapter 5) in which deaf children are specifically taught ASL. The goal of Total Communication is to take the best of both oral and manual approaches and tailor them, as far as possible, to the communication needs of individual students. However, as put into practice by many schools a "total" approach has too often been wrongly equated simply with simultaneous communication. Too many programs have ended up using both oral and manual methods inadequately. That is, listening skills and speech are not taught sufficiently, while the information carried by the manual and nonvocal components of most teachers' communication is linguistically incomplete and nonsystematic (Marmor and Petitto, 1979).

Other significant changes among the teachers of the deaf that occurred during the 1960s and 1970s are undoubtedly related to what might be called the Total Communication revolution in deaf education. Federal stipends for teacher training in deaf education in the early 1960s provided the impetus for the establishment of several special education programs at colleges and universities across the country (Brill, 1974). Earlier the major sources of teachers of the deaf had been the teacher training programs developed at the residential schools themselves (Moores, 1978). This development of so many totally new teacher training programs at different college and university settings, and away from the schools for the deaf, may have provided an opportunity to include innovative approaches in the field such as the Total Communication philosophy and simultaneous communication instruction.

Also, although the changed attitude toward signing did not herald a noticeable increase in the percentage of deaf teachers, there were some significant changes in this area as well. Whereas in 1961 almost all the deaf teachers were employed in the public residential schools, fully 30% of deaf teachers were teaching in public day programs by 1974 (Moores, 1978). Furthermore, until recently, most deaf teachers were restricted to teaching at the junior and senior high school levels. With the greater acceptance of manual communication, the numbers of deaf teachers who are teaching and being sought to teach at the elementary and preschool levels is increasing.

Conclusion

From a narrow perspective, the course of language use among deaf persons and in deaf education appears to have been determined by chance events or by the actions of significant individuals. Taking a broader view, however, one might see this history as having been influenced by and reflecting larger national and even international trends. Factors that have been intimately linked with the language used in the education of the deaf include the numbers and quality of teachers in the field, the numbers of deaf teachers in the profession, the educational starting age of students, the etiology of hearing impairment, hearing aid technology, day and residential programs, and language teaching approaches.

The struggle between oral English forces and manual ASL forces has been popularly referred to among the Deaf as the Hundred Years War, and unquestionably, the feelings in each camp have matched those of enemies engaged in mortal combat. The Total Communication philosophy was a call to lay down arms – requesting that concern return to the deaf child and advocating that neither oral nor manual approaches be excluded, but rather that they be mixed and selectively emphasized according to the capabilities of each child. Unfortunately, this position was compromised and misinterpreted as it was translated in practice to mean simultaneous communication for all. In this form, it is now viewed by many as just a third camp in an expanded war between oral and manual approaches, and between English and ASL forces.

This is not the first time that an individual approach has been advocated in contrast to the universal pure oral or manual-only approach. Edward M. Gallaudet attempted to win acceptance for this "combined method" as oralism was reaching ascendancy at the turn of the century. In the same way his father, Thomas Gallaudet, had hoped to learn the best of both oral and manual approaches when the first permanent school for deaf children in America was still at the planning stage.

Why, then, was this most reasonable approach repeatedly rejected in favor of one or the other opposing method advocated as the universal approach for deaf children? The extremism of the pure oral camp, which has argued against any use of manual methods, is at least partly due to the fear that children who are exposed to visual-manual communication will not develop the motivation needed for the difficult tasks of lipreading, listening, and speaking understandably, and thus will be inhibited if not entirely prevented from pursuing oral English skills. This possibility might be enough to scare the hearing parents of over 90% of deaf children into permitting pure oral methods to be used exclusively with their young children.

The position of the pure oralists, no matter how extreme, is still only one of the reasons that the combined and individually tailored approaches failed to take hold. Another is that educational programs designed to meet the individual communication capabilities and needs of deaf children involved enormous costs. In addition to the regular curriculum, school programs would need to be able to offer deaf students training in oral/aural skills — speech, speechreading, and listening/residual hearing — as well as instruction in ASL. Each deaf student might not require all these services in any given school year; in some years no students may require any one of these services. Nevertheless, for a true Total Communication program, all these kinds of training must be available. The qualifications demanded of teachers in such programs must also be greater than those required of teachers for hearing children. Not only must teachers of the deaf have elementary or secondary credentials, they must also either be able to teach oral English skills or be fluent signers. Even those teachers using one of the formalized systems of simultaneous communication need the flexibility in manual communication, ranging from a signed English to ASL, to communicate effectively with each deaf student.

There are no shortcuts to Total Communication: If the communication needs of each deaf student are to be met so that general education (in English, mathematics, science, history, social studies and so on) can proceed, and if the communication capabilities of all students are to be developed to their fullest potential, then each child will require different services and different teachers with different qualifications. If anything, despite the institution of individualized educational programs (IEPs) since 1975, the trend seems to be away from providing instruction and communication according to the requirements of individual students, and toward offering all hearing-impaired students the same services under the name of Total Communication. The implication of simultaneous communication is that all approaches are covered, just as the implication of mainstreaming and integration is that the quality of instruction and education offered to deaf children is equal to that of their hearing schoolmates. The reality in the schools is something quite different, and it is the deaf students who suffer as a result of the discrepancy.

History has shown that no single language approach is best for all deaf students. If we are truly to offer a combined or Total Communication approach in the education of deaf children, then we must acknowledge that this means an individual approach. Although such an approach may appear far more costly than other approaches in the short run, when one considers that the average reading ability of deaf high school seniors at present is at the 3.6 grade level and that almost half of these students score between second and third grade in tests of academic achievement, then surely the cost of raising the levels of achievement and language to hearing standards is lower than the cost to society of vocationally wasted individuals who must receive social security benefits throughout their adult lives.

References

Bell, A. G. (1883). *Memoir: Upon the Formation of a Deaf Variety of the Human Race*. New Haven, Conn.: National Academy of Sciences.

Berger, K. W. (1975). History and development of hearing aid. In M. C. Pollack (Ed.), *Amplification for the Hearing Impaired*. New York: Grune & Stratton.

Best, H. (1943). *Deafness and the Deaf in the United States*. New York: Macmillan.

Brill, R. G. (1974). *Education of the Deaf, Administrative and Professional Developments*. Washington, D.C.: Gallaudet College Press.

Cokely, D., and C. Baker. (1980). Sign language in the 20th century: A chronology. In C. Baker and R. Battison (Eds.), *Sign Language and the Deaf Community: Essays in Honor of William C. Stokoe*. Silver Spring, Md.: National Association of the Deaf.

Evans, L. (1982). *Total Communication: Structure and Strategy*. Washington, D.C.: Gallaudet College Press.

Galloway, V. H. (1973). Les misérables. In D. Watson (Ed.), *Readings in Deafness*. New York: Deafness Research & Training Center.

Gannon, J. R. (1981). *Deaf Heritage: A Narrative History of Deaf America*. Silver Spring, Md.: National Association of the Deaf.

Garretson, M. D. (1976a). Committee report defining total communication. *Proceedings of the Forty-Eighth Meeting of the Conference of Executives of American Schools for the Deaf*. Rochester, New York.

(1976b). Total communication. In R. Frisina (Ed.), *Bicentennial Monograph on Hearing Impairment: Trends in the U.S.A. Volta Review* 78 (4).

Jordan, I. K., G. Gustason, and R. Rosen. (1976). Current communication trends at programs for the Deaf. *American Annals of the Deaf 121*, 527–532.

(1979). An update on communication trends at programs for the Deaf. *American Annals of the Deaf 124*, 350–357.

Kluwin, T. (1981). The grammaticality of manual representations of English in classroom settings. *American Annals of the Deaf 126*, 417–421.

Kohl, H. R. (1966). *Language and the Education of the Deaf*. New York: Center for Urban Education.

Lane, H. (1977). Notes for a psycho-history of American Sign Language. *The Deaf American 30* (3–7).

(1980). A chronology of the oppression of sign language in France and the United States. In H. Lane and F. Grosjean (Eds.), *Recent Perspectives on American Sign Language*. Hillsdale, N.J.: Lawrence Erlbaum.

(1984). *When the Mind Hears: A History of the Deaf*. New York: Random House.

Lane, H., and F. Grosjean. (Eds.) (1980). *Recent Perspectives on American Sign Language*. Hillsdale, N.J.: Lawrence Erlbaum.

Markowicz, H. (1974). Sign English: Is it really English? Unpublished manuscript. Washington, D.C.: Gallaudet College, Linguistic Research Laboratory.

Marmor, G., and L. Petitto. (1979). Simultaneous communication in the class-room: How well is English grammar represented? *Sign Language Studies* 23, 99–136.

Moores, D. F. (1978). *Educating the Deaf: Psychology, Principles, and Practices.* Boston: Houghton Mifflin.

Paul, M. E. (1972). American Sign Language and deaf persons: A statement of the problem. *Deafpride Papers: Perspectives & Options.* Washington, D.C.: Deafpride.

Quigley, S. P., and P. V. Paul. (1984). *Language and Deafness.* San Diego: College Hill Press.

Ries, P. (1973). Further studies in achievement testing, hearing impaired students, spring, 1971. *Annual Survey of Hearing Impaired Children and Youth.* Gallaudet College Office of Demographic Studies, ser. D. no. 13. Washington, D.C.

Savage, R. D., L. Evans, and J. F. Savage. (1981). *Psychology and Communication in Deaf Children.* Sydney, Australia: Grune & Stratton.

Schein, J. D., and M. T. Delk, Jr. (1974). *The Deaf Population of the United States.* Silver Spring, Md.: National Association of the Deaf.

Strong, M., and E. S. Charlson. (In press). Simultaneous communication: Are teachers attempting an impossible task? *American Annals of the Deaf.*

Tervoort, B. T. (1983). The status of sign language in education in Europe and the prospects for the future. In J. G. Kyle and B. Woll (Eds.), *Language in sign: An International Perspective on Sign Language.* London: Croom Helm.

Woodward, J. (1975). How you gonna get to heaven if you can't talk with Jesus: The educational establishment vs. the deaf community. A paper presented at the annual meeting of the Society for Applied Anthropology, Amsterdam.

(1978). Historical bases of American Sign Language. In Patricia Siple (Ed.), *Understanding Language through Sign Language Research.* New York: Academic Press.

4 Sign language instruction and its implications for the Deaf

Steven Fritsch Rudser

Editor's introduction

Rudser describes the history of sign language instruction in the United States and paints a rather gloomy picture of the state of affairs today, particularly with regard to the training of interpreters. Rudser identifies three distinct groups of people who seek sign language instruction: hearing parents of deaf children, teachers of the deaf, and students of sign language interpreting. Each of these groups has different needs with regard to the kind of sign language, level of skill, and term of instruction. Rudser, himself an experienced interpreter fluent in ASL and signed English, takes strong positions on many of the issues he raises. He argues that hearing parents, in the interests of speed, are best advised to learn PSE (although it seems he feels ASL might be ideally more appropriate). He maintains that teachers must have ASL as well as English in order to communicate more effectively with their students and use ASL as a medium of instruction, a point also made by Lou in Chapter 3 with regard to Total Communication. Rudser is concerned that the procedures used in training and selecting sign language interpreters are not as rigorous as those for spoken language interpreters. Higher entrance standards and a longer training program (in conjunction, presumably, with higher rates of pay) might serve both to raise the level of interpreting and to facilitate integration between the Deaf and Hearing populations.

Currently over 300 postsecondary institutions in the United States offer sign language instruction *(Reflector,* 1984), and a number of publishing companies and bookstores specialize in sign language and deafness. Several journals relating to sign language have been published. *Sign Language Studies,* a quarterly publication for sign language research, has been published since 1972. The *Reflector,* a journal for sign language teachers and interpreters, was published between 1981 and 1984. The National Symposium on Sign Language Research and Teaching has held a number of major conferences since its inception in 1977. There are national organizations for sign language instructors, interpreters, and parents and teachers of deaf children.

All of these activities give an impression of maturity and organization. In fact the discipline of sign language instruction is still in its infancy, and probably has not developed sufficiently even to address the needs of target populations. This chapter covers issues relating to the teaching of manual communication to several distinct groups of hearing people. The first part describes the history of sign language instruction. The second part focuses on hearing parents and teachers of deaf children and the issues of language modeling and early communication. The third section discusses sign language interpreters, summarizing the history of interpreter education up to the present, and makes some recommendations for a new approach.

History of sign language classes

There is little information on formal sign language classes before the middle of the twentieth century. By the 1940s sign language classes were not uncommon in seminaries, and sign language instruction was used as a means of preparing clergy to work with deaf people (Gannon, 1981), but it was not until the 1970s that sign language classes were commonly available.

The first texts on sign language were picture dictionaries that included lists of English words and photographs or drawings of sign equivalents. The two earliest examples were Long's book published in 1909 and Michael's book in 1923 (Gannon, 1981). In the early 1960s there was a proliferation of sign language books. The difficulty with both the texts and the instruction in this initial period was that they taught only vocabulary. Although the students might be able to express their own language (i.e., English) in the manual symbols of sign language, they did not learn to communicate with deaf people in the way that deaf people themselves use sign language. An additional difficulty was that instruction focused on learning to produce signs, not necessarily on learning to recognize them in context. Students had great difficulty understanding deaf signers, even when the deaf person signed in English. This is contrary to normal language learning situations, where receptive skills develop before expressive skills. Some of the texts published in the 1960s and early 1970s, such as Falberg's *The Language of Silence,* Babbini's *Manual Communication,* and Madsen's *Conversational Sign Language II,* attempted to teach some aspects of American Sign Language (ASL) by including information on what was often referred to as "idiomatic" sign language. However, ASL was not recognized as a language independent of English.

Stokoe published his work *Sign Language Structure* in 1960. Although the book had little immediate effect, it came to have a profound influence on both texts and methods for sign language instruction. It was not until 1972 and the publication of Fant's *Ameslan: An Introduction to American Sign Language* that the real influence of Stokoe and subsequent linguistic researchers was apparent. Fant's book was the first to begin with the premise that English and ASL were distinct languages. Furthermore, although this book did teach vocabulary, the emphasis had changed from vocabulary to grammatical structures. Other books on ASL followed, as well as a number of books by linguists describing various aspects of ASL grammar, and teachers were quick to make use of this rapidly expanding body of information on ASL. One of the many positive aspects of this trend was the general recognition of the complexity of the language. However, the problem was that students often learned how to describe grammatical features of ASL in linguistic terms, but they did not necessarily develop comparable sophistication in producing and recognizing those grammatical features.

The next stage of instruction focused on the ability to use ASL rather than describe it. Texts such as *A Basic Course in American Sign Language* by Padden, Humphries, and O'Rourke and the *American Sign Language* series by Baker and Cokely attempt to teach ASL as a second language rather than a foreign language. Classes are conducted only in the target language from the very beginning of instruction. The goal behind this teaching methodology is to simulate the natural progress of children's acquisition of their first language. Even though these three stages in the development of sign language instruction are quite distinct and the movement through them is easily traced, it is safe to say that all three methods can still be found in sign language classes today.

The linguistic analysis of ASL was taking place at the same time that educators were creating the manually coded English (MCE) systems such as SEE I, SEE II, LOVE, and Signed English. In these invented systems, root signs were borrowed from ASL, and other signs were invented to represent English morphemes. The objective of these systems was to present the English language in a manual mode that would make it easier for deaf children to learn English. Sign classes in these systems are given primarily by teachers of the deaf for parents of the deaf children who are taught these systems in school. Classroom instruction is most similar to the first stage of ASL teaching, focusing primarily on vocabulary acquisition, since the student already knows the language and only needs to learn new symbols to express it. It was also during this period of intensive research on ASL and the development of the MCE systems that researchers began to study and describe Pidgin Sign English (PSE), which is the variety of sign language commonly used between deaf and hearing people.

The combination of the several methods of instruction with the different varieties of sign (ASL, PSE, and the artificial English systems) make sign language instruction today a very complicated endeavor. Obviously the approach suited to an instructor teaching ASL as a second language may not be the most appropriate one for another who is teaching a manually coded English system to native speakers of English. In addition, the method of instruction will be influenced by the student population and by their reasons for learning sign language. Those simply wanting to develop the ability to communicate on a basic level with deaf people will have different needs from hearing parents who discover their infant is deaf or individuals who would like to work as interpreters. The rest of this chapter is about the special situations of hearing parents and teachers of deaf children and of those interested in becoming sign language interpreters.

Sign language and parents and teachers of deaf children

The most important factor distinguishing parents from other groups of sign language students relates to motivation. Most students are motivated to learn sign language because of a desire to communicate with deaf people or an attraction to the language itself. Parents, on the other hand, are under pressure to learn sign language because they need it to communicate with their children. Hearing parents of deaf children typically go through a series of strong emotional reactions to the diagnosis of their child's disability (Schlesinger and Meadow, 1972). With the increase in Total Communication programs, many parents have begun learning some form of manual communication very early, whereas others may be doing so only after a painful failure with oral education. Whether the decision to use sign language was a positive first choice or a last resort, in neither case are the parents studying sign language simply for personal enjoyment. Many are well aware that their early communication with their young child can have major linguistic and psychological implications for the child's life. In addition, the parents feel a time pressure that other students do not feel, in that the child cannot wait for the parents to become proficient at their own pace. All too often, communication with the child is severely restricted by the parents' level of skill. For these reasons, the learning of sign language often becomes emotionally loaded for the parents, and this situation obviously complicates the regular learning process.

Another important distinction between parents and other groups of students is that parents are not learning sign language to communicate with adults who are already fluent, but rather with their own children, for whom they would ordinarily serve as primary language models. In this case, however, the parents' native speech is inaccessible to the child. Until the child begins some kind of educational program, the parents will be the major linguistic influence, but they will be using a language or mode that is foreign to them. Although most sign language students can be satisfied with skills that make basic communication possible, parents with young deaf children are usually aware that the child's future linguistic development depends to some extent on the level of skill they are themselves able to attain.

Once the parents have decided to use a manual approach with the child, they must decide which of the available sign systems they will learn. Should it be ASL, PSE, or one of the manually coded English systems such as SEE (Signing Exact English)? Although the idea of using ASL as the primary language of instruction is finally beginning to receive the attention it deserves, it is not clear that hearing parents should try to use ASL as the manual system for communicating with their children. Deaf children exposed to ASL acquire fluency in the same way that hearing children master their native language. Deaf children exposed to manual English systems, however, do not typically become fluent in English, in spite of school curricula that focus heavily on English acquisition. Thus ASL would seem to be the ideal at home, but if the parents are not already fluent in it before the birth of the deaf child, they will be attempting to model a language that they themselves are trying to learn. The ordinary difficulties in learning a second language after childhood, combined with the emotional stresses discussed above, make it highly unlikely that the parents will succeed in providing a good language model for their children. Children need consistent language input to develop their own linguistic potential.

It is for this very reason that educators often argue that the appropriate choice for parents is one of the forms of manually coded English, such as the popular SEE II, since they are based on English, which is usually the parents' native language. Because these invented systems are simply codes for expressing the English language, the student only needs to master a set of new symbols, much like learning a new writing system. The artificial systems, however, are in fact very cumbersome. Bellugi and Fischer (1972) have demonstrated that bilingual individuals relaying the same anecdote in both ASL and spoken English take equal time to express equivalent ideas, but the signed version contains approximately half as many signs as the English version has words, since it takes longer to produce a sign than a word. ASL exploits the fact that the body, unlike the voice, can produce more than one symbol at a time; for example, it can produce one sign on the hands and negate it facially or produce two signs simultaneously. In this way ASL can convey the same amount of information with fewer signs. In contrast, the artificial systems for representing English not only operate on the principle of a sign for every English word, but many words require more than one sign. Furthermore, since the users of these systems are encouraged to speak and sign simultaneously, they must either drastically reduce their normal speech rate or leave out some of the signs. Research shows that skilled MCE signers do omit many signs for English words or morphemes, especially those representing English function words and affixes (Kluwin, 1981; Marmor and Petitto, 1979; Swisher, 1984). Thus the model of English presented to the children is at best incomplete and at worst grossly ungrammatical. This degraded form of English is probably no better a linguistic model than the imperfect ASL the parents would have acquired had they decided to try to use that.

A third alternative for the parents is to use Pidgin Sign English. Because pidgins are typically easier to learn than full languages, it would take less time to become fluent in PSE than ASL, and it would be easier to use than MCE, since it is not an artificially created system that violates the principles of visual/gestural languages. While the child is young, the parents' PSE can lean heavily on English, thereby enabling them to communicate as freely as possible. Over the years the parents' PSE will probably be influenced more and more by ASL. Their general signing skills will almost certainly improve with time, and they will probably come into contact with more and more deaf adults. The most important influence will come from the child, who, as he or she grows, will interact more frequently with other deaf children and with deaf adults, and whose language will move steadily toward ASL. The parents slowly become less important language models. Eventually they resemble other sign language students who want to learn sign language to communicate with deaf people. The more ASL they learn the more it can enhance their communication with their children; the issues of linguistic modeling are no longer so crucial. In fact, at this stage roles may be reversed and the child may become the language model for the parent attempting to acquire better sign language skills.

The question of which sign language or system to use in the education of deaf children is at least as significant as the choice of communication in the home, but there is an important distinction between parents and educators. The parents' ability to learn a new communication mode for their deaf child is affected by their socioeconomic status, intelligence, language-learning aptitude, amount of available time, as well as the emotional issues discussed above. In the home there must be a compromise between what is best for the child and what is realistic for the parents. Teachers, on the other hand, are professionals who have trained for years to develop the necessary skills and knowledge to educate deaf children. They have already demonstrated a high level of academic achievement. Hence the decision of what language or mode is used in the classroom need not be influenced by the kinds of pressures that are felt by emotionally stressed parents. Rather, the choice of MCE, PSE, or ASL should be based on what is most effective for the students.

The various MCE systems are certainly the most frequently used at present. The rationale for this is that the children live in an English-speaking environment and need to have the ability to read and write English, and that MCE is the most complete method available for representing English visually. But are the children in MCE classrooms really being exposed to English? Research demonstrates that teachers signing and speaking simultaneously produce grammatically correct manual English only a very small percentage of the time. Deletions of function words and grammatical morphemes are very common, and even omissions of subjects and main verbs are frequent. Marmor and Petitto (1979) suggest that attempting to produce spontaneous spoken English simultaneously with manually coded English may be unrealistic because of linguistic overload. Significantly better English and reading levels for deaf children educated with MCE have not been documented. Although the visual representation of English seems reasonable, the deaf child's attempt to acquire MCE in the classroom is in no way analogous to the hearing child's acquisition of English as a primary language in the home. Deaf children continue to recreate and use their own dialect, which is more similar to ASL than to English (e.g., see Chapter 5). Unfortunately, standards and expectations in deaf education are so low that the failure of MCE to produce deaf children fluent in English is largely ignored.

Since PSE is a pidgin, it is also not the appropriate language for instruction. PSE has many varieties and cannot substitute for a full language system, and the only reason for using PSE in the classroom would be the relative ease with which the teachers could learn it. The goal, however, is obviously not ease of teacher preparation, but the enrichment of the lives of deaf people through quality education. Instructors communicating fluently in a true language is the way to provide this.

ASL is a naturally occurring visual/gestural language that, in a Deaf community such as a residential school, deaf children typically acquire to a sophisticated level for communication, without a single hour of formal instruction. In spite of this, educators of the deaf continue to ignore the Deaf community and its language. In so doing they prevent those Deaf children with Deaf parents from being educated in their native language, and prevent the other children from being educated in the language that they can most reasonably be expected to master. Hence the children are denied the strong linguistic base that could be their greatest support in learning English as a second language. Although manually coded English has largely replaced oralism as the most common means of educating deaf students, it is no more successful than oralism at turning the average deaf child into a native or near-native speaker (or signer) of English. In fact, the average deaf student graduates from high school with a fourth grade reading level, in spite of many years of instruction in English and reading. The fact that education in ASL has been discussed only very recently belies the fact that the issue is charged with emotion and prejudice.

Many adult members of the Deaf community are to some extent bilingual in ASL and English, but it is a bilingualism too often born of frustration and pain. Planned bilingual education for deaf children, with the language of their community as the first language, and the language of the majority community second, is a reasonable approach to the problems facing deaf education today.

Perhaps the most immediate impediment to bilingual education is the signing ability of the educators. Deaf people today make up only a very small percentage of teachers of the deaf (see Chapter 8). Bilingual education would rely much more heavily on deaf teachers and would require hearing teachers to acquire nativelike skills in ASL. MCE would have its place in English classes, where students would study it as a second language, but even the English teacher should have at least receptive understanding of ASL to assist in his or her students' acquisition of English.

Developing fluency in nonnative signers is not impossible, but it would require an approach radically different from the one used in teacher training programs today. Maxwell (1985) documents the lack of emphasis on sign language skills in teacher preparation where, in many programs, sign language classes are electives rather than requirements. The fact that teachers of the deaf are graduating with minimal sign language skills is having profound effects on deaf education. The heavy emphasis on English in the average deaf classroom demonstrates the value attached to that language, and the minimal sign language competency of the average hearing teacher shows equally clearly the value, or more accurately the lack of value, attached to sign language. Deaf children have the right to be educated by instructors who are skilled signers communicating in a language in which they are fluent. It can be argued that until this happens, until deaf children really have free and accessible communication in the classroom, they cannot be expected to attain their full intellectual and linguistic potential, and teachers of the deaf cannot be said to truly serve the community for whom their profession exists.

Sign language and interpreters

Formal education of sign language interpreters began as a by-product of higher education for deaf people. As long as the majority of deaf college students were educated at Gallaudet College (the liberal arts college for the deaf created by an act of Congress in 1864), the need for interpreters was not great. However, in the late 1960s and early 1970s the concept of educating deaf students alongside hearing students became popular, and a number of programs for deaf students appeared at other institutions. In 1964, the Leadership Training Program (LTP) at California State University, Northridge (CSUN), accepted its first deaf student and hired an interpreter. The LTP is a master's program in administration for the field of deafness. In 1965, Congress mandated the creation of a technical college for deaf students to complement the liberal arts education available at Gallaudet. This time, rather than establish a separate institution for deaf students only, the National Technical Institute for the Deaf was made part of another school, the Rochester Institute of Technology in Rochester, New York. In 1968 and 1969 federal money established regional deaf programs at three community colleges and augmented the program already begun at CSUN. The three community colleges were Delgado College in New Orleans, Seattle Central Community College (SCCC) in Seattle, and Technical Vocational Institute (TVI) in St. Paul. By 1985 there were over 50 postsecondary programs for the deaf in the United States.

Before this move toward integrating deaf college students with hearing students took place, there were probably very few people who made their living as sign language interpreters. When interpreting services were needed, they were often provided on a volunteer basis by people who had deaf parents, who were teachers of deaf children, or who had learned sign language from relatives, friends, or religious groups. Integration in education meant that interpreters were needed, and professional interpreting became more common. In the beginning, most of the people who interpreted professionally were the same people who had previously interpreted as volunteers, those who had already had some occasion in their lives to learn sign language. As the postsecondary programs increased in both size and number, the demand for interpreters also increased. Before long the demand exceeded the supply of signers. Some of the educational programs began to train their own interpreters. These initial efforts focused on hearing college students, who were usually trained in intensive summer programs lasting approximately eight weeks. The most successful individuals completing the program would then be hired to provide interpreting services at that school. Recruiting potential interpreters from the college's student body meant that the institution had an ongoing source of new trainees, and the students could earn money to help pay for their education. Both NTID and TVI began their programs in this way.

Student trainees were accepted into these programs with minimal or no knowledge of sign language. American Sign Language had not yet been recognized as anything other than a defective form of English peculiar to deaf people, so the curricula naturally concentrated on signed English. During the course of the training, students were taught a core vocabulary of several hundred signs (in comparison, the ASL vocabulary has thousands of signs) and were taught to fingerspell words for which they did not know a signed equivalent. Instruction was weighted heavily toward working from English to sign language, since the task that the students would encounter most often would be signing a hearing instructor's lecture. Individuals trained in this manner often had to work for several years before they developed enough knowledge of the language to be able to transmit material from sign language to English. This, of course, had major implications for the deaf consumers, since real two-way communication between teacher and deaf student was out of the question. A further problem was that by the time the student interpreter had enough on-the-job experience to compensate in some measure for the lack of real training, he or she would graduate.

Realizing the severe limitations of this approach to preparing interpreters, the federal government funded three regional interpreter training programs in 1974. These programs were housed in the three community colleges with deaf programs mentioned above, namely, Delgado, SCCC, and TVI. The programs were to offer certificates and Associate of Arts (A.A.) degrees in interpreting and would be able to develop more extensive curricula encompassing various aspects of interpreting and the field of deafness. The benefits of the two-year program over the summer intensive course were immediately apparent. Within a few years there were similar programs in community colleges across the nation.

In recent years there has been some move to award bachelor's degrees in interpreting. CSUN (Northridge, California), Madonna College (Livonia, Michigan), Bloomsburg University (Bloomsburg, Pennsylvania), Maryville College (Maryville, Tennessee), and the University of Wisconsin-Milwaukee all offer bachelor's degrees (*American Annals of the Deaf*, 1985). Most of these programs, however, offer the degree in a related field such as deaf studies (CSUN), educational studies (University of Wisconsin), or sign language studies (Madonna) and allow students the option of a concentration in interpreting. A four-year program creates a more extensive exposure to ASL and allows the student to have a more sophisticated knowledge of sign language before beginning interpreter training. It is obvious that the four-year colleges and universities are more appropriate places to educate interpreters, but, unfortunately, they remain the exception to the rule. McIntire (1984) has described well the challenges that sign language interpreting faces in seeking acceptance as a new discipline within academia.

At the same time that these rapid changes in the education of interpreters were taking place, linguistic research on American Sign Language was blossoming. The fact that Deaf people shared a language that differed from English in more than just mode became common knowledge. This new understanding of ASL was reflected in the courses that were being offered in the curricula of the various programs. Instruction was no longer limited to signed English. Courses such as conversational ASL, grammar of ASL, and deaf culture appeared. It was, however, this same linguistic research that led people to look critically at the feasibility of preparing competent interpreters in two years. Before it was understood that ASL was indeed a language, interpreting was considered analogous to court reporting and stenography, which are technical skills that can be learned in a relatively short period of time. This new research made it clear that the only activity really analogous to sign language interpreting is foreign language interpreting. Unfortunately, even though the skills required in both types of interpreting are essentially the same, the attitudes and practicalities of professional preparation are not equivalent.

There are very few spoken language-interpreting programs in the United States, but a comparison between the programs that do exist and the sign language interpreting programs is very revealing. Most of the differences in training reflect the implications of entrance requirements. At the Monterey Institute of International Studies (MIIS), in California, requirements for admission are quite rigorous. The student must have native fluency in two languages, one of which must be English. The student must have lived for at least six months in a country where the non-English language is spoken, or must have received part of his or her education in that language. For certain programs, such as the degree in conference interpreting, a third language is required. The student must already have a bachelor's degree. Thus, MIIS admits students who are bilingual, bicultural, and highly educated.

In stark contrast to this is the situation in sign language interpreting programs. Many of these programs are housed in community colleges that have a so-called open-door policy. Open-door policies are interpreted differently in various states, but the basic idea is that students should be able to enter the program directly, the only prerequisite being a high school diploma or General Education Diploma (GED). Most of these schools also require that individual programs be no longer than two years, which means that the average training program has only a minimal amount of time, both to teach sign language and to develop interpreting skills. Understandably, at the present time interpreter education still focuses mainly on language instruction, rather than or actually teaching the highly complex art of interpreting. A few programs have been lucky enough to establish sign language prerequisites to interpreter training, but even these programs must usually be content with one year of sign language instruction or the equivalent. The difference between one year of classroom instruction and native fluency is painfully obvious.

The fact that students entering interpreting programs usually do not know ASL, although serious enough in itself, is not the only problem interpreter educators face. Since few community colleges test English ability as a prerequisite for admission, a high level of sophistication in the English language also cannot be taken for granted. In spite of the fact that English is the native tongue of the majority of the students, many do not have the heightened mastery of the language that is needed to understand and transmit a wide range of material in a variety of settings. Since an individual's language can be influenced by a host of different factors, such as gender, race, age, intellect, and regional and cultural background, an individual aspiring to work as an interpreter must be familiar with a wide range of linguistic styles. This presupposes a broad mastery of the English language that is beyond the capabilities of the students in many of the interpreting programs.

Few individuals graduating from two-year interpreter training programs are able to pass the Registry of Interpreters for the Deaf certification evaluation. Graduates usually work for several years before they develop enough skill to become certified. This, in itself, is proof of the inadequacy of current interpreter education. Two years may in fact be enough time to prepare a student for professional employment, if the student comes to the training with the necessary above-average skills in both ASL and English. Then, as in programs for spoken language interpreters, the curriculum would be free to shift from teaching language to addressing the complicated issues of transmitting human communication from one language to another.

The present educational situation is unsatisfactory from the point of view of students, teachers, and consumers. It is patently unfair to admit students to programs that are of too short a duration to teach the skills and knowledge they purport to impart. Interpreting is a rigorous and demanding profession, and two years, when that time must also include teaching one of the two languages, is not enough time. Yet the fact that the vast majority of interpreting programs exist within community colleges suggests that those in the field believe that it is possible to prepare interpreters in two years. If interpreter education is to be offered, as, of course it must be, then programs and timetables must reflect reality. If it takes four years to prepare an interpreter (e.g., two years to learn the language and two years to learn to interpret), then programs must be four years long.

The educator is also robbed of a sense of success by the current state of affairs. Asked to do an impossible job, he or she can only fail. This is disheartening and eventually leads educators to lower their standards, which are otherwise constantly unattainable for the students. A lowering of standards, however, is not an acceptable solution to the problems in interpreter education. The interpreting profession needs to strive for excellence, not mediocrity.

Ultimately, the most serious consequence of the present state of affairs is the effect on consumers. Consumers of interpreting services, both hearing and deaf, have a right to the best services that diligently trained professionals can provide. At present, decisions on whether deaf and hearing people will interact in a given situation are all too often made on the basis of whether competent interpreting services will be available. It must always be remembered that interpreter education is the means to an end: to provide an opportunity for deaf people to integrate into the larger community to the extent they desire. If unrealistic training is inhibiting the development of professionals who could make this goal possible, then a grave disservice is being done to the Deaf community.

Summary

Since the early 1960s there has been a steady move to depathologize deafness. Strong similarities between the Deaf community and ethnic and linguistic minorities have been noted, and these observations enhance our understanding of deaf people, their language, and their experience in a sometimes hostile majority culture. But this new sensitivity has not yet been integrated into the institutions and professions serving the Deaf community. It is now time for this to happen. Deaf children born to hearing parents may not have the advantage of learning ASL from their parents, but they can be exposed to the next best thing, PSE, at an early age. Deaf children should be educated in the language of their community, ASL, and taught English as a second language through the medium of their first language. Educational programs for teachers of the deaf and sign language interpreters must adequately teach the linguistic expertise necessary for those roles. If this does not happen, the gulf between the understanding of the deaf experience and the actual services provided to deaf people will continue to widen, so that although we will continue to understand better the damage inflicted by unchallenged policies and assumptions of the status quo, we will fail to do anything about it.

References

Babbini, B. E. (1974). *Manual Communication: Fingerspelling and the Language of Signs*. Urbana: University of Illinois Press.

Bellugi, U., and S. Fischer. (1972). A comparison of sign language and spoken language. *Cognition* 1, 173–200.

112   *Steven Fritsch Rudser*

Cokely, D., and C. Baker. (1980). *American Sign Language: A Student Text.* Silver Spring, Md.: T.J. Publishers.

Falberg, R. M. (1963). *The Language of Silence.* Wichita, Kans.: Wichita Social Services for the Deaf.

Fant, L. J., Jr. (1972). *Ameslan: An Introduction to American Sign Language.* Silver Spring, Md.: National Association of the Deaf.

Gannon, J. R. (1981). *Deaf Heritage: A Narrative History of Deaf America.* Silver Spring, Md.: National Association of the Deaf.

Humphries, T., C. Padden, and T. J. O'Rourke. (1980). *A Basic Course in American Sign Language.* Silver Spring, Md.: T.J. Publishers.

Kluwin, T. (1981). The grammaticality of manual representations of English in classroom settings. *American Annals of the Deaf 126,* 417–421.

McIntire, M. (1984). Achieving academic acceptance. *The Reflector 8,* 5–6.

Madsen, W. J. (1972). *Conversational Sign Language II.* Washington, D.C.: Gallaudet College.

Marmor, G. S., and L. Petitto. (1979). Simultaneous communication in the classroom: how well is English grammar represented? *Sign Language Studies 23,* 99–136.

Maxwell, M. M. (1985). Sign language instruction and teacher preparation. *Sign Language Studies 47,* 173–180.

Padden, C., Humphries, T., and T. O'Rourke. (1981). *A Basic Course in American Sign Language.* Silver Spring, Md.: T. J. Publishers.

Programs for training interpreters for the deaf. (1985). *American Annals of the Deaf 130,* (2), 150–151.

Schlesinger, H. S., and K. P. Meadow. (1972). *Sound and Sign.* Berkeley: University of California Press.

Sign course inventory. (1984). *The Reflector 8,* 12–17.

Stokoe, W. C. Jr. (1960). *Sign Language Structure.* Studies in Linguistics Occasional Papers 8. Buffalo: University of Buffalo Press.

Swisher, V. (1984). Signed input of hearing mothers to deaf children. *Language Learning 34* (2), 69–85.

5 A bilingual approach to the education of young deaf children: ASL and English

Michael Strong

Editor's introduction

One educational approach that has never been attempted officially with deaf children is bilingual education. Uncertainties about whether ASL constitutes a language and about the number of children who learn that language at home, the lack of trained teachers who know ASL, and the fact that it has no written form, in conjunction with negative feelings in general about bilingual education, probably account for the reluctance to try it with the deaf. This chapter describes a pioneering effort to design and execute an experimental bilingual curriculum for young deaf children. The justification for adopting a bilingual educational approach for this special population is three-pronged: Evidence from existing research has shown the alternatives to be unsuccessful, Cummins's linguistic interdependence model provides theoretical support, and findings from an earlier observational study of residential school children has shown that children from both hearing and deaf families use more ASL-like structures than English forms in their spontaneous language.

There follows a brief description of the experimental curriculum, which uses a storytelling format first to introduce ASL into the classroom and later to teach English through the medium of ASL. Emphasis is on both language learning and the enhancement of metalinguistic awareness. This program, although limited, is the first of its kind to be researched and evaluated in the United States.

Probably the most difficult problem deaf children must face is the acquisition of language. The long-standing failure of educators in this area is evident from the poor oral English skills and low reading levels of these children. Recently, the acceptance of signing in classrooms for the deaf in America has legitimized a second means of communication for Deaf children, one that hitherto was restricted to covert interactions between students and conversations out of sight of school personnel. Furthermore, the formal study of ASL by contemporary linguists has confirmed its status as a genuine linguistic system distinct from English. However, the sign system used in classrooms that have adopted a Total Communication approach is not ASL, but one of the signed varieties of English developed as an artificial code for the representation of spoken (or more accurately written) English in a visual-gestural mode.

Although most deaf people consider the widespread acceptance of signing a great step forward in deaf education, many educators of the deaf are still opposed to the use of ASL. The reasons for this are complex and often politically motivated, but the fact remains that no attempt has yet been made to test the efficacy of using ASL formally in the classroom (in the manner of many bilingual programs throughout the world) as a medium of communication through which other school subjects, notably English, might be taught. There is, however, ample theoretical and re-search evidence to support this kind of approach, although apparently it has not been convincing enough to those who make programmatic decisions to outweigh the competing political perspectives, threats to existing teachers, demands on time, and potential disruptions to estab-lished curricula. This chapter describes an initial attempt to overcome some of these problems and the rationale used for eliciting the necessary cooperation from members of the educational establishment.

Justification for the approach

Previous research

One way to distinguish the different kinds of programs for deaf children is to look at the kinds of communication systems they employ. Oral programs use spoken English only and place great emphasis on speech training, lipreading, and maximal use of hearing aids and residual hear-ing. A second approach combines manual communication with spoken English so that the teachers use both sign and speech simultaneously. Simultaneous communication has been in use for many years, but re-cently has become the backbone of the relatively new Total Commu-nication approach to educating the deaf. Total Communication officially proclaims the right of a deaf child "to learn to use all forms of com-munication available to develop language competence" (Denton, 1970). As Quigley and Kretschmer (1982) subsequently noted, this definition may refer to practically any communication method and may, in many cases, simply be a way of giving a positive label to a program that otherwise has no coherent philosophy attached to it. A third kind of program uses manual communication only, either a manual form of English or ASL. This last variety is uncommon and is confined largely to preschool programs for children of deaf parents. (However, there are programs in Sweden that use Swedish Sign Language and Swedish bilingually, and in England there is at least one experimental program using British Sign Language and English.) ASL is permissible in Total Communication programs in this country, but tends to be the last resort of a teacher who is unable to make a child understand in any other way. The low incidence of deaf teachers, coupled with official policy, accounts for this situation.

In general, very little research has been done on the relative effects of different systems. Positive results have been demonstrated for oral programs only when subjects were selected from one of the few model oral programs in the United States (Quigley and Kretschmer, 1982, p. 22). However, the oral method was used almost exclusively for many years before people began to admit that it was by and large a failure. When researchers initiated studies into various forms of manual communication, results generally favored the sign systems over the oral approach. Russian studies (e.g., Morazova, 1954) reported the benefits of using fingerspelling over a strictly oral method, and Quigley (1969) confirmed those findings in this country. Moores (1978) reported that preschool programs using total communication or fingerspelling outperformed oral programs.

Some researchers have investigated the effects of parental language use on the language development of deaf children. The hearing status of the parents has been well established as a predictor of future linguistic and academic success (Meadow 1968; Quigley and Frisina 1961; Stevenson, 1964; Stuckless and Birch, 1966), the advantage being enjoyed by fewer than 10% of the deaf children who have deaf parents. Researchers have been unable to pinpoint the reason for this advantage. That it might be entirely due to early exposure to ASL is somewhat difficult to accept in view of the findings on parental attitudes (Corson 1973) suggesting that deaf parents are better prepared to cope with deaf children and therefore provide better emotional and educational support. Corson's study included both oral and manual deaf parents, and both groups showed significantly more positive acceptance of deafness than hearing parents. Furthermore, some signing deaf parents use as much manual English as they do ASL with their children, so it might be more an issue of comprehensible native signing than of ASL per se.

Brasel and Quigley (1977) attempted to address this issue by assessing the effects of four different home language environments on academic performance through a comparison of scores on the Stanford Achievement Test and the Test of Synthetic Abilities. The four groups consisted of children aged 10–19 who had received oral English with intensive training, oral English with no special training, manual English (PSE), and ASL. The authors found that the manual English group scored highest in all measures of achievement, reading, and grammatical ability.

The oral group with no special training scored lowest on all measures, and the ASL group scored higher than the intensive oral group. Thus, Brasel and Quigley concluded that manual communication has an advantage over oral communication, and that manual English is preferable to ASL.

This carefully designed study leaves unanswered one important question concerning the language varieties of the manual English group. It is not clear to what extent the parents excluded ASL from their communication. One would expect that, as the children were from deaf families, their PSE would have tended toward the ASL end of the continuum. It follows, too, that deaf parents who describe themselves as using English are likely to be better educated than parents using only ASL at home. Conversely, if the ASL parents were well educated, it is probable that they used English to some extent as well. Unfortunately, the groups were established on the basis of self-report, with no verification by the researchers, so that the reality of the distinctions between groups is in doubt.

Bilingual education theory

The fact remains that more than 90% of deaf children have hearing parents, most of whom are not fluent enough in any form of sign language to provide native user input. These children then arrive at school with, at best, minimal communication skills. In this way deaf children are unlike hearing speakers of other languages, who come to school fluent in a first language. Whereas the question for hearing children centers on whether to incorporate this primary language in their formal schooling, for most deaf children the issue is which form of which language should be considered their primary means of communication. As we have seen, the choice is between various forms of signed or spoken English. However, now that linguists have recognized ASL as a language (e.g., Klima and Bellugi, 1979), researchers are beginning to view the education of the deaf as an issue centering on bilingualism (e.g., Barnum, 1984; Champie, 1984; Erting, 1978; Kannapell, 1974; Marmor and Petitto, 1979; Quigley and Paul, 1984). This is a positive shift in that deafness as a handicap is being deemphasized, and attention is turning instead to language acquisition. Such a change also brings the acquisition of language by deaf individuals into the realm of legitimate concern for those who conduct research into bilinguilism, bilingual education, and second language acquisition, and for those who teach English to speakers of other languages.

This change in thinking is not yet reflected in school programs for a number of reasons. First, there may still be some skepticism among educators of the deaf as to the status of ASL as a language. Second, most teachers in elementary schools for the deaf are themselves hearing, and consequently few are native users of ASL. Third, children cannot learn to read ASL as it does not have a written form. Lastly, there are no published ASL curricula.

In spite of these problems, much of the theoretical justification for bilingual education is applicable to the special case of deaf children. The Cummins (1981) model of Common Underlying Proficiency, for example, is particularly appropriate. Cummins uses this model to illustrate that experience with either of two languages can promote development of the proficiency applicable to both languages. Elsewhere, Cummins (1979, 1980) argues that in order to keep up in subject matter and maintain normal cognitive development, students need to develop high levels of first language competence. Moreover, they need to develop not only basic interpersonal and communicative skills in the first language, but also the ability to use language effectively "as an instrument of thought and to represent cognitive operations by means of language" (Cummins, 1978, p. 397). Cummins further suggests that a lack of development in the CALP (Cognitive/Academic Language Proficiency) aspect of first language competence may explain why some minority children have problems in school. Thus, low first language skills can exert a limiting effect on the development of the second language. Given this interdependence hypothesis, Cummins argues that education in the first language develops CALP in any other. Thus, for example, in the case of children from Latin America, those who have learned to use Spanish for academic purposes will have developed an ability that aids them in using any other language in an academic setting. On the other hand, those who have not fully developed CALP skills in their first language have more trouble in acquiring second language CALP skills and perform academically below the level of other children their age.

The issue of common underlying proficiency clearly has bearing on the education of deaf children. Deaf children, even more than non- or limited-English-speaking hearing children, have consistently performed far below the level of their hearing English-speaking peers throughout their school careers (DiFrancesca, 1972; Furth, 1966; Wrightstone, Aronow, and Moskowitz, 1963). The handicap of deafness alone cannot account for this failure, because there are group and individual differences in the academic achievement of deaf students exposed to the same educational conditions. One variable that possibly does account for many of these differences is the home language experience of the child. A large number of research studies (summarized by Moores, 1978), show that deaf children of deaf parents outperform deaf children of hearing parents in many aspects of academic work. One may hypothesize from such findings that the advantage enjoyed by deaf children of deaf parents derives largely from the consistent input they receive in the first language.

Children of hearing parents rarely have this opportunity and must learn to communicate as much as they can either from oral English, pantomime, or from nonnative signs that their mothers and sometimes their fathers are attempting to learn themselves.

Evidence cited by Cummins in support of his theory of common underlying proficiency resembles these findings, which demonstrate the value of fluency in the parental language for deaf children of deaf parents. Cummins's evidence stresses the advantage of good first language skills for learing the L2, English. Although bilingual education, as an educational institution, has not gained widespread approval in the United States, findings of available, well-controlled research are strongly supportive of the basic principle upon which it rests, namely, the interdependence of skills across languages. For example, Troike (1978) reviewed 12 evaluations and several research studies in which bilingual instruction was found to be more effective than English-only instruction in promoting English academic skills. Cummins (1981) reviews six other program evaluations from both the United States and abroad, all of which clearly show the benefits for second language performance of programs emphasizing the use of the first language.

Other research evidence derives from the study of primary language development in the home. In essence, these studies show that the use of a minority language in the home is not a handicap to children's academic progress. Cummins and Mulcahy (1978) studied a Ukrainian bilingual program in which first and third grade students who used Ukrainian consistently were better able to detect ambiguities in English sentence structure. Chesarek (1981; quoted in Cummins 1981) studied elementary students on a Crow reservation in Montana and found that a subgroup of students, who had one or more Crow-speaking parents but who were raised as English speakers, scored significantly lower both on a nonverbal ability test and on several aspects of English achievement than the native Crow-speaking group, who had been learning English for three years in a bilingual program.

Bhatnager (1980; quoted in Cummins 1981, but without reference) traced the academic progress of Italian immigrant children in French and English schools in Montreal. He found that the children who used Italian and either French or English interchangeably were better at speaking and writing their second language than children who used English or French all the time. These findings are explained by the fact that the quality of the second language used in the home by parents may have been lower than was necessary to provide beneficial input for the children's academic development. Wells's (1979) study has shown that the quality of interaction children experience with adults is more important for academic success than whether that language is English or something else.

This wealth of evidence strongly suggests that deaf children of hearing parents are suffering, not from their lack of English input, but from a lack of *any* language input that is of high enough quality to aid cognitive/ academic language proficiency. This problem has not gone unrecognized by educators, but the solution in the past has been to attempt to find some way to improve the teaching of English as a first language, and efforts ranging from oral approaches, through new-oralism to manual English and Total Communication, have all failed to raise significantly the reading levels of deaf children in comparison with their hearing peers. The disappointing results from these approaches may stem from the fact that none represents a complete language system in itself to the deaf child. Very little spoken English can be processed by most deaf children, either through aided hearing or lipreading, and manual systems of English of the type used in Total Communication programs are not taught accurately or consistently (see Kluwin, 1981, on junior high teachers; Marmor and Petitto, 1979, on high school teachers; Strong and Charlson, in press, on elementary school teachers; Swisher, 1984, on hearing parents).

Thus, a bilingual approach would certainly seem to be applicable to deaf children of deaf parents who use ASL in the home, although this is only a small proportion of deaf children. However, deaf children of hearing parents who associate with deaf adults and children of deaf parents – for example, in a residential school – have as much chance of acquiring ASL as a means of social communication and group identity, as they do English. Under these circumstances, they, too, are suitable candidates for this approach. The following section describes the findings of a study that examined the language patterns of children at a residential school and provides empirical evidence to support this line of reasoning.

Data on the language patterns of young deaf children at a residential school

A study (Strong, 1985) of the spontaneous sign language of young deaf children was recently carried out at a residential elementary school for the deaf. Data from this study provide the third kind of justification for a program that teaches and uses ASL.

The subjects were 19 children aged 4–7 from the four most junior classes at the residential school. Eleven children were of deaf parents, 8 had hearing parents. All the subjects were deaf from birth and had no other impairments. All were described as profoundly deaf, with hearing loss greater than 80 DB in the better ear, 4 were in the preschool class that met each morning, 11 were in two kindergarten classes, and 4 were in the first grade class. Three of the four teachers (all female) were hearing and one (the preschool teacher) was deaf. The official school policy espouses total communication, with teachers speaking and signing simultaneously; the signs are loosely based on the system known as SEE 2. The teachers themselves do not feel bound either to the SEE 2 system or to simultaneous communication and readily admit to using any kind of language they feel will help the children to understand. The children represented all levels of signing ability from rudimentary skill to exceptional fluency.

The children were videotaped at regular intervals over the course of one school year. Spontaneous samples of sign language were collected in the classroom and in the cafeteria as the children went about their daily tasks. In addition, special sessions of "weekend news" were recorded. These consisted of reports on the events of the weekend that each child presented to the class every Monday. In all, between 50 and 60 hours of tapes were recorded.

The study sought to examine the observed language of the children to determine the extent to which it could be characterized as either ASL or English. The tapes were transcribed on coding sheets that made it possible to record each observed utterance, along with instances of particular grammatical structures, identified in advance as acceptable in one language but not in the other by a team of experts in linguistics and ASL.

This analysis revealed an overwhelming majority of ASL over English elements, regardless of situation or skill level and in spite of constant English input from the teachers throughout the year. Signs for English verb inflections, determiners, and forms of the verb *to be* were rarely used whereas ASL markers for directionality and temporal aspect were very common. Classifiers were widely used, as were indexic reference and facial questions and negatives. Overall, children seemed to be more motivated to acquire and use the social language of their peers than the English forms modeled by the teachers. This finding might have been predictable from the evidence of studies of simultaneous communication cited earlier (Kluwin, 1981; Marmor and Petitto, 1979; Strong and Charlson, in press; Swisher, 1984), which showed teacher and parent language as incomplete, inconsistent, and nonstandard, and thus as potentially impeding the learners' acquisition process.

Since ASL is accessible to deaf individuals, is used by many deaf adults and deaf children, and might be considered the most appropriate full language system available to the Deaf, it is surprising that no formal school programs have yet been based on ASL. Since it also appears that, at least in the environment of a residential school such as that observed in the above-mentioned study, deaf children from all backgrounds appear to use language that is more like ASL than English, there is even more reason to consider it as a likely medium for classroom instruction. Deaf children differ from hearing non-English speakers mainly in the poor quality of input they receive in their primary language (unless they have deaf parents who use ASL). The aim, then, of the program described below was to provide good quality primary language input and establish the viability of using ASL as a means of teaching English.

The experimental bilingual/ESL program

The present program was seen as a first step toward creating a bilingual educational environment in which ASL is used as the primary language and English the second language. Owing to its limited resources and the fact that only a small part of the school day was available to work with, the program's goals were conservative. They were defined as follows:

1. To develop and expand ASL skills and then to use that language as a medium for teaching English.
2. To develop an awareness of ASL and English as equal but separate languages together with an ability to recognize some of the differences between the two languages.

These goal statements were also transformed into research hypotheses that were to be tested by using a matched pair design to compare the experimental group with a second group of children who had not been exposed to the experimental syllabus. This research is being evaluated at the time of writing. (For a report, please contact the author directly.)

The experimental class contained eight profoundly, prelingually deaf children from a variety of backgrounds. Two had deaf parents and were fluent in ASL, three had parents who were skilled signers, two had almost no communication skills when they arrived at the school, and the last one was somewhere in between. The class differed from traditional bilingual models in that there were no native speakers of another language in the group, but may be considered bilingual in that two languages (ASL and English) were used. The teacher was a deaf, native user of ASL (and bilingual in English), who visited the class to teach the special syllabus. She had more than ten years of teaching experience and had been coached in the art of storytelling by a professional storyteller.

The syllabus (see the appendix) was appropriate for children aged 4–7 and was constructed around a series of children's stories that were culturally adapted, where necessary, for an audience of deaf children. Thus, characters do not listen and talk on the phone, they communicate on a TTY; characters do not overhear a conversation, they watch it from a distance, and so on. The syllabus is divided into two parts. The first part deals with ASL only, the second part introduces English. Part 1 is divided into 10 units. Each unit centers on a different story and focuses on a separate aspect of the language. A unit is expected to take

5–10 one-hour sessions and begins with the introduction to and telling of the story in ASL (either live or on videotape); this is followed by a variety of activities, including role playing, story retelling, drawing pictures, question-and-answer sessions, quiz games, and so on. Part 2 also consists of 10 units with similarly structured activities. However, Part 2 focuses on structures and functions that are realized very differently in ASL and English. In this part, stories are presented on videotape, first in ASL and then in a strict manual version of English (i.e., not PSE). Children are encouraged to look for differences in the two versions, with the teacher guiding them toward those that pertain to the theme of that particular unit. The lessons are still conducted in ASL, but now the goal is to introduce English and to show some of the ways in which it differs from ASL with a view to stimulating a metalinguistic awareness in the learners.

Although considerable attention is given to form as well as function, the overall emphasis is on the use of language in real situations, in this case the language of telling or acting a story, and on asking or giving information. The grammatical aspects are kept simple and elementary. Teacher evaluation can be effected in a number of ways. Children may retell the story one-on-one with the teacher, the teacher may pose questions in either ASL or English and have the child respond in the appropriate language, the teacher may ask information questions about the story, and so on. For research purposes, the children were given a signed repetition task (Strong, Gold, and Woodward, 1986) to measure vocabulary and structural knowledge, and a recognition task to measure metalinguistic awareness. Both of these kinds of tests, which had stimulus items recorded on videotape, could also be used for teaching purposes.

The experimental program ran in this form for a year and a half, starting in January; the first part was repeated after the summer break. The children, who had already experienced some storytelling events in the classroom, were enthusiastic participants. The parents, who all gave special permission for their children to be involved, were also enthusiastic. Even some parents of nonparticipating children who heard about the program asked whether their offspring might be involved. For the most part the children's regular classroom teachers were cooperative, or at least tolerant of the program. It did, after all, represent a certain amount of disruption to the normal schedule and involved using ASL, a language in which most hearing teachers are not completely comfortable. One teacher was very much in favor, one ambivalent, and one basically against the idea. The school administration were at first skeptical, but later wholly supportive. In view of the fact that some people react emotionally when ASL is recommended for use in school, this generally positive reception was encouraging.

Summary

Deaf children educated under the commonly available programs that use either an oral approach or total communication, with or without some measure of mainstreaming into regular classrooms, continue to perform well below their hearing peers, especially in English. In many ways, deaf children can be likened to hearing speakers of other languages for whom bilingual education is one available option. Although increasing numbers of researchers, parents, and others associated with the Deaf have suggested that bilingual approaches should be developed for deaf children, few, if any, such programs are in operation in the United States. This chapter describes an attempt to design and implement an experimental program of this type, which is justified by findings from previous research on alternative methods, bilingual education theory, and a study of language use in a residential school for the Deaf. Although the program described here is necessarily limited in scope, it may encourage others to explore more extensively the potential benefits of applying the principles and practices of bilingual/ESL education in programs for deaf children.

Acknowledgments

The research for this chapter was funded by NIHR grant #Goo8300146 to the University of California, Center on Deafness, and by a grant to the author from the UCSF Academic Senate. The author would like to thank Dr. Henry Klopping, Jacob Arcanin, Marianne Deluca, and Pat Dorrance for making it possible to conduct the study at their school, and Linda Cox-Kuntze, Nancy Eldridge, Norma Richards, and Rosemary Marshall, the teachers who welcomed us into their classrooms with such good humor. Suzy Bank-Schamberg provided much help on storytelling techniques. Most of all, the experimental program owes its success to Joyann Burdett, teacher extraordinaire and tireless supporter of this approach. Thanks, too, to the children who both accepted and ignored us in just the right proportions, who willingly took part in extra tests, and who at times stayed on after school so that the program might continue. The chapter has also benefited from the careful comments of Virginia Swisher and other colleagues, who should not feel responsible for any errors.

Appendix: *ASL/English Storytelling Syllabus*

(Created by Michael Strong, James Woodward, and Suzy Bank-Schamberg, University of California, San Francisco, Center on Deafness)

Part 1: ASL

This syllabus has been designed for deaf children, aged 4–7, who are in an environment such as a residential school where ASL tends to be the principal language of social interaction. Part 1 is divided into 10 units, each of which focuses on one or more functional/grammatical features of ASL. Part 2 also has 10 units, each of which serves as a very elementary introduction to an aspect of English structure that differs greatly from ASL in its surface features. Each unit is based on a different story, which incorporates the linguistic material to be introduced. The purpose is, first, to introduce ASL into the classroom curriculum and thereby to provide reinforcement for those children of deaf parents who are already fluent in the language, at least in conversational settings, and to give other children who have less developed linguistic skills instruction in the language; second, to introduce English as a language distinct from ASL, by teaching a few basic examples of how the two languages might express the same idea differently.

UNIT ONE: STORY: "GOLDILOCKS AND THE THREE BEARS"

1. Referring to people and things (pronouns).
   This focuses on indexic reference with referents present and absent, scene setting, and includes possessives (your, his, etc.), reflexives (yourself, myself), and number incorporation (the three of you, etc.).
2. Describing (word order).
   This illustrates the sign order of noun followed by descriptor, which is common in ASL but not acceptable in English.

UNIT TWO: STORY: "ONE FINE DAY"

Expressing location and direction (locational and directional verbs).
   This unit will introduce verbs that maintain the same orientation, such as *give, show, tell, go sit,* and those that involve a change in orientation, such as *ask, say no, fly.*

UNIT THREE: STORY: "THE LITTLE RED HEN"

1. Asking questions.
   This part of the unit focuses on how to ask yes/no questions in ASL with appropriate sign order and facial expression.
2. Saying "no."
   Various forms of the negative are introduced here.

UNIT FOUR: STORY: "THE HARE AND THE TORTOISE"

1. Locating and moving living and inanimate things (classifiers).
   This will focus on location and movement in classifiers, while ignoring handshape.
2. Describing action (adverb incorporation).
   This focuses on how to modulate verbs of action to indicate movements (e.g., fast, slow, stop/start) and nature (e.g, careless).

UNIT FIVE: STORY: "AMOS AND BORIS"

Representing people and things (handshape classifiers and some size and shape specifiers).

This unit focuses on the different handshapes used in ASL to represent persons, cars, and objects of varying sizes, shapes, and patterns.

UNIT SIX: STORY: "THE BOY WHO CRIED WOLF"

Talking about events that have already happened, are happening now, or will happen sooner or later (time line).

This unit introduces the ASL time line, or the way tense is marked in that language. The story introduces different points on the time line such as yesterday, ago, distant past, a few days, weeks ago, recently, tomorrow, will, a few days from now, soon, and so on.

UNIT SEVEN: STORY: "THE THREE LITTLE PIGS"

1. Describing how you do things (temporal aspect).
   This focuses on the facial expressions and sign movements that represent the marking of verbs for temporal aspect to express ideas such as "again and again," "continuously."
2. Describing the order in which actions are carried out (distributional aspect).
   This covers the movements attached to verb signs when marked for distributional aspect, for example, "you, then you, then you"; or "all of you together."
3. Expressing completion or incompletion (aspect marked syntactically).
   This introduces the important ASL concepts "finish," and "not yet."

UNIT EIGHT: STORY: "THE THREE BILLY GOATS GRUFF"

Identifying and emphsizing topics (topicalization).

This focuses on word order adjustments and facial expressions that are used to emphasize or draw attention to particular aspects of an utterance.

UNIT NINE: STORY: "SYLVESTER AND THE MAGIC PEBBLE"

1. Expressing doubt or uncertainty (conditionals).
   Simple conditionals are introduced using the correct sign order and facial expression.
2. Giving more information about persons or things (relative clauses).
   Again, sign order and facial expression are the means to relativize in ASL.
3. Asking questions (Wh-questions).
   This focuses on how to form Wh-questions in ASL using the correct vocabulary, facial expression, and sign order (e.g., repetition of question word at the end of the sentence).

UNIT TEN: STORY: "THE LION AND THE RAT"

1. Specifying action (object incorporation).
   This introduces some ASL verbs that can be modified to incorporate the object, such as *chop tree, close window.*

2. Noun–verb distinction. Finally, some noun/verb pairs are introduced that share the same sign but are distinguished only by an additional movement, for example, *sit/chair, drive/car, fly/plane*.

A unit normally takes at least one week and possibly two weeks of classroom time, at one hour per day. Stories have been chosen to facilitate the appropriate focus/foci for the particular unit, but frequently include elements from other units.

Part 2: English

Part 2 introduces several elementary English constructions and shows how the same function is performed differently in ASL and English. Each story is told first in English then in ASL, with the teacher continuing to use ASL as the medium of instruction.

UNIT ONE: STORY: "THE LITTLE GIRL AND THE BIG BEAR"

Referring to people and things (pronouns).
   This unit introduces the English nominative pronouns, as represented by the English sign system Signing Exact English (SEE 2).

UNIT TWO: STORY: "THE BEAUTIFUL RAT"

Describing (basic word order of the English noun phrase: article, adjective, noun).
   The purpose of this Unit is to introduce the definite article and focus on the English word order adjective + noun in comparison with the ASL word order noun + adjective. (Although the English word order is acceptable in ASL also, the differing forms are presented in order to reinforce the concept of two distinct languages).

UNIT THREE: STORY: "WHERE CAN AN ELEPHANT HIDE?"

Saying "no" (negatives).
   This unit introduces the English forms *no* and *not*, and the contractions *can't, don't,* and *won't*.

UNIT FOUR: STORY: "CINDERELLA"

Asking questions.
   This unit introduces the *wh*-question words with the verb *to be*, and yes/no questions of the form "do you...," "did you...," and "can I...."

UNIT FIVE: STORY: "THE HORSE, THE FOX, AND THE LION"

This unit introduces a number of English adverbs, most of which carry the suffix *-ly*, which in SEE 2 is represented as a separate sign tagged on to the adjective sign (e.g., SLOW-LY; HAPPY-LY, etc.).

UNIT SIX: STORY: "HANSEL AND GRETEL"

Describing things that have happened or will happen (past and future tenses.
The simplest forms of the past and future tense are introduced in this Unit.
Thus, the sign PAST following an English verb is used to indicate past time,
and the sign FUTURE before the verb is used for future time, in accordance
with the SEE 2 system.

UNIT SEVEN: STORY: "THE MAGIC PORRIDGE POT"

Talking about things that are happening now (present progressive; habitual).
This unit introduces the two verb inflections -*ing*, and -*s* for the third person singular, and also the verb *to be* (copula) in the present tense.

UNIT EIGHT: STORY: "JACK AND THE BEANSTALK"

Prepositions.
Some of the most frequently used English prepositions are introduced here,
particularly in environments where ASL would normally incorporate them
into the verb.

UNIT NINE: STORY: "LITTLE WOOD DUCK"

Giving more information about persons or things (relative clauses).
This introduces the use of "who" and "that" in English relative clauses.

UNIT TEN: STORY: "LEO THE LOP"

Expressing doubt or uncertainty (conditionals).
This is difficult and should be included only if the children have mastered
the present and future tense forms.

References

Barnum, M. (1984). In support of bilingual/bicultural education for deaf children. *American Annals of the Deaf 129*, 404–408.

Brasel, K., and S. Quigley. (1977). The influence of certain language and
communication environments in early childhood on the development of
language in deaf individuals. *Journal of Speech and Hearing Research 20*,
95–107.

Champie, J. (1984). Is total communication enough? The hidden curriculum.
American Annals of the Deaf 129, 317–318.

Chasarek, S. (1981). Cognitive consequences of home or school education in a
limited second language: A case study in the Crow Indian bilingual community. A paper presented at Language Proficiency Assessment Symposium,
March, Airlie House, Virginia.

Corson, H. (1973). Comparing deaf children of oral deaf parents and deaf
parents using manual communication with deaf children of hearing parents
on academic, social, and communication functioning. Unpublished doctoral
dissertation. University of Cincinnati, Ohio.

Cummins, J. (1978). Educational implications of mother tongue maintenance in minority language groups. *Canadian Modern Language Review 34*, 395–416.

(1979). Cognitive/academic language proficiency, linguistic interdependence, the optimal age question and some other matters. Working Papers on Bilingualism, no. 19. Toronto: Ontario Institute for Studies in Education.

(1980). The cross-lingual dimensions of language proficiency: Implications for bilingual education and the optimal age issue. *TESOL Quarterly 14* (2), 175–187.

(1981). The role of primary language development in promoting educational success for language minority students. In *Schooling and Language Minority Students: A Theoretical Framework*. Los Angeles, Calif.: California State University, Evaluation, Dissemination and Assessment Center.

Cummins, J., and R. Mulcahy. (1978). Orientation to language in Ukrainian-English bilingual children. *Child Development 49*, 1239–1242.

Denton, D. (1970). Remarks in support of a system of total communication for deaf children. In *Communication Symposium*. Frederick: Maryland School for the Deaf.

DiFrancesca, S. (1972). Academic achievement test results of a national testing program for hearing-impaired students: United States, Spring, 1971. Office of Demographic Studies Series D, no. 9. Washington D.C.: Gallaudet College.

Erting, C. (1978). Language policy and deaf ethnicity. *Sign Language Studies 19*, 139–152.

Furth, H. (1966). *Thinking without Language: Psychological Implications of Deafness*. New York: Free Press.

Kannapell, B. (1974). Bilingualism: A new direction in the education of the deaf. *The Deaf American 26* (June), 9–15.

Klima, E., and U. Bellugi. (1979). *The Signs of Language*. Cambridge, Mass.: Harvard University Press.

Kluwin, T. (1981). The grammaticality of manual representations of English in classroom settings. *American Annals of the Deaf 126*, 193–286.

Marmor, G. and L. Petitto. (1979). Simultaneous communication in the classroom: How well is English represented? *Sign Language Studies 23*, 99–136.

Meadow, K. (1968). Early manual communication in relation to the deaf child's intellectual, social, and communicative functioning. *American Annals of the Deaf 113*, 29–41.

Moores, D. (1978). *Educating the Deaf: Psychology, Principles and Practice*. Boston: Houghton Mifflin.

Morazova, N. (1954). *Development of the Theory of Preschool Education of the Deaf and Dumb*. Moscow: Institute of Defectology.

Quigley, S. (1969). The influence of fingerspelling on the development of language, communication, and educational achievement in deaf children. Urbana, Ill.: Institute for Research on Exceptional Children.

Quigley, S., and R. Frisina. (1961). *Institutionalization and Psychoeducational Development of Deaf Children*. CEC Research Monograph. Washington D.C.: Council on Exceptional Children.

Quigley, S. and R. Kretschmer. (1982). *The Education of Deaf Children*. Baltimore, Md.: University Park Press.

Quigley, S., and P. Paul. (1984). ASL and ESL? *Topics in Early Childhood Special Education* 3(4), 17–26.

Stevenson, E. (1964). A study of the educational achievement of deaf children of deaf parents. *California News 80,* 143.

Strong, M. (1985). A study of sign language among young deaf children. A paper presented at the nineteenth annual TESOL Convention, New York, N.Y.

Strong, M., and E. Charlson. (In press). Simultaneous communication: How teachers approach an impossible task. *American Annals of the Deaf.*

Strong, M., R. Gold, and J. Woodward. (1986). A signed repetition task for deaf children. (Videotape). San Francisco: University of California, Center of Deafness.

Stuckless, R., and J. Birch. (1966). The influence of early manual communication on the linguistic development of deaf children. *American Annals of the Deaf 106,* 436–480.

Swisher, M. V. (1984). Signed input of hearing mothers to deaf children. *Language Learning 34,* 2, 69–85.

Troike, R. (1978). Research evidence for the effectiveness of bilingual education. *Nabe Journal 3,* 13–24.

Wells, G. (1979). Describing children's linguistic development at home and at school. *British Educational Research Journal 5,* 75–89.

Wrightstone, J., M. Aronow, and S. Moskowitz. (1963). Developing reading test norms for deaf children. *American Annals of the Deaf 108,* 311–316.

SECTION II:
RESEARCH REPORTS

6 An assessment of syntactic capabilities

Gerald P. Berent

Editor's introduction

In this chapter Berent discusses the performance of adult deaf learners of English on different syntactic structures using the interlanguage perspective that is currently in favor among second language acquisition researchers. With Chomsky's government-binding theory as a framework, Berent discovers a strong general preference for an explicit expression of the canonical NVN (SVO) word order of English finite clauses, which has also been reported in other studies. Possibly suffering from the limitations of a restricted working memory, deaf children, Berent suggests, are thus limited in their ability to extend core grammar to peripheral forms that are marked for various syntactic features. In the second part of the chapter, Berent reports on an attempt to teach certain syntactic structures to a group of students who had failed to show gains in English ability despite continued regular instruction. He found that the ceiling effect persisted among this group and suggests that the difference between deaf students that typically make slow gains and those that reach a ceiling may be related to the degree and nature of the processing limitations that they experience as a result of their hearing loss. The implications of this phenomenon for educators of the deaf are profound. It may be that the goal of teaching a nativelike fluency in English to deaf individuals is, with very few exceptions, an unrealistic one, and that research, as Berent implies, should focus on determining exactly which areas of English grammar are and are not amenable to deaf learners, a task that would certainly be anathema to most ESL teachers.

In the context of second language (L2) acquisition, the notion of *interlanguage* has developed to designate the "separate linguistic system based on observable output which results from a learner's attempted production of a [target language] norm" (Selinker, 1972). The basis for positing the existence of learner interlanguages as the objects of study within a theory of L2 acquisition is the fact that, for the most part, learner utterances will not be identical to the utterances of native speakers, even when both attempt to express the same intended meaning. Selinker therefore argues that the surface structures of interlanguage sentences constitute the relevant data with which theoretical predictions about L2 acquisition must be made.

Although interlanguage has been approached from a variety of theoretical perspectives since Selinker's original article appeared (for an overview, see Rutherford, 1984), those who have studied L2 acquisition generally agree that the learner's performance in the target language at any given stage is not haphazard, even if it is variable, and that learner interlanguages are governed by principles of some sort. The goal of L2 acquisition theory is to establish the principles that account for the character of learner interlanguages.

In first language (L1) acquisition, the notion of interlanguage would seem to have no relevance, since the nature of an interlanguage is determined, in part, by the interaction of features of the learner's native language and features of the target language. In L1 acquisition, cognitive development and other processes of maturation influence the learner's linguistic development and determine the nature of various stages in that development. With regard to the acquisition of English by deaf individuals, the notion of interlanguage would also have no relevance if English were considered the L1 in such cases. However, according to Quigley and Paul (1984), many of the 75% of deaf American adults who use American Sign Language (ASL) regard ASL as their native language. Yet, as Quigley and Paul point out, since only 3 or 4% of deaf children are born to two deaf parents and fewer than 10% have one deaf parent, only a small percentage of deaf children really acquire ASL naturally in infancy and early childhood. For these children English may be legitimately considered an L2. However, it is during their school years that most deaf children begin to learn ASL actively from their deaf peers. The situation is obviously a complex one; the status of ASL as an L1 and its interaction with the acquisition of English are only beginning to receive the attention they deserve (for an overview see Quigley and King, 1982).

For those deaf children for whom ASL is in no sense an L1, the acquisition of English nevertheless begins to take on the character of L2 acquisition. Once the deaf child reaches the point when he or she has a functional – though only partial – L1 (English), learning proceeds educationally and environmentally in much the same way that L2 learning proceeds. Therefore, the deaf individual's linguistic behavior can be understood both in terms of delayed L1 development and in terms of a continual, less naturalistic L2 development, wherein the L2 is the standard, ideal model that has not been attained. Under these circumstances we might be tempted to speak of this situation as "L1.5 acquisition."

Actually, acquisition research is demonstrating more and more that the processes of L1 acquisition and L2 acquisition are more alike than had once been thought (see, e.g., Dulay and Burt, 1974; Ervin-Tripp, 1974). Where interference from L1 had once been thought to heavily influence the course of the learner's L2 development, it is now understood that universal principles of grammar and the principles of independent theories, such as theories of markedness (see Rutherford, 1982), play a central role in both L1 and L2 acquisition. Accordingly, stages of L2 interlanguage development and stages of L1 development have a great deal in common, even if use of the term *interlanguage* presupposes an L1 that is distinct from the target L2. Under the reasonable assumption that the linguistic behavior of (language-impaired) deaf individuals is governed by the same kinds of linguistic and other principles that govern L1 and L2 acquisition, the present study approaches the linguistic output of deaf young adults as rule-governed interlanguages.

Just as there is great variability and instability within L2 interlanguages (Tarone, 1979), there is likewise variability and instability within the interlanguages of deaf learners. In his review of the descriptive literature on English in the deaf population, Bochner (1982) notes that the "range of linguistic diversity found in the deaf population probably exceeds that found in any subgroup of the normally hearing population." He attributes this diversity to the complex interaction of biological and environmental variables uniquely affecting deaf individuals. In view of this diversity, the present study seeks generalizations about the inter-languages of deaf individuals on the basis of the collective performance of groups of deaf young adult college students, under the full realization that not all aspects of the detail and variability of interlanguage are available in such a setting. Since an interlanguage is really the linguistic system responsible for the output of an individual learner at a given point in time, individual interlanguages will have to be studied carefully to verify the general principles identified in a group study such as this one.

The concern of this chapter is actually interlanguage syntax. Drawing on certain notions of current linguistic and acquisition theories, the study identifies general principles that seem to guide the syntactic behavior of deaf learners. In particular, the notion of "explicitness" is explored, which here refers to the presence or absence of explicit nominal and verbal constituents in a sentence. It is shown that deaf learners' relative abilities to process specific English structures correlate with the degree to which those structures deviate from the explicit representation of grammatical relations. Serving to define degrees of explicitness are certain categories that are presumably "visible" to the hearing user of English but that may be "invisible" to certain deaf learners. The analysis of interlanguage syntax is followed by a description of an instructional experiment designed to improve the syntactic performance of a group of deaf learners who seemed to have reached a ceiling in their syntactic capabilities.

Assessing syntactic performance

The *Test of Ability to Subordinate* (Davidson, 1978) (hereafter, the TAS) was chosen as a diagnostic tool for gaining insight into the nature of the syntactic capabilities of deaf young adult college students. This test was originally developed to assess the abilities of intermediate and advanced students of English as a second language (ESL) to use subordinate structures in writing. Since writing is generally a more common mode of linguistic expression for deaf individuals than it is for normally hearing individuals, the gap between written expression and general linguistic competence is narrower with respect to the former group than it is with respect to the latter (Goda, 1959; Bochner, 1982). Therefore, it was assumed that the TAS would be an appropriate tool for analyzing the syntactic capabilities of deaf individuals.

Davidson (1978) provides information about the reliability and validity of the TAS in his test manual. The structures and items of the TAS were based on composition texts, writing samples, and literature on language acquisition and writing maturity. The test items were verified by linguists, English teachers, and ESL teachers and were pretested on hundreds of native and nonnative speakers of English. The reliability of the TAS – that is, its measure of consistency – was determined by the Spearman–Brown split-half technique, which yielded a reliability coefficient of .90, and by the Kuder-Richardson Formula 20, a measure of inter-item consistency, which yielded a reliability coefficient of .88.

The 45-item test utilizes a sentence-combining format wherein, for a given item, students read two or three simple sentences that they must combine into one sentence exhibiting a particular target structure. They do this by filling in missing words in a given sentence frame. In the test item in 1, for example, the correct written response is *Mary's*.

(1) a. Mary has an idea.   b. I like the idea.
    I like _____ idea.

The TAS was designed around nine target structures, five tokens of each structure, which are generally found in the mature writing of native speakers of English. The nine structures are as follows:

(2) a. prenominal adjectives
    b. adverbs
    c. prepositional phrases
    d. infinitive phrases

e. participial phrases
f. gerund phrases
g. adverbial clauses
h. relative clauses
i. noun clauses.

In selecting the target structures, Davidson (1978) drew on the theoretical assumptions of early versions of transformational grammar (e.g., see Chomsky, 1965), according to which most of the structures contained in 2 derive via rather intricate transformations from deep structures that are more primitive than those posted recently in Extended Standard Theory (EST) (e.g., see Chomsky, 1980, 1981). Thus, although Davidson labeled all of these structures as subordinate, 2a, 2b, and 2c (which lack subordinate verb forms) would not now be considered so. Furthermore, structures 2d, 2e, and 2f, which are considered "phrases" in traditional grammar, are analyzed as "clauses" in EST because those verbal forms have logical "subjects" associated with them. Despite other changes in EST – for example, the fact that the noun clause tokens on the TAS are now considered "complements" of verbs – Davidson's TAS labels will be retained for the sake of simplicity in referring to the test.

For purposes of the present study, the TAS was revised with the permission of the author and publisher. The revised experimental test, which will be referred to as the *Revised Test of Ability to Subordinate* (RTAS), retains the original sentence-combing format and the specific items of the TAS but utilizes a multiple-choice answer format rather than a sentence completion format. Thus, in the RTAS item 1 is rendered as in 3, where the subjects are required to write the letter of their choice to the left of the item number.

____ (3) a. Mary has an idea. b. I like the idea.
        I like ___ idea.

    A. Mary   D. the Mary's
    B. Mary's   E. Mary has an
    C. the Mary

Correct answers were chosen from the list of acceptable answers in the TAS Teacher's Manual (p. 9). Foils were chosen on the basis of likely errors that L2 learners or deaf learners of English might be expected to make on the target structures. Foils that reflect less likely L2 or deaf learner errors are other logical faulty combinations of propositions expressed in the simple sentences.

For the purpose of pre- and posttesting, a second version of the RTAS were constructed, parallel to the first. The two tests will be referred to as Test A and Test B. Item per item, Test B. contains the same structures and foil types as Test A but uses different lexical items. The Test B item that parallels 3 is shown as item 4.

_____ (4) a. Tom has a car.   b. I drove the car.
    I drove _____ car.

    A. Tom's   D. the Tom's
    B. Tom   E. Tom has a
    C. the Tom

Following are sample items from the RTAS Test A. Whereas 3 and 4 are examples of one token of target structure 2a, items 5 through 12 below are sample tokens of target structures 2b through 2i, respectively.

(5) a. You have to be strong to lift it.   b. Do you have enough strength?
    Are you _____ to lift it?

    A. strong   D. enough strength
    B. enough strength   E. strength enough
    C. strong enough

(6) a. He has children.   b. He gives them a lot of money.
    He gives a lot of money _____.

    A. children   D. on his children
    B. his children   E. has children
    C. to his children

(7) a. She bought a new car.   b. Her sister persuaded her.
    Her sister persuaded her _____.

    A. buy a new car   D. she buy a new car
    B. to buy a new car   E. to buying a new car
    C. bought a new car

(8) a. We have a map.   b. The map clearly shows this street.
    We have a map clearly _____.

    A. shows this street   D. that showing this street
    B. for show this street   E. showing this street
    C. of showing this street

(9) a. She is always asking for money.   b. I am tired of that.
    I am tired of _____.

    A. she is always asking   D. her always asks
        for money   for money
    B. she always asking   E. that she is always
        for money   asking for money
    C. her always asking
        for money

(10) a. He does not smoke.   b. Smoking makes him sick.
    He does not smoke _____.

    A. makes him sick   D. because smoking makes

B. and makes him sick   him sick
C. because makes him sick   E. why smoking makes him sick

(11) a. We have a doctor.   b. We like him very much.
We have a doctor _____ very much.

A. we like   D. who that we like
B. which we like   E. that we like him
C. who we like him

(12) a. They have a feeling.   b. He will get better.
They feel _____.

A. get better   D. that he will get better
B. will get better   E. that his getting better
C. that will get better

The sentence completion frames of Davidson's (1978) TAS allow for any acceptable response within certain limitations established in the Teacher's Manual. Thus, acceptable responses to relative clause item 11 would be *whom we like, who we like, that we like,* and *we like,* but not *and we like him,* since the last choice was not one of the subordinate structures that the majority of educated native speakers provided during the preparation of the test. As can be seen, the multiple-choice format of the RTAS forces one possible correct response and thus allows for both ease of scoring and analysis of performance on very specific target structures.

Actually, the five tokens representing a given structure on the TAS (and RTAS) differ linguistically from one another in significant ways. For example, whereas item 11 contains a relative clause whose (deleted) relative pronoun object modifies a (human) object antecedent, the other relative clause tokens exhibit other combinations of human/nonhuman and subject/object relative pronouns and antecedents. By virtue of this design, a subject's performance on the TAS (and the RTAS) provides information on relative degrees of success not only among the structures listed in 2 above, but also among subtypes of each of those structures. In Table 1, the target items of Test B of the RTAS are grouped by target structure. The italicized correct responses illustrate the variation in the individual tokens within a given structure.

To gain insight into the nature of the acquisition of English by deaf learners relative to the specific structures tested in the TAS, the RTAS was administered to 48 students at the National Technical Institute for the Deaf (NTID) at the Rochester Institute of Technology in Rochester, New York. These subjects were enrolled in NTID English courses at three levels of proficiency. Placement into their respective English levels was based on scores attained on the *Michigan Test of English Language Proficiency* (1962). The mean score out of

TABLE I. TARGET ITEMS OF TEST B OF THE "REVISED TEST OF ABILITY TO SUBORDINATE"

PRENOMINAL ADJECTIVES

1. I drove *Tom's* car.
2. Bill lost *his* books.
3. The *little German* car was sold.
4. John took *our new* chairs.
5. The teacher returned the *corrected* homework.

ADVERBS

6. They *usually* meet on Monday.
7. The child disappeared *today*.
8. He was *seriously* injured.
9. Is it long *enough* to reach it?
10. He laughed *rudely* at the woman.

PREPOSITIONAL PHRASES

11. She sends a lot of gifts *to her brothers*.
12. The President *of France* travels a lot.
13. Lay the clothes down *on the bed*.
14. He got married *in October*.
15. She talks to her students *in a loud voice*.

INFINITIVE PHRASES

16. It is hard for me *to write letters*.
17. His parents forced him *to sell the motorcycle*.
18. It was her choice not *to take the test*.
19. We allowed Mary *to leave school*.
20. He goes there *to buy vegetables* every day.

PARTICIPIAL PHRASES

21. Have you ever talked about people not *following rules*?
22. Only *invited yesterday*, Tom did not want to go to the party.
23. I found a lesson clearly *explaining the grammar*.
24. Slowly *pouring the milk*, I filled my cup.
25. We are talking about the man just *seen in the park*.

GERUND PHRASES

26. Instead *of watching television*, they went to sleep.
27. I am bored with *his always talking about himself*.
28. She has an interesting custom *of sleeping in the afternoon*.
29. She was accused *of stealing it*.
30. They are responsible *for cleaning the house*.

TABLE I. *(cont.)*

ADVERBIAL CLAUSES

31. It started to rain *while they were playing baseball.*
32. She can't clean the house *because she doesn't have any time.*
33. *When we came home from work*, it was cold in the house.
34. I will cry *if you hit me.*
35. He does not drive *because driving makes him nervous.*

RELATIVE CLAUSES

36. The woman *who visited the school* last week is leaving tomorrow.
37. Football is a sport *that many people watch.*
38. The noise *which scared him* was caused by an airplane.
39. I called a man *who might visit us.*
40. That is the man *we saw* on television.

NOUN CLAUSES

41. We think *that she will go away.*
42. They thought *they were smart.*
43. They do not know *why he is always working.*
44. They don't remember *if the movie started on time.*
45. She felt *the answer was wrong.*

Note: Target structures are italicized.
Source: Based on Davidson (1978).

100 points on the *Michigan Test* for the level I group (N = 16) was 46.81 (SD = 3.33); the mean score for the level II group (N = 16) was 57.06 (SD = 1.95); and the mean score for the level III group (N = 16) was 66.94 (SD = 3.04).

Half of the subjects in each group completed the RTAS Test A and half completed Test B. When the A and B scores for each group were combined, the level I group achieved a mean score (out of 45 total points) of 21.56 (SD = 5.99), the level II group achieved a mean score of 30.44 (SD = 4.21), and the level III group achieved a mean score of 35.25 (SD = 3.84). The RTAS scores of those subjects who completed Test A, correlated .86 with their *Michigan Test* scores, using a Pearson product–moment correlation. The RTAS and *Michigan Test* scores of those who completed Test B correlated .84. Thus, there is an association between global performance as measured by the *Michigan Test* and performance on the nine sets of structures that make up the RTAS.

Table 2 shows the percentages of correct responses, overall and by group, on the nine structures tested by the RTAS. The higher the percentage, the greater the success on a given structure.

TABLE 2. PERCENTAGES OF CORRECT RESPONSES, OVERALL AND BY GROUP, ON
THE NINE STRUCTURES OF THE "REVISED TEST OF ABILITY TO SUBORDINATE"

Structure	Overall	Level I	Level II	Level III
Prenominal adjectives	74.6	57.5	80.0	86.2
Adverbs	66.7	45.0	67.5	87.5
Prepositional phrases	77.9	71.2	77.5	85.0
Infinitive phrases	74.2	53.7	80.0	88.7
Participial phrases	38.7	25.0	31.2	60.0
Gerund phrases	54.6	30.0	58.7	75.0
Adverbial clauses	85.4	68.7	91.2	96.2
Relative clauses	45.4	32.5	47.5	56.2
Noun clauses	65.8	47.5	75.0	75.0

A comparison of the level I, II, and III percentages reveals that
performance on most structures gradually improves as the level of
proficiency rises. Apparent the only structures on which performance
does not change between levels II and III are the noun clauses,
where success rate for both groups is 75.0%. A noticeable improvement of 20% or more occurs between levels I and II on prenominal
adjectives, adverbs, infinitive phrases, gerund phrases, adverbial
clauses, and noun clauses. An improvement of 20% or more occurs
between levels II and III only on adverbs and participial phrases. If a
criterion of 80% or greater is used to define "mastery" of a particular structure, the level III group appears to have mastered the prenominal adjectives, adverbs, prepositional phrases, infinitive phrases,
and adverbial clauses. The level II group has mastered the prenominal adjectives, infinitive phrases, and adverbial clauses, whereas the
level I group has mastered none of the structures.

Performance on nonclausal structures

Before considering the relative orders of difficulty among the structures of the RTAS, let us examine the three categories that are considered "nonclausal" within current conceptions of EST, namely, the
adjectives, adverbs, and prepositional phrases. On the basis of the
80% criterion for success, the most proficient group, level III, performed successfully and much the same on all three of these structures. The least proficient group, level I, was least successful on the
adverbs (45.0% success rate) and most successful on the prepositional phrases (71.2%).

Overall performance on these three structures in the RTAS Tests A
and B (combined) is indicated in Table 3. These percentages are matched

TABLE 3. OVERALL SUCCESS RATES ON TABLE I ITEM TYPES FOR PRENOMINAL
ADJECTIVES, ADVERBS, AND PREPOSITIONAL PHRASES

Prenominal adjectives (%)	Adverbs (%)	Prepositional phrases (%)
(1) 93.7	(6) 95.8	(11) 93.7
(2) 100.0	(7) 81.2	(12) 87.5
(3) 70.8	(8) 54.2	(13) 91.7
(4) 68.7	(9) 58.3	(14) 60.4
(5) 39.6	(10) 43.7	(15) 56.2

Note: Table 1 item numbers are shown in parentheses.

with the numbers of the sentences in Table 1. By analyzing individual items we gain insight into the process of acquisition and are able to formulate hypotheses about acquisition orders, learnability, and the nature of learner interlanguages.

Of the prenominal adjective structures, possessive nouns and pronouns (represented as 1 and 2, respectively, in Table 1) posed no difficulty, according to their success rates of 93.7% and 100% (see Table 3). Items 3 and 4, with two prenominal constituents, posed greater difficulty. In the case of item 3, 14.6% of the subjects chose the foil type *little and German* to complete the sentence frame, showing a preference for an explicit expression of conjoined constituents. As for item 5, this prenominal adjective is actually a derived participle (see the discussion of participial phrases later in the chapter), hence the lower rate of 39.6%. Over half the subjects (52.1%) chose the foil *correction* rather than *corrected*.

In the sentences requiring adverbs, subjects were quite successful on item types 6 and 7, which contain the high-frequency adverbs *usually* and *today* (on Test A, *always* and *yesterday*). Subjects were not so successful on items 8 (54.2%) and 10 (43.7%), which required the derivational suffix *-ly* (see Lichtenstein, 1983, with regard to deaf learners' recoding of morphological suffixes during the reading process). Finally, item type 9 would be expected to present considerable difficulty for language learners by virtue of the idiomatic nature of the syntactic structure ADJECTIVE + *enough* + INFINITIVE.

With respect to the prepositional phrases, subjects were most successful on item types 11 (93.7%) and 13 (91.7%), both of which contain prepositional phrases (PPs) for which the main verbs of the sentences are "subcategorized." That is, a certain preposition may be associated with a certain verb as an intrinsic feature of that verb. Thus, the verb *send* (Test A, *give*) is subcategorized for a PP governed by *to*, and the verb *lay* (Test A, *put*) is subcategorized for a PP governed by *on*. Subjects were also successful on item type 12 (87.5%), in which the PP *of NP* is part of the intrinsic noun phrase

144 *Gerald P. Berent*

(NP) constituency of such "relational nouns" as *president, mayor, uncle* and so on (on the constituency of relational nouns, see Hornstein, 1977). The phrases that caused the most difficulty were of the type in items 14 (60.4%) and 15 (56.%). Unlike the prepositions in 11 and 13, which the language learner no doubt closely associates with the lexical items (verbs) that subcategorize those PPs, the prepositions in 14 and 15 appear in idiomatic PPs of time and manner, respectively, for which no verbs are specifically subcategorized. In that case they are much less predictable than the prepositions in 11 and 13, which express basic "dative" and "locative" relations.

Relative performance on clausal structures

As stated above, the remaining six structures of the RTAS are considered clausal structures within current formulations of EST (see Chomsky, 1981) and as such are true instances of subordination. Before the relative orders of success on these six structures are evaluated, the performance on one of the structures needs to be reexamined. One of the items in the noun clause category actually taps more than subjects' knowledge of the constituency of noun clauses and, accordingly, overall performance on the noun clause category is confounded by this fact.

Specifically, item type 45 (see Table 1) is the only noun clause item that tests the subjects' awareness of noun clause constituency as well as their knowledge of the sequence-of-tense rule associated with such sentences. If the main verb is past in sentences like 45, the subordinate verb must often also be past. Item type 41, on which there was an 85.4% success rate, tests the subjects' knowledge of the structure of "*that*-complements" (see the Test A item shown in 12 in the earlier discussion of sample items and foils). Item type 42 also contains a *that*-complement, but one from which the "complementizer" *that* has been deleted, which should account for the slightly lower success rate of 70.8%. Neither 41 nor 42 addresses the sequence-of-tense rule; however, item 45, which does, carries a success rate of 39.6%. Actually, 45.8% of all subjects chose the foil *She felt the answer is wrong* (rather than ... *was wrong*), which was counted as incorrect.

Under an assumption that those subjects would have made the correct choice if the sequence-of-tense foil were not included, the noun clause rates shown in Table 2 would be instead as in 13:

(13) Overall   Level I   Level II   Level III
     75.0%   58.7%   82.5%   83.7%

These figures give a more accurate picture of the subjects' knowledge

TABLE 4. RELATIVE ORDERS OF SUCCESS, OVERALL AND BY PROFICIENCY
LEVEL, AMONG THE SIX CLAUSAL STRUCTURES OF THE "REVISED TEST OF
ABILITY TO SUBORDINATE"

Overall	Level I	Level II	Level III
ADV. CL.	ADV. CL.	ADV. CL.	ADV. CL.
NOUN CL.	NOUN CL.	NOUN CL.	INF. PHR.
INF. PHR.	INF. PHR.	INF. PHR.	NOUN CL.
GER. PHR.	REL. CL.	GER. PHR.	GER. PHR.
REL. CL.	GER. PHR.	REL. CL.	PPL. PHR.
PPL. PHR.	PPL. PHR.	PPL. PHR.	REL. CL.

Note: PHR. = phrase, CL. = clause, PPL. = participial, REL. = relative,
GER. = gerund, INF. = infinitive, ADV. = adverbial.

of these structures, since the tense change is an adjustment rule that is
applied independently of knowledge of the constituency of noun clauses.
In fact, in an instructional experiment on the learning of *that*-comple-
ments in reported speech by NTID students at basic and low intermediate
levels of English, the most frequent error that subjects made was to
violate the sequence-of-tense rule that applies in such sentences (Albertini
and Samar, 1983).

On the basis of subjects' success rates shown in Table 2 but taking
into account the revised figures of 13 above, Table 4 depicts the relative
orders of success among the six clausal structures of the RTAS. The
structures on which subjects were most successful appear at the top,
those on which they were least successful at the bottom.[1]

Overall, the largest gap in performance (19.6 percentage points) occurs
between the gerund phrases and the infinitive phrases, clearly setting
apart the participial phrases, relative clauses, and gerund phrases as the
least mastered structures. The gap between the participial phrases and
the relative clauses is only 6.7 percentage points, and the gap between
the latter and the gerund phrases is 9.2 percentage points. As can be
seen in Table 4, the relative orders among those three structures differ
at each proficiency level. There is virtually no difference in overall per-

---

1 Ioup (1983) conducted a study on adult second language learners in which she administered the original TAS (Davidson, 1978). Despite the difference in design between that study and this one, the relative orders of performance by Ioup's subjects
closely parallel the performance orders reported here. One notable exception is the
fact that, for her subjects, performance on infinitive phrases was relatively lower
and performance on relative clauses was relatively higher than in this study. Nevertheless, the analysis here accounts in many respects for the results of Ioup (1983), at
least with regard to predictions of linguistic theory. As will be seen, there are additional constraints in operation that might further restrict the processing of English
structures by certain deaf individuals.

formance (0.8 percentage points) between the infinitive phrases and the noun clauses, but there is a 10.4% difference between the noun clauses and the adverbial clauses. The only other noteworthy difference among the three levels is that, at level III, performance on infinitive phrases seems to have surpassed performance on noun clauses.

Adverbial clauses and noun clauses

What the most mastered adverbial clauses and the noun clauses have in common is an *explicit* representation of subject noun phrase (NP) and verb phrase (VP) constituents. That is, the adverbial clauses conform to the pattern 14a and the noun clauses conform to the pattern 14b, where NP and VP each minimally contain explicit nominal and verbal elements, respectively.

(14) a. ...CONJUNCTION + NP + VP
     b. ...COMPLEMENTIZER + NP + VP

In L2 acquisition research, "explicitness" of expression has been invoked to explain certain acquisition orders, relative orders of difficulty, ease of processing, and so on (for discussion of this notion and references, see Rutherford, 1982, 1984). In view of the relative orders reflected in the subjects performance on the RTAS and in view of less explicit properties that will be attributed to the other structures, it is reasonable to investigate the extent to which explicitness influences the interlanguages of deaf learners.

Although greater explicitness is associated with adverbial clauses and noun clauses, the two structures differ in certain respects. Whereas adverbial clauses are optional sentence constituents, noun clauses are not. That is, noun clauses are associated with (subcategorized by) specific main verbs and are therefore obligatory in certain structures. In Table 1, if the italicized clauses are deleted from items 41–45, the resulting portions are incomplete. The same is not true of the adverbial clause items 31–35. If the italicized clauses are deleted from those sentences, the resulting portions remain independent, grammatical sentences.

In interpreting the two kinds of structures, the learner is generally confronted with surface strings of nominal (N) and verbal (V) constituents of the following forms:

(15) a. N V (N) CONJUNCTION N V (N).
     b. N V COMPLEMENTIZER N V (N).

In view of the common tendency of deaf learners to interpret the grammatical relations of the nearest NVN sequence as "subject," "verb," "object" (see Bochner, 1978; Quigley and King, 1980), the NV(N) sequences on either side of the subordinating conjunction in sentences containing adverbial clauses are more balanced and hence more interpretable, at least from the standpoint of syntactic parsing, than those on either side of the complementizer in sentences containing noun clauses (see Bever, 1970, for a discussion of the NVN processing strategy in L1 acquisition).[2] This fact helps to explain the observed 10.4% difference in overall performance on these two otherwise most mastered clausal structures.

Aside from these general differences that distinguish adverbial clause sentences from noun clause sentences, there are explanations for the relative differences in performance on a few of the individual items. Among the adverbial clauses, there were relatively lower success rates on item types 34 (70.8%) and 35 (77.1%) than there were on the other items (see Table 1). Item 34 contained the only conditional adverbial clause on the RTAS. Conditional sentences, because of their presuppositions and other features, tend to confuse the language learner far more than sentences with certain other types of adverbial clauses (see Berent, 1985a, b). Since one of the sentences to combine in that test item contained a negative command (*Don't hit me*) and since one of the foils also contained a negated verb, this item should prove to be more troublesome than the others, which did not contain a conditional clause. Another test item, item 35, had a lower success rate no doubt because the NP subject of the adverbial clause was a gerund (V-*ing*), which some would interpret as a verbal rather than as a nominal constituent. The subjects of all the other adverbial clauses were clearly of the category N.

Noun clause items 41, 42, and 45 have already been analyzed in the discussion of the sequence-of-tense rule above. It should be pointed out that there was a success rate of 56.2% on item type 43. As with item 45, however, the difficulty seems to be connected not with noun clause constituency but rather with the form of the verb (progressive aspect) contained in the noun clause: 31.3% of all subjects chose the foil yielding *They do not know why he always working* rather than the correct choice with . . . *is working*. Thus, although the verb form is incorrect, the foil in question is the only one with explicit COMPLEMENTIZER + N + V constituency.

Violations of NV(N) constituency

Unlike the adverbial clauses and noun clauses, the remaining four clausal categories on the RTAS violate basic NV(N) constituency in that they

2 The parenthetic (N) in the sequence NV(N) reflects the optionality of the verbal object, since transitive verbs require objects and intransitive verbs do not.

do not conform to the patterns illustrated in 15 above. Items 19, 29, and 24 of Table 1 can be considered examples of structures containing infinitive, gerund, and participial phrases, respectively:

(16) a. We allowed Mary to leave school.
     b. She was accused of stealing it.
     c. Slowly pouring the milk, I filled my cup.

The nominal and verbal constituents in those sentences conform to the patterns shown in 17, where V includes V-ing and where adverbs, prepositions, and auxiliary verbs are ignored.

(17) a. N V N V N.
     b. N V V N.
     c. V N N V N.

Given the tendency to assign the grammatical relations of subject-verb-object to contiguous NVN sequences, it is easy to understand why the elusive patterns in 17 might be more difficult to interpret than the balanced and explicit N V (N) patterns of 15. Will the deaf learner interpret the middle N in 17a as the object of the first V or the subject of the second V? In 17b, if the first N and V function as subject and verb, then what is the role of the second V? Where is its subject? And in 17c, what is the role of the first V? Why is there no N to its left?

In the theoretical linguistic framework of EST, infinitives, gerunds, and participles in sentences like 16 are analyzed as having abstract, underlying subjects. These subjects are represented by the symbol "PRO," which is a placeholder for the logical subject of such nonfinite verbs.[3] Incorporating PRO, the sentences in 16 are represented roughly as in 18, where PRO in the bracketed portions is an NP serving as the logical subject of *to leave, stealing,* and *pouring,* respectively.

(18) a. We allowed Mary [PRO to leave school]
     b. She was accused of [PRO stealing it]
     c. [PRO slowly pouring the milk] I filled my cup

To the hearing adult user of English, PRO is presumably accessible to interpretation, just as any other lexical item is. In other words, although PRO is "invisible" on the surface, it is somehow "visible" to the mind; otherwise, users of the language would not know that infinitives, gerunds, and participles were constituents to which logical subjects must

---

3 The incorporation of PRO, an abstract pronominal element, into EST has simplified the theory in many respects and has increased the theory's explanatory power. For one thing, PRO establishes a parallelism between finite and nonfinite clauses. In the sequence NP VP, when the V contained in VP has tense (i.e., is finite), then NP is a fully specified lexical item; when the V does not have tense (i.e., is nonfinite), then NP = PRO. In either case, the structure of the clause is the same. For details, see Chomsky (1977, 1980, 1981), Lightfoot (1980), and Reuland (1983).

be assigned. Assuming the visibility of PRO, the nominal and verbal constituents of the sentences in 16 would be represented as in 19, rather than as in 17.

(19) a. N V N [N V N].
    b. N V [N V N].
    c. [N V N] N V N.

Under this analysis, the NV(N) sequences characteristic of the RTAS sentences containing infinitive, gerund, and participial phrases are no different from the explicit NV(N) sequence of the adverbial and noun clause sentences illustrated in 15 in their reflection of basic subject-verb-object relations.

Not only must PRO somehow be "visible" to the language user as the nominal subject of an infinitive, gerund, or participle, but certain principles must guide the language user in assigning a referent to PRO. That is, the user must be able to determine which constituent in a sentence is the "logical subject" of the infinitive, gerund, or participle. In other words, which constituent does PRO represent?

In sentences with infinitive phrases, the NP most immediately to the left of PRO is generally assigned as its referent. For example, in sentence 18a PRO represents *Mary* rather than *we* because *Mary* is the NP to the immediate left of PRO. Accordingly, it is understood that *Mary* did the leaving and not *we*. This principle whereby the referent of PRO is the closest NP to the left of PRO is known as the "minimal distance principle." Although the majority of sentences containing infinitive phrases conform to this principle, some sentences "violate" it, depending on the nature of the main verb of the sentence. So, in contrast to 18a, the logical subject of *to fix* (i.e., the referent of PRO) in sentence 20 is *we,* and not *Mary,* even though *Mary* is immediately to the left of PRO.

(20) We promised Mary [PRO to fix the car].

It is an exceptional property of a few verbs like *promise* that guides the interpretation of PRO in 20.[4]

Unlike infinitive phrases, which are generally complements to specific main verbs, gerund phrases regularly appear in noun phrase positions, either as subjects, objects of verbs, or objects of prepositions. All of the gerund phrases on the RTAS (Table 1, items 26–30) are objects of prepositions. The interpretation of PRO in gerund phrases does not follow the minimal distance principle as systematically as in the case of

---

4 Berent (1983) has shown that both prelingually deaf young adult learners of English and adult second language learners of English overextend the minimal distance principle in interpreting the referent of PRO in sentences containing infinitive structures. Therefore, in a sentence like 20, many of these learners would incorrectly interpret *Mary* as the logical subject of *to fix.*

infinitive phrases. Although it often does, other semantic or pragmatic factors can determine the reference of PRO. In the following sentence, for example, PRO can represent either *John* or *Bill,* depending on the situation.

(21) John talked to Bill about [PRO borrowing money].

In sentences with participial phrases, still other factors determine the reference of PRO. PRO often precedes its referent, as in 18c, and there are additional syntactic facts that the language user must know. For example, in certain participial constructions, only the subject of the main clause may serve as the referent of PRO, as in 22, where PRO can only refer to *John.*

(22) John talked to Bill on the phone, [PRO explaining what had happened].

It thus appears that, with regard to the interpretation of PRO, infinitive phrases are the most systematic, gerund phrases are somewhat less systematic, and participial phrases are the least systematic from the standpoint of the language learner. These relative degrees of systematicity correlate with the relative orders of success illustrated in Table 4. That is, subjects were most successful on the infinitive phrases, less successful on the gerund phrases, and least successful on the participial phrases. This was true overall and within each of the three proficiency categories. But other distinguishing characteristics of the three PRO structures also contribute to their relative degrees of complexity and help to explain why deaf learners might perform differentially on them.

First, when only the "visible" nominal and verbal constituents are considered, as in the patterns of 17, the degree of deviation from explicit NV(N) constituency is greater in sentences containing gerunds and participles than in sentences containing infinitives. Also, to the extent that prepositions are accessible to deaf learners for processing (see the next section), the gerund phrases would appear to be more explicit than the participial phrases, which function more as "free agents" in the sense that they modify other NPs and do not by themselves express grammatical relations such as "subject" or "object."

It is now clear why there was such a small difference in overall performance (0.8 percentage points) between the infinitive phrases and the noun clauses and why the infinitive phrases actually surpassed the noun clauses (Table 4) at the highest proficiency level. First, the two structures actually deviate from explicit NV(N) constituency almost to the same extent (compare 17a, for example, with 15b, ignoring the complementizer). Second, one would expect greater facility at higher proficiency levels on the least complex and most systematic of the three PRO structures, namely, the infinitive phrases.

Although the constituency of the three PRO structures has been discussed at length, the morphological differences of the forms involved have not. The infinitive consists of *to* followed by the basic form of the verb. Both the gerunds and participles employ V-*ing*, which is more complex morphologically than V alone. In addition, two of the RTAS sentences containing participial phrases use the passive participle expressed as V-*ed* and V-*en* (Table 1, items 22 and 25). The fact that deaf learners have difficulty with passive structures is well documented (Quigley and King, 1980). Regarding "morphological skills," Lichtenstein (1983) conducted a study of deaf learners' English language abilities as they relate to working memory capacities. He reported that only a small percentage of his subjects recoded the suffixes -*ing* and -*ed* during the reading process and that the tendency not to recode these suffixes to speech was significantly associated with lower morphological skills. With regard to "function words" such as prepositions, articles, and pronouns, Lichtenstein reported "selective recoding" by his subjects. That is, they recoded these free morphemes to varying extents. This, he suggests, may be a "strategy for dealing with English linguistic materials which is adapted to the individual's [working memory] capacities."[5] It is therefore likely that the infinitive structure, with its free morpheme *to* and its basic form of the verb, will be accessible for processing to more deaf learners than the suffixed forms of the gerund and participle. Furthermore, the gerund ought to be more accessible than the participle because it appears in regular NP positions, often governed by prepositions, which are free morphemes. Accordingly, its constituency will be more inferable than that of the participle.

Relative clauses

Relative clauses are the only remaining RTAS structures to be discussed. In both L1 and L2 acquisition research, relative clauses have received a great deal of attention.[6] They have received at least some attention in the literature on the acquisition of English by deaf learners (see, e.g., (Bochner, 1978; Quigley, Smith, and Wilbur, 1974; Wilbur, Montanelli, and Quigley, 1976). Like PRO structures, relative clauses also violate basic NV(N) constituency and therefore interfere with the deaf learner's assignment of the basic grammatical relations of subject, verb, and object. But they violate NV(N) constituency in a different way. In PRO

5 Some research indicates that deaf individuals generally have a shorter working memory span than hearing individuals (e.g., Belmont and Karchmer, 1978; Wallace and Corballis, 1973).
6 For references and an overview of the L1 acquisition of relative clauses, see Bowerman (1979). For some discussions on the L2 acquisition of relative clauses, see Chiang (1980), Gass (1980), and Schumann (1980).

structures, PRO always represents the "subject" of an infinitive, gerund, or participle. In relative clauses there is a different kind of "invisible" category called "trace," which can represent any NP in the relative clause, that is, the subject, the object, or the object of a preposition (on the details of trace within EST, see Chomsky, 1977).

Consider relative clause items 39, 37, and 40 (Table 1), which are repeated below with traces, indicated by the symbol *t* in the relevant NP positions.

(23) a. I called a man [who [*t* might visit us]].
     b. Football is a sport [that [many people watch *t*]].
     c. That is the man [_ [we saw *t* on television]].

Within EST, the relative pronoun (*who, which, that,* etc.) is moved to a position just to the left of the inner brackets in 23 and the trace then occupies the position that the relative pronoun vacated. In 23a, *who* was moved from the position of the subject of the verb *might visit* and, in 23b, *that* was moved from the position of the object of the verb *watch*. In 23c, the relative pronoun was also moved from the position of the object of the verb *(saw)*, but it was subsequently deleted (an optional alternative in the case of object relative pronouns in English). As with PRO, the "invisible" trace must somehow be visible to the minds of hearing adult users of English; otherwise, they could not assign the appropriate grammatical relations to the NPs contained in relative clauses.

Under the assumption that traces are not visible to certain deaf learners, the explicit N/V constituency of sentences 23a,b,c would be as in 24a,b,c, respectively (where the prepositional phrase *on television* in 23c is ignored).

(24) a. N V N [N V N].
     b. N V N [N N V].
     c. N V N [N V].

In terms of the explicitness of subject and object nominal constituents, the bracketed relative clause represented in 24a conforms to basic subject-verb-object word order. Not surprisingly, there was a relatively high success rate on this sentence (70.8%). The relative clause in 24b explicitly contains the subject and the object of the verb, but basic word order has been violated: [NNV] expresses the order as object-subject-verb. As a result, there was a much lower success rate on that sentence (27.1%). Sentence 23c received the very low rate of 6.2%, obviously because of the deleted relative pronoun. If the object trace in 23c is invisible to the deaf learner, then [NV] excludes any explicit representation of the required object of *saw*.[7]

---

7 There were other relative differences in performance among the relative clause

The language learner must not only recognize the ways in which relative clauses violate the explicit expression of basic subject-verb-object word order, but also be able to associate the relative pronoun with some other NP in the main clause of the sentence. For example, in the sentences of 23, the learner must know that *who* represents *a man* in 23a, that *that* represents *a sport* in 23b, and, what is more difficult, that some missing relative pronoun represents *the man* in 23c. Given these complexities, it is obvious why relative clauses were among the more problematic RTAS structures, as shown in Table 4. Although both the relative clauses and the PRO structures contain "invisible" categories, the role of trace, the leftward movement of the relative pronoun, and so on distinguish the relative clause structures from the PRO structures. Accordingly, each proficiency level handled relative clauses slightly differently, as evidenced by their relative positions among the other difficult structures shown in Table 4.

Learners' preferences for explicit expression

Learners' preferences for the explicit expression of grammatical relations through NV(N) constituency are apparent in the choice of foils on individual RTAS items. On the relative clause items, for example, those tested chose foils in which explicit object NPs appeared in the positions filled by *t* in sentences 23b and 23c. Thus, for item 23b, 20.8% of the subjects chose the foil resulting in 25a, 25.0% chose 25b, and 25.0% chose 25c:

(25) a. Football is a sport *that many people watch this sport.*
      b. Football is a sport *that many people watch it.*
      c. Football is a sport *which many people watch it.*

Similarly, for sentence 23c, the foils resulting in 26a and 26b were each chosen by 37.5% of the subjects.

(26) a. That is the man *who we saw him* on television.
      b. That is the man *that we saw him* on television.

On the three PRO structures, many subjects opted for foils in which NV(N) sequences resembled finite clause structure rather than nonfinite clause structure. For example, on the infinitive phrase item 19 (Table 1), repeated as 27a, 14.6% of the subjects chose the foil yielding 27b and 12.5% chose 27c.

items. Subjects were more successful on Table 1 items 36 (64.6%) and 39 (70.8%), which contained the "+ human" relative pronoun *who*, than they were on item 38 (58.3%), which contained *which*. This fact is consistent with the findings of Bochner (1978) and Wilbur et al. (1976).

(27) a. We allowed Mary *to leave school.*
   b. We allowed Mary *left school.*
   c. We allowed Mary *that she left school.*

On gerund phrase item 27 (Table 1), repeated here as 28a, 35.4% of the subjects chose the foil resulting in 28b.

(28) a. I am bored with *his always talking about himself.*
   b. I am bored with *that he is always talking about himself.*

And on participial phrase item 21 (Table 1), repeated here as 29a, 54.2% of the subjects chose the foil that results in 29b.

(29) a. Have you ever talked about people not *following rules?*
   b. Have you ever talked about people not *follow rules?*

All of these choices show a preference for explicit NP subjects, finite verb forms, and explicit NP objects.

The interlanguages of deaf learners

The collective performance by deaf learners on the structures of the RTAS provides valuable evidence for building hypotheses about deaf learner interlanguages. With respect to notion of explicitness, deaf learners clearly seem to prefer the explicit expression of NV(N) constituency as a representation of the basic grammatical relations, subject-verb-object. This preference is verified not only in the relative order of success on the six clausal structures of the RTAS but also in the nature of the foils that subjects chose to complete the target sentences.

The adverbial clause sentences, on which subjects were the most successful, provide the most explicit expression of basic NV(N) constituency and the greatest balance across clauses. The other clausal structures deviate from explicit constituency in various ways. For example, although the constituency of noun clause sentences is nearly as explicit as that of adverbial clause sentences, the former lose some of their explicitness and balance by virtue of their status as the complements of specific verbs.

Of the three PRO structures, the infinitive phrases deviate from NV(N) constituency the least and are furthermore the most systematic in being assigned a logical subject. In terms of morphology, the free morpheme *to* and the infinitive's basic, unsuffixed verb form suggest that the structure is less complex than the other PRO structures and no doubt easier for deaf learners to process. The other PRO structures were shown to deviate from NV(N) constituency to a greater extent. However, since gerund phrases occupy regular NP positions (objects of prepositions on the RTAS), their constituency should be somewhat clearer to deaf learners than participial phrases, which do not occupy NP positions. Moreover, some of the participial phrase items contain passive participles, which contribute to their complexity. With regard to the assignment of logical subjects, the gerund was shown to be less systematic than the infinitive and the participle less systematic than the gerund.

Finally, it was seen that relative clauses deviate from NV(N) constituency by virtue of the position of the relative pronoun or by virtue of its absence. The fact that the relative pronoun must be associated with some NP in the main clause adds to the complexity of relative clauses.

Explicitness alone comes very close to serving as a guiding principle in the interlanguage behavior of deaf learners. The extent to which a structure deviates from basic NV(N) constituency seems to dictate the degree of difficulty the deaf learner will experience with that structure. Factors such as the more limited working memory capacities of certain deaf learners may very well induce deviation. For example, if the suffix *-ing* is unavailable for processing, then the form V-*ing* will be perceived no differently than V alone. Since the role of V-*ing* is, among other things, to signal that a verb is functioning as a noun or as a modifier, the obvious consequence is that the deaf learner encounters VVN, NVV, for example, instead of the anticipated NVN. What appear to be violations of the logic of the language to the deaf learner are not violations to the hearing adult user, who in processing forms like V-*ing* accordingly infers the appropriate constituency and assigns the relevant "invisible" categories as placeholders of the required grammatical relations. Whereas PRO and trace are somehow a mental reality to the hearing adult user of the language, these "invisible" categories seem to be absent from the interlanguage systems of many deaf learners.

In seeking a framework for the description and explanation of deaf learner interlanguages, however, we must consider factors other than the power of explicitness. How, for instance, do deaf learners interpret the relatedness of two NPs in a sentence, as in the case of a pronoun and its antecedent? How do they perceive the various "government" relations, as in the case of verbs and prepositions that govern their objects? How do they handle "agreement" phenomena, as in the case of subject–verb agreement? And so on. A promising approach to such questions might be found in the framework of Chomsky (1981), in whose highly elaborated theory of grammar these phenomena are analyzed in terms of several interacting subsystems of grammar. By extending this framework to the exploration of deaf learner interlanguages – as has been done here to a limited extent in the discussion of PRO and trace – we may arrive at a more meaningful understanding of the acquisition of English by deaf individuals.

Finally, it should be emphasized that an interlanguage system is really the system of a single language learner. Although the collective performance of many learners on a test such as the RTAS reveals general tendencies that are no doubt characteristic of interlanguage behavior, these generalizations must be tested further on individual learners. Moreover, these generalizations must be examined in language generated by deaf learners themselves, since it is productive language that truly reflects a learner's interlanguage system. In these investigations, however, it must be remembered that a learner's interlanguage is in a constant state of flux and that one will always be confronted with the kind of variability and instability that has been reported in Tarone (1979). The investigator's job is to identify principled behavior amidst what sometimes appears to be chaos.

An instructional experiment

Many believe that deaf adults receiving remediative language instruction will continue to make gains in their syntactic abilities, even though these gains may be only gradual (see Quigley and King, 1980). Nevertheless, there are always students who seem to have reached a ceiling in their syntactic capabilities despite ongoing English instruction. In order to determine whether a focused syntactic treatment might make a difference for such students, an experimental course was designed to provide concentrated instruction in a finite set of syntactic structures, namely, the nine structures tested on the TAS (Davidson, 1978).

Nine young adult deaf students were identified at NTID who had failed to show significant gains in English language ability beyond the fourth of five levels of English instruction. Until the spring of 1983, students at NTID were placed into their appropriate English levels on the basis of an "English-Score," or "E-Score," that was derived by combining a student's scores on the Reading Comprehension Subtest of the California Achievement Tests – Junior High Level (Tiegs and Clark, 1957) and the NTID Written Language Test (Crandall, 1976). The latter is a test of productive English language ability, which is scored primarily on the basis of syntactic well-formedness and lexical appropriateness. The E-Score was used both for initial placement of students into English levels and for subsequent advancement to higher English levels. The nine students who agreed to take the experimental course had remained at English level four for at least their last two academic quarters of instruction and failed to test out of that level even at the end of five quarters of instruction, during which they had received approximately six contact hours of English instruction per week.

The experimental course lasted one academic quarter (i.e., 10 weeks), and during this time three contact hours per week were devoted to concentrated instruction in the nine structures of the TAS. *Sentence*

TABLE 5. PRETEST/POSTTEST PERFORMANCE ON NONCLAUSAL STRUCTURES

Structure	Pretest (%)	Posttest (%)
Prenominal adjectives	66.7	64.4
Adverbs	66.7	68.9
Prepositional phrases	80.0	93.3

Making by Robert G. Bander (1982) was chosen as the course textbook because it provides ample drill and practice on all of the nine structures of the TAS (plus many other structures). It was hypothesized that systematic explanations and exercises involving the nine structures might have an impact on the students' syntactic abilities, since instruction in most NTID English courses at the time covered a broad range of reading, writing, and grammar skills.

At the beginning of the 10-week course, the RTAS was administered to the nine students as a pretest measure. Five completed Test A, four Test B. In order to gauge their improvement on the nine structures, the RTAS was again administered at the end of the 10-week course. This time those who were pretested with Test A completed Test B and vice versa. On the pretest, the students received a mean score of 27.33 (SD = 5.20), and on the posttest they received a mean score of 29.44 (SD = 3.40), out of a total of 45 points on each test. This small difference between the means suggests that, overall, there was probably little or no improvement in performance on the nine structures of the RTAS after 10 weeks of concentrated instruction on those very structures.

Differences between the means of individual structures, however, indicate that the students may have improved significantly on some of them. Pretest and posttest performance on the three nonclausal structures of the RTAS is shown in Table 5; scores reflect percentage correct.

The greatest improvement between pretest and posttest performance occurred on the prepositional phrases, which were the only nonclausal structures on which the students demonstrated "success" when the 80% or greater criterion was used. Unlike the performance by the larger group of 48 subjects who took the RTAS, the performance here showed little variation between prenominal adjectives and adverbs, the latter of which were the most troublesome overall for the larger group (see Table 2).

With regard to the clausal structures of the RTAS, the order of success on the pretest is shown in Table 6. The pretest and posttest success rates are indicated next to each structure.

The fact that the relative orders of performance in Table 6 closely parallel the relative orders of performance by the larger group of 48 subjects reported in Table 4 lends further support to the analysis of interlanguage behavior presented in this chapter. Under the 80% criterion, the nine students did demonstrate "success" on the adverbial

TABLE 6. RELATIVE ORDERS OF SUCCESS AMONG THE SIX CLAUSAL
STRUCTURES OF THE RTAS (PRETEST) WITH PERCENTAGE SUCCESS RATES
SHOWN FOR BOTH PRETEST AND POSTTEST

Structure	Pretest	Posttest
ADV. CL.	71.1	86.7
NOUN CL.	66.7	71.1
INF. PHR.	64.4	75.6
REL. CL.	51.1	62.2
GER. PHR.	46.7	35.6
PPL. PHR.	44.4	35.6

Note: PHR. = phrase, CL. = clause, PPL. = participial, REL. = relative, GER. = gerund, INF. = infinitive, ADV. = adverbial.

clauses (86.7%) by the end of the experimental course. They improved on these structures by 15.6 percentage points. Thus, their facility on the structures that are the most explicit in the expression of NV(N) constituency and on which they already demonstrated the most success seems to have been further sharpened through focused drill and practice.

Note that performance on the infinitive phrases improved by 11.2 percentage points at posttesting, surpassing performance on the noun clauses, on which there was only slight improvement. Focused instruction seems to have had some effect on the most explicit and morphologically least complex of the three PRO structures. The only other positive change of more than 10 percentage points occurred on the relative clauses (11.1 percentage points). In spite of the manner in which they deviate from basic NV(N) constituency, relative clauses do usually retain their constituents, except in the case of a deleted object relative pronoun. Therefore, it may be possible to train students to analyze structures with moved explicit constituents, such as relative clauses, more successfully than structures with "invisible" constituents, such as gerunds and participles.

There was actually a considerable negative change in performance on both the gerund phrases and the participial phrases. These are, of course, the less explicit and less systematic of the PRO structures and the ones that employ the suffixed V-*ing* form.

Exactly why some students seem to reach a ceiling in their syntactic capabilities, either in general or with respect to specific structures, while others continue to make gradual gains is not clear. There may be an "explicitness threshold" beyond which certain structures with less explicit representation of grammatical relations are simply inaccessible. Of possible relevance to this notion are the results of Dulay and Burt (1978), who argue on cognitive grounds that it is impossible to teach certain structures that are beyond the language learner's internal level of linguistic development. A more principled approach to the investigation of deaf learner interlanguages should provide greater insight not only into the theoretical issues of language acquisition by deaf learners, but into the instructional implications as well. Success in teaching English as an "L1.5" may depend on how amenable learners are to the structures being taught to them.

Acknowledgments

This research was conducted at the National Technical Institute for the Deaf at the Rochester Institute of Technology as part of an agreement with the U.S. Department of Education. I am grateful to Margaret C. Brophy, who taught the experimental English course with me, the results of which are reported in this chapter. I am also grateful to David Davidson and Language Innovations, Inc., for allowing me to alter the design of the *Test of Ability to Subordinate* (Davidson, 1978) for experimental purposes.

References

Albertini, J. A., and V. J. Samar. (1983). Early instruction of object complements to hearing-impaired college students. *Applied Psycholinguistics* 4, 345–357.

Bander, R. G. (1982). *Sentence Making: A Writing Workbook in English as a Second Language.* New York: CBS College Publishing.

Belmont, J. M., and M. A. Karchmer. (1978). Deaf people's memory: There are problems testing special populations. In M. M. Gruneberg, P. E. Morris, and R. N. Sykes (Eds.), *Practical Aspects of Memory.* London: Academic Press.

Berent, G. P. (1983). Contol judgments by deaf adults and by second language learners. *Language Learning* 33, 37–53.

(1985a). Markedness considerations in the acquisition of conditional sentences. *Language Learning* 35, 337–372.

(1985b). Differences in L2 and deaf learners' processing of conditionals. Presented at the nineteenth annual convention, Teachers of English to Speakers of Other Languages, April 8–14, New York.

Bever, T. G. (1970). The cognitive basis for linguistic structures. In J. R. Hayes (Ed.), *Cognition and the Development of Language.* New York: Wiley.

Bochner, J. (1978). Error, anomaly, and variation in the English of deaf individuals. *Language and Speech* 21, 174–189.

(1982). English in the deaf population. In D. G. Sims, G. G. Walter, and R. L. Whitehead (Eds.), *Deafness and Communication: Assessment and Training.* Baltimore, Md.: Williams and Wilkins.

Bowerman, M. (1979). The acquisition of complex sentences. In P. Fletcher and M. Garman (Eds.), *Language Acquisition.* Cambridge: Cambridge University Press.

Chiang, D. L. (1980). Predictors of relative clause production. In R. C. Scarcella and S. D. Krashen (Eds.), *Research in Second Language Acquisition: Selected Papers of the Los Angeles Second Language Acquisition Research Forum.* Rowley, Mass.: Newbury House.

Chomsky, N. (1965). *Aspects of the Theory of Syntax*. Cambridge, Mass.: MIT Press.
  (1977). On wh-movement. In P. W. Culicover, T. Wasow, and A. Akmajian (Eds.), *Formal Syntax*. New York: Academic Press.
  (1980). On binding. *Linguistic Inquiry* 11, 1–46.
  (1981). *Lectures on Government and Binding*. Dordrecht: Foris Publications.
Crandall, K. E. (1976). NTID Written Language Test: Procedures and reliability. A paper presented at the annual convention of the American Speech and Hearing Association, Houston.
Davidson, D. M. (1978). *Test of Ability to Subordinate: A Diagnostic Test of Ability to Subordinate in Writing for Intermediate and Advanced ESL Students*. New York: Language Innovations, Inc.
Dulay, H. C., and M. K. Burt. (1974). You can't learn without goofing: An analysis of children's second language "errors." In J. C. Richards (Ed.), *Error Analysis: Perspectives on Second Language Acquisition*. London: Longman.
  (1978). Some remarks on creativity in language acquisition. In W. Ritchie (Ed.), *Second Language Acquisition Research*. New York: Academic Press.
Ervin-Tripp, S. M. (1974). Is second language learning like the first? *TESOL Quarterly* 8, 111–128.
Gass, S. (1980). An investigation of syntactic transfer in adult second language learners. In R. C. Scarcella and S. D. Krashen (Eds.), *Research in Second Language Acquisition: Selected Papers of the Los Angeles Second Language Acquisition Research Forum*. Rowley, Mass.: Newbury House.
Goda, S. (1959). Language skills of profoundly deaf adolescent children. *Journal of Speech and Hearing Research* 2, 369–376.
Hornstein, N. (1977). S and X' Convention. *Linguistic Analysis* 3, 137–176.
Ioup, G. (1983). Acquiring complex sentences in ESL. In K. M. Bailey, M. C. Long, and S. Peck (Eds.), *Second Language Acquisition Studies*. Rowley, Mass.: Newbury House.
Lichtenstein, E. (1983). Deaf working memory processes and English language skills. Manuscript. Rochester, N.Y.: National Technical Institute for the Deaf.
Lightfoot, D. (1980). Trace theory and explanation. In E. A. Moravcsik and J. R. Wirth (Eds.), *Current Approaches to Syntax*, vol. 13, *Syntax and Semantics*. New York: Academic Press.
Michigan Test of English Language Proficiency (Form A). (1962). Ann Arbor: University of Michigan, English Language Institute.
Quigley, S. P., and C. M. King. (1980). Syntactic performance of hearing impaired and normal hearing individuals. *Applied Psycholinguistics* 1, 329–356.
  (1982). The language development of deaf children and youth. In S. Rosenberg (Ed.), *Handbook of Applied Psycholinguistics*. Hillsdale, N. J.: Lawrence Erlbaum.
Quigley, S. P., and P. V. Paul. (1984). *Language and Deafness*. San Diego: College-Hill Press.
Quigley, S. P., H. L. Smith, and R. B. Wilbur. (1974). Comprehension of relativized sentences by deaf students. *Journal of Speech and Hearing Research* 17, 699–713.

Reuland, E. (1983). Governing -*ing*. *Linquistic Inquiry* 14, 101–136.

Rutherford, W. E. (1982). Markedness in second language acquisition. *Language Learning* 32, 85–105.

1984. Description and explanation in interlanguage syntax: State of the art. *Language Learning* 34, 127–155.

Schumann, J. (1980). The acquisition of English relative clauses by second language learners. In R. C. Scarcella and S. D. Krashen (Eds.), *Research in Second Language Acquisition: Selected Papers of the Los Angeles Second Language Acquisition Research Forum*. Rowley, Mass.: Newbury House.

Selinker, L. (1972). Interlanguage. *International Review of Applied Linguistics* 10, 209–231.

Tarone, E. (1979). Interlanguage as chameleon. *Language Learning* 29, 181–191.

Tiegs, E. W., and W. W. Clark. (1957). *California Achievement Tests—Junior High Level*. Monterey, Calif.: California Test Bureau.

Wallace, G., and M. C. Corballis. (1973). Short-term memory and coding strategies of the deaf. *Journal of Experimental Psychology* 99, 334–348.

Wilbur, R. B., D. S. Montanelli, and S. P. Quigley. (1976). Pronominalization in the language of deaf students. *Journal of Speech and Hearing Research* 19, 120–140.

7 Children's new sign creations

Diane Lillo-Martin

Editor's introduction

*Lillo-Martin, for several years a researcher in Ursula Bellugi's labora-
tory at the Salk Institute, is interested in lexical innovations in ASL.
Her study reported in this chapter examines the responses of groups
of deaf children of deaf parents (whose native language is ASL) and
deaf adults to two kinds of intriguing tests designed to elicit sign creations for new objects, persons, or machines. She analyzes the responses from her subjects in terms of a set of principles established by
researchers working with English- and Hebrew-speaking children responding to similar tests, and finds that deaf children go through several stages in their acquisition of appropriated use of word-formation
devices, differing in some important ways from those experienced by
hearing children. For the sign language users, certain of the tasks
often elicited responses that were non-word-based (in contrast to the
responses from hearing subjects). This suggests that the visual modality can have a major effect on the structure and acquisition of visual
languages.*

One enduring aspect of language is change. Pronunciations change;
structures change; and perhaps most rapidly of all, the lexicon changes.
As new concepts enter the society in which a language is spoken and
old ones die away or take on new importance, the vocabulary of a
language grows and shifts. Speakers of every language know this (at
least implicitly), and they all know what kinds of devices are used in
their language to create new words and the relative productivity of each
of these devices under a variety of circumstances. This, therefore, is
knowledge that children must obtain when they are learning their native
language. They must learn which word-formation devices are used in
their language, which ones are used most often, and, most important,
how to use the devices appropriately.

The process of the acquisition of word-formation devices in young
deaf children learning American Sign Language as their native language

162

has been examined in several experiments in which such children were asked to create a new name for an object that they had never heard of or seen before (Lillo-Martin, 1984). The children responded to these tasks in various ways, depending on their age and the method of presentation. Two major types of word-formation devices were used: (a) word-based devices, such as compounding and forming derivations, and (b) non-word-based devices, which combine meaningful morphological units. This chapter describes these word-formation devices and the tests used to elicit them and investigates the nature of the signs created by the young subjects.

Word-formation devices in American Sign Language

Certain patterns in American Sign Language serve as bases for creating new signs (Bellugi and Newkirk, 1981). Several of these are equivalent to the word-formation devices found in many spoken languages. For example, one common means of creating new words is compounding. ASL has its own system of compounding, which does not directly relate to the compounding found in English (Klima and Bellugi, 1979, ch. 9). ASL compounds have characteristic stress patterns: The first element is reduced, often it is made close to the place of articulation of the second element, and the transition between the two elements is reduced. In addition, the handshapes of the two parts tend to merge.

There are also various derivational processes for creating new words in ASL. Some are idiomatic or figurative. One that is relevant here is a well-studied derivation of related nouns from verbs and vice versa. As Supalla and Newport (1978) have shown, pairs of nouns and verbs are related by this derivation such that the verbs are made with a longer, continuous movement, and the nouns with smaller, repeated, and restrained movement.

Third, although the structure of ASL is quite distinct from that of English, one way of forming words in ASL is to borrow from English. Most pertinent to this discussion is the agentive -ER suffix. Although this borrowing has been reduced and incorporated into some standard lexical items such as TEACHER and STUDENT, its most productive use is still in academic and other English-oriented situations.[1]

The final device that I would like to discuss here is one sometimes

---

1 *Notation Conventions.* I am following the general practice of writing ASL using upper case English glosses with approximately the same meaning. Compounds are glossed with ˆ between the two independent sign glosses, and the agentive affix is glossed as -ER. Derivations are marked with square brackets following the gloss, SIGN[D:noun]. Sign handshapes are indicated using the corresponding English letter in the fingerspelling system, enclosed in slashes, as in /A/.

called "mimetic depiction." Signs in ASL are made by forming the hand(s) into one of a specifiable set of hand configurations (HC), articulating them with a specific movement (MOV), at a specific location (LOC) on the body or in the signing space in front of the body (see, e.g., Stokoe, Casterline, and Croneberg, 1965).[2] The combinations of HC, MOV, and LOC allowed in signs obey certain arbitrary constraints, such as the phonotactic rules of spoken languages, but in general, elements from all three of these parameters are necessary for a meaningful unit. However, there exist in ASL some HCs, MOVs, and LOCs that are partly meaningful subunits in and of themselves. Therefore, when these units are combined to produce a sign, its meaning can be determined from the meaning of its components. These signs are called "mimetic" because the configurations of the hands usually represent something visually salient about the new object, and the movement generally represents the movement inherent in the new object or its use, or traces an outline of the object.

Although this type of device is in some sense mimetic, in that many of the components are visually motivated, it is nevertheless not mime, nor an analogue representation of continuous form. Rather, the signs so formed are still constrained by formal properties of lexeme formation in ASL. These signs are morphologically complex, and the handshapes and movements used can also be morphologically complex and be composed of meaningful units themselves. Supalla (1982, in press) and Newport (1982; Newport and Supalla, 1980) have argued for this morphological complexity, describing the sets of features found as the components of the handshapes and movements. Newport and Supalla call the signs composed in this way "verbs of movement and location," and they provide an account of several types of elements used in this process.

Handshapes

The handshapes used in the ASL verbs of movement and location have been called "classifiers," of which there are several types (for an overview, see Newport, 1982; Newport and Supalla, 1980; Supalla, 1980, 1982, in press; and Ryder, 1984). The two most frequently cited types are size and shape specifiers (SASSes) and semantic classifiers. In static size and shape specifiers, the number of fingers extended and the shape of the extension combine to classify aspects of the "visual-geometric structure of the noun referent" (Supalla, in press). Thus, the index finger

2 This is the classical description of ASL signs as simultaneous bundles of information. Current phonological analyses have since expanded the description of signs to include reference to sequential aspects as well as additional information (see, for example, Liddell, 1984).

extended straight out from the hand indicates a thin and straight object, while all four fingers extended curving toward the bent curving thumb indicates a deep cylindrical object. Another kind of SASS traces an outline of the object, using one of a more limited set of hand configurations. The semantic classifiers, rather than describing aspects of the appearance of an object, pick out specific semantic groups as their referents. For example, the /3/ handshape picks out land and sea vehicles of transportation (cars, ships, bicycles, etc.) as its possible referents.

Movements

The movements used in these signs have also been catalogued by Supalla and Newport, who report seven basic movement roots (including contact, linear, and circular). These are combined in sequence and simultaneously to produce the variety of movements seen in these verbs of movement and location. From this limited set of movement roots, an individual can derive quite complicated patterns of movement.

Because meaningful elements can be combined in systematic ways, ASL has a vast amount of productivity for a variety of purposes. As Supalla and Newport have shown, one of these purposes is to indicate the path of movement that an object takes ("verbs of movement"). Some of the possible combinations of these units have become standardized lexical elements. When this process occurs, the meaning can change from that picked out by the original combination. The standard sign for FALL, which is now used for any object falling, is made with the /V/ handshape, which productively chooses only two-legged objects as referents; thus the meaning has been broadened in the lexicalization. As will be seen from the results of the test described here, these meaningful units can be combined for the purpose of describing and naming of objects. Because signs formed in this way are composed of meaningful sign parameters, I call them "compositions."

Word-formation tests

Two tests were given to deaf children and adults to examine their use of the various word-formation devices described in the preceding section. The first of these tests was modeled after one developed by Clark and Hecht (1982) and Clark and Berman (1984) and given by them to English- and Hebrew-speaking children, respectively. The second test, which has so far been given only to the signing children, turned out to be especially relevant to the visual-spatial modality. In both of these tests, subjects were asked to create a sign for a new object, person, or activity. In the first test, the subjects were asked to create the sign on the basis of what the objects and people do. In the second test, they were merely shown a picture of the object or person using the object and asked to create the sign on the basis of the picture. These two tests are discussed in the next two sections.

People and machines

Clark and Hecht (1982) conducted a study of the coining of new words by children learning English as their native language. When the deaf children in this study, were asked to make up a name for a machine or person performing a particular activity, the youngest (ages 3;0–3;8), responded in two ways: They would coin new compounds, such as a *build-man* for a man who builds, and *cleaner-people* for a person who cleans; or they would use already known lexical items such as *camera* for a machine that looks, and *trampoline* for a machine that jumps. The oldest children (5;3–6;0) and the adults used the affix -*er*, to produce names such as *builder cleaner, looker,* and *jumper*.

Later, Clark and Berman (1984) used the same study to examine the acquisition of word formation in young children learning Hebrew as their native language. The youngest children in this study (3 years) most often used suppletives and a zero conversion device that nominalizes the present-tense participial verb form; the older children used one of a few devices involving affixation of -*an* (a nominalizing suffix similar to English -*er*) and compounding. The adults in the Hebrew study used one of the -*an* affixing devices.

The results of these two studies led Clark and her colleagues to conclude that four principles govern the acquisition of word formation:

I. *Principle of Transparency:* Known elements with one-to-one matches of meanings to forms are more transparent for constructing and interpreting new words than elements with one-many or many-one matches. (Clark and Hecht, 1982, p. 4)

II. *Principle of Formal Simplicity:* Simpler forms are easier to acquire than more complex ones, where simplicity is measured by the degree of change in a form. The less a word-form changes, the simpler it is. (Clark and Berman, 1984, p. 9)

III. *Principle of Productivity:* Those word-formation devices used most often by adults in word innovations are the most productive in the language for constructing new word-forms. (Clark and Hecht, 1982, p. 6)

IV. *Principle of Conventionality:* For certain meanings, there is a conventional word or word-formation device that should be used in the language community. (Clark and Hecht, 1982, p. 8)

The principle of transparency was postulated to explain the early occurrence of compounds such as *build-man* in the English experiment.

Since compounds combine known meanings and forms in a one-to-one manner, they are supposed to be transparent and thus easily learned. The principle of simplicity underlies the fact that the youngest Hebrew-speaking children used zero conversion rather than compounding to respond to the test. Transparency correctly predicts the use of the transparent *-an* device early on for the Hebrew-speaking children. The last two principles are postulated to account for the child's development into conformity with adult usage.

The results of the two tests for Hebrew and English suggest that

[F]ormal simplicity appears to carry more weight for the younger children than semantic transparency.... The general shift, from age four on, to word-forms that were semantically transparent in addition to being relatively simple in form suggests that by that age, children have become conscious of the need for novel words to be transparent to addressees as well as simple for speakers. (Clark and Berman, 1984, p. 51)

In order to examine the applicability of these proposed principles for a third language, and to investigate the acquisition of word-formation in American Sign Language, this test was given to young deaf children learning ASL as their native language.

Subjects

This test was given to 24 deaf children having deaf parents and learning ASL as their first language. The children were divided into four age groups as follows: Group I: four children aged 3–4; Group II: five children aged 5–6; Group III: six children aged 7–8; and Group IV: nine children aged 9–10. In addition, 16 deaf adults were tested.

Procedure

In this test (as in the studies done by Clark and Berman, 1984; and Clark and Hecht, 1982), the children were told what the characteristic activity of a certain machine is, and they were asked to create a new sign for this machine. For example, the child might be told in ASL, "I have a picture of a machine that feeds babies. What would you call a machine that feeds babies?" At this point, the children are expected to coin a new name for this novel object. After they respond, they are shown a picture of the object. Half of the questions involved novel machines and the other half people. For example, "I have a picture of a girl who tears paper. What would you call a girl who tears paper?" Again, a new name is expected.

TABLE I. WORD-FORMATION DEVICES USED IN THE "PEOPLE AND
MACHINES TEST"

Group/Age	Compounding	Affixation	Derivation	Other
I (3–4)	15.0	30.0	50.0	5.0
II (5–6)	25.0	21.7	46.7	6.6
III (7–8)	23.6	9.7	43.1	23.6
IV (9–10)	25.9	42.6	24.0	7.4
Adults	36.6	16.4	23.3	23.7

Results

The results from the People and Machines test are presented as percentages for each response type in Table 1. Three devices were used to create new nouns by all age levels. The groups differed, however, in the percentage using the three devices.

Unlike the children in the English study, the youngest children in this study did not use compounds very often. The older children used compounding slightly more often, and the adults used it rather frequently. If the principle of transparency alone were at work here, then we might expect to see compounding used often by the young children, as it was in the English study, especially given its relative productivity for the adults.

The agentive affix borrowed from English, -ER, was mostly used by the older children. The adults did not use it to a large extent. This disparity could be explained by the situation in which the tests were done: The children were tested at their school, and the oldest ones might have used this device because of the English environment.[3]

In the initial analysis, it seemed as though deverbal derivation in ASL was not used much by the youngest children. The nouns derived by this process have the same handshapes and locations as their related verbs, but the verbs are made with a longer, continuous movement and the nouns with smaller, repeated, and restrained movement (Supalla and Newport, 1978). However, for the youngest group of children, most of the responses in the "other" category were single forms that matched the stimulus verb in handshape and locations. The movement used was a combination of the standard movements used to signal the verb form and deverbal derivation. Launer (1982) found that young deaf children do not always use the correct movement parameters to distinguish between related nouns and verbs. Rather, she found that they sometimes use a combination of correct and incorrect aspects of movement. In this

3 It should be noted that only a few children used this device and that they used it almost exclusively, whereas others seldom used it.

study, the older groups of children and the adults used this kind of response much less often (the responses in the "other" category for them were mostly noun phrases describing the objects or established lexical items whose meanings were extended to cover the new items).

In many cases, the youngest children were obviously basing their noun signs on the same root as the verb stimulus, but their responses were not initially scored as derivations because the movement they used was improper for a deverbal derivation. Therefore, the number of these same root quasi-derivations was added to the initial derivation score to produce the scores given in Table 1. Of all the age groups, youngest children used these derivations and quasi-derivations most frequently, and the use of these forms gradually declined with age.

Some of the test responses that relied mainly on these word-based devices are given in Figure 1. For example, a machine that laughed might be called a LAUGH^MACHINE, or a girl that tears paper, a PAPER-^TEAR, using compounds. A boy that reads was called a READ[D:noun], using the deverbal derivation, and a machine that feeds babies was called a FEED-ER, using the agentive affix. These signs, and the pictures used in the test to elicit them, are illustrated in Figure 1.

Discussion

In their discussion of the proposed principles for the acquisition of word-formation devices, Clark and Berman (1984) describe the strategies attending each principle. Of greatest interest here are the strategies for transparency and simplicity, which are, respectively,

a. In production, look for word-formation devices that use whole words as their elements and add them to your repertoire for constructing new words.
b. Make as few changes as possible in forming a new word from an old one.
(Clark and Berman, 1984, pp. 8–9)

According to these strategies, the ASL options of compounding and affixation would be considered transparent. The minimal movement change in the derivations and quasi-derivations could be considered simple. This breakdown and the results from the test given in ASL would support, along with the Hebrew data, the notion that the principle of simplicity takes precedence over the principle of transparency for the youngest children. The gradual decrease in the use of derivations and increase in the use of compounding further support the suggestion that transparency, productivity, and conventionality soon come into play when the child is acquiring word-formation devices.

These results seem relatively straightforward. However, in the literature on word formation in adult signers (e.g., Bellugi and Newkirk,

Stimulus   **Sign creation**

LAUGH^MACHINE

PAPER^TEAR

READ [D:noun]

FEED-ER

Figure 1. Example stimuli and responses to the People and Machines Test

"CINNAMON ROLL"   "MILKSHAKE"   "SAND-CRABS"

Figure 2. Signs invented by a deaf child

1981), it is clear that the compositional device is quite productive. In addition, Klima and Bellugi (1979) report on signs spontaneously invented by a 3-year-old deaf child that also are mimetic, or compositional. In one such sign for a cinnamon roll, the child used a /C/ handshape in the base hand, with a /1/ hand moving in a circular direction above the base, "indicating the swirls of cinnamon sugar on top" (Klima and Bellugi, 1979, p. 11). (This sign and two others invented by this deaf child are illustrated in Figure 2.) It is surprising that the subjects in this study did not use this device. Since it was suspected that the first test did not tap all of the children's word-formation potentials, the following test was given to investigate further the word-formation abilities of young deaf children.

Invented objects

The second test used different stimuli and presented them in a different manner than did the People and Machines test. The responses to this test were quite different from those in the first test and greatly favored the non-word-based device for creating new signs.

Subjects

This test was given to 30 deaf children having deaf parents, and attending the same residential school for the deaf. All of the children were tested individually in the same testing situation. The subjects were divided into four groups by age for the initial analysis: Group I, 4 children aged 3–4; Group II, 5 children aged 5–6; Group III, 11 children aged 7–8; and Group IV, 11 children aged 9–10. Twenty-four deaf adults were also given this test.

TABLE 2. WORD-FORMATION DEVICES USED IN THE "INVENTED OBJECTS TEST"

Group/Age	Compounds	Extensions	Composition
I (3–4)	7.4	40.0	52.6
II (5–6)	14.2	25.8	60.0
III (7–8)	16.7	30.3	52.7
IV (9–10)	12.5	40.8	45.8
Adults	20.9	17.0	61.8

Procedure

In this test, the subjects were shown a picture of an odd, invented object without being told its function. The children were asked to create a name for the object simply on the basis of its appearance in this picture. After making the sign, the children were shown a picture of a person using the object in some way. When shown this picture, they were asked to create a verb sign for the activity.

This method of presentation was used in the first half of the test only. In the second half, the order was reversed: The children were shown pictures of someone using an odd object first and then asked to create a verb sign. After the children looked at the activity picture, they were shown a picture of the object alone and were asked to create the noun sign. Examples of these pictures are given in Figure 3.

Results

The responses to this test were initally catalogued according to the type of word-formation device used. It was found that *compounds* were used sparingly by the children, but they made up almost 20% of adult responses. If a picture resembled a commonly known object, the sign for that object might be used, *extending* the meaning to cover the invented object (for example, calling item 6 a "football"). Most frequently, a new sign was created using the *compositional* type of word-formation device described earlier. These results are given in Table 2.

The compositional responses are divided into two categories. In one category, specific handshapes specifying size and shape (SASSes) are conjoined in such a way as to *describe* explicitly what the item looks like. In the other category, the handshapes and movements *represent* the appearance of the object, or the grip in using the object; here, the movement primes employed are closer in length to those for established lexical signs. This kind of response is called a neologism. Table 3 indicates what percentage of the compositions in Table 2 are descriptions or neologisms.

The size and shape specifiers used in the descriptions are all in the

TABLE 3. RESPONSES FORMED BY COMPOSITION

Group/Age	Neologisms	Descriptions
I (3–4)	96.0	4.0
II (5–6)	97.2	2.8
III (7–8)	95.6	4.4
IV (9–10)	91.9	8.1
Adults	54.5	45.5

subset labeled "free morphemes" by Ryder (1984). These descriptions are thus more like phrases than single word or compound responses. The primes used in the neologisms, on the other hand, are in the set of Ryder's "bound morphemes." These responses are thus more like multimorphemic words.

Considered together, the compositional devices were most often used in responses to this test. These kinds of non-word-based devices, in which a new word is constructed from meaningful sublexical elements, are quite different from the word-based responses to the People and Machines test. Although they were not used in the earlier test, they were heavily relied on in the second test, where the subjects were told the function of the object they were naming, but only saw its size, shape, and movement in a picture. Unlike the responses to the People and Machines test, which were most often derivations made with minimal change, the responses here were highly complex and clearly different from the earlier ones.

After the initial categorial analysis, the new signs created by the children in this test were examined more closely. Representative responses from a few of the subjects are described below.

Children's new sign creations for invented objects

Subjects

The specific responses analyzed in this section come from 18 children, aged 2–10, and four adults. There are two children at each age level 2, 3, 4, 5, 6, 7, 8, 9, and 10. All except four of these children were tested in the same situation as the children included in the initial results. The four who were not tested in this situation attended different schools from the main group, and so were tested separately by the same experimenters, who used the same procedure for both groups. All of the children included here have deaf, signing parents, except for one 10-year-old who was tested with the main group although her results were not included in the initial analysis. The children included in this analysis

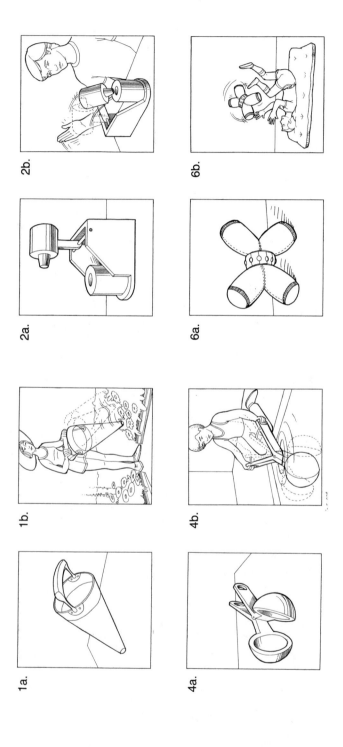

2b.

6b.

2a.

6a.

1b.

4b.

1a.

4a.

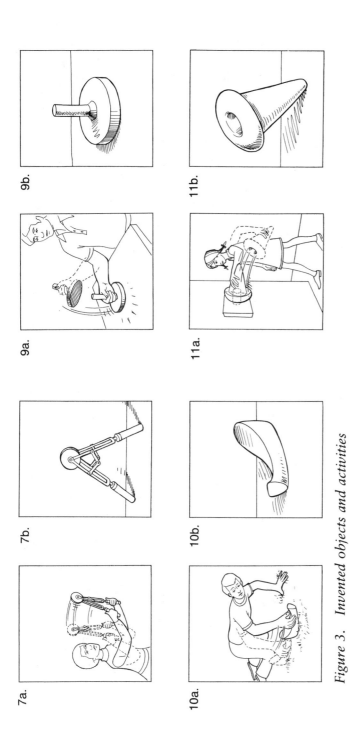

Figure 3. Invented objects and activities

were randomly selected from the main group and the additional children
brought in whenever they were needed to make up two at each age level.
The four adults were randomly selected from the total group of adults
used in the initial analysis, but constrained so that all were deaf adults
who had had deaf parents and who had been individually tested in the
same testing situation.

TWO- AND THREE-YEAR-OLDS

The 2- and 3-year-old subjects were able to attend and respond to this
task. However, the responses of the 2- and 3-year-olds, unlike those for
any other age level, were sometimes completely unrelated to the stimulus
pictures (at least, no relation was discernible). The 2- and 3-year-olds
were also more likely than any other group to use an existing sign only,
rather than create a new sign. For example, item 1a was called a "hat"
by one 2-year-old and one 3-year-old, and "ice cream" (as in "ice cream
cone") by the other two.[4]

Although the 2- and 3-year-olds did make some unrelated responses
(21 out of 90 responses) and did give some existing lexical items as
names for the new objects, they also succeeded in using the compositional
word-formation device to create certain neologisms. For example, for
item 4b, the youngest subject was able to produce a sign with the two
hands in /S/ handshapes as a grip classifier, and the hands moving together toward one another indicating the movement the person in the
picture was making. This kind of response for item 4b was made by 17
of the 22 subjects in this analysis (including all four of the adults). Also,
a 3-year-old used her two hands in /C/ handshape size and shape specifiers, placed close to each other, to indicate the shape of object 2.

The 2- and 3-year-olds did not usually capture the relation between
the object and activity pictures in their signs. However, most seemed to
understand that the two were related. As an example, one of the 2-year-
olds, who got into a short streak of producing totally irrelevant signs,
still produced the same irrelevant sign for both the object and activity
pictures for an item, then a new one for the next pair. For example, she
signed BREAK for both 10a and 10b, then a sign like ALLIGATOR for
both 11a and 11b. Only the 3-year-olds were able to produce some
invented pairs beginning to look like deverbal derivations. For example,
for item 7a, the oldest 3-year-old had her two hands in /A/ handshapes
as grip classifiers, moving the hands together to represent squeezing the

4 Note, however, that in the initial analysis adults often gave more than one response.
  One of those responses was an existing lexicalized sign, and another an invented
  sign; the figures in Table 1, showing more 'extensions' for the adults, reflect this
  difference.

two handles of the device together. For 7b, she used the same handshape with quicker, smaller movement of the hands together.

When the youngest children produced invented signs, these were usually made with large, extended movements, and loosely formed handshapes. However, this exaggeration in pronunciation is characteristic of children's signing in general. Aside from this factor, deaf native signing consultants considered that when the children did make new sign creations, they were in general not violating the combinatorial rules of ASL phonology; in fact, the signs were sometimes very similar to the signs that the older children and adults formed. Note, however, that some errors in sign formation were produced by the youngest children. These errors were almost exclusively errors in the orientation of the hand. Orientation, although used to distinguish some minimal sign pairs, is often considered a "minor" parameter of sign formation (Klima and Bellugi, 1979), and its realization can sometimes be predicted on the basis of the features of the other parameters.

FOUR- AND FIVE-YEAR-OLDS

The 4- and 5-year-olds were more on task than the younger children. Their responses were somewhat more uniform than those of the youngest group, although still more varied than those of the older children. They also made more innovative signs than the youngest group, rather than rely on existing lexical items.

An example of the range of answers given can be seen in their response to the first item. A 4-year-old used tracing SASSes to describe the shape of the object. A 5-year-old used an /S/ grip classifier moving slightly up and down. This is like the sign for SUITCASE, and reflects the handle on the object.

When shown the activity picture for 1, a 4-year-old responded with a compound of FLOWER, and the sign for putting something inside a container, all the while holding her left hand in a /C/ handshape SASS signifying the outer edge of the container. She seemed to have picked up on the appearance of flowers in the drawing, and imagined a possible function for the object, although not what is depicted in the picture. Note, too, that it is physically infeasible to interpret the object as a sort of container since it has a hole in the bottom. A 5-year-old used both hands in an /S/ grip handshape, hands together and palms facing downward, with the hands moving back and forth and sideways. This sign, like many of the invented signs given by the 5-year-olds and older children, captures the movement that a person makes when using the object. These four examples are illustrated in Figure 4.

The 4- and 5-year-olds were also somewhat better than the 2- and 3-year-olds at using deverbal derivations to relate the noun (object) and

Stimulus (Item #1)   **Sign creation**

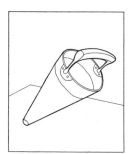

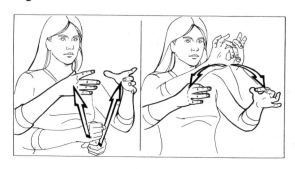

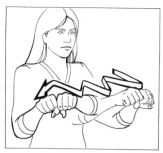

Figure 4.   Example stimuli and responses to the Invented Objects Test: 4- and 5-year-olds

verb (activity) responses. As with the older subjects, such derivations occurred more often in the second part of the test, where the activity picture was seen before the object picture, than in the first part of the test, in which the order was reversed.

SIX- AND SEVEN-YEAR-OLDS

By age 6 and 7, the responses begin to look more and more alike across subjects. For some items, certain aspects are highly salient and are captured in a similar way for most of the adults and oldest children. These standard responses begin to appear also at this age. Such a standard response usually is made with the hands in a grip classifier, the movement representing the movement of the person using the object. In the second half of the test, the object response is often a deverbal form of this sign.

For verbs and nouns with a basis in the movement of the person using the object, however, the signs are still constrained by the formal properties of ASL sign formation and thus differ from mime. For example, many responses to item 10 involved a /C/ handshape, palm down, moving from right to left repeatedly. A mime of this action would need to include kneeling on the floor to represent the fact that the object is brushed across the ground. In the invented signs, the ground is conveyed by using the nondominant hand in a /B/ handshape, palm up, and the movement of the active /C/ is on the base /B/. One of the errors that the children younger than 6 made was to follow this aspect of a restrained area for ASL signs. One 4-year-old actually stood up and walked to the wall for item 11. Even the 6- and 7-year-olds occasionally made movements outside of the signing space, as four children aged 3–7 produced large kicking movements with their legs for item 6.

Although there are more commonalities in the responses of the 6- and 7-year-olds than in those of the younger subjects, the answers do vary somewhat in the salient aspects of the picture represented. For example, although almost all of the responses to item 9 involved a downward stamping movement of an /S/ hand (half of them to a /B/ hand, palm up, for the base), like the movement in the picture, one 6-year-old looked at the shape of the item and called it a joystick, like the ones used in videogames.

EIGHT- TO TEN-YEAR OLDS

The responses of the 8- to 10-year-olds were most like those of the adults. Deverbal derivations, in which the noun signs were formed by reducing and restraining the movement of a verb sign, were quite common. This is also the most common age at which to find deverbal derivations encoded in reverse. That is, when the object was seen before the activity, subjects at this age could deduce the movement from the picture and encode it in a proper nounlike form. For example, for item

Stimulus (Item #2)   **Sign creation**

Noun

Verb

Figure 5.   Example stimuli and responses to the Invented Objects Test:
Derivationally related noun and verb

2, an 8-year-old used his right hand in an /X/ handshape, as an SASS for the extended portion of the top of the item, and moved it into the left hand, which was in an /O/ handshape, representing the base of the item. Although a 4-year-old was able to produce this sign with a long movement for the verb, it was not until 8 that a small, repeated, re-strained movement was used for this item first for the noun in response to the object picture seen first. These signs are illustrated in Figure 5.[5]

Like the adults, the 8- to 10-year-olds referred to the function or

5   The 8- to 10-year-olds were also most like the adults in their attitude toward the test. Like the adults, they tended to be a little puzzled and hesitant about naming these bizarre objects, whereas the younger children responded without pause. Fur-thermore, the oldest children and adults were also more concerned about giving the "correct" response than the youngest children were, and sometimes felt they had given the "wrong" answer when they saw the second picture. This kind of response was also observed, but to a lesser degree, in the People and Machines test, in that subjects would want their responses to properly match the picture. Apparently, adults want to know information about function and appearance before deciding on a new sign.

possible function of the object more than the younger children did. Their signs were well formed, and for many of the items a particular response was used consistently across all of the older children and the adults.

Conclusion

Several conclusions can be drawn from the results of these tests. First, children learning ASL go through several steps in acquiring the appropriate use of word-formation devices. At the youngest ages, they use more extensions than the older children, yet do create a few new words by using mostly unmarked handshapes and some large, awkward movements. They also make some errors in sign phonology. As they get older, their productions approximate those of the adults more and more, both in form and in the aspects represented. The older children and the adults incorporated a notion of the function of the objects much more than did the younger children.

Second, children learn relatively early the types of word-formation devices that are appropriate for a given situation. The children as well as the adults used the word-based devices for the first test and the compositional devices for the second test.

Third, these tests have shown that the HC and MOV components Supalla and Newport (1978) described for verbs of movement can also be used in creating nouns for novel objects and verbs for the actions of these objects.

Fourth, it may be necessary to use more than one task to elicit the full range of desired structures. If the Invented Objects test had not been carried out, the children's use of the compositional word-formation device might have gone unnoticed. Differences appeared even in the Invented Objects test, depending on the order of presentation of the related object and activity pictures. If the People and Machines test had not been conducted, the productivity of the word-based devices would not have been seen.

We see that specific tasks call for specific word-formation processes. The use of these processes may be acquired following the principles of formal simplicity and semantic transparency, at least for some word-formation tasks and devices. In addition, the results of the tests discussed here suggest that tasks involving verbal description of stimuli call for word-based morphological devices, whereas, at least for a visual language, a task involving nonverbal pictural presentation of stimuli calls for word-formation devices that are not word based. The special effects of nonverbal stimuli and the use of word-formation devices that are not word based are quite possibly prime examples of effects that the visual modality can have on the structure and acquisition of a visual language.

Acknowledgments

This work was supported in part by National Institutes of Health Grants NS15175, NS19096, and HD13249, and National Science Foundation Grant BNS83–09860 to Drs. Ursula Bellugi and Howard Poizner at the Salk Institute for Biological Studies. Illustrations were made by Frank A. Paul, copyright Dr. Ursula Bellugi, the Salk Institute.

We are grateful to the following people and institutions for allowing the subjects to participate in the experiments and for providing facilities: George Attletweed, Ohlone College, Fremont, California; Dr. Ray Jones, California State University at Northridge; Dr. Henry Klopping, California School for the Deaf, Fremont, California.

Many thanks go to those subjects who participated in this experiment and to those who helped with it, including Maureen O'Grady, Lucinda Struxness, and Dennis Schemenauer. Special thanks go to Ursula Bellugi, Edward Klima, Mary Ellen Ryder, and Michael Strong for their support and beneficial discussions about this experiment.

References

Bellugi, U., and D. Newkirk. (1981). Formal devices for creating new sign in American Sign Language. *Sign Language Studies 30*, 1–35.

Clark, E., and R. Berman. (1984). Structure and use in the acquisition of word-formation. *Language 60*, 542–590.

Clark, E., and B. Hecht. (1982). Learning to coin agent and instrument nouns. *Cognition 12*, 1–24.

Klima, E., and U. Bellugi. (1979). *The Signs of Language.* Cambridge: Harvard University Press.

Launer, P. (1982). A plane is not to fly. Unpublished doctoral dissertation, New York University.

Liddell, S. (1984). Think and believe: Sequentiality in American Sign Language. *Language 60*, 372–399.

Lillo-Martin, D. (1984). The acquisition of task-specific word formation devices in American Sign Language. *Papers and Reports on Child Language Development 23*, 74–81.

Newport, E. (1982). Task specificity in language learning? Evidence from speech perception and American Sign Language. In E. Wanner and L. Gleitman (Eds.), *Language Acquisition: The State of the Art.* Cambridge: Cambridge University Press.

Newport, E., and T. Supalla. (1980). Clues from the acquisition of signed and spoken language. In U. Bellugi and M. Studdert-Kennedy (Eds.), *Signed and Spoken Language: Biological Constraints on Linguistic Form.* Dahlem Workshop Reports, Life Science Research Report Series, No. 19.

Ryder, M. (1984). A classification of classifiers in American Sign Language. A paper presented at the Annual Linguistics Society of American Meeting, Baltimore.

Stokoe, W., D. Casterline, and C. Croneberg. (1965). *A Dictionary of American Sign Language.* Washington, D.C.: Gallaudet College Press.

Supalla, T. (1982). Structure and acquisition of verbs of motion and location in American Sign Language. Unpublished dissertation. University of California, San Diego.

(In press). The Classifier System in American Sign Language. In C. Craig (Ed.), *Noun Classification and Categorization*. Philadelphia: Benjamins.

Supalla, T., and E. Newport. (1978). How many seats in a chair: The derivation of nouns and verbs in ASL. In P. Siple (Ed.), *Understanding Language through Sign Language Research*. New York: Academic Press.

8 Linguistic and cultural role models for hearing-impaired children in elementary school programs

James Woodward, Thomas Allen, *and* Arthur Schildroth

Editor's introduction

This brief report of part of the data from a large-scale survey of teachers of the deaf by researchers at the Gallaudet Center of Assessment and Demographic Studies provides some information on teacher background variables that confirms otherwise anecdotal evidence, revealing the extreme homogeneity of teachers of the deaf and raising the issue of teachers as cultural role models. Woodward, Allen, and Schildroth looked at data on 609 elementary school teachers of the deaf, 85% of whom turn out to be hearing females. Using an ingeniously designed questionnaire, they were able to collect data on the teachers' classroom language characteristics. In addition to direct questions about language use, they provided a sample English sentence and asked the respondents to indicate, morpheme by morpheme, which elements they would include manually, either by fingerspelling, or by separate or inclusive sign. From the answers to these questions, the authors could deduce what language or sign system (if any) the teachers used. Not one of the teachers reported using ASL as a primary means of communication in the classroom. Nearly 60% used simultaneous communication and over 40% used no signs at all. The distribution of language use varied according to the kind of school, with more signing being used in the special schools. The authors infer from these data that deaf children are exposed largely to Hearing cultural role models, except in residential or day schools for the Deaf, and thus that an assimilationist approach dominates education of the Deaf. The implication of this state of affairs is that deaf children are treated much like children from other countries in that they are submerged into mainstream American society in a single generation. It is not clear whether such a goal is realistic when applied to deaf children, even if it were desirable. Profound hearing loss, in most cases, presents fundamental communication difficulties between deaf and hearing people that can only be overcome if both groups make a concerted effort to understand the culture and language of the other. If access to deaf chil-

dren's own culture and language is restricted, then problems of
social identity and self-esteem, in addition to language difficulties,
will probably be impossible to avoid.

Since less than 5% of hearing-impaired children have two deaf parents
(Rawlings and Jensema, 1977), most hearing-impaired children are not
meaningfully exposed to American Sign Language and Deaf cultural
values at home (De Santis, 1979; Padden, 1980). The very large majority
of hearing-impaired children who have two hearing parents often experience severe communication difficulties with their parents and as a
result learn very little English at home (Charrow and Fletcher, 1974;
Furth, 1966). Without this knowledge of English, most hearing-
impaired children of hearing parents are often unable to fully learn
Hearing cultural values in the home.

School, therefore, becomes a crucial place for enculturation (Meadow,
1972) and language acquisition (Markowicz and Woodward, 1978) for
most deaf children. From linguistic and anthropological perspectives,
the elementary school, because of the age factor, is more important for
language acquisition and for enculturation than any higher level of education. Research has shown that the time from birth until puberty is
critical for language acquisition (Chomsky, 1969; Hoffmeister and Wilbur, 1980) and for enculturation (Bock, 1969).

This means that elementary school teachers are often the first adult
role models with whom hearing-impaired children can successfully communicate, and their impact on the children's socialization therefore as-
sumes even greater significance than for teachers of hearing children.

The purpose of the present study is to examine background information on elementary school teachers of hearing-impaired students and
on the type of communication these teachers use in the classroom. From
these data we draw several conclusions about how these elementary
classroom teachers serve as linguistic and cultural role models for their
hearing-impaired students.

Data collection

Data from this study were collected in the spring of 1985 by the
Gallaudet Research Institute's Center for Assessment and Demographic Studies (CADS). The population for the study was drawn
from those programs supplying data to the Annual Survey of Hearing Impaired Children and Youth, which each year collects demographic and educationally relevant data on more than 50,000
hearing-impaired students.

TABLE I. ELEMENTARY SCHOOL TEACHERS BY GENDER, HEARING STATUS, AND
TYPE OF PROGRAM, 1985

Hearing status and gender	Special school		Local school program	
	N	(%)	N	(%)
Hearing female	186	83.0	333	86.5
Hearing male	13	5.9	35	9.1
Deaf female	13	5.9	1	0.3
Deaf male	1	0.3	1	0.3
Hard-of-hearing female	7	3.1	8	2.1
Hard-of-hearing male	4	1.8	7	1.7
Totals	224	100.0	385	100.0

From the 1983–1984 annual survey data base, we randomly selected
4,500 students and assigned them to one of three subject area stratifi-
cation groups: reading, mathematics, and social studies. Questionnaires
were sent to the programs enrolling these students, with instructions to
distribute them to the reading, mathematics, or social studies teachers
of the students. Students were stratified in this way to ensure that teachers
in a variety of academic contexts were represented in the data base.
Since sampling was carried out on an individual student basis, some
teachers received two or more questionnaires. The primary aim of the
analysis being to describe the communication patterns of teachers, the
duplicate responses for these teachers were eliminated from the analysis.
In addition, the data set was limited to teachers at the elementary school
level, since communication at this level is likely to have a greater impact
on the transmission of cultural values than communication at higher
levels. Finally, teachers with missing or incomplete data were eliminated
from the data base. The resulting file contained information on 609
teachers.

Teacher background

Of the 609 teachers in this study, 85.2% are hearing females. Only 42
teachers report themselves as hearing-impaired: 16 deaf and 26 hard-
of-hearing. Of the deaf teachers, only two are male. Twenty-five of these
42 hearing-impaired teachers teach in special schools. Table 1 indicates
the distribution of the 609 teachers in terms of sex, hearing status, and
type of program in which they are teaching.

Of the 25 hearing-impaired teachers working in special schools, 14
classify themselves as deaf, 11 as hard-of-hearing. On the other hand,

15 of the 17 hearing-impaired teachers in local school programs consider themselves hard-of-hearing rather than deaf.

Classroom communication of teachers

Teachers were asked if they signed, spoke, or signed and spoke during their instruction of the individual students randomly selected for the survey. For teachers who signed, the following questions were asked to determine the degree to which the signing was in English or American Sign Language (ASL) and the extent to which various channels were used:

1. When teaching this student in the classroom, do you normally:
   A. Speak and sign at the same time
   B. Sign only
   C. Other
2. If you sign only, do you use lip movements for most or all English words?
   A. Yes
   B. No
3. The following list consists of phrases which have been used to characterize types of signing. Which of these best describes the signing that you use when teaching this student? (Choose only one.)
   A. American Sign Language (ASL or Ameslan)
   B. Pidgin Sign English (PSE)
   C. Seeing Essential English (SEE I)
   D. Signing Exact English (SEE II)
   E. Signed English
   F. Linguistics of Visual English (LOVE)
   G. Other
4. Read the following two English sentences:
   He is looking at me.
   I am looking for him.
   A. When communicating the meaning of the two English sentences above to the *named student* in the classroom, indicate how you would communicate each of the following:
      (a. Would fingerspell; b. Would use separate sign or gesture; c. Would include as part of another sign; d. Would omit)

He	(a, b, c, or d?)	**I**	(a, b, c, or d?)
is	(a, b, c, or d?)	**am**	(a, b, c, or d?)
look	(a, b, c, or d?)	**look**	(a, b, c, or d?)
-ing	(a, b, c, or d?)	**-ing**	(a, b, c, or d?)
at	(a, b, c, or d?)	**for**	(a, b, c, or d?)
me	(a, b, c, or d?)	**him**	(a, b, c, or d?)

   B. When communicating the meaning of the two English sentences above to *this* student in the classroom, indicate how you would normally sign the following words:
      (a. Would use the same sign for each; b. Would use a different sign for each; c. Would not sign one or both of these words)

He and **Him**   (a, b, or c?)
I and **Me**   (a, b, or c?)
Am and **Is**   (a, b, or c?)
Look in both sentences   (a, b, or c?)

To determine code preferences, we first assumed that the nonsigning teachers were communicating in English. For signing teachers, code was a little more difficult to determine. Although Question 3 specifically asked teachers whether they communicated in ASL or in a manually coded form of English, the teachers' responses to this question were, in many cases, invalidated by their responses to other questions. For the current analysis, signing teachers were assumed to be signing in English unless they met the following three conditions: (a) They responded "sign only" to Question 1 (i.e., they did not sign and speak at the same time); (b) they responded "no" to Question 2 (i.e., they did not use lip movements); and (c) they responded "would include as part of another sign" or "would omit" to the sentence items *-ing* (in both sentences), *is,* and *am.* Teachers who met these three conditions were classified as being true ASL communicators.

To further specify channel differences, we examined various subchannels. English signers were classified according to whether or not they used simultaneous communication (i.e., whether they spoke and signed at the same time; see Question 1). Those English signers not using the simultaneous communication method were classified by the use of lip movements with their signs (Question 2). ASL signers, by definition, used a single channel (signing only).

None of the teachers in the survey normally uses ASL as the preferred form of classroom communication. The majority of teachers (57.5%) report using speech and signs at the same time. These teachers cannot be using ASL. An additional 41.7% of the teachers report using no signs at all. This group of teachers also cannot be using ASL. Only six teachers report signing without voice. However, these six teachers also report mouthing most or all English words while signing. In addition, most of them reported using English inflections and/or function words when signing in the instructional context.

There are, however, important differences in the use of these methods as reported by teachers in the two school settings. A large majority (almost 89%) of teachers in special schools use speech and signs, with a much smaller percentage using speech only. (Only five teachers in these special schools use signs without speech.) The use of the two methods – speech only and a combination of sign and speech – is more evenly divided in the local school setting, with a majority (60.1%) reporting the use of speech only over the simultaneous method (39.7%). One teacher at a local school program reports the use of sign without speech.

Table 2 indicates a close association between method of communi-

TABLE 2. TYPE OF COMMUNICATION USED BY ELEMENTARY SCHOOL TEACHERS
BY PROGRAM TYPE AND HEARING STATUS, 1985

| Type of communication | Special school | | | | | | Local school program | | | |
| | Hearing | | Hard of hearing | | Deaf | | Hearing | | Hearing-impaired | |
	N	%	N	%	N	%	N	%	N	%
Speech only	21	10.6	0	0	1	7.1	222	60.3	9	52.9
Signs only	1	0.5	2	18.2	2	14.3	1	0.3	0	0
Speech and signs	177	88.9	9	81.8	11	78.6	145	39.4	8	47.1
Totals	199	100.0	11	100.0	14	100.0	368	100.0	17	100.0

cation, program type, and hearing status of the teachers. Hearing teachers in special schools use speech and signs much more frequently (89.8%) than do hearing teachers in local school programs (39.4%). Conversely, hearing teachers in the local school setting report using speech without signs more often (60.3%) than do hearing teachers in special schools (10.6%).[1]

Summary and implications

This study examined the background information of 609 elementary school teachers of hearing-impaired students and the type of communication used by these teachers in the classroom.

This study produced several prominent results. Almost 9 of every 10 of these elementary school teachers of hearing-impaired children are hearing women; deaf women account for less than 3% of the total, and only 2 deaf males are among the 609 teachers. Fourteen of the 16 deaf teachers in the sample are in a special school environment; only 2 deaf teachers are in a local school setting.

The findings on teacher background strongly suggest that elementary school hearing-impaired children are almost exclusively exposed to Hearing cultural role models and have very limited contact with male teachers, especially deaf male teachers. Further, among the hearing-impaired teachers in the local school programs in this sample, none

---

1 Much of this information detailing the relationship between communication method and school setting undoubtedly reflects the different types of students enrolled in these two very different educational settings. Such student variables as degree of hearing loss and age at onset of hearing loss influence the type of communication used by teachers in elementary schools.

appears to be culturally Deaf: 15 of the 17 hearing-impaired teachers in this setting classify themselves as hard-of-hearing rather than deaf, and 9 indicate they did not use any form of signing in the classroom.

The only apparent culturally Deaf role models with whom elementary school hearing-impaired youngsters have classroom contact are in the residential or day schools for these students. In these special schools the majority of the 25 hearing-impaired teachers classify themselves as deaf, all report some form of signing in the classroom, and all rate their signing skills as very good.

The results regarding communication used by teachers appear quite clear: Elementary school hearing-impaired children are almost exclusively exposed to English in the classroom. None of the 609 teachers in the 1985 CADS Communication Study are using ASL as their preferred form of communication in the classroom.

In conclusion, these data very strongly suggest that the great majority of teachers in elementary school programs for hearing-impaired students serve as role models of Hearing cultural values and of English. Very few hearing-impaired students at the elementary school level are receiving meaningful exposure to adult Deaf cultural role models and fewer still to formal instruction in American Sign Language. Although it is impossible to say from this study how much of the present approach is due to conscious decision and how much is due to other factors such as teacher shortages and funding problems, it is clear that elementary school programs are utilizing an assimilationist approach rather than a bilingual-bicultural approach. Assimilation has clearly been the goal of deaf education at the elementary school level for many years (Corbett and Jensema, 1981; Moores, 1978; Woodward, 1982). Judging from assessments of administrators in deaf education (Prickett and Hunt, 1977) and studies like the present one, we see little indication of any drastic change in approach in the near future.

Acknowledgment

The research described in this chapter was supported in part by Sign Language Research, Inc.

References

Bock, P. (1969). *Modern Cultural Anthropology.* New York: Alfred A. Knopf.

Charrow, V., and J. Fletcher. (1974). English as the second language of deaf students. *Developmental Psychology* 10 (4), 463–470.

Chomsky, C. (1969). *The Acquisition of Syntax in Children from 5 to 10.* Cambridge, Mass.: MIT Press.

Corbett, E., and C. Jensema. (1981). *Teachers of the Deaf.* Washington, D.C.: Gallaudet College Press.

De Santis, S. (1979). *The deaf community in the United States.* A paper presented at the American Anthropological Association meeting, November, Cincinnati, Ohio.

Furth, H. (1966). A comparison of reading test norms for deaf and hearing children. *American Annals of the Deaf,* 111, 461–462.

Hoffmeister, R., and R. Wilbur. (1980). The acquisition of sign language. In H. Lane and F. Grosjean (Eds.), *Recent Perspectives on American Sign Language.* Hillsdale, N.J.: Lawrence Erlbaum.

Jordan, I. K., G. Gustason and R. Rosen. (1976). Current communication trends at programs for the deaf. *American Annals of the Deaf.*

(1979). An update on communication trends at programs for the deaf. *American Annals of the Deaf.*

Markowicz, H., and J. Woodward. (1978). Language and maintenance of ethnic boundaries in the deaf community. *Communication and Cognition 11* (1), 29–38.

Meadow, K. (1972). Sociolinguistics, sign language, and the deaf subculture. In T. O'Rourke (Ed.), *Psycholinguistics and Total Communication: The State of the Art.* Silver Spring, Md.: National Association of the Deaf.

Moores, D. (1978). *Educating the Deaf: Psychology, Principles, and Practices.* Boston: Houghton Mifflin.

Padden, C. (1980). The deaf community and the culture of deaf people. In C. Baker and R. Battison (Eds.), *Sign Language and the Deaf Community.* Silver Spring, Md.: National Association of the Deaf.

Prickett, H., and J. Hunt. (1977). Education of the deaf—The next ten years. *American Annals of the Deaf 9,* 153–160.

Rawlings, B., and C. Jensema. (1977). *Two Studies of the Families of Hearing-Impaired Children.* Washington, D.C.: Office of Demographic Studies.

Woodward, J. (1982). *How you gonna get to heaven if you can't talk with Jesus: On depathologizing Deafness.* Silver Spring, Md.: T.J. Publishers.

9 Acquiring linguistic and social identity: interactions of deaf children with a hearing teacher and a deaf adult

Carol J. Erting

Editor's introduction

The topic of role models, raised in Chapter 8, is explored in depth by Erting. She reports here on an ethnographic study of three deaf pre-school children interacting with their hearing teacher and a visiting deaf adult. From her examination of the videotaped interactions and from interviews, Erting was able to distinguish clear differences in orientation between the deaf and hearing adults. In spite of her training and experience working with deaf children, the hearing teacher consistently adopted hearing strategies in her interactions that often led to misunderstandings and miscommunication. This apparent refusal by the teacher to accept fully that the children were deaf, and a tendency to treat them as trainees for a hearing society rather than as deaf children, distinguished her from the deaf adult whose orientation was appropriately visual and Deaf. This detailed observation and analysis of a single situation complements nicely the survey data presented by Woodward, Allen, and Schildroth in Chapter 8 and adds strength to their concerns about the ramifications of their findings. If Erting's findings are typical — and there is no reason to suspect that they are not — her recommendation that more deaf teachers be hired would help to ameliorate the problem, as would the better training of educators of the deaf in cultural, linguistic, and cognitive aspects of deafness. Erting's preference for a team teaching approach with one deaf and one hearing teacher is a particularly good one and lends itself readily to the kind of bilingual approach advocated by Strong in Chapter 5.

Deaf children need deaf adult role models. Psychologists, linguists, social scientists, teachers, deaf adults, and parents of deaf children have all argued that interaction with older deaf children and adults helps the deaf child develop a positive self-image and acquire communicative competence (Erting, 1978, 1980; Johnson and Erting, 1984; Kannapell, 1974; Luetke-Stahlman, 1983; Meadow, 1980; Mindel and Vernon,

1971; Moores, 1982). Nevertheless, most deaf children have little access to adult deaf individuals on a regular basis. A recent study (Corbett and Jensema, 1981) reported that only 13.6% of the teachers of deaf students in the United States themselves have hearing losses. Almost half of these hearing-impaired teachers are at the high school level or, in other words, 22% of the high school teachers of deaf students are hearing impaired. At the preschool level, only 5% of the teachers are hearing impaired.

Preschool programs for deaf children that label themselves Total Communication usually claim to include both American Sign Language (ASL) and some variety of manually encoded English (MCE) in their repertoire of strategies for communicating with the students. Since most of the teachers are hearing and since most hearing people are not fluent signers of ASL, preschool deaf children do not usually have the opportunity to communicate with skilled users of American Sign Language. Although this situation is particularly problematic for preschool children who have Deaf parents and are learning and using ASL as their native home language, access to a fluent user of ASL is also an issue for most other deaf children. Preschool deaf children who have hearing parents learn a variety of ASL from their ASL-using peers (Erting, 1985; Johnson and Erting, 1984). Thus if the children are to be active participants in the kind of dialogue necessary for linguistic, cognitive, and emotional development, at least one key adult in the educational environment should be fluent in ASL. Frequently, not only are hearing teachers unable to use ASL productively, but they are unable to understand the children when they use ASL or ASL-like signing (Erting, 1982). Although there has been little research on the communicative interactions of preschool deaf children with their hearing teachers and little is known about communication between preschool deaf children and Deaf adults, the few studies that exist suggest that hearing teachers who use simultaneous communication with preschool deaf children communicate quite differently from Deaf adults, whether they are using ASL or some variety of English signing (Erting, 1978, 1980, 1982; Johnson and Erting, 1984).

For example, in one study where there was a hearing teacher and a Deaf assistant in a preschool classroom, the Deaf assistant frequently signed English to the Deaf preschoolers but her English signing was markedly different from the hearing teacher's MCE (Johnson and Erting, 1984). The Deaf woman rarely mistranslated English words into signs and she always produced signs for words that were critical to the understanding of the sentences. The hearing teacher, on the other hand, often signed sentences that were incomprehensible because her sign productions were inaccurate and incongruous alongside the spoken English accompanying the signs. These data suggested that in the case of this classroom, the Deaf assistant was producing English signing that was a more consistent and accurate model for learning English than the MCE produced by the native English speaker. Furthermore, whereas the hearing teacher seemed to assume that the children would learn to sign English simply by being exposed to the MCE model, the Deaf woman used contrastive examples. She frequently showed the children different ways of signing the same thing, presenting information first in signing that was more like English and then in signing that was more ASL-like, or vice versa.

The study

The study on which this chapter is based was undertaken in part to investigate and describe the ways in which Deaf and hearing adults communicate with preschool deaf children. Ethnographic and microanalytical methods were used to study the interaction among parents, teachers, and deaf children in a preschool.

The setting

Ten teachers worked in the preschool; they were mostly young, white, highly educated (all held master's degrees) females with normal hearing who fit the profile of a "typical" teacher of deaf children based on data gathered by Corbett and Jensema (1981). One was a white male, one was a black female, one was a hearing-impaired female, and the others were white females ranging in age from the mid-20s to 30s. All of the 24 children attending the preschool had some degree of hearing loss; the majority were profoundly deaf. This preschool population was unusual in at least one important respect: Approximately half of the children had Deaf parents.[1] Since the preschool encouraged the parents to come to the school for sign language classes and parent meetings, the deaf children of hearing parents had some opportunity to see their classmates interacting with their deaf parents and to participate in the interaction with deaf adults themselves.

Research questions

The principal research question was a descriptive one: What are the communication patterns that emerge when Deaf and hearing parents and teachers interact with deaf preschoolers. If we assume, as Berger and Luckmann (1966, p. 153) do, that "language constitutes both the most important content and the most important instrument of sociali-

---

1 One study estimates that about 4% of all deaf children have two deaf parents (Jordan and Karchmer, 1986).

zation," these patterns should give an indication of the interactional processes that enable deaf children to acquire some understanding of their deafness.

Analysis of field notes gathered during the participant-observation phase of the research revealed that deaf children were learning about themselves and their places in the world through interactions with both Deaf and Hearing adults. These interactions were shaped by competing social identities ("Deaf" and "Hearing") symbolized by competing linguistic systems (ASL and MCE).

The goal then was to study the communicative interaction of selected Deaf and Hearing adults with three deaf children in order to identify emerging patterns of language use during the socialization process and to understand the implications of these findings for the developing social identity of the child.

Methodology and data collection

After approximately 18 months of participant observation in the preschool, one teacher and three children were chosen for intensive study. They were selected on the basis of the ethnographic research using the method of theoretical sampling defined by Glaser and Strauss (1967), wherein participants in the research are chosen according to criteria thought to be theoretically important with respect to the questions being addressed. The hearing teacher, for example, fit the profile of the typical teacher of deaf children presented by Corbett and Jensema (1981): She was a normally-hearing, highly educated female in her mid- to late 20s with no deaf relatives. The three preschool children were selected because they differed with respect to variables that have been shown to be important in studies of sign language use: degree of hearing loss, parental hearing stuatus, language used at home, and language preference of the parents (Woodward, 1973).

Participant observation had indicated that mothers, fathers, and teachers were the three categories of adults with whom these young deaf children interacted most frequently. Therefore, the children were each videotaped in an unstructured dyadic play situation with their mothers, their fathers, and the hearing teacher. Since one of the deaf children had hearing parents, a fourth adult was added to the study so that she would have the opportunity to interact with a Deaf adult.

The discussion below is concerned with the communicative interaction between the children and only two of the adults: the hearing teacher and the Deaf adult. Data on the interactions of the children and their parents have been reported elsewhere (Erting, 1985). Before I discuss the findings, I should say something about the characteristics, skills, and experiences of the participants with respect to deafness and communication.

Subjects

THE HEARING TEACHER[2]

The hearing teacher's first contact with deaf people occurred when she was in college, and at that time she began learning to sign. She described her classroom signing as "exact English," which she learned when she was working toward her master's degree in deaf education. The exact English signing she described did not follow any particular manually encoded English system such as those developed by Anthony (1971), Gustason, Pfetzing, and Zawolkow (1972), or Bornstein (1975). Rather, exact English was the label that her two deaf teachers at the university used for the type of sign communication they were teaching. This teacher, unlike many of the teachers at the preschool, had good receptive and some expressive skills in American Sign Language, which she had acquired primarily during informal interaction with her deaf teachers outside of the classroom. During her interaction with the preschool children in the classroom as well as during videotaped interaction, the teacher used simultaneous communication. She placed a high value on developing the speech and auditory potential of the children and expressed concern that she had not consistently required speech from the children during the videotaped interaction. She was also preoccupied with the adequacy of her simultaneous communication, commenting frequently on the clarity, completeness, and correctness of her signs as she watched the tapes.

The teacher had frequent contact with the parents of the three children. She was able to observe the children and parents communicating with each other and talk with the parents about their goals and expectations for their children. The parents with whom she had the most contact expressed generally positive opinions about her. The Deaf parents agreed that the teacher's signing of English was different from their own, but they regarded her signing skills as better than those of most hearing teachers. They especially appreciated her use of facial expressions, even though these, too, were different from their own. They were concerned, however, about the teacher's inability to understand their children's signing as well as their children's inability to understand her communication much of the time.

2 Parts of this description of the participants and the discussion of teacher–child interactions are taken from Erting (1985) and used with permission of the publisher.

THE DEAF ADULT

The Deaf adult who interacted with each of the three children was the mother of two preschool hearing-impaired children, one of whom was audiologically hard-of-hearing and the other profoundly deaf. Her own parents and grandparents were Deaf as well as her brother and several members of her extended family. She was audiologically hard-of-hearing, wore hearing aids, could use the telephone, and was a student at Gallaudet College. At the age of about 3 years she began attending the oral residential school for deaf children, where her brother was already a student. She learned sign language from her parents and communicated with her family through signs, speech, and lipreading. Although the language of the home was primarily American Sign Language, her parents encouraged her to develop her oral skills since she had some hearing and was attending an oral school. She is married to a hard-of-hearing man whose parents are hearing. Unlike his wife, he attended public school, has no other deaf family members, and did not learn sign language until he attended college.

This Deaf woman was chosen to interact with the three deaf children because, like many college-educated Deaf adults in this community, she had a wide repertoire of communication skills. Furthermore, she had preschool deaf children herself, had participated in the parents' groups at the school, had been videotaped before, and was not a complete stranger to the children. The parents of the children also knew the Deaf woman. When the Deaf parents viewed the videotapes of their children interacting with her, they stated that she was using ASL with some English signing but not "exact English." They also agreed that the Deaf woman and the children understood each other very well. The hearing parents described the Deaf adult's signing as "faster (than their own signing) and not complete signed English," but they agreed that their child understood her communication. They commented that the Deaf adult was not using her voice with their child, but then added, "Well, then again, deaf people don't talk to deaf people. Why use their voices?"

THE DEAF CHILDREN

Tommy, 3 years 9 months old, was the profoundly deaf son of two Deaf parents. His three older siblings had normal hearing. Tommy's parents had both attended Gallaudet College and preferred to use manually encoded English signing with Tommy at home. Tommy's father had Deaf parents himself and had attended residential schools for deaf children; Tommy's mother had hearing parents and was educated orally in both public and private schools. Tommy's parents believed American Sign Language was important for Tommy to learn, but only after he had mastered MCE. Tommy used his voice and wore his hearing aid inconsistently. He also attended the preschool program sporadically.

Mary, also the child of Deaf parents, was 3 years 7 months old at the time of the taping. Unlike the other two children, however, she was audiologically severely hard-of-hearing. She had both hearing and deaf siblings. Her parents were both Gallaudet College graduates and, like Tommy, her father's parents were Deaf and her mother's parents were hearing. Mary's father had attended a residential school for deaf children; Mary's mother was educated at a private, residential oral school for deaf children until she was 12 years old. At that time, she transferred to a state residential school where sign language was used. Mary's parents preferred to use American Sign Language at home but they also used a variety of fluent English signing with Mary. (Fluent English signing refers to a variety of signing commonly labeled Pidgin Sign English, or PSE.) Although Mary had more residual hearing and a more normal-sounding voice than the other two children, she wore her hearing aid and used her voice for speech inconsistently.

Cathy, who was 4 years and 1 month old when the videotapes were made, was an only child of hearing parents. Her parents had been using signs with her since she was approximately 2 years old. Cathy was profoundly deaf but she wore her hearing aid consistently at home and at school. Her response to sound was minimal and her speech unintelligible. Nevertheless, she used her voice much more consistently than the other two children. Her parents preferred to use simultaneous communication (spoken English and MCE) with Cathy in the home, but they made a conscious effort to give Cathy experience with Deaf adults. Their goal was to help her to feel comfortable with both Deaf and hearing people.

Data collection

The three deaf children were videotaped once with the hearing teacher and once with the Deaf adult. The taping sessions lasted 30–40 minutes and took place in a room in the school that had been converted into a videotaping studio designed for preschool children. Two cameras were partly concealed and mounted on the wall at a height of approximately 4 feet. One camera was remotely controlled; the other was operated by the researcher from behind a wall in which a window had been cut to accommodate the camera. The researchers operating the video equipment were in an adjacent room and could not be seen by the participants; in addition, the cameras were draped with black felt so that only the lenses remained visible.

It was assumed that, at least for the adults, the laboratory setting within the school would exert such a strong pressure for English that both of them would use some variety of English signing rather than a variety of ASL even if ASL was the preferred and usual language choice for interaction with the children outside of school. There are, however, various ways of signing English. In addition to the systems that have been devised for encoding English manually, a type of fluent English signing generally known as Pidgin Sign English (PSE) has developed as a result of the Deaf–Hearing contact situation. These types of signing cannot be placed on a simple, unidirectional continuum of discrete linguistic varieties, however. Sociolinguists and others have suggested that variation is multidimensional rather than unidirectional from the native or preferred language to the target language, that is, in the case of Deaf signers, from ASL to MCE (Baker and Cokely, 1980; Johnson and Erting, 1984; Washabaugh, 1981). According to this view, linguistic features from both languages may be combined in a variety of ways to produce forms of English signing.

Since participant observation had shown that the school setting was defined as a domain in which some variety of English signing was usual and had also revealed that the Deaf participants all signed varieties of ASL, especially outside of the school and in their own homes, an attempt was made to create some contexts in the laboratory setting that might encourage the use of ASL features by the adults.

Before each videotaping session, the adult was asked to play with the child and was told that the most important point was that they understand each other, not how much the child knew or the "correctness" of his or her language. The hope was that this instruction as well as the researcher's expressed positive attitude toward all sign language varieties would induce the adults to accept the use of ASL in situations where, either consciously or unconsciously, they might judge ASL to be the best language to facilitate understanding. Furthermore, participant observation had indicated that the child could provide a pressure for the use of ASL if the adult and child normally used that language for social interaction.

During the 30–40 minutes of videotaped interaction for each adult–child dyad, two of the interactional events that occurred were food sharing and free play. Observations in the classroom and in the homes of the children suggested that communicative interaction in these two broad types of situations were structured differently and elicited a range of linguistic variation. For example, food sharing, also known as "juice and cookie time" in the preschool classroom, has been characterized as an activity that carries a pressure for the use of MCE (see Johnson and Erting, 1984). Teachers of deaf children often explicitly designate such food-sharing activity as an opportunity for teaching appropriate social behavior – connected with receiving and eating food – along with the use of proper English language forms. Free play, on the other hand, is usually associated with a more casual communicative style; in this situation, the child usually initiates the play and often directs it.

Data analysis

The analytic goal was to identify linguistic features of the participants' signing that might be acting as social markers of Hearing or Deaf identity during face-to-face interaction. Studies of language variation suggest that linguistic features act as social markers in speech (or signing) and that the probability of their occurrence increases or decreases with the presence of related social variables. Furthermore, there is likely to be systematic variation evidenced by the co-occurrence of sets of markers that are important as socially significant linguistic variations. In order to determine whether the English signing of the adults and children constituted different varieties that were in part the result of different selections and combinations of linguistic features, the analysis focused on a limited set of linguistic features from ASL and from manually encoded English. The features were selected with three considerations in mind: (1) the participants' own statements about defining features of ASL and English, (2) linguists' formal definitions, and (3) constraints imposed by the form of the data.

Statements about ASL and manually encoded English taken from field notes and interview records showed that MCE was most often associated with English word order, initialized signs (especially those representing the English copula), invented signs to represent English grammatical affixes, fingerspelling, and mouthing or speaking English words while signing. ASL was most often associated with action, pictures, facial expression, and the absence of the features mentioned above for manually encoded English. The decision was made to identify linguistic features from the manual component of the signing only since the videotaped data did not permit complete retrieval of nonmanual information. In addition, the analysis was begun at the level of the sign rather than the sentence, which controls most of the nonmanual signals (Baker, 1980; Baker-Shenk, 1983; Liddell, 1977, 1980; McIntire, 1980; Wilbur, 1979).

With analysis focused on the manual component of the signing at the level of the individual sign, the decision was made to target those features of MCE mentioned most often by the Deaf and hearing adults in the study and also included as parts of most sign systems for representing English: (1) initialized signs – specifically initialized copula, articles, and initialized pronouns (ASL handles the grammatical functions performed by these linguistic features very differently from manually encoded English); (2) the invented signs for affixes, usually initialized, and added to signs to show verb tense, possession, plural, and word class (these grammatical functions are also performed quite differently in ASL); and (3) fingerspelling, a manual encoding of the individual letters of the English alphabet so that English words can be "spelled in the air."

For ASL features, the decision was made to focus on (1) grammatical processes that are performed on ASL signs, especially verbs; and (2) proforms referred to in the ASL linguistics literature as classifiers and a subset of classifiers known as size and shape specifiers (SASS) (see Kegl and Wilbur, 1976). The grammatical processes have been described by linguists as modulations and inflections (Fischer and Gough, 1978; Klima and Bellugi, 1979; McIntire, 1980). They result in internal modifications of the sign related to orientation and position in space and movement. Classifiers, according to Stokoe, might be viewed as a type of pronoun,

a special class of signs that share some of the functions of collective nouns and indefinite pronouns in English.... ASL like many languages requires special forms to go with antecedents semantically classified; e.g. "something long and thin," "something hollow," "something self-propelled." In ASL these classifiers serve differentially in slots where English allows only *it, he/him,* or *she/her.* (Stokoe, 1980, p. 379).

By focusing on these ASL features, then, we take into account the participants' notions of ASL as action and pictures and the linguists' formal descriptions of certain central grammatical devices and processes in ASL that differ from the devices used to signal the same grammatical functions in MCE. ASL inflections and modulations included as target features were those for (1) manner and degree, (2) location, (3) numerosity, (4) temporal aspect, (5) subject-verb-object agreement, (6) distributional aspect, (7) reciprocity, and (8) reduplication. The proforms known as classifiers, including size and shape specifiers, were also counted as targeted features of ASL.

Results

TEACHER–CHILD INTERACTION

In view of the sociolinguistic research on the adjustments speakers make to a variety of listener characteristics (Ervin-Tripp, 1964; McClure, 1977), the teacher's own communicative skill, and the differing linguistic experiences and skills of the three deaf children, we expected the teacher to adjust her communication behaviors in predictable ways when interacting with each child. For example, to the extent that the teacher could use American Sign Language, we expected to see her using more ASL-like signing with the child of Deaf parents who used ASL in the home. Similarly, during interaction with the child of hearing parents who used simultaneous communication, we predicted that the teacher would use few if any ASL-like structures. With regard to auditory/vocal communication, we anticipated seeing more use of this mode with the hard-of-hearing child than with the two profoundly deaf children.

The communication behaviors we expected did not occur. Instead, the teacher's communication behavior was actually quite similar with all three children in the following ways:

1. As seen in Table 1, she used more signs marked with MCE features than signs marked with ASL features, and voice accompanied the signs most of the time.
2. In order to attract the children's attention, the teacher often used their name signs and simultaneously called their names; sometimes she also waved her hand or touched the children, but she usually attempted to get their attention without any visual or tactile signal, even when their backs were turned.
3. The teacher repeatedly asked all three children to accompany their signs with voice. When the children began to communicate with her by signing without simultaneously vocalizing, she often interrupted the communication by cupping her hand at her ear and breaking eye contact until the children began vocalizing. At other times, she responded to the children's questions or statements by signing or gesturing and saying, "I can't hear you," "let me hear," "tell me," or "I want to hear you, too." Her response to the meaning of their statements or inquiries was delayed until they produced the utterance in the desired form, that is, with voice.
4. She often began signing and talking before the children were looking at her. Frequently, she neither repeated the portion of the communication that the children had missed nor showed any awareness that the children's lack of access to part of the message had disrupted the interaction.

Tables 1 and 2 show that the teacher's communication behavior differed from child to child in the following unexpected ways:

1. She used no targeted ASL features with Mary, the child with whom she claimed to communicate in ASL most often and for whom ASL was the primary language of the home.
2. Although she used similar percentages of targeted MCE features with each child, the teacher used features from a greater number of targeted categories with Mary than she did with the two children who had the most MCE input at home.
3. On the other hand, the teacher used features from more of the different targeted ASL categories with Cathy, the child of hearing parents, than she did with the two children of deaf parents.

These communication behaviors contradicted the teacher's descriptions of her own behavior with each child, which she provided during an interview conducted in the weeks following the videotaping. At that time, the teacher said that she used her voice all the time when she was signing with the children and that her signing was "exact English" 80% of the time and ASL 20% of the time. With Tommy, she said she used

TABLE 1. DISCOURSE FEATURES, TARGETED LINGUISTIC FEATURES, AND SIGNS ACCOMPANIED BY VOICE FOR CHILDREN AND TEACHER

	Total interaction						
	Discourse features				Linguistic features		Signs accompanied by voice (%)
	Duration	Total glosses	Initiations	Turns	MCE	ASL	
Tommy	5:57	64	9	26	15 (23%)	2 (3%)	42
Teacher		122	10	28	21 (17%)	4 (3%)	82
Mary	15:57	135	16	56	8 (6%)	0 (0%)	42
Teacher		351	17	68	54 (15%)	0 (0%)	78
Cathy	15:27	58	1	45	9 (16%)	0 (0%)	66
Teacher		370	24	75	51 (14%)	8 (2%)	79

TABLE 2. TEACHER'S USE OF TARGETED MCE AND ASL FEATURES WITH EACH
CHILD, TOTAL INTERACTION

	With Tommy		With Mary		With Cathy	
	N	%[a]	N	%	N	%
MCE *features*						
Initialized copula	7	33	14	26	13	25
Articles	4	19	12	22	10	20
Initialized pronouns	4	19	11	20	18	35
+S	0	0	1	2	1	2
+'S	0	0	1	2	0	0
+ING	1	5	0	0	3	6
+PAST	0	0	7	13	0	0
+LY	0	0	0	0	0	0
+N	0	0	1	2	0	0
Fingerspelling	5	24	7	13	6	12
Total	21/122	17	54/351	15	51/370	14
ASL *features*						
Manner, degree	0	0	0	0	1	13
Location	0	0	0	0	1	13
Numerical incorp.	0	0	0	0	0	0
Temporal aspect	0	0	0	0	0	0
S-V-O agreement	4	100	0	0	3	38
Distributive	0	0	0	0	0	0
Classifiers	0	0	0	0	2	25
SASS	0	0	0	0	1	13
Negative incorp.	0	0	0	0	0	0
Plural	0	0	0	0	0	0
Reciprocal	0	0	0	0	0	0
Total	4/122	3	0/351	0	8/370	2

[a]Totals within percentage columns do not always equal 100 because of rounding. Percentages based on total number of sign glosses transcribed for the teacher with each child.

"exact English" most of the time with some ASL, although not as much as with Mary. All of these descriptions of her own communicative behavior were contradicted by analysis of the videotapes.

In addition to the quantitative differences just noted, the teacher's interaction with Mary was noticeably different in quality from her interaction with Tommy and Cathy. Not only was there greater mutuality during the interaction between Mary and the teacher, there was also more information exchange than with the other two children. With Cathy and Tommy, the teacher frequently asked questions to elicit labels from the children or she intentionally mislabeled something in an attempt to elicit a correction from the child. This type of behavior did not appear in the videotaped segments analyzed for Mary and the teacher.

The teacher's comments about each child as she viewed the videotapes are important to take into account. Remarks about Mary were primarily positive, whereas comments about Tommy and Cathy pointed out difficulties. For example, when the teacher watched the videotape of her interaction with Mary, the first comment she made was, "When she speaks, she sounds so cute. She has pretty decent speech and she doesn't use it." Later, she added, "I think that she's so cute.... She's a very considerate child. Look at all the stuff she does to help you. Very, very thoughtful kid.... We have a good time together, Mary and I."

Regarding Tommy's behavior, the teacher commented that Tommy rarely used his voice, he "tuned [her] out" or he answered questions with short one- or two-word responses. She said he was not interested in communicating with her so that she had to "pull everything out of him." When viewing the videotape of her interaction with Cathy, she stated that Cathy used her voice "mostly all the time," and that "her language [was] excellent." Regarding Cathy's behavior, she said, "She's always testing.... she just refuses to answer questions. She won't help at all. Even if she knows ... she won't help."

Most of the teacher's remarks while viewing the videotapes were spontaneous comments about her own performance. One of her first remarks indicated her concern about her own signing, "I was really wondering about my signing – if my signing was clear." Later, she interrupted a conversation about Tommy's behavior with the following remark: "My signing is pretty clear here. I thought I had dropped a lot of signs." A few times she interrupted a conversation about another subject to comment on her misunderstanding of Tommy's signing or her own signing mistakes. For example, one time she picked up a toy carrot and said "carrot" but signed ORANGE. When she saw the mistake she had made, she was clearly annoyed with herself. Then she noticed that she misread Tommy's fingerspelling, "I thought he said L-O-W. I saw O-W ... it was D-O-W-N." While viewing Mary's videotape, the teacher made similar comments, exclaiming, "I'm watching myself make mistakes!"

DEAF ADULT–CHILD INTERACTION

The Deaf adult's communicative behaviors with the children showed more of the speaker adjustments to interlocutor that sociolinguistic research predicts. Yet her interaction was similar with all three children in the following ways and indicated that her interactions with these deaf children were governed by norms of Deaf in-group communication:

1. She attempted to get the children's attention by visual or tactile signals. She waved at or touched the children but never used the children's name signs or called their names.
2. Throughout the communicative interaction with each child, she frequently checked to see that she had the child's visual attention and did not begin signing until she was certain the child was looking at her.
3. She never asked the children to use their voices.
4. She responded to the meaning of the children's utterances and never to the form. That is, she never asked the children to repeat an utterance or response except when seeking clarification of the message.
5. At least 90% of the signs she produced with each child were unmarked for targeted linguistic features.

Tables 3 and 4 show that the Deaf adult's communication behavior differed from child to child in the following ways:

1. She used more signs with targeted ASL features during interaction with Mary and Cathy than she did with Tommy. Furthermore, she used five different types of ASL features with Mary and with Cathy, but only one type with Tommy.
2. She used the most signs marked with targeted MCE features during interaction with Tommy, somewhat fewer with Cathy, and the fewest with Mary. These features included initialized pronouns and invented signs for affixes that were used with Tommy and Cathy but not with Mary.
3. She used her voice to accompany more signs when she interacted with Mary and Cathy than with Tommy.

The Deaf adult's comments when she viewed the videotapes of her interaction with each child were in agreement with the quantitative findings. When she reviewed Tommy's tape she stated that she was trying to find some way to relate to him because he was resisting and felt angry that his mother had left him with a stranger. Tommy had only seen her a few times around the school and they had not interacted frequently. The adult explained that she knew that Tommy really understood signs, so she tried to sign clearly and not talk much. When told that Tommy's mother signed and used her voice simultaneously with Tommy, the Deaf woman explained that she did not like to use her voice with a deaf person who couldn't hear her and she assumed Tommy was profoundly deaf. Later, she added that Tommy had not used his voice during their interaction. She continued, "When he really communicated he used signed English. But when he's playing [instead of really concentrating on communicating] he really uses more ASL." When asked what kind of signing Tommy was using during the play segment that was analyzed, she replied,

I was using signed English. This was a conversation. He was using signed English with me. He asked if my boy had toys and he asked me if he could go over to my house.... He was asking me what color is my house. He's us-

TABLE 3. DISCOURSE FEATURES, TARGETED LINGUISTIC FEATURES, AND SIGNS ACCOMPANIED BY VOICE FOR CHILDREN AND DEAF ADULT

	Total interaction						
	Discourse features				Linguistic features		Signs accompanied by voice (%)
	Duration	Total glosses	Initiations	Turns	MCE	ASL	
Tommy	5:40	79	10	23	12 (15%)	2 (3%)	25
Deaf adult		187	8	28	14 (7%)	1 (1%)	1
Mary	13:56	89	18	53	5 (6%)	6 (7%)	21
Deaf adult		303	24	63	7 (2%)	16 (5%)	14
Cathy	13:25	42	2	24	2 (5%)	1 (2%)	95
Deaf adult		185	18	43	7 (4%)	11 (6%)	15

TABLE 4. DEAF ADULT'S USE OF TARGETED MCE AND ASL FEATURES WITH
EACH CHILD, TOTAL INTERACTION

	With Tommy		With Mary		With Cathy	
	N	%	N	%	N	%
MCE features						
Initialized copula	5	36[a]	2	29	4	57
Articles	3	21	3	43	1	14
Initialized pronouns	3	21	0	0	1	14
+S	2	14	0	0	0	0
+'S	0	0	0	0	0	0
+ING	0	0	0	0	0	0
+PAST	0	0	0	0	0	0
+LY	0	0	0	0	0	0
N	0	0	0	0	0	0
Fingerspelling	1	7	2	29	1	14
Total	14/187	7	7/303	2	7/185	4
ASL features						
Manner, degree	0	0	7	44	2	18
Location	0	0	0	0	1	9
Numerical incorp.	0	0	0	0	0	0
Temporal aspect	0	0	0	0	0	0
S-V-O agreement	0	0	2	13	5	45
Distributive	0	0	3	19	1	9
Classifiers	1	100	3	19	0	0
SASS	0	0	0	0	2	18
Negative incorp.	0	0	0	0	0	0
Plural	0	0	0	0	0	0
Reciprocal	0	0	1	6	0	0
Total	1/187	1	16/303	5	11/185	6

[a]Totals within percentage columns do not always equal 100% because of rounding. Percentages based on total number of sign glosses transcribed for the Deaf
adult with each child.

ing signed English. . . . That's ASL – he pretended he was really drawing my
house.

When the Deaf adult was watching Mary's videotape, she stated that
she knew Mary much better than the other two children and that the
interaction was very comfortable. When asked how much hearing she
thought Mary had, she said:

I would say a good guess is about 60 dB. She does have a lot of hearing
because . . . when I decide to drop my hands and talk to her she understands
me when she's watching me. And when she's not looking at me and I call
her, she turns around right away. I'm wondering if I used my voice with her.

When asked about the kind of signing Mary was doing during the play interaction, she responded that she was not really talking in sentences; most of the time she was responding to the adult's questions, "either one- or two-word responses. It's hard for me to say."

The Deaf adult knew Cathy somewhat better than she knew Tommy. She said that during the videotaping she wanted to make sure that she and Cathy enjoyed themselves; she knew "what a temper she has" and did not want to make Cathy angry. She described her own communication as a combination of signed English and ASL – and noted that it was different from the communication used by Cathy's parents, which is "just signed English." Cathy did not use much ASL, according to the Deaf adult. She also stated she did not think Cathy's understanding of signs was as good as Mary's and Tommy's, "maybe more than half but not fully." She admitted that she was confused by Cathy's lack of response on several occasions: "She often just looks at me.... Does she really understand me or is she ignoring me? I know she can understand communication, but I still have my doubts." When Cathy pretended to talk on the telephone and refused to sign, the adult stated, "She's using her voice.... She's copying what she sees her mother and father do on the telephone."

When the deaf adult's use of the initialized copula ARE with Cathy was pointed out to her, she stated, "I use Pidgin Sign." She elaborated on her communication behavior explaining that with one of her own deaf children, the one who had better hearing, she used more signed English, talking and signing simultaneously, and with the other child she used more ASL; "I keep my mouth closed and just sign." When asked why, she stated she did not know; it is just a habit she could not explain when people asked her why she talked different ways. She explained that she noticed the same thing happening with the preschool children she knew at school. With Mary, Cathy, and Tommy she tended to use more signed English, but she used ASL with other children whose parents tended to use ASL because she believed it was the only way for them to understand her.

Discussion

Three factors appeared to exert the most influence on the teacher's communication behavior during these videotaped interactions with the three children – her belief system about deafness and language as shaped by her training as a teacher of deaf children, her relative comfort and enjoyment of the interaction with each child, and her identity and experience as a hearing–speaking person. Teacher-training programs for prospective teachers of deaf children as well as the philosophy of this preschool promote the point of view that the primary problem deafness imposes is an English language deficit. According to this view, the deficit is so great and the obstacles are of such magnitude that every situation, every communicative exchange between teacher and child, should be treated as an opportunity to teach English, often through rote memory and drill, or at least as an opportunity to provide a model of English for the children. Furthermore, a central goal of most educational programs for deaf children is to teach them to behave as much as possible like hearing people, that is, to use intelligible speech. The teacher used targeted MCE features to a similar extent with each child, she frequently and fairly consistently used her voice along with her signs, she required vocalization from the children, asked questions to elicit labels, and intentionally mislabeled objects to elicit corrections from the children – all of these behaviors indicated that she defined her role as English language teacher and that she focused on form and language structure, sometimes at the expense of meaning. Thus, the teacher's communication showed little of the variation that might have been anticipated as a response to individual communication differences among the children.

It has been pointed out that the teacher's interaction with Mary, the hard-of-hearing child of Deaf parents, was noticeably different from her interaction with the other two children. The teacher's own comments provide some insight into the reasons for the qualitative differences. The teacher identified difficulties that she experienced with both Tommy and Cathy, whereas her comments about Mary were positive. According to the teacher, Tommy and Cathy presented her with problems, but Mary was a considerate and thoughtful child with whom she had a lot of fun. Thus, the teacher, according to her own report as well as the videotape record, had to coax both Tommy and Cathy to interact with her. One strategy was asking questions that elicited labels from the children and intentional mislabeling of objects, since Cathy enjoyed taking the role of teacher and correcting her. Control was another issue with both Tommy and Cathy and such a question–answer format allowed the teacher some degree of control with minimal interaction. Mary, on the other hand, did not challenge the teacher's control, nor did she challenge the teacher's sense of success in the same way Tommy and Cathy did. Perhaps a clue to this aspect of the teacher's view of Mary is the statement, "When she speaks she sounds so cute." Mary had a more normal-sounding voice than the other children and frequently her speech could be understood. Tommy used his voice very little; Cathy used her voice much more, but both Tommy and Cathy had unintelligible speech. Although Mary's speech skills were primarily due to her better hearing, every time Mary used her voice and could be understood she probably contributed to the teacher's positive feelings about her own efforts in the classroom. In view of the fact that the teacher received very little positive reinforcement for her efforts to teach speech to the profoundly deaf children in her class, it is likely that her interaction with Mary provided an opportunity for her to feel positive and hopeful about her work. It is not surprising then that the teacher seemed to relax and enjoy her interaction more with Mary than she did with the other children.[3]

It is interesting that the teacher did not respond to the children during the videotaped interactions in the manner that would have been predicted from her statements about them and her descriptions of her own behavior. Recall that she used the lowest percentage of targeted MCE features with Cathy, the child she evaluated as having the best English and no ASL skills, and she used no targeted ASL features with Mary, the child with whom she claimed to communicate in ASL most often and for whom ASL was the primary language at home. A number of interactional factors probably operated to produce the patterns that emerged. Throughout the videotapes, the teacher began communicative interactions using simultaneous communication (MCE + voice). When the children failed to respond to her communication or did not respond in the desired way, the teacher used more targeted ASL features and fewer simultaneous communication features in her subsequent efforts to communicate. This strategy was successful and it was one that she used in the classroom according to her own report and classroom observations. Through such behavior, deafness (translated as the inability to hear and talk), communication difficulty, and lack of English skills were linked in one conceptual domain, represented symbolically by ASL. Similarly, speech, hearing, ease of interaction, and English skills were linked within another conceptual domain, represented symbolically by MCE usually in the form of simultaneous communication. Thus, when Cathy and Tommy did not cooperate with the teacher during the videotaped interaction and there was an apparent communication difficulty, they were probably viewed as more deaflike and responded to on the basis of Deaf social identity. That is, they needed ASL, or at least less MCE-like signing. Mary, on the other hand, cooperated with the teacher, used her voice, and responded to some auditory stimuli. The combined effect of the relative ease of the interaction, Mary's more normal sounding voice and intelligible speech, and her ability to respond to some sounds, caused the teacher to move toward simultaneous communication and

---

3 Support for this interpretation appears in interview records and field notes of conversations with deaf adults recounting their experiences in school. Profoundly deaf adults recalled their feelings of resentment when their hearing teachers would praise the hard-of-hearing students for their success, especially in speech skills, and criticize the other students for not working hard enough. The hard-of-hearing students were frequently held up as bright, hard-working, and successful, according to these accounts, whereas the profoundly deaf students were made to feel incompetent and less intelligent.

away from ASL, and to respond to Mary on the basis of a more hear-inglike social identity.

It appears, then, that the use of voice by the children and by the teacher had a significant influence on the teacher's perception of the interaction and her communication behavior with the children as com-pared with other features of the interaction. In part, this was a result of the teacher's professional training as well as her own identity as a hearing–speaking person. Interaction with a preschool deaf child who uses very little vocalization to communicate unless reminded, or whose speech is unintelligible, is a continual reminder to the teacher that she is not succeeding in her efforts to make the child "normal." She has been taught that only through continual exposure to speech and a correct model of English (that is, MCE) will the children acquire speech and English skills. However, to continue to use simultaneous communication when it is not facilitating meaningful interaction must be quite difficult. Certainly, when children attempt to communicate in any way they can, it is compelling to follow their lead and disregard form in the interest of meaning. Perhaps one strategy the hearing teacher used to meet the demands of the school, the hearing parents, and her own professional beliefs was to construct her interaction more like a performance than a finely-tuned communicative interaction. If the teacher was using such a strategy, it would help to explain why certain aspects of her commu-nication appeared to be so similar with each child and why she did seemingly irrational things such as call the names of profoundly deaf children when their backs were turned.

The Deaf adult, on the other hand, interacted with the children on the basis of their shared Deaf social identity, that is, on the basis of her own experience as a Deaf person and her view of the children as members of the same sociocultural group. The result was a visual rather than auditory orientation to interaction. Her comments coupled with the results of the quantitative analysis support the conclusion that the Deaf adult varied her communicative behavior with each child as a result of her perception of individual differences in communication skills and preferences among the children. For example, it appears that the pro-duction of 15% of her signs with voice while interacting with Cathy and 1% of her signs with voice while interacting with Tommy was a result of her differing perceptions of these children. She saw Tommy as a profoundly deaf child who never used his voice alone. Cathy, although she too was profoundly deaf, insisted on using her voice alone at times during the interaction, and the Deaf adult was aware of that behavior. The Deaf woman's use of voice with Mary 14% of the time is probably a result of her knowledge of Mary's hearing status, her past commu-nication experience with Mary, and her own ability to hear Mary's voice. Interestingly, there was a decrease of voice with signs, from 25% in food sharing to 6% in play for the Deaf adult interacting with Mary. This decrease was probably a result both of the increase in Mary's targeted ASL features during play (from 0% in food sharing to 12% in play) and of Mary's decreased use of voice in play (from 30% in food sharing to 15% in play). Familiarity of interactants with each other also seems to have influenced the interaction. The Deaf adult was well acquainted with Mary and her family. She therefore came to the interaction with prior knowledge of Mary's communicative skills. There was no awkwardness or resistance for either of them to overcome and not much uncertainty on the part of the woman as to the language Mary would understand. The Deaf woman had less experience with the other two children and was more uncertain as to their communication abilities. These children were also more resistant to her attempts to interact with them.

Conclusion

When considering the communication behavior of the two adults in this study it is important to note that the teacher and the Deaf adult probably had different perspectives on the meaning of their participation in the videotaped session. The school had told the teacher what she should be doing with the children in order to ensure the development of linguistic skills; thus, her own behavior on the videotapes as well as the children's might be perceived by her as reflecting upon the quality of her performance as a teacher. The Deaf adult, however, did not have duties to fulfill with respect to such a status; it is likely that her behavior with the children was a close approximation of the behavior of Deaf adults with deaf children outside of the school setting.

One theme that emerges from the interview data from the Deaf adults in this study is the difficulty that hearing people have in shifting from an auditory to a visual orientation when interacting with deaf children. It first appeared when the Deaf parents repeatedly expressed concern about the receptive sign language skills of the hearing teachers. Although the parents encouraged their children to use the most elaborated language they could, the fact that the teachers often could not understand the signing of the preschoolers encouraged the children to use any means possible to communicate. As a result, the children pointed and gestured to make themselves understood and eventually lost interest in communicating with the teacher except to meet the necessary requirements of life in the classroom. Other comments from the Deaf parents suggested that the problem was not simply one of receptive sign language skill. Rather it was one of visual connection with the deaf child. The hearing teacher was criticized by one set of Deaf parents for the way she managed a story-telling interaction. In these parents' view, she did not take into account the deaf child's need to look first at the picture in the book and then at the teacher to receive her communication about that picture. Instead, the hearing teacher began to sign before the child looked at her, as if he could, like a hearing child, process language information and visual information from the picture simultaneously.

The differences between the hearing teacher and the Deaf adult during videotaped interaction with the deaf children illustrate the contrast between a hearing, auditory orientation during interaction with deaf children, and a Deaf visual one. These two adults attempted to attract the children's attention in strikingly different ways. The teacher used her voice and the children's name signs whether or not the children were visually attending to her. These were strategies that could not only have been successful if the child was looking directly at her or if the child could have seen the movement of her hands by using peripheral vision. Even though Mary was the only child who had enough residual hearing to respond to the vocal call, the teacher used this strategy with all three children. The Deaf adult never sought the children's attention in any way other than by means of visual or tactile strategies. Unlike the hearing teacher, the Deaf adult frequently checked to see that the children were paying attention to her when she began to communicate and, if they were not, she either repeated what they had missed or waited to begin until there was eye contact. The hearing teacher, however, frequently began signing before the children were looking at her and often did not repeat or show any awareness that they might have missed some of the communication. In several cases, this behavior on the part of the teacher appeared to be the cause of misunderstanding between herself and the children.

Another essential difference between the communicative interaction of the hearing teacher and the Deaf adult is illustrated in an example of miscommunication between the teacher and Tommy. During one segment of the videotape, the teacher and Tommy were engaged in a conversation but about different topics. The teacher did not show any awareness of the problem, interpreting Tommy's communication about playing with toys as if it were about her topic, preparing for a story. It is difficult to know how much of the problem resulted from the teacher's lack of visual contact with Tommy and how much resulted from her difficulties understanding the small and rapid signs of the preschool child. The Deaf adult, however, did not have this problem with any of the children. If a misunderstanding occurred, she usually demonstrated her awareness of it by taking steps to repair the conversation. It is not likely that a conversation consisting of several exchanges with the child on one topic and the adult on another could have occurred without the Deaf adult realizing it and taking steps to repair the conversation.

The hearing teacher interacted with the children on the basis of her status as a hearing person and on the basis of her status as a teacher of deaf children. The Deaf adult, however, interacted with the children on the basis of her status as a Deaf person. She was neither parent nor teacher to the children, but rather a person with a shared social identity. Prescriptions and policies guided the behavior of the hearing teacher to a large extent, whereas her own experience as a Deaf person and as a parent of deaf children guided the behavior of the Deaf adult. The result was that the teacher interacted in much the same way with each child whereas the Deaf adult did not; rather, she adjusted her communication style to the perceived needs and abilities of the children as well as to the interactional demands presented by the particular situations.

The difference in the children's response to the teacher and the Deaf adult as interactional partners is perhaps best illustrated by Tommy. During most of the interaction with both the teacher and the Deaf adult, Tommy did not communicate readily nor at length. He responded minimally to the teacher's questions and made short, simple requests or statements to her; in the case of the Deaf adult, he was obviously resistant and uncommunicative. This behavior was in contrast to Tommy's behavior with his parents, both at home and on videotape. Whereas there was no significant change in Tommy's behavior with the teacher throughout the videotaped interaction, there was a dramatic change in his communicative behavior with the Deaf adult during the final five minutes of the interaction. Tommy's parents explained the change in terms of Tommy's growing awareness of and respect for the Deaf woman's receptive sign language skills. Tommy had been testing and discovering the interactional competencies of this woman during the first 25 minutes of the interaction; then he began to sign with her as if he expected her to be able to understand him and she did. In the case of the teacher, however, Tommy knew from previous experience in the classroom that she did not understand his signing beyond a certain level. During the videotaped interaction, his previous conclusions about her communicative skills were probably confirmed by episodes such as the one recounted above, when the teacher misinterpreted Tommy's comments about playing with the toys, responding to him as if he were suggesting a place to sit for the story, which was her topic. Furthermore, the teacher's interactional strategies seemed geared to the elicitation of labels and speech rather than conversations about meaningful topics. It is likely that these behaviors reflected her ideas about her responsibilities as a teacher of deaf children. The Deaf adult, on the other hand, did not have a goal other than successful, happy interaction with the child. In fact, rather than asking the children to adjust their communication to her expectations, she adjusted hers to each child's abilities and preferences. This particular skill was one that seemed to be shared by most of the Deaf parents at the preschool. Because such highly educated Deaf persons interact all of their lives with a variety of people, hearing and deaf, with a range of linguistic and interactional abilities, it is likely that they acquire an understanding of the requirements of communication situations and develop strategies for achieving successful interaction. The sensitivity and communicative skill of the Deaf adult coupled with the basic visual orientation shared and understood by the two of them was probably perceived by Tommy, encouraging him to take the risk and sign with her in a much more elaborated style than he used with the hearing teacher.

Implications

Deaf children need the same basic things any child does – love and acceptance, communication with others, the opportunity to explore and discover. Before these needs can be met, however, adjustments need to be made in the environment. Care must be taken that these adjustments do not become the focus of the interaction with the child but that they remain tools to help accomplish the essential tasks of childhood. When the teacher in this study became concerned about the form of the children's expressions, especially about whether they were using their voices, she overlooked the content of the children's statements. Not only did she miss the opportunity to interact with them about subjects that were important to them, but she also repeatedly gave them the message that they were behaving unacceptably. This teacher's behavior was not unusual. Very often, even in preschool classrooms, teachers place a great deal of emphasis on proper form, most often focussing on the grammaticality of manually encoded English sentences. The recommendation being made here is not to disregard linguistic skills but to shift the focus from skills in a particular language to the range of skills required to be a good communicator. Deaf children can begin acquiring these more general and immediately useful interactional skills from infancy if they are provided with skilled communicators as interactional partners. Later, when it is more appropriate from a cognitive and developmental point of view, they should receive direct instruction in linguistic skills.

One way in which schools might provide an environment of skilled communicators for deaf children is to use a team-teaching approach with one Deaf teacher and one hearing teacher in each classroom. Not only would such an arrangement provide the deaf children with native speakers, skilled signers, and positive role models, it would also demonstrate productive cooperation between hearing and deaf people who respect each other and each other's competencies. In addition, it would provide the teachers themselves with an ongoing opportunity to learn about each other's language and culture.

Hearing teachers need to be taught to be better visual communicators, beginning at the fundamental level of visual awareness and sensitivity. Miscommunication occurred several times during the videotaped interaction of the teacher and the children because the teacher broke eye contact at a critical moment or because she did not see small manual or nonmanual behaviors such as eye gaze shifts and one-handed signing. Currently, teacher training programs provide prospective teachers with very little help in this area. Training programs also need to provide prospective teachers with more course work in linguistic and sociocultural aspects of deafness and schooling as well as more direct experience with Deaf adults, especially Deaf parents of deaf children. Instead of placing so much emphasis on the auditory sense deaf children do not have, training programs should place more emphasis on vision and on understanding the fundamental difference between an auditory and a visual orientation in perceiving and structuring the life experience. At the same time, every effort should be made to recruit more Deaf students interested in becoming teachers, in particular, preschool teachers.

Schools as policy-making institutions can do their part to facilitate some of these recommendations. First, they can begin by recruiting and hiring more Deaf teachers and administrators. Second, they can reassess the foundations upon which their current programs are built. Schools for deaf children tend to adopt policies concerning the education of deaf children that are detailed prescriptions for treatment in areas where knowledge is inadequate and insufficient. The result is often a dramatic swing of the pendulum every few years to new policies, equally detailed in their prescriptions and equally inadequate. Perhaps if school administrators were to officially recognize the lack of knowledge about many aspects of deafness, language, and cognition, for example, teachers would be able to admit their difficulties and successes more freely and make some progress toward understanding and asking unanswered questions. When teachers must constantly strive to meet an unattainable goal, and policies and goals have been formulated without sufficient knowledge about their feasibility or desirability, tremendous amounts of energy are spent unproductively, even destructively. Schools, through their policies and resource allocation, should shift some of the focus away from the implementation of policy based on little or no research toward research efforts involving Deaf and hearing school personnel, Deaf and hearing parents, and deaf children. It is only through such efforts that more effective policies can be designed.

References

Anthony, D. (1971). *Seeing Essential English*. Vols. 1, 2. Anaheim, Calif.: Educational Services Division, Anaheim Union School District.

218   *Carol J. Erting*

Baker, C. (1980). Sentences in American Sign Language. In C. Baker and R. Battison (Eds.), *Sign Language and the Deaf Community*. Silver Spring, Md.: National Association of the Deaf.

Baker-Shenk, C. (1983). A microanalysis of the nonmanual components of Questions in American Sign Language. Unpublished doctoral dissertation. Berkeley: University of California.

Baker, C., and D. Cokely. (1980). *American Sign Language: A Teacher's Resource Text on Grammar and Culture*. Silver Spring, Md.: National Association of the Deaf.

Berger, P., and T. Luckmann. (1966). *The Social Construction of Reality: A Treatise in the Sociology of Knowledge*. Middlesex, England: Penguin Books.

Bornstein, H. (1975). *The Signed English Dictionary for Preschool and Elementary Levels*. Washington, D.C.: Gallaudet College Press.

Corbett, E., and C. Jensema. (1981). *Teachers of the Hearing Impaired: Descriptive Profiles*. Washington, D.C.: Gallaudet College Press.

Erting, C. (1978). Language policy and deaf ethnicity in the United States. *Sign Language Studies, 19*, 139–152.

   (1980). Sign language and communication between adults and children. In C. Baker and R. Battison (Eds.), *Sign Language and the Deaf Community*. Silver Spring, Md.: National Association of the Deaf.

   (1982). Deafness, communication, and social identity: An anthropological analysis of interaction among parents, teachers, and deaf children in a preschool. Unpublished doctoral dissertation, Anthropology Department, Washington, D.C.: The American University.

   (1985). Linguistic variation in a school for deaf children. In W. Stokoe and V. Volterra (Eds.), *Proceedings of the Third International Symposium on Sign Language Research*. Rome: Consiglio Nazionale delle Ricerche.

Ervin-Tripp, S. (1964). An analysis of the interaction of language, topic, and listener. In J. Gumperz and D. Hymes (Eds.), *The Ethnography of Communication, American Anthropologist 66*, 86–102.

Fischer, S., and B. Gough. (1978). Verbs in American Sign Language. *Sign Language Studies 18*, 17–48.

Glaser, B., and A. Strauss. (1967). *The Discovery of Grounded Theory: Strategies for Qualitative Research*. Chicago: Aldine.

Gustason, G., D. Pfefzing, and E. Zawolkow. (1972). *Signing Exact English*. Rossmoor, Calif.: Modern Signs Press.

Johnson, R., and C. Erting. (1984). Linguistic socialization in the context of emergent deaf ethnicity. Wenner-Gren Foundation Working Papers in Anthropology. New York.

Jordan, I. K., and M. A. Karchmer. (1986). Patterns of sign use among hearing impaired students. In A. N. Schildroth and M. A. Karchmer (Eds.), *Deaf Children in America*. San Diego, Calif.: College-Hill Press.

Kannapell, B. (1974). Bilingualism: A new direction in the education of the Deaf. *The Deaf American*, June, 9–15.

Kegl, J., and R. Wilbur. (1976). When does structure stop and style begin? Syntax, morphology, and phonology vs. stylistic variation in American Sign Language. In *Papers from the Twelfth Regional Meeting of the Chicago Linguistic Society*. Chicago: University of Chicago Press.

Klima, E., and U. Bellugi. (1979). *The Signs of Language.* Cambridge, Mass.: Harvard University Press.

Lidell, S. (1977). An investigation into the syntactic structure of American Sign Language. Unpublished doctoral dissertation. San Diego: University of California.

(1980). *American Sign Language Syntax.* The Hague: Mouton.

Luetke-Stahlman, B. (1983). Using bilingual instructional models in teaching hearing-impaired students. *American Annals of the Deaf 128,* 873–877.

McClure, E. (1977). Aspects of code-switching in the discourse of bilingual Mexican-American children. In M. Saville-Troike (Ed.), *Linguistics and Anthropology.* Washington, D.C.: Georgetown University Press.

McIntire, M. (1980). Locatives in American Sign Language. Unpublished doctoral dissertation, Linguistics Department. Los Angeles: University of California.

Meadow, K. (1980). *Deafness and Child Development.* Berkeley: University of California Press.

Mindel, E., and M. Vernon. (1971). *They Grow in Silence.* Silver Spring, Md.: National Association of the Deaf.

Moores, D. (1982). *Educating the Deaf.* Boston: Houghton Mifflin.

Stokoe, W. (1980). Sign language structure. *Annual Review of Anthropology 9,* 365–390.

Washabaugh, W. (1981). Sign language and its social context. *Annual Review of Anthropology 10,* 237–252.

Wilbur, R. (1979). *American Sign Language and Sign Systems.* Baltimore, Md.: University Park Press.

Woodward, J. (1972). Implications for sociolinguistic research among the deaf. *Sign Language Studies 1,* 1–7.

(1973). Some observations on sociolinguistic variation and American Sign Language. *Kansas Journal of Sociology 9,* 191–199.

10 Development of vocal and signed communication in deaf and hearing twins of deaf parents

Martha Gonter Gaustad

Editor's introduction

Gaustad's research focuses on the special case of a pair of twins of deaf parents, one of whom is hearing, the other deaf. This is a particularly interesting scenario, with considerable theoretical importance, since the study of fraternal deaf–hearing twins provides a natural laboratory in which to consider questions of the role of modality versus handicap in the acquisition of language. Gaustad was interested in the effects of hearing status on the pragmatic effects of communication, communication mode, and language functions. She studied the twins as they interacted with each other and with deaf and hearing adults. Gaustad found that the hearing twin received more input than the deaf twin, that the parents code-switched to accommodate to the hearing status of the children, and that hearing status did not seem to affect the children's functional use of language. Furthermore, the children's output modality matched that of the parents quite consistently. This sensitivity to mode and hearing status of the interlocutor observed in both children and adults provides further evidence of the importance of deaf teachers in schools, both as sources of input and as role models for the children.

By adulthood, most deaf persons have attained some skills in both English and American Sign Language (ASL). Although English is required for literacy in a hearing society, sign language is the social and cultural bond within the Deaf community. Given these facts, a few professionals have advocated a bilingual approach to education of the deaf (Cokely, 1979; Quigley and Paul, 1984; Stokoe, 1976). Yet standard English and ASL represent not only two distinct languages but two separate modes of communication: aural/oral and visual/manual. The reluctance of educators to consider a bilingual approach centers on the diagnostic and language delay suffered by most deaf children. Bilingual instruction in what amounts to two nonnative languages might only further interrupt the process of language acquisition (especially English).

220

Complicating the concern about language choice in education is the body of evidence demonstrating the benefits for a deaf child of having deaf parents. Opportunity for early exposure to language (sign) does not completely explain the superiority of such children across a broad range of educational, psychological, social, personal, and career variables. Perhaps it is what deaf parents do when they interact that may hold the key to these children's success (Bodner-Johnson, 1982; Meadow et al., 1981).

Current practice in education of the deaf relies heavily on classroom use, primarily by hearing teachers, of systems of manually coded English (MCE): sign codes for representing semantic and syntactic features of spoken English. The philosophical emphasis is on total communication, the integration of MCE systems with traditional oral methods (such as speech and lipreading). Notions of communication, as opposed to language, and of the deaf learner as interactor are predominant. Studies of normally-hearing children have highlighted both the role of interaction as a medium for language acquisition (Moerk, 1977; Ochs and Schieffelin, 1979) and the complex manner in which features of the communication context affect the nature and product of that interaction (Moerk, 1977; Snow and Ferguson, 1977). Communicative intent, style, and linguistic structure are manipulated by children, as well as adults, to suit requirements of situation and listener (Berko-Gleason, 1973; Cross, 1977; and Lieven, 1978). In their world, deaf youngsters must learn from a kaleidoscope of discourse with both deaf and hearing interactors, through both manual and vocal modalities and, for those with deaf parents, in two dissimilar languages. The common factor in this varied communication is the social and personal impetus to communicate: "The child communicates before he has language. He does so in order to carry out certain functions that are vital to the species. These primitive communication acts are effected by gesture, vocalization, and the exploitation of context" (Bruner, 1978, p. 65).

To date, most research that is pertinent to signed instructional methodology has been conducted with school-age children. Usually such examinations have been restricted either to English or sign, to deaf or hearing environments, and results have been confounded by the interaction of language and environment (deaf:sign/hearing:English). Furthermore, language analyses have focused principally on semantic and syntactic aspects and development. Results of ASL studies have revealed parallels to the development of spoken language (Klima and Bellugi, 1979; McIntire, 1977; Skarakis and Prutting, 1977). Studies of MCE have noted increases in the English competencies of deaf students (Brasel and Quigley, 1977; Weiss et al. 1975). However, MCE effectiveness appears also to be related to age at intervention (Gonter, 1983; Raffin, Davis, and Gilman, 1978) and to levels of parental skill and usage, which are frequently not high owing to the foreign nature of the signed medium (Crandall, 1978). Unfortunately, there is little information on which to base specific classroom intervention policies or parent training techniques, especially in regard to the deaf child under the age of 4. Only very recently have pragmatic features become the subject of sign research (Curtiss, Prutting, and Lowell, 1979; Maestas y Moores, 1980; Meadow et al., 1981; Miller, 1982; Van Metre and Maxwell, 1981). More information is needed to describe the deaf child as interactor relative to varying characteristics of the communication process and environment. Only when the development of communicative competencies, style, and flexibility is outlined can realistic goals and procedures for home or school intervention be formulated.

The present study concerns the development of communication skills in a set of twins, a deaf male and a hearing female,[1] from the age of 16 to 24 months. The twins have hearing-impaired parents and an older deaf sibling. The unusual subject family and the structure of the study environment have provided unique opportunities to follow the concurrent development of speech and sign communication. Deaf family members and close deaf adult friends, almost exclusively within the Deaf community, provided signed models and interactions. Ongoing contacts with hearing relatives and the hearing researchers provided models of and interactions in vocal and manual English. Differences in environmental and child-rearing variables, which have confounded most comparisons of language systems between deaf and hearing subjects, have been minimized. The research questions for this study stem primarily from characteristics of the subjects themselves and the pragmatics of their interaction, rather than from theory.

Method

Subjects

This case study involves a five-member family within the deaf subculture of a metropolitan area in Ohio. Father, in his late 30s, is a blue-collar laborer. He lost his hearing at about age four as a result of illness. Although he has a severe loss, his early exposure to language and good speechreading ability enable him to function somewhat more easily with hearing nonsigners than his wife does. He attended programs for the hearing-impaired in a public school system and graduated from high school at the age of 20. In communicating, he varies his language from

1 Although it was later determined that this subject has a hearing impairment, lack of severity should permit regular educational placement and functioning as a hearing individual, especially by comparison with her profoundly deaf twin.

American Sign Language to spoken English, depending on his interactor. His use of voice is frequent and reasonably understandable to persons accustomed to deaf speech. He does not use a hearing aid.

Mother, in her early 30s, was adopted as an infant after her father died. The cause of her profound deafness is undetermined, although it is presumed she was deaf at birth. Her natural and adoptive parents and three natural siblings all had normal hearing. At first, she attended a public day school program for the hearing impaired that emphasized oral language skills. She reports that she was unsuccessful in using speech and speechreading to communicate. From the age of nine until graduation, she attended a residential school for the deaf where she learned to sign. American Sign Language is her preferred form of communication. She relies on an interpreter or writing for communicating with nonsigners. Her use of voice is infrequent and her speech is not intelligible. Mother works occasionally as a typist.

Ann, seven years older than the twins and profoundly deaf since birth, is the mother's child by a previous marriage. Her natural father is also deaf. Although exposed to sign language from infancy, mother reports that Ann did not use signs until the age of four, when she began school. She was first fitted for a hearing aid also at that time. Ann previously attended both state and private institutions for the deaf as a resident student but currently is living with the family and is enrolled in public day classes. In general, her role in this research has been very limited.

The primary subjects of study are dizygotic twins, Terri (female) and Timmy (male), whose communication skills were followed from the age of 16 to 24 months. Timmy is profoundly deaf (100 + dB in the speech frequencies, both ears). Although mother attributes his hearing loss to illness and high fever at the age of 2 months, the immediate family history provides evidence of a genetic origin. He was tested and fitted for a hearing aid before the study began, but use was reportedly postponed owing to recurrent ear infections. (He is currently in a signing class.)

At the time Timmy was diagnosed, Terri was thought to have normal hearing and so was not tested. Speech was delayed, but this was attributed to the lack of stimulation for speech at home. It was obvious during the early tapings that she responded to speech as well as other vocal and nonvocal auditory stimuli (e.g., whistling and musical toys). When she was 3 1/2 a moderate hearing impairment (50 dB in the speech frequencies, both ears) was diagnosed, although by that time spoken language was developing. Terri was fitted with a hearing aid, not worn at home, and with it she functions normally. (She is currently in an oral class.)

The twins were born one to two weeks prematurely, Timmy first (7 lb. 8 oz., 20½ inches) and Terri (6 lb. 6 oz., 19½ inches) minutes later.

He was the larger of the twins at birth and years later exceeds her still in both height and weight. Mother reports that motor development proceeded normally; Timmy walked first at 10½ months, a couple of weeks before Terri, and both demonstrate right-hand dominance. From the beginning, both children appeared to possess normal intellectual ability and mother reports that they learned at about the same rate.[2] Socially, Timmy is initially friendlier with strangers than Terri, but overall spends less time interacting with adults and more time in solitary play than she does. Neither child gives evidence of any additional handicap.

Research questions

This study includes nearly all of the types of adult–child combinations used in communication research pertaining to deafness:

2 At intervals during the study, standardized measures of the twins' intellectual, social, and motor development were obtained for purposes of better evaluating differences in language or communication behavior. The Minnesota Child Development Inventory (MCDI) was used to examine the children's social-adaptive development. The inventory yields scale scores in the skill areas of general development, gross motor, fine motor, expressive language (sign), comprehension conceptual, situation comprehension, self-help, and personal/social. Scores were obtained on six occasions (chronological age 22, 27, 34, 39, and 59 months). The children's parents served as informants for the inventory. They reported their responses to the items to a sign language interpreter, who recorded them on the answer sheet. This inventory is believed to be a valuable descriptor of the children's social-adaptive skills. It is not being used as an indicator of normal social development because of its lack of extensive deaf norms.

The children's intellectual abilities were also examined on several occasions during their first 60 months of life. The twins' ages at each testing were the same as for the administrations of the MCDI. Because testing started with infancy, several intelligence scales have been used with the children, including the Bayley Scales of Infant Development, the Cattel Infant Intelligence Scale, the Stanford-Binet Intelligence Scale, the Wechsler Preschool and Primary Scale of Intelligence, and the Leiter International Performance Scale. Tests were administered by trained clinical psychologists with the assistance of a sign language interpreter. At each testing age no more than two intelligence scales were administered to the children.

Collectively, these psychological measurements have shown the twins to possess similar general intellectual ability, the latest tests indicating that both are above average. Expected discrepancies between performance on verbal versus nonverbal measures (lower verbal) are attributed to effects of hearing loss. More specifically, the testing series showed that (1) in the area of fine motor development, Terri outperformed Timmy and both surpassed age (hearing) norms from the earliest to the latest measurement (this advantage is attributed to signing behavior); (2) in the areas of gross motor development, self-help skills, and situation comprehension, Timmy initially outperformed Terri, and both surpassed age norms (at the latest testing they were at similar levels, which were slightly below age norms); (3) in the areas of personal/social development and language (expression and comprehension) the twins have consistently performed at about the same levels, but those levels have been below age (hearing) norms from the beginning.

a. deaf parent–deaf child
b. deaf parent–child with hearing
c. parent with hearing–deaf child
d. parent with hearing–child with hearing
e. hearing (signing) adults–deaf child
f. hearing adults–child with hearing

The general purpose of the study was to probe the effects of hearing status on pragmatic aspects of the interactors' communications. More specifically, the following questions regarding communication modality and communication function were examined.

1. Do interlocutors vary in the use of communication modes according to the child's hearing status and does this pattern change with time? On the basis of research that showed accommodation of adults to hearing children, it was hypothesized that the child's status (hearing) would be the major controlling factor in mode use; that proportionately more vocal input would be provided to the hearing female and more manual input to the deaf male. This relationship was expected to be fairly stable over time.

2. Does mode of communication used by the children differ according to their own or interlocutors' hearing status and does this pattern change with time? It was hypothesized that initially expression of mode by the children would depend heavily on their own constraints (his hearing loss, her lack of vocal experience) and be primarily manual. It was anticipated that each would develop responses to interlocutor status with time, but that the hearing twin would be able to adjust sooner.

3. Do interlocutors vary in the use of communication mode according to their own hearing status? Research on the accomodation of many types and ages of interlocutors to the communication needs of young children leads to the hypothesis that interlocutor hearing status would not be an important factor.

4. Do the children's communications exhibit differences in pragmatic function according to hearing status, and does this relationship change over time? Similarities between deaf and hearing children in the development of pragmatic functions have been documented (Carmichael and Greenberg, 1980; Meadow et al., 1981). However, it was hypothesized that the availability of two input modalities and the consequent likelihood of greater and more varied input might lead to more diversity in function sooner for the hearing than the deaf twin.

Data collection

Videotaped recordings of the twins were made at least once a month, usually for one hour, from the ages of 16 to 24 months. These taped samples included occasional interaction with deaf neighbors and friends as well as regular interaction with family members and the hearing researchers. Most interactors used gesture and sign to some degree. Use of voice varied greatly. Activities were typical for children of preschool age and included manipulative and social play, book sharing, snacks, holiday activities, and, infrequently, personal hygiene. Emphasis was placed on natural communication and the language used in these situations. The camera was placed at an advantageous location and usually left stationary and running continuously. Once the routine was familiar, these practices had the effect of lessening the intrusiveness of the equipment.

The study was conducted by a certified teacher of the deaf, who is a fluent user of manual English, and a graduate assistant, who is a hearing native signer of ASL and also certified to teach the deaf. Since it is in the nature of children to interact with anyone present, this shared fluency in sign gave the researcher and assistant the flexibility to alternate interacting and recording roles.[3]

Some stimulus items were brought to taping sessions to supplement materials already available in the home. These provided some content continuity across time and allowed for interaction about novel, as well as familiar, objects and activities. These outside materials usually were preschool toys, educational kits, books, manipulative and art materials, selected sound-producing items and, occasionally, testing materials.

Data coding and analysis

Videotapes were transcribed to include contextual, nonverbal, vocal, and sign content and to provide description or interpretation where necessary. In addition to this content, the English gloss had to accommodate the unique capability for simultaneity in three-dimensional manual communication, its incidence, and gross timing. Two types of simultaneity were coded: first, the co-occurrence of separate productions in one or more modalities by a single communicator (i.e., a word with a different sign, or different signs with each hand) and, second, the co-occurrence of separate utterances by two or more interactors.

The transcription system (see Appendix A) specified the initiator and addressee of each utterance, the presence or absence of eye contact at the beginning of an utterance, the manual and/or vocal portions, pauses

---

3 The phenomenon of "observer paradox" is a recognized difficulty of this study; that is, some results may have been different had the hearing interactors been persons other than the researchers. However, regular interaction with other hearing people was not a feature of the twins' natural environment until they began school at the age of 43 months. Differences between the twins' interactions with hearing persons at school versus deaf parents at home will be one focus of analysis of later videotape samples taken during alternate months at school and at home.

within an utterance as well as pauses while another signs, individual and interactive simultaneity, reduplication of elements, questioning intonation, utterance termination, and a few specific notations not required for all utterances. Some elements of this transcription system were adapted from a system used at the Salk Institute and reported by Reilly and McIntire (1980). Additional notational devices were developed by the researcher during past work with videotaped manual language samples.

Two analyses of the transcripts were performed: the first for communication mode and the second for pragmatic function. Appendix B presents one coded page from an actual transcript that was selected for the range of modalities and functions it contains.

Examination of communication mode included both receptive and expressive aspects with regard to each twin. Each communication to the children (receptive) and by the children (expressive) was classified as one of four types: (a) gestural (GES): nonverbal, which included headshakes and attention-getting devices; (b) voice-only (VO): words or interpretable approximations; (c) sign-only (SO): signs or interpretable approximations, pointing, and so on; and (d) combined vocal and manual (VM): speech (approximation) accompanying sign (approximation). Consider the following example from an actual transcript:

"CAN YOU find the" FOOD?/

The elements "CAN, YOU" were each spoken and signed simultaneously, "find, the" were spoken only, and FOOD was signed only. This communication, with both vocal and manual elements would have been classified as combined modalities (VM). Since the categories represent discrete phenomena, no difficulties were encountered with reliability (95%–100%) and no uncodable instances were noted. Frequencies were tallied by category and interactor for each month.

Owing to the young age of the twins and the unpredictability of natural situations, low frequencies and zeros occurred for some interactors, categories, and months. For further analysis, data were collapsed in two ways. The nine months of study were divided into thirds, 16–18, 19–21, and 22–24 months. Communications with nonregular interactors (neighbors, psychologist, and so on) were eliminated, as were communications in which the addressee could not be specified. Also, since Terri and Timmy produced a very small number of utterances to one another, those were examined separately.

For the pragmatic function analysis, each twin communication was coded by combining elements from Day (1982) and Greenberg and Carmichael (1980). Eight categories, some with subcategories, were defined (see Appendix C): performative, request, behavioral response, verbal response, description, statement, conversational device, and miscellaneous (unclassifiable). In the case of verbal responses to questions, double coding was used, one to identify the type of question (e.g., wh- or yes/no) and the second to characterize the nature of the response itself (e.g., location). Consider the following exchange from an actual transcript:

adult: "want another one?"/
twin: THIS (index balloon in bag)/

The twin response would have been coded YNR/REF to indicate the yes—no nature of the question as well as the referent nature of the verbal response. Other examples of coding can be found in the transcript sample, Appendix B. Intra-rater reliability was calculated for the single coder. After a period of more than six months from the time of the first coding, the reliability was 85% calculated over a randomly selected sample of four transcripts: number of agreements divided by the number of agreements plus disagreements in codings (Greenberg, 1980). Again, owing to low and zero frequencies for some categories, the data were collapsed by dividing the study period into the same three time segments: 16–18, 19–21, and 22–24 months.

Results

The twins' communications to their hearing-impaired parents and the hearing researchers were analyzed to determine possible communicative differences between the two children, which were hypothesized to result from the important difference in their hearing status. Modality findings are presented first, followed by the pragmatic function analysis and a synopsis of twin-to-twin communication.

Overall, the volume of communication from all interactors to Terri, the hearing female (924 utterances) exceeded that to Timmy, the deaf male (653 utterances). At the same time, utterance production to all interactors over the nine-month period of study was greater for Terri (566 utterances) than for Timmy (363 utterances). The children were both just starting to imitate formal signs at 16 months when the study began. Their spontaneous communications at that time were mainly nonverbal, consisting of pointing, gestures, mime, and facial expression. At 16 months the amount of communication produced by each twin was about the same. However, nine months later Terri's production had increased approximately 50%, whereas Timmy's remained near his original level.

Modality

The modality analysis was undertaken to determine whether adults who interacted with the twins would adjust their communication style according to their own or the child's hearing status and whether the children would make similar adjustments for the same reasons. Tables 1 and 2 contain summaries of modality use by all interactors. Communications received by the twins from deaf and hearing adults are presented in Table 1 and those expressed by the twins to these various interactors are presented in Table 2. Related data have been tabulated together for ready comparison.

Child hearing status: effects on interlocutors' language mode

There were general differences not only in the amount of communication provided to each twin, but also in the kinds of input directed to the deaf and hearing twins. These differences were comparatively stable over time, although the actual sources of difference varied from age period to age period. In Table 1 communications to Timmy (DM) and Terri (HF), receptive, are categorized by modality (gesture, GES; voice only, VO; sign only, SO; and combined vocal and manual, VM) as well as by interlocutor (mother, M; father, F; and hearing adults, H). Percentages rather than frequencies were used throughout the analysis to accommodate differences between the twins in total numbers of utterances.

A review of Timmy's interlocutors revealed that, across time, communication from mother was most often sign only (69%) followed by combined. Father's communication to his deaf son was most often sign only (56%) followed by combined. The overwhelming majority of utterances from hearing interlocutors to Timmy combined vocal and manual modalities simultaneously (81%), the next most used modality changing from voice only at 16 months to sign only by the time he reached 24 months.

A review of Terri's interlocutors showed that, over time, hearing adults most frequently communicated with her using combined vocal and manual modalities (65%), their second most frequent modality being voice only. Father communicated with Terri most often like the hearing interlocutors, by using combined modalities (40%). His second most frequent modality varied between voice only and sign only. Terri's input from mother gradually changed from combined vocal and manual early (57%) to sign only (67%) by 24 months.

To obtain a fundamental comparison of differences in input to the twins, the categories in Table 1 labeled gestural, sign only, and combined were totaled to represent *manual* input. *Vocal* input was obtained by

TABLE I. PERCENTAGE OF RECEPTIVE COMMUNICATION TO EACH TWIN BY MODALITY AND INTERLOCUTOR, AT THREE AGE PERIODS

	Gestural	Sign only	Combined	Voice only
(To) DM				
16–18 months (N = 274)				
M[a]	15	56	29	0
F	6	34	57	3
H	1	3	87	9
% total	7	31	58	4
19–21 months (N = 177)				
M	0	100	0	0
F	0	58	42	0
H	1	1	89	9
% total	0	53	44	3
22–24 months (N = 202)				
M	3	52	45	0
F	9	77	9	5
H	3	17	67	13
% total	5	49	40	6
Means (%) (N = 653)				
M	6	69	25	0
F	5	56	36	3
H	2	7	81	10
% total	4	44	48	4
(To) HF				
16–18 months (N = 337)				
M	12	30	57	1
F	1	18	56	25
H	1	1	57	41
% total	5	16	57	22
19–21 months (N = 254)				
M	0	44	50	6
F	6	49	35	10
H	0	1	68	31
% total	2	31	51	16
22–24 months (N = 333)				
M	0	67	31	2
F	13	28	31	28
H	2	7	70	21
% total	5	34	44	17
Means (%) (N = 924)				
M	4	47	46	3
F	7	32	40	21
H	1	3	65	31
% total	4	27	51	18

[a]M, Mother; F, Father; H, Hearing adults (researchers).

TABLE 2. PERCENTAGE OF EXPRESSIVE COMMUNICATION FROM EACH TWIN BY
MODALITY AND INTERLOCUTOR, AT THREE AGE PERIODS

	Gestural	*Sign only*	*Combined*	*Voice only*
(From) DM				
16–18 months (N = 115)				
M	7	93	0	0
F	10	90	0	0
H	27	73	0	0
% total	15	85	0	0
19–21 months (N = 131)				
M	25	75	0	0
F	12	88	0	0
H	13	85	2	0
% total	17	82	1	0
22–24 months (N = 117)				
M	12	88	0	0
F	28	72	0	0
H	18	81	1	0
% total	19	81	0	0
Means (%) (N = 363)				
M	15	85	0	0
F	17	83	0	0
H	19	80	1	0
% total	17	83	0	0
(From) HF				
16–18 months (N = 137)				
M	18	64	7	11
F	6	70	12	12
H	19	59	8	14
% total	14	65	9	12
19–21 months (N = 185)				
M	33	67	0	0
F	6	84	10	0
H	9	53	14	24
% total	16	68	8	8
22–24 months (N = 244)				
M	2	89	6	3
F	13	72	9	6
H	6	85	4	5
% total	7	82	6	5
Means (%) (N = 566)				
M	18	73	4	5
F	8	76	10	6
H	11	66	9	14
% total	12	72	8	8

*a*M, Mother; F, Father, H, Hearing adults (researchers).

totaling the categories of voice only and combined. Across the months, the manual input to Timmy (DM) exceeded that to Terri (HF) and exceeded the vocal input to him. Conversely, vocal input to Terri exceeded that to Timmy as well as the manual input to her. Finer details exemplify this basic difference: The average sign-only input to Timmy almost doubled that to Terri (44% to 27%), whereas the average voice-only input to her was four times that to him (18% to 4%).

Ratios of *vocal* to *manual* receptive and expressive language for each twin at each of the three periods are plotted in Figure 1. Individually, for Timmy (DM) the ratio of total vocal to manual input (in percentages) from all interlocutors remained moderately low across time: 66:95 at 16–18 months, 84:92 at 19–21 months, and 68:90 at 22–24 months. The change at 19–21 months was a function of a disproportionate increase in frequency of interaction with the hearing researchers (almost all the vocal input to Timmy was from hearing interlocutors).

Individually, for Terri (HF) the ratio of total vocal to manual input (in percentages) from all interlocutors (Figure 1) was fairly high and stable over time: 82:75 at 16–18 months, 85:75 at 19–21 months and 77:81 at 22–24 months. The variation at 22–24 months resulted from a switch away from voice-only communication to combined by hearing interlocutors and a substantial change from combined to sign-only communication by mother.

These data support the importance of the child's hearing status, as it is perceived by interlocutors, as a controlling factor in the nature of the input the child receives. In this instance deafness resulted in both heightened manual input and a lower vocal input than did hearing, and the distinction was maintained over time. These results confirm the original hypotheses.

Child hearing status: effects on child's language mode

Differences also exist between the twins in the modality of their communications to others. The magnitude of these differences fluctuates over time, although in general there was much more vocal behavior by the hearing female than by her deaf twin. Percentages of use of the four modality categories by the twins to the various interlocutors over the three time periods are presented in Table 2.

The ratio of vocal to manual communication from Timmy (DM) at each of the three time periods was calculated in the same way as for the adult interlocutors: *vocal* included the categories of voice only and combined; *manual* included gestural, sign only, and combined. Timmy's ratio of total vocal to manual output (in percentages) to all interlocutors was 0:100 at 16–18 months, 1:100 at 19–21 months, and 1.5:100 at 22–

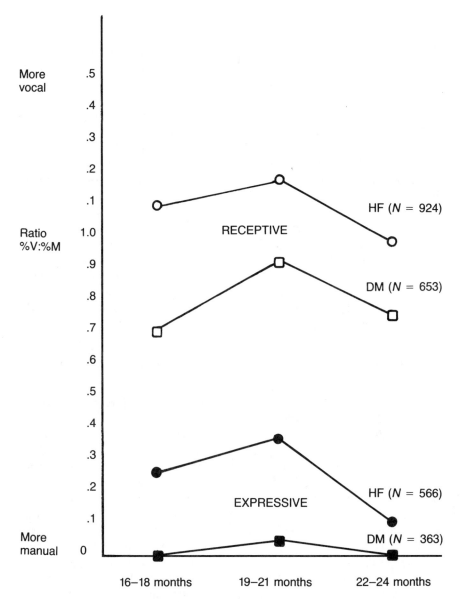

Figure 1. Ratio of the percentage of vocal (V) communication to the percentage of manual (M) communication for all interlocutors to and from each twin, at three age periods

24 months. This rigidly fixed behavior is reflected in an almost flat plot of these ratios in Figure 1.

In contrast, the ratio of total vocal to manual output (in percentages) from Terri (HF) to all interlocutors varied considerably over the study periods. Her ratios are also plotted in Figure 1. At 16–18 months the ratio was 20:80; at 19–21 months the ratio shifted to 29:83, and then to 10:96 at 22–24 months. The greatly reduced ratio at time three appears to be accounted for in large measure by a decrease in vocal communication to hearing adults and an increase in sign-only communication to hearing interlocutors as well as to mother.

Differences between the twins in their expression of modality change over time. This variability is primarily a result of fluctuation in Terri's expressive behavior. As hypothesized, both twins rely most heavily on manual communication, owing to their own limitations as communicators, his deafness, and her (presumed) lack of experience. The fact that Terri does use more vocal communication than Timmy may reflect her awarness of sound and/or the levels of vocal input presented both by her parents and by hearing interlocutors.

Interlocutor hearing status: effects on child's language mode

In spite of the strong reliance on manual communication by both children, the twins did differ in their expression of modality as a function of interlocutor hearing status. The original hypothesis is confirmed. A closer examination of Table 2 shows this well. The expressive modality Timmy (DM) used with all interactors was nearly always manual ($N = 357$). His very few utterances with a vocal component ($N = 6$) were to hearing adults, although all interlocutors had vocalized to him at some time. From the beginning, Terri (HF) used a broader range of expressive modalities across interlocutors than her twin. As can be seen in Table 2, her most frequently used modality, like Timmy's, was sign-only. In addition, she also made good use of the vocal categories. The data show that generally she used a greater percentage of both voice-only and combined communication to hearing interlocutors than to her parents and usually a greater percentage of these vocal categories to father than to mother.

The interaction of modalities between the twins and their deaf and hearing interlocutors is plotted separately in Figures 2a and 2b. The vocal/manual ratios for parent–child communications are contained in Figure 2a, and those for hearing adult–child communications are plotted in Figure 2b. Timmy's expressive communication to both sets of interlocutors looks nearly identical. However, Terri's is different, especially at 19–21 months, when communications to hearing interlocutors were higher in frequency than at other age periods. What is more remarkable is the overall mutuality in pattern of the parents' and children's communications to each other.

These observations support the hypothesized advantage of awareness of sound as a factor in communicative flexibility, in the appropriate adjustment of communication to recognized characteristics or needs of the listener. Further evidence of this may be hidden in the sharp decrease of appropriate vocalization by Terri (HF) to hearing interlocutors at the 22–24 months period. This result was unexpected. However, a year and a half later it was determined that she, too, had a hearing loss, much milder than her brother's. Because audiological testing of young children is unreliable, a word of caution should be added. Terri's second testing showed an 8–10 dB deterioration in her audiogram. This may indicate that her loss was progressive and therefore that, during the period currently being reported, she was gradually losing auditory sensitivity. This is supported by anecdotal notes and observations of the researchers that as an infant Terri seemed more responsive to sounds such as whistling and whispering than she was later.

Interlocutor hearing status: effects on interlocutor's language mode

Summaries of communication by all interlocutors to the twins are contained in Table 1. In general the patterns of behavior by both deaf and hearing interlocutors to each child are very similar. Both hearing and deaf adults communicated more with the hearing female than with the deaf male. Both groups also discriminated between the twins on modality used for input, providing more manual input to Timmy (DM) and more vocal input to Terri (HF). These ratios of vocal to manual (receptive) input provided to each twin are plotted in Figure 2a for the parents and Figure 2b for hearing interlocutors. Comparison of these plots shows that from both groups the vocal/manual ratio for input to Timmy was fairly stable over time, whereas from both the parents and hearing interlocutors the same ratios for input to Terri decline sharply. In general, the behavior of hearing and deaf interlocutors is similar. These observations would seem to confirm the original hypothesis that it is the child's and not the parents' status that regulates adult behavior. However, there were differences between deaf and hearing interlocutors in the degree to which they responded to each child. Although both groups communicated to Timmy with similar and stable ratios of vocal to manual communication (more manual), the actual ratios were, on the average, twice as high for hearing interlocutors as they were for his deaf parents. To Terri the ratios for both groups were similar (more vocal) but the actual ratios were almost three times as high for hearing interlocutors as for her parents. Furthermore, although both parents and hearing

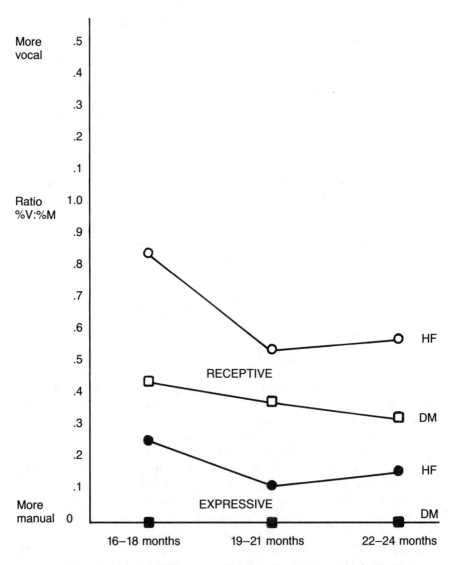

Figure 2a.   Ratio of the percentage of vocal (V) communication to the percentage of manual (M) communication for hearing impaired parents to and from each twin, at three age periods

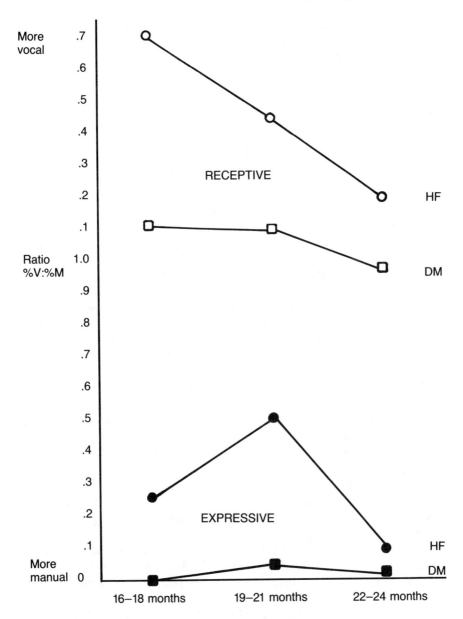

Figure 2b.   Ratio of the percentage of vocal (V) communication to the percentage of manual (M) communication for hearing interlocutors to and from each twin, at three age periods

TABLE 3. PERCENTAGE OF EIGHT COMMUNICATION FUNCTIONS FOR EACH
TWIN, AT THREE AGE PERIODS

Category	16–18 months		19–21 months		22–24 months	
	DM	HF	DM	HF	DM	HF
Request	43	39	33	39	39	45
Performative	10	2	5	1	1	1
Behavioral response	7	0	2	0	2	2
Verbal response (to questions)	12	16	12	16	9	14
Statement	1	10	4	2	6	1
Description	14	13	22	20	20	12
Conversational device	11	10	20	15	18	20
Miscellaneous (unclassifiable)	2	10	2	7	5	5
N^a =	152	188	163	254	194	347

[a]Some utterances (verbal responses) were double coded.

adults decreased vocal input to her over time, this decrease was more
pronounced with the hearing interlocutors. Thus adult hearing status
may not have affected differences in input to the children in a qualitative
sense, but it may well have had a quantitative impact.

Function

The issue with regard to language function was whether or not the
difference in their hearing status would affect the uses to which the
children put their communication skills. Would Terri and Timmy differ,
in what ways would they differ, and would their comparative use of
functions change with time?

The transcripts were coded for pragmatic function. Each twin utterance was categorized as one of eight major types: performative, request,
responses (behavioral and verbal), description, statement, conversational
device or miscellaneous (unclassifiable). Data for the comparison of
pragmatic functions are contained in Table 3. In general, there is a
remarkable similarity between the twins in both the types of functions
expressed and the distribution of functions across their communications.

Request (e.g., "more eat") is by far the most expressed communicative
function (> 33%) for both twins at all age periods. Functions with a
substantial nonverbal component, such as performatives (e.g., "bye
bye"), and compliant/noncompliant behavioral responses to requests or
questions (e.g., retrieving an object without comment), occurred infrequently (< 10%) compared with verbal functions for both twins. Purely
behavioral responding tended to decrease over the period of the study

(except during a tantrum by Terri at 22 months). Both children's verbal responses to requests and questions (e.g., "You want more?" "What do you want?") were higher in frequency (9%–16%) than nonverbal responding at 16–18 months and this relationship remained fairly stable over time. Also for both twins, responses in the form of statements of agreement or disagreement (e.g., yes or no) occurred very infrequently (1%–6%) except during a single activity with Terri at 18 months. When the twins are compared on the ratio of their use of these nonverbal/ verbal categories, Timmy (DM) exhibits higher percentages of nonverbal communication (behavioral responses, performatives) than Terri (HF), whereas she exhibits comparatively higher percentages of verbal responding (to questions, requests, statements) than he does.

The categories of description (e.g., "that balloon," "all gone") and conversational device (e.g., pointing at "him") were used moderately by both twins (10%–22%) and increased for both children from the ages of 16 to 24 months. Timmy's use is slightly higher than that of his hearing twin at 16–18 months and remains so except for the use of conversational devices at 22–24 months. The frequency of unclassifiable utterances (e.g., certain gestures, sounds) is somewhat higher for Terri but overall decreases for both twins, except for Timmy at 22–24 months. This last increase is attributed to unsuccessful attempts at vocal communication.

Just as patterns of communication expressed by pragmatic function are similar for the twins during the period studied, there are more similarities than differences between the twins with regard to variety within functional categories. This can be seen by examining the percentage of occurrences for each functional subcategory presented in Table 4.

The categories of behavioral response and statement had only two subfunctions each and, in addition, were of very low frequency. Therefore, any judgment of real differences between the twins would be unwarranted. The percentage of requests for objects and actions was always very high for both twins and very consistent over time. The exception was at 19–21 months, when a hide-and-seek activity elicited many information-seeking requests from Terri (HF). Overall frequencies of the various types of requests ranked highest to lowest were object, action, attention, information, confirmation. Performatives were almost always either greetings or games for both twins. Verbal responses were always to adult Wh- or yes/no questions, requests for information, or confirmation. No occurrences were noted of responses by either twin to adult requests for clarification or choice. In the category of description the deaf male used more variety at a younger age than his hearing twin, although the difference that existed was minimal by age 24 months. Overall frequencies of the various descriptive subfunctions, highest to lowest, were reference and location about equal, then discuss self and

TABLE 4. PERCENTAGE OF OCCURRENCE OF THE MOST FREQUENT VERSUS INFREQUENT SUBCATEGORIES OF PRAGMATIC FUNCTION

Category		16–18 months		19–21 months		22–24 months	
		DM	HF	DM	HF	DM	HF
Request	object	91	94	92	82	91	91
	action						
	attention						
	information						
	confirmation	9	6	8	18	9	9
Performative	greeting game	81	100	100	50	100	100
	polite–scold						
	warn–claim						
	protest pattern						
	role play–joke	19	0	0	50	0	0
Response behavior	compliance	82	0	50	0	25	50
	noncompliance	18	100	50	0	75	50
Response verbal	(to): Wh-						
	yes–no	100	100	100	100	100	100
	clarification choice	0	0	0	0	0	0
Statement	agree/disagree	100	100	100	100	100	100
	explain	0	0	0	0	0	0

Description							
reference location	90	92	81	96	72	72
discuss self discuss other property possession	10	8	19	4	28	28
Conversational device							
acknowledge direct attention	81	84	97	100	89	83
offer continuer	19	16	3	0	11	17
Miscellaneous (unclassifiable)							
vocalization	0	94	0	82	11	81
gesture sign	100	6	100	18	89	19

242 Martha Gonter Gaustad

discuss other about equal, then property and possession, both with few instances. Again, with conversational devices, Timmy used some variety earlier than Terri did, but by 22–24 months she surpassed him. The two most frequent conversational devices for both twins were acknowledgement and directing attention followed by offer (continuer was never noted). Unclassifiable utterances consisted of communication attempts in which the content (and therefore the intent) was indeterminable, usually because of lack of precision in either vocal or manual production. The difference between the twins' unclassifiable utterances is consistent with the results of the modality analysis: Those of the deaf male twin were all of a gestural nature until 22–24 months, when vocal attempts were made, whereas those of his hearing female counterpart were predominantly vocal productions.

In summary, it can be said that although the children may differ considerably in the modalities they use, the purposes for which they engage in communication are certainly similar. This similarity was expected. However, and somewhat unexpectedly, the slight differences that were evident in diversity of function or the timing of changes in distribution were not always to the advantage of the hearing twin.

Twin-twin communication

The amount of direct twin-to-twin communication was very low during all periods of this study, as might have been expected since the children were very young. Table 5 contains a summary of the modalities used by each twin (as speaker) along with the functions of their communications. Because the number of utterances is small, the data are reported in actual frequencies of occurrence. Timmy's and Terri's communication to each other reflected patterns described earlier in their interaction with adults. Although both used predominantly sign-only modality, Terri (HF) also used vocal expression, whereas Timmy (DM) did not. There was no evidence in his communication by the age of 24 months to show that he knew she could hear. Both twins used a variety of pragmatic functions, with a high proportion of them requests or descriptions. Both of these functions appeared frequently in their communications to adults.

Discussion

The analysis of the data from the first year of this longitudinal study illustrates both the constancy of language processes and the uniqueness of the situation and subjects in this study. Parental response to the communication needs of the twins and the children's use of pragmatic

TABLE 5. FREQUENCIES OF MODALITY USE AND PRAGMATIC FUNCTION FOR
COMMUNICATIONS EXPRESSED BY EACH TWIN TO THE OTHER

	DM	HF		DM	HF
Gestural	1	2	Request	5	21
Sign only	10	22	Performative	1	
Combined		5	Response behavioral		
Voice only		1	Response verbal		
			Statement		2
Totals	11	30	Description	4	3
			Conversational device	1	2
			Miscellaneous		2
			Totals	11	30

functions both conform to established patterns of communicative behavior. Some aspects of the children's language productions, however,
especially level and type of output, result from their status as bimodal
twins.

Although they apparently possess normal intelligence, both twins were
somewhat delayed in language development at age 16 months when the
study began. Appearance of the first recognizable sign between 15 and
16 months was later than the 8–10 months reported by other investigators for deaf children of deaf parents (Bonvillian, Orlansky, and Novack, 1983; McIntire, 1977; Prinz and Prinz, 1981; Schlesinger, 1972).
By age eighteen months deaf children of deaf parents are reported to
have anywhere from a 10- to 117-sign vocabulary and to be producing
multisign utterances (Bonvillian et al., 1983; Prinz and Prinz, 1981;
Schlesinger, 1972). Although at 16 months the twins both occasionally
used gestures in combination with a sign (e.g., POINT + SIGN; Hoffmeister, 1982), even their pointing was simpler in form (-B- or flat hand
instead of a -G-hand) than has been reported elsewhere. By age two they
were producing fewer multi-unit utterances than would have been anticipated. In many instances what they did produce might better be
labeled as successive utterances (Bloom, 1973) or vertical constructions
(Scollon, 1979).

Since the volume of parent–child communication also seemed low and
since both children were equally affected, the delay may be explained
by their communication environment. Galenson et al. (1979) reported
language delays in young deaf children of deaf parents. They attributed
the delay to an impoverished and disrupted maternal-child relationship
arising from a combination of the hearing loss itself and poor parenting.
Regarding hearing children of deaf parents, there has been disagreement
about whether delays or interference in speech and language development exist (Schiff and Ventry, 1976; Sachs and Johnson, 1976; Todd,

1976) or don't exist (Lenneberg, 1967; Mayberry, 1976). Considerations have included both reduced stimulation for vocal language and effects of bilingual learning (Prinz and Prinz, 1981).

In Timmy's and Terri's cases the delay may be due to effects of "twinning," which have been reported to be stronger than factors of socioeconomic status or mother's educational level (Lytton, 1980). Lytton reports that the volume of communication that might be expected from parents to a single offspring is adversely affected by the reduced availability of time for social interaction and then further by the twins' sharing of interactive language opportunities actually afforded by the parents. He stresses the reciprocal interaction of parent and twins' communicative behaviors: Twins seek out parental interaction less than do singletons, and parents communicate less with twins than singletons (Lytton, 1980).

Another general and quantitative finding was the comparatively greater amount of communication to and from the hearing female twin. This difference may reflect the relative ease of communication and language learning with a hearing as opposed to a deaf child. However, since in this instance hearing status compounds possible sex differences in linguistic behavior, it should simply be noted that this phenomenon seems to correlate with a more generalized perception of differences between the twins' operational styles: He takes, she asks. Further evidence of this difference lies in the comparative frequencies of the twins' use of nonverbal versus verbal categories for pragmatic functioning.

Modality

The analysis of communication modality corroborates and extends existing knowledge on modality use and code switching. Studies to date have shown that hearing parents adjust their speech in various ways to accommodate communication levels and needs of young hearing children (e.g., Berko-Gleason 1973; Schiff-Meyers, 1982). Obviously, hearing and deaf parents using forms of manual communication with young deaf children, especially in households with hearing children, represents such an accommodation. Studies have examined code switching by deaf adults with other adults (Hoffmeister and Moores, in press; Maestas y Moores, 1980; Schiff-Meyers, 1982; Woodward, 1972) and provided anecdotal evidence of modality and code switching by deaf children (Erting, 1980; Prinz and Prinz, 1981; Schlesinger, 1972). But there has been a lack of detail specific to the interaction of adults with children regarding modality adjustment, proportions in input, changes in the process over time, etc. Uniquely, in this study, modality use has been observed longitudinally with deaf and hearing subjects side by side. Parental accommodation to hearing status has been shown to be very distinct and, throughout the extent of this study, very consistent. (One could speculate that the drop in "vocal" to "manual" ratio to Terri between 16 and 24 months of age represents adult adjustment to a formally undiagnosed hearing loss.) Although it is too early yet for the children to be code switching between ASL and English (Priesler, 1981; Schlesinger, 1972), the beginnings of requisite behaviors are in evidence, especially in Terri's apparent discrimination between interlocutors on the basis of their preferred communication modality. A few actual examples of adult and child modality switching from a single, multiperson interaction highlight some of the patterns that have been discussed: more vocal (in " ") than manual input by adults to Terri (HF, see 4, 6, 9), more manual than vocal input to Timmy (DM, see 12, 13, 18), more vocal expression to hearing adults by the hearing female (see 2, 8) than by her deaf brother (see 1), and more vocal output by Terri to hearing adults (MAG, see 2, 8) than to her parents (F, see 11, 20, 22). The following sample is from the transcript at 21 months (see Appendix A for additional coding conventions):

MAG has tossed box	1	DM → MAG⁺:	THERE (index – behind MAG)/
of raisins to F.	2	HF → MAG⁺:	"ah ———" QUESTION GESTURE ('where/all gone')/
	3	MAG→ HF +:	"all gone" QUESTION GESTURE/
MAG gives a clue....	4	MAG→ HF⁺:	"terri i THINK daddy has them"/ ME FATHER HAVE
DM moves to look in bag behind F.	5 ⌠ 6 ⌡	DM → ?: MAG→ HF⁺:	THERE (index – rear dad)/ "terri . . . terri daddy has the FOOD/FATHER
		MAG→ HF: HF → MAG⁰:	"terri . . ."/ "wa" ('what')/
	9	MAG→ HF⁰:	"daddy has the food"/
HF goes to F.	10 ⌠ 11 ⌡ 12	F → HF⁺: HF → F⁺:	EAT (3)/ EAT (3)/ EAT (2)... "EAT" (4)...
		F →DM⁺: F continued	"EAT (3) ATTENTION GETTER (taps DM chest) EAT (3)/
	13	DM → F⁺:	EAT ———/
DM wants a raisin.	14	F →DM⁺: F continued	"EAT" (6)... (F prompts DM to sign – pushes hands) "EAT" (3)/
	15	DM → F⁺:	GESTURE (uninterpretable – "give"?)/
	16	F → DM⁺	"EAT" (3)/

F holds up box of	17	DM	→ F$^+$:	THAT (index – box raisins)
raisins.	18	F	→ DM$^+$:	———/
				----- EAT (2) THAT (index-box)/ (F molds *eat* with DM *THAT* hand – holds DM wrist and pushes finger side of D-hand to DM mouth)
HF walks over to F	19	F	→ HF$^+$:	"EAT" (3)/
and DM.	20	HF	→ F$^+$:	EAT (3)/
F works on sign for	21	F	→ HF$^+$:	"daddy"/
"father."...				FATHER/ (F molds "*Father*" with HF hand on HF head with voice – "daddy," 2)
	22	HF	→ F$^+$:	You... GIVE.../

It is significant that accommodation to interlocutor occurs in a child as young as Terri, in modality of communication if not in specific language. Whether this modality switching was facilitated by her hearing and whether Terri's apparent lead in making such adjustments has extended effects may be determined by future analysis of the twins' communication at later ages.

Function

Similarity between the twins in the functions of their utterances seems particularly noteworthy in the light of the striking differences between them in both amount and modality of communication. The functional analysis revealed a gradually increasing sophistication of each twin as a communicator during the period from 16 to 24 months. The longitudinal data show a shift from early nonverbal responding to a greater frequency of response accompanied by language, along with decreasing numbers of uninterpretable responses and increasing variety and use of conversational devices. Both twins responded verbally to questions throughout the study period, and although such responses did not increase dramatically in number, they did become more pragmatically appropriate. Specific evidence of this was the growing use of statements of agreement and disagreement (yes–no questions) and different types of description (Wh- questions).

In terms of pragmatic function, the twins' performance was very similar to what we know of deaf and hearing children (Carmichael and Greenberg, 1980; Curtiss et al., 1979; Day, 1982; Meadow et al., 1981). Requests accounted for a high percentage of the twins' communications, followed by descriptions. Studies with deaf and hearing children aged 3 and older show these two functions to be used about equally, so the twins may have been functioning at an earlier stage. For deaf and younger (less sophisticated) hearing children, it was noted that attention to objects rather than actions predominated. This was as true of the requests by both twins. Also, hearing children are more likely to answer and ask yes/no questions at younger ages than deaf children. This tendency may be reflected in the greater percentage of verbal question responses by Terri than Timmy. In general, where comparisons with categories analyzed in previous studies are possible, the distribution of functions for the twins appears consistent.

Conclusion

The very uniqueness of this study situation reduces its generalizability. However, it does serve to isolate certain aspects of adult–child interaction that may be important in the development of deaf children, perhaps providing direction for later research.

Terri's behavior demonstrates the perceptiveness of young children to characteristic differences in their communication partners. Although at such a young age children do not have many skills with which to accomplish listener accommodation, the perception of differences may set the stage for the development of that flexibility. It was not possible to determine from Timmy's early behavior whether he failed to recognize a difference in hearing status or did not acknowledge the difference, perhaps owing to the lack of feedback for his own vocal productions. However, this reduced accommodation may also be evident in the behavior of his hearing-impaired parents. It is interesting to note that changes in their communication to Terri over time, perhaps a response to her hearing loss, was less marked than that of hearing interlocutors.

The importance of the characteristics of parental input is highlighted in this study too. The effects of reduced opportunities for parent–child interaction are clear, but the precision with which the children's (especially Terri's) output matched modality characteristics of the parents' input (Figure 2a) were unexpected and remarkable. Considering the circumstances of the majority of deaf children who have hearing parents, more research on actual and optimal input to these children at home is badly needed if we are to design effective intervention.

The response of hearing interactors to differences in the twins' hearing status is also significant because it reveals a communication dilemma. Most special classes for the deaf consist of a hearing teacher and severely to profoundly deaf students. For a teacher of the deaf, the modeling and encouragement of good speech skills is an important goal. However, there is abundant evidence from this and other studies (Cross, 1977; Penman et al., 1983; Shatz and Gelman, 1977; Schiff-Meyers, 1982) that adults communicating with children have a natural and strong tendency to alter their language to reflect the child's actual communication characteristics and skills (rather than potentialities). This results in some conflict between different aspects of the teacher's role. Recent recognition of pragmatic deficits of deaf children as communicators (Brackett, 1983; Wilbur, 1979) focuses additional attention on the teacher as model communicator, which only increases the complexity of the problem.

The communicative situation of young deaf children, their parents, and their teachers is an intricate weaving of individual needs, styles, and skills. This study has shown minimal effects of hearing status differences on the early expression of communication functions, but greater effects on communicative style and flexibility. Although the long-range effects of these early experiences are unpredictable, further research is needed to determine advantageous methods for training both parents and teachers to make maximal use of deaf children's potential as communicators.

Acknowledgments

This investigation was supported in part by NIH Research Grant NS-09590–10 from the National Institute of Neurological and Communicative Disorders and Stroke. Preparation of this chapter was supported, in part, by the Center for Studies in Education and Human Development at Gallaudet College while the author was a Visiting Scholar there. Portions of this material were presented at the annual meeting of the American Educational Research Association, New Orleans, 1984.

The kind and helpful comments of Dr. Kay Meadow and Dr. Fran Bridges-Cline in the preparation of this chapter and the research assistance of Ms. Cheryl Schmidt are gratefully acknowledged.

Appendix A: Transcription system

SIGN	uppercase manuscript = manual only (English glosses)
"speech"	lowercase in quotation = vocal only
"SIGN"	uppercase in quotation = sign and voice simultaneously
F-I-N-G-E-R	uppercase with dashes = fingerspelling
YES^H NO^H	indicate unaccompanied affirmative/negative head movements
( )	contain approximate glosses and descriptions of nonlexicalized GESTURES; number of repetitions of previous sign; variations from citation form of a sign; clarifications of signs as required.
SIGN^R SIGN^L	designate hand executing the sign (where this is significant)
...	significant pause within an utterance
x———	gesture (e.g., pointing) or sign (e.g., eat) held for some period of time (grossly specified by length of line)

?	questioning intonation (holding or raising the previous sign, raised-furrowed eyebrows, etc.)
/	end of utterance, hands return to neutral or resting position
interactors	identified at beginning of transcript, specified by initials for each utterance
→	direction of address, "speaker" to "listener" (S→L)
eye contact	+ contact made, − not made, 0 undetermined (all as superscripts to addressee)
indexing	glossed as appropriate for the content followed by explanation: YOU AND I (dual index)

Individual simultaneity

x	simultaneous execution of two signs or sign and speech
x	e.g., BOY dominant hand e.g., "daddy" spoken
	ME nondominant hand FATHER signed

Interactive simultaneity (also labeled "overlapping")

In addition to other notations:

| —————— | pause during which another interactor signs |
| { | simultaneously executed utterances of two or more interactors (may include continuations) |

Appendix B: *Transcript Sample*

INTERACTORS: Timmy (DM)   Terri (HF)   Marti (MAG)
          AGE: 23.5 months   p. 21

	Utterance number		
Context	*HF*	*DM*	
MAG attempts to blow up another balloon.			MAG→ DM⁺:
		35	DM → MAG⁺:
MAG stretches balloon.			MAG→ DM⁺:
		36	DM → MAG⁻:
MAG blows up balloon.	86		HF → MAG⁻:
			MAG→ DM⁺:
		37	DM → MAG⁺:
			MAG→ HF⁺:
	87		HF → MAG⁺:
MAG gives DM the balloon.			
DM tries to bite the balloon.			MAG→ HF⁺:
		88	HF → MAG⁻:
MAG holds out another balloon.			MAG→ HF⁻:
		89	{ HF → MAG⁻:
			{ MAG→ HF⁺:
			{ HF continued:
			{ MAG continued:
			HF continued:
			HF continued:
			HF continued:
MAG stretches balloon.			MAG→ DM⁺:
DM holds his blown balloon to his mouth.		38	DM → ?:
MAG beings blowing up balloon.	90		HF → MAG⁻:
			HF continued:
			MAG→ HF⁻:
			MAG continued:
	91		{ HF → MAG⁺:
			{ MAG→ HF⁻:
			HF continued:
	92		HF → DM:
			HF continued:
Mag blows up the balloon, hits it into air.			
HF tries to catch it.			
HF gets balloon, squeezes it, and breaks it.			

Interchange

"i CAN'T"/	VM	
QUESTION GESTURE[R] (palm raised, 2)/	GES	RIN
"MAKE it BLOW up"/	VM	
GESTURE[R] (S hand contacts mouth)/	GES	ACK
THAT[L] (arm extend to balloon)/	SO	ROB
"this one's FOR YOU"/	VM	
ME[R] (index chest) ME[R] (index chin, 3)/	SO	ACK
"FOR HIM" (index DM)/	VM	
THAT[R] (arm extends to balloon)————/	SO	ROB
"you want one?"/	VO	
THAT[R] (excitedly indexes balloon)/	SO	YNR/RB
"want this one?"/	VO	
THAT[L] (arm extend to balloon) EAT	SO	YNR/DIS
———— "THIS (index balloon) this is RED	VM	
(standard, 2) MORE (standard, 4) BALLOON		
......RED"...BALLOON/		
(0-hands to mouth, index edge[R] strokes		
mouth, 2; back of hand[R] contacts mouth,		
tilts back—like DM's DRINK sign)/		
"READY?"/	VM	
YES[H]	GES	YNR/SAD
THAT[L] (arm extended to balloon)...	SO	CDA
ATTENTION GETTER[L] (taps MAG)/		
"WHOSE?...hey terri...WHOSE?	VM	
...WHOSE?...this YOURS?"/		
EAT[L] (standard, 1)...EAT[L] (same, 1)	SO	WHR/DIS
————"is this YOURS?"/	VM	
MORE (standard, 9)/		
ATTENTION GETTER (waves at DM)	SO	SGN
...YOU[R] (index DM)/		

Appendix C: Pragmatic function codes and definitions

Requests (for:)

ROB	object	Used when obtaining any object or substance is the goal of the communication exchange, regardless of whether action will be required of the partner to fulfill the request. Child signs, "want more." (Mother hands child a cookie).
RAC	action	Used when activity on the part of the communication partner is itself the goal. Child signs "push" and touches mother's hand. (Mother replies, "say, you push, Mama.")
ATN	attention	Used when the goal of the communication is to gain the attention of the listener for the purpose of further communication. Child waves at mother, then taps her arm. When eye contact is made the child begins to sign.
RIN	information (Wh)	Questions, when the goal is to obtain specific information: what, where, when, why etc. Child signs "where" repeatedly while looking around on floor for toy.
RCF	confirmation (yes/no)	Expression similar in communicative intent to "Is that okay? Is this right? Do you want this?" This category includes expressions through which the child asks to be allowed to do something. (Mother and child have been pretending to drink from toy cups. Child reaches for mother's cup and signs "more." Mother replies, "No, I am finished. No more for me.")

Performatives

This next major category of communicative intent is that of performative. A performative is a communicative expression that through its production actually performs the function represented in its communicative intent. For example, saying "hello" constitutes the act of "greeting" someone.

GRE	greeting/ parting	Socially conventionalized communication. Child acknowledges arrival of a person or shows notice of that person ("hi", or "goodbye").
PGM	game	This behavior is just like that in PERFOR-MATIVE/JOKE, but the behavior must be at least the second in a sequence in which child or partner repeats the amusing behavior.
PPL	polite	Use of specific politeness markers, such as "sorry, please, thank you."
PSC	scold	Child reprimands another for an action or event (e.g., shaking index finger).
PWN	warn	Child alerts or reminds partner of possible harm ("be careful").
PCL	claim	Child establishes the right to have control of an object or activity ("my turn").
PRO	protest	The child expresses objection to an action or state ("No, that's not the way").
PRP	role play	The child establishes an imaginary role or identity for himself or herself or some object. (This code was used only for initially establishing a role; e.g., points to rabbit in book, says "me.")
PJO	joke	This kind of communication must include a laugh or a smile as one of its elements. Essentially, the child intentionally does something he or she considers to be funny and shares this feeling with the communi-

		cation partner. The child must be the first to do this and not be responding to mother's joke.
PAT	pattern	Child rote counts or signs an alphabet sequence (numbers – memory).

Response behavioral

CMP	compliance	Used when the interlocutor's request requires a behavioral response (whether or not accompanied by verbalization). Child complies, or attempts to comply, rather than demonstrating a refusal to comply.
NCP	noncompliance	Child refuses to give attention to the speaker, disagrees, complains, has a tantrum. Attempts to comply, even if unsuccessful, are coded as compliance.

Response verbal (to:) [double-coded]

WHR	Wh-question	Child's response to a Wh-question from the partner. This response will be double-coded, since such a response will simultaneously be filling the function of Description.
		(Mother holds up an object asks, "What is that?") Child signs "green."
YNR	yes/no question	Child responds to a yes/no question from partner, such as "Do you want . . . ?" Is it hot?"
		(Mother asks, "Is that okay?") Child nods yes.
CLR	clarify request	Child restates communication by repeating or altering a previous utterance after response from partner indicates confusion.
		Child signs "gimme" to mother who is sitting with many toys. When

mother doesn't know which toy the child wants and shrugs the child signs "car."

CAR	choice answer request	Used when the question or request calls for a selection among alternatives or some decision or judgment on the part of the child. "Is the clown happy or sad?" Child says "happy."

Statements

SAD	evaluate (agree/ disagree)	Used when child expresses his or her own feelings about another's behavior or some situation. (Usually accompanied by positive or negative affect.) Mother puts puzzle piece in the wrong way, child signs "wrong" and shakes head.
SEP	explain (causality)	Child expresses knowledge of a causal relationship between object or action and event. (Child has touched hot bowl.) Child shows hand to mother, points to bowl, grimaces, nods yes while signing "hurt."

Description

REF	reference (identify, name)	Child gives label for a person or object. Child points to a picture of a bird, signs, and says, "bird."
DLO	location	Location may be expressed through a formal linguistic element (sign) or through pointing. A point may also represent a demonstrative, signifying the equivalent of "this" or "that." Includes only "distal" pointing, indicating objects or persons that are not present in the immediate environment, or that are at a distance from the signer, as representing location.

		Investigator asks "Sister?" Child points to door and signs "school."
DIS	discuss self (action, thought)	Used when the description refers to characteristics, behaviors, thoughts, or actions of the speaker. Child bites candy, laughs, and signs "bite."
DIO	discuss other (attribution)	Used when describing actions, thoughts, or characteristics of another. Child points to picture in book, signs, "scare." (Mother replies, "Scared? Scared rabbit.")
DPR	property (quality)	Child refers to property of an object such as "hot, cold, empty, pink ..." Child looks at steam from soup cooking, signs, "hot."
DPO	possession	Child indicates the owner of a particular object. While having a tea party, child places cup in front of mother, looks at mother, and signs, "Mama," pointing to cup.

Conversational devices

ACK	acknowledgement	These are communications without specific information content that serve to mark completion of an activity or to acknowledge notice of an event or message. Investigator looks at child's shirt, signs, and says, "dirty." Child looks down at shirt, then shrugs shoulders and looks away.
	may take the form of imitation	Mother indicates jar of paint and says, "What color is this?" Child touches jar with fingers and signs, "color."
CDA	direct attention	The child holds up an object or points to an object in order to direct the

		partner's attention to that object (perhaps person).
		(Mother brings out a copy of a poem the child is learning to sign.) Child smiles at investigator and points to poem.
CDO	offer	Child holds object up at parent, parent takes object or performs action (like drinking) with object. Child must hold object within parent's reach or make some attempt to allow the parent access to it.
		Child looks at mother and holds up a card within mother's reach. (Mother takes card, saying, "That's mine.")
COR	continuer (nonverbal)	Used when the function of the communication is to promote continuation of another's communication by providing cues that it is being understood or accepted.
		"unhuh, mmhm," head nodding.

Miscellaneous

VOC	unclassifiable	Vocalizations, gestures or signs whose
GES	communications	communication content and purpose are
SGN		unclear because of the speaker's execution or deficiencies of recording.

Note: Most of the definitions and examples used here are courtesy of Dr. Patricia Spencer Day, Gallaudet College (Day, 1982).

References

Berko-Gleason, J. (1973). Code switching in children's language. In T. Moore (Ed.), *Cognitive Development and the Acquisition of Language*. New York: Academic Press.

Bloom, L. (1973). *One Word at a Time*. The Hague: Mouton.

Bodner-Johnson, B. (1982). Describing the home as a learning environment for hearing-impaired children. *Volta Review 84*, December, 329–337.

Bonvillian, J., M. Orlansky, and L. Novack. (1983). Developmental milestones: Sign language acquisition and motor development. *Child Development 54*, 1435–1445.

Brackett, D. (1983). Group communication strategies for the hearing-impaired. *Volta Review 85*, 117–128.

Brasel, K., and S. Quigley. (1977). Influence of certain language and communication environments in early childhood on the development of language in deaf individuals. *Journal of Speech and Hearing Research 20*, 95–107.

Bruner, J. (1978). Learning how to do things with words. In J. S. Bruner and A. Garton (Eds.), *Human Growth and Development*. London: Oxford University Press.

Carmichael, H., and M. Greenberg. (1980 February). Rev. A comparison of functional communication in deaf vs. hearing mother–child dyads: Descriptive analysis and intervention implications. A paper presented at the Annual International Interdisciplinary Conference on Piagetian Theory and the Helping Professions, Los Angeles.

Cokely, D. (1979). *Pre-college Programs: Guidelines for Manual Communication.* Washington, D.C.: Gallaudet College Press.

Crandall, K. (1978). Inflectional morphemes in the manual English of young hearing-impaired children and their mothers. *Journal of Speech and Hearing Research 21,* 372–386.

Cross, T. (1977). Mother's speech adjustment: The contribution of selected child variables. In C. Snow and C. Ferguson (Eds.), *Talking to Children: Language Input and Acquisition.* England: Cambridge University Press.

Curtiss, S., C. Prutting, and E. Lowell. (1979). Pragmatic and semantic development in young children with impaired hearing. *Journal of Speech and Hearing Research 22,* 534–552.

Day, P. (1982). The expression of communicative intention: Deaf children and their hearing mothers. *Monograph I: Socialization of the Deaf Child.* Washington, D.C.: Gallaudet College.

Erting, C. (1980). Sign language and communication between adults and children. In C. Baker and R. Battison (Eds.), *Sign Language and the Deaf Community.* Silver Spring, Md.: National Association for the Deaf.

Galenson, E., R. Miller, E. Kaplan, and A. Rothstein. (1979). Assessment of development of the deaf child. *Journal of the American Academy of Psychiatry 18,* 128–142.

Gonter, M. (1983). Effects of instruction through total communication on deaf children's English language development. A paper presented at the Annual Conference of the American Educational Research Association, April, Montreal, Canada.

Greenberg, M. (1980). Mode use in deaf children: The effects of communication method and communication competence. *Applied Psycholinguistics 1,* 65–79.

Greenberg, M., and H. Carmichael. (1980). Rev. *Coding Manual for Functional Communication.* Washington: University of Washington.

Hoffmeister, R. (1982). Acquisition of signed language by deaf children. A paper presented at the Annual Conference of the American Educational Research Association, April, New York.

Hoffmeister, R., and D. Moores. (In press). Code switching in deaf adults: The influence of audience characteristics on rated signing behavior. *American Annals of the Deaf.*

Klima, E., and U. Bellugi. (1979). *The Signs of Language.* Boston, Mass.: Harvard University Press.

Lenneberg, E. (1967). *Biological Foundations of Language.* New York: Wiley.

Lieven, E. (1978). Conversations between mothers and young children: Individual differences and their possible implication for the study of language learning. In N. Waterson and C. Snow (Eds.), *The Development of Communication: Social and Pragmatic Factors in Language Acquisition.* New York: Wiley & Sons.

Lytton, H. (1980). *Parent–Child Interaction: The Socialization Process Observed in Twin and Singleton Families.* New York: Plenum Press.

McIntire, M. (1977). The acquisition of American Sign Language configurations. *Sign Language Studies 16*, 247–266.

Maestas y Moores, J. (1980). Early linguistic environment: Interactions of deaf parents with their infants. *Sign Language Studies 26*, 1–13.

Mayberry, R. (1976). An assessment of some oral- and manual-language skills of hearing children of deaf parents. *American Annals of the Deaf 121*, 507–512.

Meadow, K., M. Greenberg, C. Erting, and H. Carmichael. (1981). Interactions of deaf mothers and deaf preschool children: Comparisons with three other groups of deaf and hearing dyads. *American Annals of the Deaf 126*, 454–468.

Miller, L. (1982). Pragmatics and sign language: Characteristics and acquisition. *Audiology 7*, 49–61.

Moerk, E. L. (1977). *Pragmatic and Semantic Aspects of Early Language Development*. Baltimore, Md.: University Park Press.

Ochs, E., and B. Schieffelin. (1979). *Developmental Pragmatics*. New York: Academic Press.

Penman, R., T. Cross, J. Milgram-Friedman, and R. Meares. (1983). Mothers' speech to prelingual infants: A pragmatic analysis. *Journal of Child Language 10*, 17–34.

Priesler, G. (1981). Modification of communication by a small deaf girl. *American Annals of the Deaf 126*, 411–416.

Prinz, P., and E. Prinz. (1981). Acquisition of ASL and spoken English by a hearing child of a deaf mother and a hearing father: Phase II, early combinatorial patterns. *Sign Language Studies 30*, 78–88.

Quigley, S., and P. Paul. (1984). ASL and ESL? *Topics in Early Childhood Special Education 3*, 17–26.

Raffin, M., J. Davis, and L. Gilman. (1978). Comprehension of inflectional morphemes by deaf children exposed to a visual English sign system. *Journal of Speech and Hearing Research 21*, 387–400.

Reilly, J., and M. McIntire. (1980). American Sign Language and Pidgin Sign English: What's the difference? *Sign Language Studies 27*, 151–192.

Sachs, J. and M. Johnson. (1976). Language development in a hearing child of deaf parents. In W. Engel and Y. Lebrun (Eds.), *Baby Talk and Infant Speech*. Lisse, Netherlands: Swets and Zeitlinger.

Schiff, N., and I. Ventry. (1976). Communication problems in hearing children of deaf parents. *Journal of Speech and Hearing Disorders 41*, 348–358.

Schiff-Meyers, N. (1982). Sign and oral language development of preschool hearing children of deaf parents in comparison with their mothers' communication systems. *American Annals of the Deaf 127*, 322–330.

Schlesinger, H. (1972). Language acquisition in four deaf children. *Hearing and Speech News 40*, 4–28.

Scollon, R. (1979). A real early stage: An unzippered condensation of a dissertation on child language. In E. Ochs and B. Schieffelin (Eds.), *Developmental Pragmatics*. New York: Academic Press.

Shatz, M., and R. Gelman. (1977). Beyond syntax: The influence of conversational constraints on speech modifications. In C. Snow and C. Ferguson (Eds.), *Talking to Children: Language Input and Acquisition*. England: Cambridge University Press.

Skarakis, M., and C. Prutting. (1977). Early communication: Semantic functions and communicative intentions in the communication of the preschool child with impaired hearing. *American Annals of the Deaf 122,* 382–391.

Snow, C., and C. Ferguson. (1977). *Talking to Children: Language Input and Acquisition.* England: Cambridge University Press.

Stokoe, W. (1976). The study of the use of sign language. *Sign Language Studies 10,* 1–36.

Todd, P. (1976). A case of structural interference across sensory modalities in second-language learning. *Word 27,* 102–118.

Van Metre, P., and M. Maxwell. (1981). Communication modes used with hearing-impaired students: Investigations and applications to a school/home program. *American Annals of the Deaf 126,* 499–505.

Weiss, K., C. McIntyre, M. Goodwin, and D. Moores. (1975). *Characteristics of Young Deaf Children and Intervention Programs.* Research Report 91. Minnesota: University of Minnesota, Research, Development and Demonstration Center in Education of Handicapped Children.

Wilbur, R. (1979). An explanation of deaf children's difficulty with certain syntactic structures of English. *Volta Review 79,* 85–92.

Woodward, J. (1972). Implications for sociolinguistic research among the deaf. *Sign Language Studies 1,* 1–8.

11 Questions and answers in the development of deaf children

Hilde Schlesinger

Editor's introduction

Schlesinger analyzes the oral/signed responses of both hearing and deaf children to a number of (mostly "why") questions in terms of her recently developed theory of powerlessness. Schlesinger, a psychiatrist who has worked with deaf children and their parents for many years, has contended that deaf children are more successful at school if their mothers do not succumb to the sense of powerlessness that often develops in the parents of children with whom they have difficulty in communicating. She traces some of the effects of powerlessness to the children's verbal responses and is able to show that the deaf children who were to become the better readers answered more often in ways similar to the hearing children. Schlesinger brings a creative and novel perspective to the analysis of the language of deaf children. Her work not only emphasizes the importance of parental input for children's language learning, but shows us, too, how this input can be severely modified by the psychological state of the mother in her reaction to the deafness of her child. This serves to remind us of the importance of parental education and counseling as a crucial component of intervention strategies for the successful habilitation of deaf children.

How and why do mothers talk that way, and what happens when they do?

"Take care of the sense, and the sounds will take care of themselves."
Lewis Carroll (1963, p. 92)

"Speak in French when you can't think of the English for a thing – turn out your toes when you walk – and remember who you are!"
Lewis Carroll (1963, pp. 166–167)

How mothers talk to their toddlers has been shown to be associated with the future academic success of their children (Clarke-Stewart, 1973; Golden and Birns, 1976; Ramey, Sparling, and Wasik, 1981), the reading

261

level of their hearing (Milner, 1951) and deaf adolescents (Borchert, 1984; Schlesinger, 1982; Schlesinger and Acree, 1984) and their socioeconomic status (Bee et al., 1982; Bronfenbrenner, 1958; Bruner, 1975; Clarke-Stewart, 1973; Schachter, 1979), Tulkin and Kagan, 1972) and, as reported in this chapter, with success, failure, and other psychological differences in deaf children's responses to questions.

How do mothers talk?

Mothers talk with their children, do so very differently, and tend to be more often at one side or the other of a series of dichotomies. Some talk *with* their youngsters and participate equally in dialogue; some primarily talk *at* their children. Some mainly support the actions of their offspring, and if not, provide reasons why not; others primarily control the actions of their children, and do not explain why. Some ask genuine questions, "Where do you want to go?"; others ask constraint questions with answers clearly known to mother and child, "What color is this?" Some are prompted by what the child does or says; others are prompted by their own inner needs or interests. Some describe a large world in which events happened in the past and will continue to happen in the future; others comment only about the here and now. Some elicit information; some mainly present it. Some teach on the fly; others drill letters, numbers, and colors.

Some mothers mediate the environment by endowing stimuli with meaning. They may do so by selecting some and placing them in time and space or by grouping others to establish causal and dependent relationships (Feuerstein, 1977, p. 366). In summary, some mothers engage in mediating dialogues; others deliver directive monologues.

Why do mothers talk that way?

Mothers tend to talk with their children with the intent either to "communicate" or to "control" (McDonald and Pien, 1982). There is increasing evidence that advantaged mothers tend to do the former, whereas disadvantaged mothers and parents of disabled children tend to do the latter.[1] Many reasons have been advanced for this pattern:

---

1 The reader will encounter the following terms throughout the chapter: "disadvantaged and advantaged," "low and high functioning," "lower class and middle class," and "Lo/Reader and Hi/Reader." Each time, the terms are those used by the authors quoted. The appropriateness of each term has been debated; nevertheless, they are somewhat but not entirely interchangeable. The present author uses the term "advantaged" not in terms of socioeconomic variables, but in terms of a sense of control of parents' lives and children's school achievement. In addition, she feels

more financial security, a more harmonious life, more education, and more books in the house (summarized in Feagans and Farran, 1982; Williams, 1970). Perhaps mothers who feel in control of their lives and have a conviction that they can influence their children *communicate* with their children. Perhaps other mothers are more often beset by powerlessness and perceive themselves as lacking "the cognitive competence, psychological skills, instrumental resources, and support systems needed to influence their environments successfully" (Schlesinger, 1987). These are the mothers who will more often feel the need to *control* their children, especially during toddlerhood when children strive toward autonomy (Barsch, 1968; Borchert, 1984; Brinich, 1980; Schachter, 1979; Schlesinger, 1982, 1985; Schlesinger and Meadow, 1972). "Controllingness" has a negative influence on language acquisition (Leifer and Lewis, 1983; Schlesinger, 1987).

Often these controlling parents are powerless; often these powerless parents are poor. Not all economically disadvantaged parents feel powerless and use "disadvantaged" dialogue styles with their children. Despite their status in society and their dependence on others for basic life supports, only those who have internalized negative attitudes of the dominant culture see themselves as powerless, helpless, and unable to influence the development of their children (Hess and Shipman, 1965; Minuchin et al., 1967; Ogbu, 1978, 1982). Many parents of deaf (and other disabled) children feel powerless because their children differ from them, because the future of their "different" children looms uncertain in their minds, and because their usual parenting practices do not result in expected behaviors on the part of their children. Although the sources of powerlessness differ, their concomitants appear identical. Parents are perplexed, lack some basic information about their child's development, question their ability to parent, and feel defeated when they are unable to answer their child's unanswerable questions (Sestini, cited in Tough, 1982) or when they fail to understand their deaf child's speech.

What happens when mothers control most of the time?

Children who are primarily subjected to directive monologues will not fare well. It will be said of them, "A number of deaf children are limited during their early years to information that is 'portrayable' by touch,

that there is some, but not an absolute, correlation between the terms simply because it is easier to be in control of one's life when not beset with monetary problems or subject to negative ascriptions by the majority culture. Moreover, in the case of this study of deaf children it must be noted that there are no significant differences for the parents of Lo and Hi/Readers in relation to their socioeconomic status, nor were the differences explained by degree of hearing loss.

smell or vision" (Blank, 1975). Later they will belong to "large masses of children and adolescents who, despite repetitive exposure to a wide range of stimuli and in spite of a rather rich set of experiences, do not seem to benefit from them in the direction of increased efficiency in handling either those stimuli or others that may appear in slightly altered form" (Feuerstein and Reimer-Jensen, 1980, p. 406). These are the children who will later become low-functioning adults, regardless of etiology and despite normal ability. They will become adults about whom it is said that they live in the present, have a unique sense of time, and use time to outwit others or to show them that they too have power (Auletta, 1982; Bettelheim, 1971; Feuerstein, 1979; Gonzales and Zimbardo, 1985; Gregory, 1976; Ogbu, 1978; Stierlin, 1977).

There is a subtle influence related to powerlessness in many different groups that leads to dialogue changes, first in the parents and later in their children.

What happens to the children early on?

The language of advantaged and disadvantaged children differs not so much in syntax as in function. Tough (1977) describes 3-year-old disadvantaged children as less likely to use language for recalling past, reasoning about present, or anticipating and predicting future experiences, or to use language for imagination or play. At ages 5 and 7, these children label their environment, do not impose central meanings on their utterances, and are less often explicit. They are less likely to note and define problems, to survey alternatives for solutions, or to project into the experiences and feelings of other people. Deaf children also have delays in using words for feelings appropriately (Greenberg et al., 1984). Disadvantaged children use language for self-main-tenance. Their sentences, "I want this" and "Go away," reflect an expression of their needs and a protection of their interests. By contrast, middle-class children are found to be more disposed to use language for extending and promoting action and for securing collaboration with others: "My daddy will be coming soon, and then I am going home with him" (Tough, 1977). In addition, "lower-class children become increasingly proficient in attending to and describing the world just before them; middle-class children become increasingly proficient in using language as a tool to restructure and reason about their perception" (Blank, Rose, and Berlin, 1978, p. 75).

Blank (1975) gave a *why* question task to high-and low-functioning children from lower-class homes who were divided on the basis of intelligence tests and found that "the well functioning 5-year old children ... achieved some level of correct response on 68% of the ... problems, while at the same age poorly functioning children achieved such responses on only 30% of the problems ... the former [enjoy] ... success experience, the latter ... overwhelming failure" (1975, p. 54). Until the low-functioning youngsters reached 11 years of age, 50% of all their errors were of the unteachable variety (either no answers or irrelevant answers indicating no understanding of the question nor of any of its contents).

Would deaf children react in similar ways, would the deaf Lo/Readers respond as low-functioning youngsters do, and would the deaf Hi/Readers respond as the well-functioning youngsters that Blank studied?

Research

Purpose of the research

The purpose of this chapter is to report a reanalysis of linguistic data collected from deaf elementary school students aged 7 1/2 to 9 who were participating in a longitudinal study initiated almost 20 years ago (Farwell, 1978; Schlesinger and Meadow, 1972, 1976). The youngsters have been followed into their adolescence, and their early responses can now be reinterpreted with respect to the theory of powerlessness and dialogue and in the light of recent research on the language of disadvantaged children.

Subjects

Forty profoundly deaf children and 20 children with normal hearing were recruited as preschoolers to participate in a long-term research project. The deaf toddlers were expected to be "advantaged": They were chosen because they had no additional handicaps, had normal intellectual potential, and were from intact English-speaking families. As adolescents, 38 of the original 40 children completed the Stanford Achievement Test. For this report, the deaf students are divided into two groups on the basis of the SAT: Those who scored above the median (6.6) for reading are identified as deaf Hi/Readers (Group 1, $N = 19$); those who scored below the median for reading on the SAT are called the deaf Lo/Readers (Group 2, $N = 19$). Group 3 comprises 20 children with normal hearing who are identified as "hearing."

The deaf adolescents retained their early advantaged status: Their average reading level was 6.6 whereas that of deaf school-leavers was 3.5 (Karchmer, 1984). However, the grade levels varied widely within the group, ranging from 1.4 to 6.3 for the Lo/Readers and from 6.6 to 12.5 for the Hi/Readers (Schlesinger and Acree, 1984).

The mother's dialogue strategies with their deaf children were studied at toddlerhood, and at 5, 8, and 16 years of age. At each of these ages, strategies that had differentiated advantaged from disadvantaged toddlers in Schachter's (1979) study also significantly differentiated deaf Hi/Readers from deaf Lo/Readers (Borchert, 1984; Schlesinger, 1982; Schlesinger, 1986; Schlesinger and Acree, 1984, 1985). Maternal responsiveness at the first three ages (p < .05) and repetition-of-child versus self-repetition at the first two ages (p < .01) were among the significant differences reported. The above data corroborate the hypothesis that early maternal dialogue is associated with different reading levels at adolescence. Theoretical strategies have been advanced by Tough, Blank, and Feuerstein to hypothesize how maternal dialogue stances relate to differences between well and low functioning children. The hypothesis tested here is that cognitive and psychological stances of elementary school children relate to their future reading status (Hi versus Lo). The underlying variable postulated to relate to different dialogue styles is powerlessness initiated by parental feelings toward the "deafness" of their children and not to the degree of their hearing loss.

Data collection

Farwell (1978) originally devised and administered a task to explore deaf children's comprehension difficulties with Wh-questions of all types. The present analysis is limited to Why-questions (see the appendix). Stories were demonstrated via playroom equipment without linguistic symbols. Thus a wooden cat was chased by a dog, climbed a tree, and was rescued by a father who climbed the tree via a ladder to get the cat down. The questions asked of the children were "Why did the cat climb the tree?" and "Why did father bring the ladder?" Another story was about a sheep that entered a car, drove away, and hit a rock, and thereby caused the car to fall down. A mother was shown waking a father in consternation to relate this unusual event. The questions included "Why did the car fall down?" and "Why did mother wake father?"

Other questions were asked without preliminary storytelling; however, concrete objects representing each concept sign or word were made available to the child. These latter questions included "Why do people get presents?" "Why are presents wrapped?" "Why do babies cry?" "Why do people need flashlights?" "Why do children go to school?" "Why do schools have blackboards?" and "Why do you wear a hearing aid?" In addition, one What-question was added: "What do you want to be when you grow up?"

Farwell asked the questions in the language modality best known to the child (oral-only or speech plus signs) and tried to make sure that each lexical item was understood. None of the children were using American Sign Language at the time of this study, nor were they tested for it. Later, as adolescents, they were tested (Lou, in press). Expressive difficulties were also taken into consideration: *Arf* was permitted to substitute for the word *dog*, and the handling of a diaper with a disgusted look was accepted as referring to a toilet accident. A flexible rephrasing of each question was implemented when an inappropriate response was given. The protocol was not rigidly experimental, but the questions were altered in a dialogue format with a hierarchy of suggested rephrasings. These included repetitions, changes in word order or syntax, and, as a last resort, a yes/no question format. The child's frustration was taken into account in considering the type and number of probes. No attempts were made to influence or correct the grammar. The answers were recorded on videotape and transcribed.

Research questions and hypotheses

The psychological development of individuals or groups of individuals may be understood directly through observation of human behaviors, or via the insights of researchers. Children's responses to the ink blot test, for example, are like windows through which we may glimpse their psyches (Ames et al., 1974). Tough (1977, 1982), on the other hand, provided insights through studies of children's use of feeling labels, while Blank (1970, 1975) looked at abstractions in children's language. The way that children respond to questions reflects the influence of perceptual, cognitive, and affective stances on linguistic output.

The research centers on two primary aspects of the children's responses to the questions. Earlier research (Borchert, 1984; Schlesinger, 1982, 1986; Schlesinger and Acree, 1984, 1985) uncovered a relationship between parental dialogue styles at toddlerhood and subsequent reading levels of their deaf adolescents. Specific linguistic differences in the responses of the three groups in elementary school were then predicted. It is hypothesized that the responses can be interpreted in terms of the theory of powerlessness and dialogue that was summarized in the introduction to this chapter. The first focus of the analysis is simply a judgment of the "appropriateness" of the content and the "correctness" of the grammar of each response and the number of modifications required to obtain appropriate responses. Correctness was judged liberally and the children did not need to meet all the demands of the task. Imprecise and oblique answers containing extraneous material were also scored as appropriate, or "correct" (Blank et al., 1978). Even appropriateness of answers is related to the theory of powerlessness, since it is predicted that hearing children and deaf Hi/Readers will have more appropriate answers and thus will produce fewer dialogue disruptions and will tug less at their mother's sense of ability and power.

The second focus of the questions is more psychological and concerns developmental, psychological, and potentially psycholinguistic issues. These issues are described earlier in the chapter and pertain to Tough's work (1977), which relates to the tendency of disadvantaged youngsters to label versus impose a "central meaning" on their environment and to use fewer labels for feelings or for the future, and the work of Blank et al. (1978), which indicates that disadvantaged children develop some language strategies at a later age than their advantaged peers and predicts similar tendencies for the deaf Lo/Readers.

A. Hypotheses Related to the Appropriateness of Responses
1. Hearing children and deaf Hi/Readers will give more appropriate answers than deaf Lo/Readers.
2. In general, deaf children will have a higher number of English grammatical errors than the hearing controls and the errors will be of a different type.
3. The three groups will differ significantly with respect to appropriate responses and correct grammar, and the differences between them.
4. Modifications of questions can lead to appropriate responses; however, deaf Lo/Readers will need the highest number of repetitions and modifications with the least number of eventually appropriate responses.
5. Deaf Lo/Readers will give more unteachable responses, as defined by Blank (1975).

B. Psychological, Developmental and Potentially Psycholinguistic Measures
1. Both groups of deaf children, but especially deaf Lo/Readers, will demonstrate some language features characteristic of younger hearing children.
2. Hearing children and deaf Hi/Readers are less likely to engage in labeling strategies only and are more likely to impose a central meaning to their responses.
3. Hearing children and deaf Hi/Readers are more likely to use feeling words in interactional ways (taking the view of the other).
4. Hearing children and deaf Hi/Readers are more likely to incorporate both the concept and the language of a sense of the future in their responses.

Results and discussion

Linguistic differences

APPROPRIATENESS OF RESPONSE

As predicted, there are striking differences in the utterances of the three groups of children. The hearing children's responses were appropriate 96% of the time, in contrast to 83% for the deaf Hi/Readers, and only 48% for the deaf Lo/Readers (Table 1). In comparison, the percentage of correct responses for Blank's high-functioning children at 5 years of age (two years earlier than our subjects) was 68%, and for the low-functioning children it was less than 30%.

TABLE I. PERCENTAGES OF APPROPRIATE/INAPPROPRIATE ANSWERS TO 10 QUESTIONS

	Deaf		All hearing
	Lo/Read	Hi/Read	All hearing
Appropriate	48	83	96
Inappropriate	52	17	4
N	19	19	20

TABLE 2. PERCENTAGES AND NUMBER OF TYPES OF ENGLISH GRAMMAR ERRORS, DEAF AND HEARING CHILDREN

	Deaf		Hearing	
Type of error	%	(N)	%	(N)
Omissions	63	(87)	47	(7)
Substitutions	4	(6)	7	(1)
Additions	4	(6)	7	(1)
Word order	8	(11)	7	(1)
Tense	15	(21)	24	(4)
Third-person singular	6	(8)	7	(1)
Totals	100	(139)	100	(15)

Note: Obviously there are too few errors by the hearing children to make comparisons meaningful. However, despite the insensitivity due to the floor effect, the two groups are remarkably similar in the distribution of types of errors made.

APPROPRIATENESS OF RESPONSE AND
CORRECTNESS OF GRAMMAR

As predicted, deaf children do have more errors of English grammar than do hearing children, but the distribution of types of errors is remarkably similar for hearing and deaf children (Table 2).

The three groups of youngsters differed significantly in their percentages of appropriate responses and correct grammar (Table 3).

No significant differences were found between deaf Hi/Readers and deaf Lo/Readers with respect to the differences between percentages of appropriate response and percentages of correct grammar, as had been predicted (Table 4).

REPETITIONS AND MODIFICATIONS OF QUESTIONS

As predicted, deaf children needed and received patient probings, repetitions, and modifications of each original question following the orig-

TABLE 3. APPROPRIATE ANSWERS AND CORRECT ENGLISH GRAMMAR

| | Deaf | | All hearing |
	Lo/Read	Hi/Read	
Answer mean	47.532	83.453	96.450
Grammar mean	8.684	50.526	84.400
S.D. Answer	30.406	17.431	7.501
S.D. Grammar	19.709	30.817	13.212

Note: *t*-tests between all three groups significant $p < .001$.

TABLE 4. DIFFERENCES BETWEEN APPROPRIATE ANSWERS AND
CORRECT GRAMMAR

| | Deaf | | All hearing |
	Lo/Read	Hi/Read	
Diff. A–G	38.847	32.926	12.050
S.D.	26.738	21.849	8.325

Note: *t*-tests significant between deaf Hi/Read and Lo/Read and hearing $p < .001$.

inal failure. Deaf Hi/Readers were exposed to a total of 92 questions, or 2.2 questions/child, whereas deaf Lo/Readers were exposed to a total of 368 questions, or 3.8 questions/child. However, not as predicted, the success/failure rate of modifications was essentially similar for deaf Lo/Readers and Hi/Readers (Table 5), and only 36% of questions asked the Lo/Readers and 30% of the questions asked the Hi/Readers led to success. Although a "rephrasing procedure, used when a child failed to answer correctly, improved group scores for all *wh* questions from about 50% to 85% correct" (Farwell, 1978, p. 2), more than 60% of the present repetitions of *why* questions led to failure. Both Hi/Readers (70%) and Lo/Readers (64%) experienced ongoing failure following the original inappropriate response.

UNTEACHABLE RESPONSES

As predicted, the percentages of unteachable answers was high. The percentages of unteachable answers are even more catastrophic (Table 6) than those reported by Blank (1975) for poorly functioning hearing children, 50% of whose inappropriate answers were also unteachable until 11 years of age. The deaf children's inappropriate answers were unteachable 79% of the time for the deaf Hi/Readers and 92% for the Lo/Readers. In sharp contrast, the hearing children's inappropriate answers were unteachable only 25% of the time.

TABLE 5. PERCENTAGE OF QUESTIONS LEADING TO SUCCESS OR TO FAILURE

| | *Deaf* | | *All hearing* |
	Lo/Read	*Hi/Read*	
Questions leading to success	36	30	n.a.
Questions leading to failure	64	70	n.a.
N	368	92	n.a.

Note: n.a. = Not applicable; repetition protocol not comparable.

TABLE 6. TEACHABLE/UNTEACHABLE INAPPROPRIATE ANSWERS TO 10 QUESTIONS (%)

| | *Deaf* | | *All hearing* |
	Lo/Read	*Hi/Read*	
Teachable	8	21	75
Unteachable	92	79	25

Psychological differences as expressed through linguistic differences

LANGUAGE FEATURES SHARED WITH THOSE OF YOUNGER HEARING CHILDREN

Deaf children gave more one-word answers, but not all their replies were laconic. Some deaf youngsters actually gave longer, more varied, and elaborated answers than did their hearing peers: for example, "Walking up the tree to get cat down and cat didn't want to come down," and "Lamb going in the old-fashioned car?" (see Table 9). The hearing subjects' productions were more monotonous and had identical content (e.g., "Cause dog chased him," and "Lamb drove car") and identical pronunciations (e.g., most of the hearing children used "cause"); the deaf children were much more likely to attempt varyingly successful approximations of "because." Divergent and innovative replies are usually typical for younger children. The hearing children's convergence to high-frequency response is found to be similar to that of older children (Entwisle, 1970). Disadvantaged black youngsters have been known to respond with innovative charm to the word "sour" with "still good," an association never given by the white children. Such "charming" divergence can later interfere with school activities (Entwisle, 1970). Thus, the deaf Lo/Readers' responses resembled those of younger or disadvantaged children.

Deaf children often gave minimal answers to questions following the

TABLE 7. PERCENTAGES OF APPROPRIATE RESPONSES REVEALING DIFFERENT STRATEGIES TO THE QUESTION "WHY DO PEOPLE GET PRESENTS?" RELATING TO ENUMERATION VERSUS CENTRAL MEANING OR SUPERORDINATES

	Deaf		All hearing
	Lo/Read	*Hi/Read*	*All hearing*
Enumeration	80	84	42
Superordinate	20	16	58
N	10	19	19

TABLE 8. PERCENTAGE OF APPROPRIATE ANSWERS ASSOCIATED WITH FEELINGS TO QUESTIONS RELATING TO WHY OF ACTION "CLIMBING CAT," OF FUNCTION "FLASHLIGHTS," AND OF INTERPERSONAL CAUSATION "PRESENTS" AND "BABY CRYING"

	Deaf		All hearing
	Lo/Read	*Hi/Read*	*All hearing*
Climb + feel	30	27	0
N	10	15	19
Flashlights + feel	18	18	5
N	11	17	19
Presents + feel	0	11	37
N	10	19	19
Babies + feel	0	26	40
N	17	19	20

acted-out stories. "Why did father get the ladder?" was frequently answered by the singleton answer "cat." Since everyone in the room had seen the wooden cat climb the tree, this answer was adequate. However, had this interchange occurred in a context-reduced environment (Cummins, 1981), this response would be characterized as an "implicit" response providing insufficient information and leading to obfuscated meaning in dialogue. When two of the questions, those concerning "flashlights" and "blackboards," required the children to combine two concepts in order to produce a more general, global, functional concept (to see in the dark, to write for all to see), the deaf children tended not to combine the two concepts available to them. This may be interpreted as difficulty in dealing with two sources of information, a hallmark of low-functioning children (Feuerstein and Reimer-Jensen, 1980).

One last result can be seen as shared with younger hearing children. In their initial reply to the question "Why do schools have blackboards?" 50% of deaf Lo/Readers and 21% of deaf Hi/Readers uttered a concrete version of "my school green, not black." Such a concrete answer was not given by any of the hearing children. This may represent the perceptually bound, egocentric, nondecentered reply usually given by more immature youngsters. In addition, recent research (Schlesinger, 1986) demonstrates that mothers of future Deaf Lo/Readers provide significantly more concrete and less abstract utterances to their children than do mothers of future Hi/Readers.

LABELING VERSUS CENTRAL MEANING

Table 7 and the discussion on explicitness indicate that deaf children's responses to the question "Why do people get presents?" tend to parallel Tough's (1977) findings for disadvantaged youngsters. As Table 7 demonstrates, more than 80% of the deaf children (80% of deaf Lo/Readers and 84% of deaf Hi/Readers) used labels, that is, enumerated a list of (up to five) different days on which people might get presents, whereas only 16% imposed a central meaning and referred to a superordinate category: "surprise" or "special days." The hearing children produced about three times as many superordinates (58%), enumerated fewer days (42%), and gave more "personal" reasons for present giving. Superordinates are words that encompass several items such as fruit, do not have a single perceptual referent, and require dialogue for acquisition. Furthermore, superordinates cannot be represented graphically and therefore cannot be tested nonverbally (Youniss, personal communication). Although, it is now well known that American Sign Language superordinates are represented by a concatenated list of various items (Bellugi, personal communication), the items are usually limited to three and have a specific cadence; furthermore, none of the children were conversant with American Sign Language at the time of this study.

In any case, more deaf children appear to perceive the reasons for gifts to be unrelated to personal experiences or causations and to arrive as if by manna from heaven on externally determined and imposed days: birthdays, Christmas, Father's day, and the like. Seven of the hearing children (37%) referred to interactional feelings as reasons for gift giving, either as a reward for good behavior of for altruistic reasons in order "to make others happy." Only 11% of the deaf Hi/Readers and none of the Lo/Readers did so (Table 8). It is of some interest that the deaf Hi/Readers also received more interpersonal explanations and justifications for events from their parents (Schachter, 1979; Schlesinger and Acree, 1984).

THE USE OF FEELING LABELS

Table 8 summarizes the use of feeling labels in the responses to four questions. The feeling labels in the first two questions both refer to fear: The cat climbed because "he was afraid," and flashlights are needed in the dark "because of monsters," and because of being "scared." There

TABLE 9. PERCENTAGE OF RESPONSES WITH ELABORATION, SELF-REVELATION, OR MENTION OF FUTURE

| | Deaf | | |
	Lo/Read	Hi/Read	All hearing
Elaboration	11	30	10
Self-revelation	21	42	60
Mention of future	32	68	70
N	19	19	20

were no differences between the two deaf groups (18%), but the hearing children gave fewer responses relating to fear (5%). There is no evidence that deaf children are more afraid than hearing children (Schlesinger and Meadow, 1976), and it is noted that the fears in the first two responses are related to animals or things. Neither the fearful quality of the "dark" nor the cat that was "afraid" is related to interactions with, or projections into, the experiences of other human beings.

The last two responses of Table 8, however, parallel Tough's (1977, 1982) differentiation between advantaged and disadvantaged toddlers. The causal, interpersonal feelings involved with the "getting of presents" has already been described. The next feeling question relates to a baby's tears: 40% of hearing children and 26% of deaf Hi/Readers cite feelings such as "shy" and "embarrassed" as reasons for a baby's tears; none of the deaf Lo/Readers do so. The ability and tendency to project into the feelings of others leads toward empathy and is a step away from Tough's "self-maintaining language" (1982).

INCORPORATION OF A SENSE OF THE FUTURE

There were two opportunities to analyze the incorporation of a sense of the future in the children's linguistic responses. During the Why questions and the general interview following the questions, the hearing children (70%) and the deaf Hi/Readers (68%) referred to a "future" twice as often as did the deaf Lo/Readers (32%) (Table 9). The maternal ability to use language with "freedom from immediacy" had been studied when these youngsters were toddlers. At that time, 95% of mother/deaf-child dyads limited their communications to topics with a visual referent of the here and now. On the other hand, 45% of the mother/hearing-child dyads made at least a passing comment about a nonvisual referent, and 15% of this latter group had prolonged conversations about objects or people distant in time or space (Schlesinger, 1972).

More hearing (60%) and deaf Hi/reading youngsters (42%) than deaf Lo/Readers (21%) use the acted-out stories and the interview as a jumping off point for self-revelatory comments. The youngsters offered "I

TABLE 10. PERCENTAGE OF APPROPRIATE RESPONSES TO THE QUESTION
"WHAT DO YOU WANT TO BE WHEN YOU GROW UP?"

	Deaf		All hearing
	Lo/Read	Hi/Read	
Adult imitations	67	7	0
Adult aspirations	22	60	67
Adult postponement	11	33	33
N	9	15	18

am very good at reading," "I got chased by Freddie," and "I live where
there are no stores" (Table 9). One might speculate that children who
display a sense of the future can also display a sense of self to inhabit
it. One youngster excitedly conveyed future dreams: "The first time I
want to be a soldier, then I want to be a police, and then I want to be
a doctor." It could be said that his need to boss was increasingly more
socialized.

The other opportunity to view the children's concept of the future
was an analysis of their responses to "What do you want to be when
you grow up?" As expected, this was a difficult question for many of
them. The sense of the future is intricately related to a sense of power,
which is in turn intimately related to socioeconomic status. Those who
have been rendered powerless by society tend to be pessimistic about
their future chances for work or other access to power and early on will
have lower aspirations (Kohn, 1969; Leacock, 1969). Thus, hearing
children (56%) and deaf Hi/Readers (39%) describe (a reality-based)
greater variability of opportunities for their future than do deaf Lo/
Readers.

An equal proportion (33%) of hearing and deaf Hi/Readers and a
lower percentage (11%) of deaf Lo/Readers are not sure about their
future or have not made up their mind (listed in Table 10 as adult
postponement). Some simply said, "I don't know"; some couched the
same thought in more elegant terminology, "I have not decided yet" or
"I haven't even thought about that." Willingness to admit to uncertainty
or to inhibit an impulsive response is more characteristic of older children
and may also be a product of middle-class upbringing.

Deaf Hi/Readers (60%) and hearing children (67%) have almost equal
aspirations for future work, but only 22% of deaf Lo/Readers have such
hopes (listed in Table 10 as adult aspirations). Sadly, deaf children (both
deaf Hi/Readers and deaf Lo/Readers) have fewer (50% fewer) aspirations toward a professional future than do the hearing children. A number of deaf children, both deaf Hi/Reader (7%), but predominantly deaf
Lo/Readers (67%), yearn only to be as tall, or as big, or as able to have

TABLE II. PERCENTAGE OF APPROPRIATE RESPONSES TO THE QUESTION "WHY
DO BABIES CRY?"

| | Deaf | | |
	Lo/Read	Hi/Read	All hearing
Describing:			
An older baby	47	42	95
A younger baby	53	58	5
N	17	19	20

loads of money as either father or mother (listed as adult imitations in
Table 10). These youngsters yearn for the advantages of adulthood
without the accompanying responsibility. Two hearing children also
yearn for the acquisition of money, but both are careful to add an
aspiration for a lucrative profession to their "I want to make money"
answers.

OTHER INITIALLY UNSPECIFIED, PSYCHOLOGICAL
DIFFERENCES

The analysis of the hypotheses above brought forth a number of other
differences possibly related to the theory of powerlessness and dialogue
and expressed in the following three post hoc hypotheses. There will
be:

1. *Linguistic Representation of Delayed Autonomy.* The responses to
the question "Why do babies cry?" revealed that deaf children and
hearing children appear to conceptualize and describe babies differently
and that developmentally different babies emerge from their utterances.
Deaf children, whose autonomy is often delayed, see in their mind's eye
a younger, more dependent baby. They describe an infant more involved
with "mother," "milk," and "bottle." Fifty-nine percent of the deaf
children (53% deaf Lo/Readers and 58% deaf Hi/Readers) characterize
such a young infant, versus only 5% of the hearing children. The older
baby, conceptualized by 95% of the hearing, but by less than one half
of the deaf youngsters (Table 11), cried for food and drink, had feelings
(see "The Use of Feeling Labels"), and had toilet accidents. Thus, more
deaf children evidenced a delay in describing a toddler struggling for
autonomy, just as their parents delay in providing autonomy for them
(Chess, Korn, and Fernandez, 1971; Schlesinger and Meadow, 1972).

2. *Linguistic Encoding of External/Internal Control, Ego/Superego
Stances.* When individuals feel powerless, they assume that control or
power resides outside, in others, or is kept in check only by a strict
conscience, often referred to as superego. When people feel in control
of their lives, the responsibility for actions resides in their very self and

TABLE 12. PERCENTAGE OF APPROPRIATE EGO/SUPEREGO ANSWERS TO THE
QUESTION "WHY DO CHILDREN GO TO SCHOOL?"

	Deaf		All hearing
	Lo/Read	Hi/Read	
Ego	40	71	89
Superego	60	29	11
N	5	14	19

their control is internal, a concept somewhat parallel to ego. Three
questions tapped the children's tendency to provide ego versus superego
responses relating to functions of school and hearing aids and the purpose of wrapping presents.

"Why do children go to school?" The children (by serendipity) were
asked a question identical to the one asked by Hess and Shipman (1965),
who found that middle-class children saw themselves as going to school
"to learn," an ego response, and lower-class children because "one had
to," a superego response. These differences are interesting and might be
expected from youngsters who must experience school activities and
their control of them quite differently. External locus of control has
generally been found to be more prevalent among children of lower
socioeconomic status (Koestner et al., 1984) and has been suspected by
clinicians to be more prevalent among low-functioning deaf children.
Only 60% of deaf children gave an appropriate answer to this question
in comparison with 100% of hearing children. Of much greater interest,
however, is the ego/superego breakdown of answers: 40% of deaf Lo/
Readers, (70%), of deaf Hi/Readers and 89% of hearing children saw
themselves as trotting off to school "to learn." The remainder of each
group saw themselves as "having to go" (Table 12).

These findings parallel Hess and Shipman's earlier findings insofar as
the deaf children, especially the deaf Lo/Readers, answer more often in
the same way as the lower-class children.

"Why do you wear a hearing aid?" This question was not asked of
the hearing children, for whom it was irrelevant. More than half of deaf
children (Table 13) saw the hearing aid as an instrument to help with
hearing (56%) rather than as a negative hallmark of deafness (44%).
Sixty-three (63%) of deaf Hi/Readers described the hearing aid as helping
them to "hear" and provided fewer (37%) negative reasons for wearing
it. Deaf Lo/Readers gave fewer ego responses (33%) and gave a higher
(67%) number of hearing aid–negative responses ("ears broken,"
"deaf," "can't hear," or "you must"). This ego/superego differentiation
was based more on the children's sense of success than on their au-

TABLE 13. PERCENTAGE OF APPROPRIATE EGO/SUPEREGO RESPONSES TO THE
QUESTION "WHY DO YOU WEAR A HEARING AID?"

| | Deaf | | All hearing |
	Lo/Read	Hi/Read	
Ego	33	63	not applicable
Superego	67	37	n.a.
N	6	19	n.a.

TABLE 14. PERCENTAGE OF APPROPRIATE EGO/SUPEREGO RESPONSES TO THE
QUESTION "WHY ARE PRESENTS WRAPPED?"

| | Deaf | | All hearing |
	Lo/Read	Hi/Read	
Ego	100	64	58
Superego	0	36	42
N	2	11	20

diological measures. More academically successful youngsters with only moderate hearing gain gave "to hear" as the reason for wearing a hearing aid than did youngsters with academic failure but good gain from their hearing aids.

"Why are presents wrapped?" This last question of the ego/superego differentiation, however, demonstrates an almost equal distribution of superego responses ("don't peek") and superordinate, ego responses ("surprise"), for two out of the three groups (Table 14). The deaf Lo/ Readers showed a superficially puzzling and unexpected 100% ego response rate. This question was the most difficult of all questions and had the lowest rate of appropriate responses for all three groups. Therefore, it was not unexpected that only two deaf Lo/Readers produced an appropriate answer; the fact that both were ego responses may be understood by the iconicity of the word *surprise* and the frequency with which it is used with deaf toddlers.

3. Linguistic Encoding of Active/Passive Orientation. One of Feuerstein's (Feuerstein et al., 1980) goals of intervention is the arousal of the low-functioning "performer from his role of passive recipient and reproducer of information to a role of active generator of new information" (p. 285). One component of a sense of powerlessness is the tendency to see oneself as object-acted-upon, rather than as agent-actively-doing. Often this self-image is based in reality, and the lives of low-functioning individuals are replete with others who act upon them.

TABLE 15. PERCENTAGES OF APPROPRIATE ACTIVE/PASSIVE RESPONSES TO THE
QUESTION "WHY DID THE CAT CLIMB THE TREE?"

	Deaf		
	Lo/Read	*Hi/Read*	*All hearing*
Active	30	73	100
Passive	70	27	0
N	10	15	19

TABLE 16. PERCENTAGE OF APPROPRIATE ACTIVE/PASSIVE ANSWERS TO THE
QUESTION "WHY DID FATHER BRING THE LADDER?"

	Deaf		
	Lo/Read	*Hi/Read*	*All hearing*
Active	33	68	90
Passive	67	31	10
N	12	19	20

TABLE 17. PERCENTAGES OF APPROPRIATE ACTIVE/PASSIVE RESPONSES TO THE
QUESTION "WHY DID THE CAR FALL OVER?"

	Deaf		
	Lo/Read	*Hi/Read*	*All hearing*
Active	27	67	80
Passive	73	33	20
N	11	18	20

Six of the questions involved actions either directly or indirectly (Tables 15–20). The hearing group typically respond with an action word or phrase: "Dog chased the cat," "children copy," and "to see in the dark." The deaf children are equally likely to employ a descriptive, passive stance ("cat afraid," "dark outside") and when they do use a verb, they do so in negation ("can't see"). Striking reversals were found between deaf Lo/Readers and deaf Hi/Readers whose linguistic contact with the world has been hypothesized to be passive and active, respectively.

"Why did mother wake father?" The children's passivity extended to animals since more deaf Lo/Readers (69%), and deaf Hi/Readers (35%) than hearing (5%) children plopped the sheep passively into the car and said only "Sheep in car" or "sheep" (Table 18). More deaf Hi/Readers

TABLE 18. PERCENTAGES OF APPROPRIATE ACTIVE/PASSIVE RESPONSES TO THE
QUESTION "WHY DID MOTHER WAKE UP FATHER?"

| | Deaf | | All hearing |
	Lo/Read	Hi/Read	
Active	31	65	95
Passive	69	35	5
N	13	17	20

TABLE 19. PERCENTAGES OF APPROPRIATE ACTIVE/PASSIVE RESPONSES TO THE
QUESTION "WHY DO PEOPLE NEED FLASHLIGHTS?"

| | Deaf | | All hearing |
	Lo/Read	Hi/Read	
Active	9	56	94
Passive	91	44	6
N	11	17	19

(65%) and even more hearing (95%) youngsters compared with deaf
Lo/Readers (31%) described a lamb more actively involved with some
driving mechanism of the car: "Lamb drives car."

"Why do people need flashlights?" All the hearing children used some linguistic version of "in order to see in the dark," and included both components necessary for the more encompassing concept – see and dark (Table
19). Forty-seven percent of deaf children simply replied "dark," a static, descriptive response, lacking the active component of the function. It may be
that some of the "dark" respondents were replying to a *When* question.
However, even when deaf children included both categories, their answers
remained passive; their passivity extended to the verb forms themselves,
since several of them used a negation of the verb, "dark *can't* see." ("can't
hear," as in the hearing aid question above).

"Why do schools have blackboards?" All the hearing children who
answered appropriately (17) gave a version of "teacher writes so that
all the children can see." All the deaf children who answered appropriately (only 2 for the Lo and 11 for the Hi/readers) replied "write,"
a teacher activity, to judge by the hearing youngsters, in which the other,
not the self, is seen as the agent. Only after considerable probing did
three of the deaf children include their own agentive activities "copy,"
"look," and "see" (Table 20).

TABLE 20. PERCENTAGE OF APPROPRIATE ACTIVE/PASSIVE ANSWERS TO THE
QUESTION "WHY DO SCHOOLS HAVE BLACKBOARDS?"

| | Deaf | | |
	Lo/Read	Hi/Read	All hearing
Active	0	0	41
Passive	100	100	59
N	2	11	17

Implications

The strained dialogue

Analyses of hearing mother/deaf-child dialogue have demonstrated that
it is possible to share "meaning and enjoyment" (Schlesinger, 1972,
1986). Only too frequently, however, it is noted that meaning is not
exchanged, maternal responsivity is low, maternal control is high, and
the interaction is strained.

It appears obvious that many of the researcher/deaf-child dialogues
are replete with response errors, and require many patient probings,
modifications, and repetitions of questions, particularly for the deaf Lo/
Readers. This finding is consistent with reports on disadvantaged
youngsters indicating that lower-class children require twice the number
of questions to provide the same amount of information as advantaged
youngsters do (Heider, Cazden, and Brown, 1968, cited in Cazden,
1970). This paucity of information is usually interpreted as "lack of
ability" or "lack of understanding" on the part of disadvantaged youngsters. However, we believe that communicational barrage (usually on
the part of the parent) or reticence (usually on the part of the child) is
being used in a desperate attempt to gain or maintain control by individuals who experience a lack of control. Individuals feel in control
when they produce the language in dialogue (Donaldson, cited in Cummins, 1981). Disadvantaged youngsters (Schachter, 1979) and deaf children (Schlesinger, 1986) have few such experiences with adults.

Also, dialogues that contain ongoing errors and repetitions are dis-
ruptive and lead to cognitive dissonance and avoidance. They may lead
to less parental reponsiveness, less complex *Why* questions, and more
constraint questions. Some authors are painfully aware that question
asking does not always enlarge horizons (Harris, 1982) and does not
extend the barren interchanges of "What is this?" "What color is this?"
questions that are ubiquitous in deaf-child/mother dyads (Mittler and
Berry, 1977).

Failures and laments

There are tragic failures among too many deaf children. Six of the deaf Lo/Readers experienced ongoing failure; they gave no answer or gave irrelevant answers to every question, or every question but one, analyzed in this chapter; eventually they were no longer given questions. The powerlessness of both child and parent, both teacher and student must increase during such dialogues. It seems probable that one quarter to one third of the deaf children in the study were not participants in early complex dialogue and did not reach their normal potential.

Children who do not reach their potential stress not only their parents, but a number of their future authority figures. Teachers of disadvantaged and deaf children participate in powerlessness and "dialogue games" and have often been noted to be very controlling (Blank, 1970; Hoeman, 1972; Ogbu, 1978; Tough, 1982). School administrators who also participate in the game are nonproductively controlling, an unfortunate outcome as it is the opposite – autonomy of caregivers – that increases children's language acquisition (Tizard, 1974).

Child powerlessness and its concomitants

A number of psychological variables are hypothesized to spring from powerlessness and to be mediated through mother/child dialogue. Delayed in their autonomy and often pressured to remain dependent, the deaf children in the study conceptualized a younger baby's tears. One consequence of feeling powerless is a tendency to seek power through association with the power of another (McClelland, 1975). In that way the "baby" continues to need mother, as an "outside power."

Powerlessness also provokes and promotes passivity. Passivity is encoded into the language productions of children and language use of their mothers. Interestingly, it has been noted that middle-class mothers use labels for actions and attributes whereas lower-class mothers tend to teach only nouns for labels for objects (Ninio, cited in Snow, Dubber, and De Blauw, 1982). Similarly, mothers of future Lo/Deaf readers use fewer verbs and attributes than do the mothers of future Hi/Readers (Schlesinger, 1986). Their children reflect this phenomenon, and most deaf Lo/Readers omit action words in their responses or only use the negation of an action. Negation as such is not an easier linguistic form, but may represent a passive avoidance of taking action. A consistent pattern evolved from questions that invited responses involving either active or passive stances. The highest level of active stances was found among hearing children, followed by deaf Hi/Readers and lastly by the more passive deaf Lo/Readers. A poignant similarity is found in Rorschach responses of children of varying socioeconomic status; static representations are more frequently seen among inner-city children, and human and animal movements are more frequently found among middle-class children (Ames et al., 1974). Another poignant example of passive language on the part of deaf children can be found in Ewing and Ewing (1964, p. 66), who describe as "errors" phrases that resemble the passive stances analyzed above. A picture depicting a girl holding her cat above her head to save it from a dog jumping up at her was described as "a girl has a baby cat in her hands and the little dog is running after it." At least the dog was active; the girl herself was not. The next picture depicts a girl trying to catch her hat, which had been blown off by the wind. This picture is described as "A little girl. Her hat's blown off her head." The wind or the hat was active, although the girl herself was not. This, too, can be an outgrowth of the internalized experiential status of passivity.

However, and not in direct contradiction, John and Goldstein (1967) stress that low SES children have difficulty with action words because they have relatively little opportunity to engage in active dialogue when learning labels, especially labels that have low stability between the word and the referent, and therefore require more "corrective feedback" from the parent. Other work (Schlesinger, 1987) notes that the crucial ingredient may be parental responsiveness to what the child says, rather than the corrective aspect of the interaction.

Accepting or internalizing a passive stance through life is related to the overall issue of control: Deaf children frequently are and see themselves under the control of others. They have been subjected to an excess of control talk from parents who have not themselves felt in control. A number of individuals have pointed to the close relationship between language and power, and have stressed the need for further study (Brown and Gillman, 1972; Harris, 1983; McClelland, 1975; Slaughter, 1983). This may relate to why blackboards are seen for others to write on, school attendance is necessary because others say you must go, and hearing aids are for broken ears, and not for the positive function of helping to hear. With regard to the question of future careers, deaf children have fewer aspirations for the professions and appear to have integrated what some researchers (Leacock, 1969; Leahy, 1983; Ogbu, 1978) refer to as early internalization of the reality of job ceilings, and of un- and underemployment. Quite clearly, the unsuccessful, and partly even the successful, deaf children begin to sense the negative ascriptions made about them first by their parents and later by the educational system and society. Depending on school placements, they also note the absence or scarcity of high-level deaf role models. This becomes even more poignant when it is noted that one-third of deaf children, predominantly deaf Lo/Readers, only desire to be as tall or as rich as father or mother. That 5 out of 24 deaf children who answered this question want to be soldiers, policemen, or "boss, soldier, boom pow" (the highest number of future aspirations) reflects the importance of the issue of control in their outlooks.

Researchers have long believed that the sense of the future is intricately related to powerlessness, which is in turn related to socioeconomic status, and that the future is mentioned less frequently by disadvantaged and deaf children (Feuerstein, 1979; Gregory, 1976; Tough, 1977). There are also innumerable references to the fact that disadvantaged and deaf children and adults live "in the present" (Auletta, 1982; Gonzales and Zimbardo, 1985; Ogbu, 1978). Some have believed this to be linguistic, others behavioral, in nature (Williams, 1970). It probably is a combination of both: The tendency to live in the here and now, the inability to delay gratification, can be related to a lack of linguistic/cognitive capacity or desire for representation of more distant goals. This lack of planning, however, may also be related to life conditions that have prevented individuals from actively determining their own future. The individual never placed in the position to predict, does not acquire the necessary skill and orientation toward planning behavior (Feuerstein et al., 1980).

A different outcome?

Deaf children and their mothers need dialogue for many reasons: "[To] embark on a path that is unique to the human community, that is the use of language as a way of transmitting information from one generation to the next" (Blank et al., 1978, p. 15). This traditional transmission is crucial. Indeed, Feuerstein (1977) defines culturally deprived individuals not as those who come from a deprived, or a depriving culture, but as those who have not had the opportunity to have the verbal concomitants of the parental culture transmitted to them. There is evidence that groups with the highest levels of cultural identity manifest the highest levels of cognitive functioning (Stodolsky and Lesser, 1967). This finding can be applied to many emigrants and to many deaf children of deaf parents. It does, however, produce a puzzle with respect to deaf children of hearing parents, who for their roots need transmission from their parents and for their wings need contact with the deaf community (this mixed metaphor obtained from Meadow, personal communication). It is important to note that anthropologists have described the possibility of some cultural transmission "totally devoid of verbal communication" (Feuerstein, 1977, p. 367), but nevertheless in a dialogue format. The mothers of the deaf Hi/Readers enjoy both verbal and nonverbal behaviors of their children, the mothers of the deaf Lo/Readers anxiously await, promote, and correct speech (Schlesinger and Acree, 1984).

The work reported here indicates that deaf children need more mediating dialogue with mothers who feel powerful. Indeed it has been shown that the most ideal caretakers are those who ascribe power to themselves and to their children (Bugental and Shennum, 1984). If mothers do not feel powerful, whatever the reasons, their interactions will shift toward directive monologues, and mothers and children will suffer. For the child, autonomy will decrease, passivity increase, and planning for the future will lessen. Conceptual skills will not flourish, for their development flows not from encounters with the physical world but rather from encounters with certain forms of complex dialogue (Blank, 1975). Similarly, inadequacy in defining the existence of problems and an inability to select relevant, as opposed to irrelevant, cues in defining a problem, or an inability to use two sources of information will interfere with cognition and stems from the lack of early mediated dialogue (Feuerstein and Reimer-Jensen, 1980).

Without mediating dialogue, English language will suffer out of proportion to the hearing loss (as language suffers in some disadvantaged hearing children). The acquisition of verbs and superordinates will be delayed, as will the understanding and use of questions, especially *why* and *how* questions. The word *why* has no physical referent and thus requires complex dialogue for acquisition. The different *why* questions – those of action, of function, of causal relationships, and of justification – are the very concepts that need to be mediated by a responsive adult to a child who initiates and sustains various exchanges (Blank, 1975). Note that Blank uses the words *initiate* and *sustain,* not *passively observe.* She predicts: "The mastery of a term such as *why* is a long and difficult process ... poor performance in this sphere is almost always a diagnostic sign that the child will experience difficulties in the academic setting" (p. 56). Those in our study who failed *why* questions at the age of 8 "failed" reading at adolescence.

Those who did well, generally deaf Hi/Readers, tended to be placed between the hearing children and the deaf Lo/Readers. It is to be noted, however, that deaf Hi/Readers are very similar to hearing children in a number of important features: in the encoding of a sense of the future and of a more external locus of control. On the other hand, deaf Hi/Readers are more nearly similar to deaf Lo/ Readers in delaying the imposition of central meanings to their responses, in conceptualizing a younger baby, and in describing feelings of fear. For the remaining variables, interpersonal feelings and passivity, they are almost exactly between the other two groups of children. Further study is necessary to spell out more completely what else needs to happen in parental dialogues to further promote a more felicitous development of deaf children.

As of now, we can state that, if psychological characterizations are encoded linguistically, as has been assumed for this chapter, and the sum of the encodings represents an individual, then, in comparison with their peers, deaf Lo/Readers appear massively passive, without much hope for the future, and either still struggling for control or despairing to get it. Deaf Hi/Readers do much better; in comparison with hearing youngsters, they are more immature and more passive, but fully as able to take charge of their lives and to set goals for their future. They may even reach the "money" they want, for it is said that "the mixture of factors that best predicts high income is future oriented work motivation, goal seeking and daily planning, coupled with low scores on fatalism" (Gonzales and Zimbardo, 1985).

Some results in the chapter are depressing, others are heartening. The future looks bright for the deaf Hi/Readers described here and for more and more deaf children able to refer to their future enthusiastically.

Summary

Striking differences occur between utterances made by deaf Hi/Readers, deaf Lo/Readers, and hearing children. Earlier research with these three groups has demonstrated that early mother/child dialogue features correlate significantly with children's later reading successes, whereas maternal monologues *at* the children correlate with their future reading failures. The research reported here suggests that cognitive and psychological stances of elementary school students as encoded linguistically are also directly related to maternal dialogue stances at toddlerhood.

Acknowledgment

Deep appreciation is expressed to Dr. Kathryn P. Meadow and Gallaudet University for their general support through peace and war since the early seventies and for their contribution to this chapter.

Appendix: Questions asked

1. Why did the cat climb the tree?
2. Why did the father bring the ladder?
3. Why did the car fall over?
4. Why did mother wake up father?
5. Why do schools have blackboards?
6. Why do people need flashlights?
7. Why do people get presents?

8. Why are presents wrapped up?
9. Why do children go to school?
10. Why do babies cry?
11. Why do you wear a hearing aid?
12. What do you want to be when you grow up?

The last two questions were analyzed individually for their psychological features, but were not included in the overall analysis. Question 11 was not asked of the hearing children, and question 12 was unscorable for correct grammar.

References

Ames, L. B., R. W. Metraux, J. L. Rodell, and R. N. Walker. (1974). *Child Rorschach Responses: Developmental Trends from Two to Ten Years.* New York: Brunner/Mazel.
Auletta, K. (1982). *The Underclass.* New York: Random House.
Barsch, R. H. (1968). *The Parent of the Handicapped Child: The Study of Child-Rearing Practices.* Springfield, Ill.: Charles C. Thomas.
Bee, H. L., K. E. Barnard, S. J. Eryes, C. A. Gray, M. A. Hammond, A. L. Spietz, C. Snyder, and B. Clark. (1982). Prediction of IQ and language skills from perinatal status, child performance, family characteristics, and mother–infant interaction. *Child Development* 53 (5), 1134–1156.
Bettelheim, B. (1971). Discussion of Alfred Flarsheim essay (resolution of the mother-child symbiosis in a psychotic adolescent). In S. C. Feinstein, P. L. Giovacchini, and A. A. Miller (Eds.), *Adolescent Psychiatry, 1.* New York: Basic Books.
Blank, M. (1970). Some philosophical influences underlying preschool intervention for disadvantaged children. In F. Williams (Ed.), *Language and Poverty: Perspectives on a Theme.* Chicago: Markham.
   (1975). Mastering the intangible through language. In D. Aaronson and R. W. Rieber (Eds.), *Developmental Psycholinguistics and Communication Disorders.* vol. 263. New York: New York Academy of Sciences.
Blank, M., S. A. Rose, and L. J. Berlin. (1978). *The Language of Learning: The Preschool Years.* Orlando, Fla.: Grune & Stratton.
Borchert, C. (1984). *Communication between mothers and their hearing-impaired toddlers: A pilot study.* Unpublished manuscript.
Brinich, P. (1980). Childhood deafness and maternal control. *Journal of Communication Disorders 13,* 75–81.
Bronfenbrenner, U. (1958). Socialization and social class through time and space. In E. E. Maccoby, T. M. Newcomb, and E. L. Hartley (Eds.), *Readings in Social Psychology.* New York: Holt, Rinehart & Winston.
Brown, R., and A. Gilman. (1972). The pronouns of power and solidarity. In P. P. Giglioli (Ed.), *Language and Social Context.* Harmondsworth: Penguin.
Bruner, J. S. (1975). From communication to language: A psychological perspective. *Cognition 3,* 255–287.
Bugental, D. B., and W. A. Shennum. (1984). "Difficult" children as elicitors

and targets of adult communication patterns: An attributional-behavioral transactional analysis. *Monographs of the Society for Research in Child Development 49* (1), ser. no. 205.

Carroll, L. (1963). *Alice in Wonderland and through the Looking Glass.* New York: Grosset & Dunlap.

Cazden, C. B. (1970). The neglected situation in child language and education. In F. Williams (Ed.), *Language and Poverty: Perspectives on a Theme.* Chicago: Markham.

Chess, S., S. J. Korn, and P. B. Fernandez. (1971). *Psychiatric Disorders of Children with Congenital Rubella.* New York: Brunner/Mazel.

Clarke-Stewart, K. A. (1973). Interactions between mothers and their young children: Characteristics and consequences. *Monographs of the Society for Research in Child Development 38,* 6–7.

Cummins, J. (1981). The role of primary language development in promoting educational success for language minority students. In California State Department of Education, Office of Bilingual Bicultural Education, *Schooling and Language Minority Students: A Theoretical Framework.* Los Angeles Calif.: California State University, Evaluation, Dissemination and Assessment Center.

Entwisle, D. (1970). Semantic systems of children: Some assessment of social class and ethnic differences. In F. Williams (Ed.), *Language and Poverty: Perspectives on a Theme.* Chicago: Markham.

Ewing, A., and E. C. Ewing. (1964). *Teaching Deaf Children to Talk.* London: Manchester University Press.

Farwell, R. (1978). Wh-question comprehension in profoundly deaf children. Unpublished doctoral dissertation. University of California, Berkeley.

Feagans, L., and D. C. Farran. (Eds.). (1982). *The Language of Children Reared in Poverty: Implications for Evaluation and Intervention.* New York: Academic Press.

Feuerstein, R. (1977). Mediated learning experience: A theoretical basis for cognitive modifiability during adolescence. In P. Mittler (Ed.), *Research to Practice in Mental Retardation: Education and Training,* Vol. 2. Baltimore, Md.: University Park Press.

(1979). Ontogeny of learning in man. In M. Brazier (Ed.), *Brain Mechanisms in Memory and Learning: From the Single Neuron to Man.* New York: Raven Press.

Feuerstein, R., Y. Rand, M. Hoffman, and R. Miller. (1980). *Instrumental Enrichment: An Intervention Program for Cognitive Modifiability.* Baltimore, Md.: University Park Press.

Feuerstein, R., and M. Reimer-Jensen. (1980, May). Instrumental enrichment: Theoretical basis, goals, and instruments. In *The Educational Forum 44,* 4, pp. 401–423.

Golden, M., and B. Birns. (1976). Social class and infant intelligence. In M. Lewis (Ed.), *Origins of Intelligence,* pp. 332–335. New York: Plenum Press.

Gonzales, A., and P. Zimbardo. (1985). Time in perspective. *Psychology Today 19* (3), 21–26.

Greenberg, M. T., C. A. Kusche, R. N. Gustafson, and R. Calderon. (1984). The paths project: A model for the prevention of psychosocial difficulties in deaf children. In G. B. Anderson and D. Watson (Eds.), *The Habilitation and Rehabilitation of Deaf Adolescents.* Washington, D.C.: The National Academy of Gallaudet College.

Gregory, S. (1976). *The Deaf Child and His Family.* New York: John Wiley & Sons.

Harris, A. (1983). Language and alienation. In B. Bain (Ed.), *Sociogenesis of Language and Human Conduct.* New York: Knopf.

Harris, D. (1982). Communicative interaction processes involving nonvocal physically handicapped children. *Topics in Language Disorders 2* (2), 21–37.

Hess, R., and V. Shipman. (1965). Early experience on the socialization of cognitive modes in children. *Child Development 34,* 869–886.

Hoeman, H. (1972). The development of communication skills in deaf and hearing children. *Child Development 43,* 990–1003.

John, V., and L. Goldstein. (1967). The social context of language acquisition. In J. Hellmuth (Ed.), *Disadvantaged Child;* vol. 1. New York: Brunner/ Mazel.

Karchmer, M. A. (1984). Demographics and deaf adolescents. In G. B. Anderson and D. Watson (Eds.), *The Habilitation and Rehabilitation of Deaf Adolescents.* Washington, D.C.: The National Academy of Gallaudet College.

Koestner, R., R. M. Ryan, F. Bernieri, and K. Holt. (1984). Setting limits on children's behavior: The differential effects of controlling vs. informational styles on intrinsic motivation and creativity. *Journal of Personality 52,* 233–248.

Kohn M. L. (1969). *Class and Conformity: A Study in Values.* Homewood, Ill.: Dorsey Press. Reprint. Chicago: University of Chicago Press, 1977.

Leacock, E. (1969). *Teaching and Learning in City Schools: A Comparative Study.* New York: Basic Books.

Leahy, R. (Ed.). (1983). *The Construction of Social Inequality.* New York: Academic Press.

Leifer, J. S., and M. Lewis. (1983). Maternal speech to normal and handicapped children: A look at question-asking behavior. *Infant Behavior and Development 6,* 175–187.

Lou, M. W. P. (1986). Assessing the language competence of deaf adolescents. In D. Watson, G. Anderson, and M. Taff-Watsen (Eds.), *Integrating Human Resources Technology and Systems in Deafness.* Monograph No. 13. Silver Spring, Md.: American Deafness and Rehabilitation Association.

McClelland, D. C. (1975). *Power: The Inner Experience.* New York: Irvington.

McDonald, L., and D. Pien. (1982). Mother conversational behavior as a function of interactional intent. *Journal of Child Language 9,* 337–358.

Milner, E. (1951). A study of the relationship between reading readiness in grade one school children and patterns of parent–child interaction. *Child Development 22,* 95–112.

Minuchin, S., B. Montalva, B. Guerney, B. Fosman, and F. Schumer. (1967). *Families of the Slums: An Exploration of Their Structure and Treatment.* New York: Basic Books.

Mittler, P., and P. Berry. (1977). Demanding language. In P. Mittler (Ed.), *Research to Practice in Mental Retardation: Education and Training,* vol. 2, pp. 245–251. Baltimore, Md.: University Park Press.

Ogbu, J. U. (1978). *Minority Education and Caste.* New York: Academic Press.
    (1982). Societal forces as a context of ghetto children's school failure. In L. Feagans and D. C. Farran (Eds.), *The Language of Children Reared in*

Poverty: Implications for Evaluation and Intervention. New York: Academic Press.

Ramey, C. T., J. J. Sparling, and B. H. Wasik. (1981). Creating social environments to facilitate language development. In R. L. Schiefelbush and D. D. Bricker (Eds.), *Early Language: Acquisition and Intervention*. Baltimore, Md.: University Park Press.

Schachter, F. (1979). *Everyday Mother Talk to Toddlers: Early Intervention*. New York: Academic Press.

Schlesinger, H. S. (1972). Meaning and enjoyment: Language acquisition of deaf children. In T. J. O'Rourke (Ed.), *Psycholinguistics and Total Communication: The State of the Art*. Washington, D.C.: American Annals of the Deaf.

(1982). Deafness, mental health and language. The Burton Lecture, Callier Center, University of Texas, November. Dallas.

(1985). The psychology of hearing loss. In H. Orlans (Ed.), *Adjustment to Adult Hearing Loss*. San Diego, Calif.: College-Hill Press.

(1986). From "What is this?" and "What Color is this?" to "What will happen next?" or "If?" A paper presented at the 1986 A. G. Bell Convention, Chicago, and the 1986 National Association of the Deaf Convention, Salt Lake City.

(1987). Effects of powerlessness on dialogue and development: Disability, poverty, and the human condition. In B. Heller, L. Flohr, and L. Zegans (Eds.), *Expanding Horizons: Psychosocial Interventions with Sensorily-Disabled Persons*. New York: Grune & Stratton.

Schlesinger, H. S., and M. C. Acree. (1984). Antecedents of achievement and adjustment in deaf adolescents: A longitudinal study of deaf children. In G. B. Anderson and D. Watson (Eds.), *The Habilitation and Rehabilitation of Deaf Adolescents*. Washington, D.C.: The National Academy of Gallaudet College.

(1985). Additional dialogue analyses. Unpublished paper.

Schlesinger, H. S., and K. P. Meadow. (1972). *Sound and Sign: Childhood Deafness and Mental Health*. Berkeley: University of California Press.

(1976). Studies of family interaction, language acquisition, and deafness. Unpublished manuscript.

Slaughter, D. T. (1983). Parental potency and the achievements of inner-city black children. *American Journal of Orthopsychiatry* 40 (3), 433–440.

Snow, C. E., C. Dubber, and A. De Blauw. (1982). In L. Feagans and D. C. Farran (Eds.), *The Language of Children Reared in Poverty: Implications for Evaluation and Intervention*. New York: Academic Press.

Stierlin, H. (1977). *Psychoanalysis and Family Therapy*. New York: Jason Aronson.

Stodolsky, S., and G. Lesser. (1967). Learning patterns in the disadvantaged. *Harvard Educational Review* 37, 546–593.

Tizard, B. (1974). Do social relationships affect language development? In K. Connolly and J. Bruner (Eds.), *The Growth of Competence*. New York: Academic Press.

Tough, J. (1977). *The Development of Meaning: A Study of Children's Use of Language*. New York: John Wiley.

(1982). Language, poverty, and disadvantage in school. In L. Feagans and D.

Farran (Eds.), *The Language of Children Reared in Poverty: Implications for Evaluation and Intervention.* New York: Academic Press.

Tulkin, S., and J. Kagan. (1972). "Compensatory education" for infants: Mother–child interaction in the first year of life. *Child Development 43*, 31–41.

Williams, F. (Ed.). (1970). *Language and Poverty: Perspectives on a Theme.* Chicago: Markham.

Index

acoustic method, 88
Acree, M., 262, 265, 266, 267, 273, 284
acrolect, 11
age, effects on language acquisition, 18–19, 24
Albertini, J., 5, 7, 32, 36, 145
Allen, T., 192
Altschuler, K., 10
American Asylum, 81
American School for the Deaf, 76, 82
American Sign Language (ASL), 3, 9, 10, 11, 12, 13, 14, 21, 25, 33–6, 75, 77, 88, 91, 92, 95, 99, 103, 107–8, 110, 111, 113, 116–17, 185, 195, 197, 198, 200, 206–9, 211–13, 220, 221, 223, 245
  agreement system in, 60
  bilingual with English, 106, 121, 220
  children's use of in school, 120–1, 266, 273
  citation forms, 22
  comparison with PSE, 27
  as a creole, 4, 56
  in education of the deaf, 114
  as first language, xi, xii, 25, 119
  instruction in, 96, 102, 109
  as a language of instruction, 80, 81, 86, 94, 105, 119–23, 190
  lexical innovations in, 162
  meso level/variety of, 25
  morphological complexity of, 57
  movement in signs, 165
  as a native language, 34
  parents' use of, 104
  relationship with English, 29, 100–1

as a second language, 101
stories in, 122
structure of, 13, 27, 54–70, 201
teacher use of, 196, 202
in total communication programs, 115, 193
verbs, 164
word-formation devices in, 163–82
Ames, L., 267, 283
Ameslan, 11, 101
Ameslish, 11
Andersen, R., 4, 12, 15, 19, 20, 25, 27, 51, 52
Anderson, J., 18, 61
Annual Survey of Hearing-Impaired Children and Youth, 185
Anthony, David, 91, 92, 196
aphasia, 25
Aronow, M., 117
articulation
  visual-gestural, 23
  vocal, 23
ASL, *see* American Sign Language
Auletta, F., 264, 284
auxiliary manual/sign systems, 8, 9, 10, 11

Babbini, B., 100
Baker, C., 57, 101, 199, 200
Baker, C.L., 50
Baker-Shenk, C., 200
Bander, Robert, 156
Barnum, M., 116
Barsch, R., 263,
Bartlett, David, 85
basilect, 11
Bayley Scales of Infant Development, 224
Bell, A., 84, 87, 88
Bellman, K., 64